D0072339

Managing Britain's Marine and Coastal Environment

Britain's maritime tradition is well documented. The management of its marine and coastal environment is therefore paramount, and offers lessons for other nations across the world. The beginning of the new millennium marks a major, long-term turning point in the historical development of Britain's maritime interest discernible by continued diversification and intensification in the uses of the sea; unprecedented and often adverse environmental impacts engendered by these uses; and the beginning of a major effort to establish a comprehensive management system which can deal with both multiple uses and environmental impacts.

This collection, featuring an impressive list of contributors, covers themes including maritime history; environmental issues; fishing; public policy; tourism; technology and resources as well as open sea development and management. Each chapter examines the present state of a particular theme before suggesting possibilities for the future.

This book will be a useful addition for those interested in geography, the environment and maritime studies, as well as engineers and policymakers.

Hance D. Smith is a Reader at Cardiff University, specializing in marine geography, marine resource management and the development of maritime communities. He is a founder member of the Commission on Marine Geography of the International Geographical Union and was Chair 1992–2000. **Jonathan S. Potts** is a Senior Specialist responsible for contemporary maritime affairs at the National Maritime Museum, Greenwich, London.

Routledge advances in maritime research
Edited by H.D. Smith, Cardiff University, UK

The oceans and seas of the world are at a critical juncture in their history. The pressures of development brought about by the globalization of the world economy continue to intensify through the major sectors of ocean use. In parallel marine management and policy issues become larger, more numerous and more urgent. The response of this series is to provide in-depth analysis of ocean development, management and policy from a multidisciplinary perspective, encompassing a wide range of aspects of inter-relationships between the oceans and seas on the one hand, and maritime human activities on the other. Several strands run through the series.

- Studies of the development and management of major ocean industries and uses including shipping and ports; strategic uses; mineral and energy resources; fisheries and aquaculture; the leisure industries; waste disposal and pollution; science and education; and conservation.
- Inter- and multidisciplinary perspectives provided by the natural sciences, geography, economics, sociology, politics, law and history.
- Responses to the need to devise integrated ocean policies and management measures which cover the deep oceans, the bordering seas, and coastal zones.
- Regional studies at a variety of geographical scales from large ocean regions to regional seas.

The series is of interest to all concerned professionally with the oceans and seas, ranging from scientists and engineers to surveyors, planners, lawyers and policy makers working in the public, private and voluntary sectors. It is also of wider public interest to all those interested in or having a stake in the world ocean and its bordering seas

1 Development and Social Change in the Pacific Islands
Edited by A.D. Couper

Managing Britain's Marine and Coastal Environment

Towards a sustainable future

Edited by Hance D. Smith and Jonathan S. Potts

LONDON AND NEW YORK

333.9164
M266

First published 2005
by Routledge and the National Maritime Museum
2 Park Square, Milton Park, Abingdon, Oxon OX14 4RN

Simultaneously published in the USA and Canada
by Routledge
270 Madison Ave, New York, NY 10016

Routledge is an imprint of the Taylor & Francis Group

© 2005 editorial matter and selection, Hance D. Smith and the
National Maritime Museum; individual chapters, the contributors

Typeset in Baskerville by Wearset Ltd, Boldon, Tyne and Wear
Printed and bound in Great Britain by MPG Books Ltd, Bodmin

All rights reserved. No part of this book may be reprinted or
reproduced or utilized in any form or by any electronic, mechanical,
or other means, now known or hereafter invented, including
photocopying and recording, or in any information storage or
retrieval system, without permission in writing from the publishers.

British Library Cataloguing in Publication Data
A catalogue record for this book is available from the British Library

Library of Congress Cataloging in Publication Data
Smith, Hance D.
    Managing Britain's marine and coastal environment : towards a
sustainable future / Hance Smith and Jonathan Potts.
        p. cm.
    Includes bibliographical references and index.
    1. Marine resources conservation—Great Britain. 2. Coastal zone
management—Great Britain. 3. Sustainable fisheries—Great Britain.
I. Potts, Jonathan. II. Title.
    GC1018.S65 2005
    333.91′6416′0941—dc22
                                                        2004010457

ISBN 0-415-32945-0

Contents

University Libraries
Carnegie Mellon University
Pittsburgh, PA 15213-3890

Figures

Tables

Boxes

Contributors

Martin V. Angel, Southampton Oceanography Centre, Southampton.

Rhoda C. Ballinger, Department of Earth Sciences, Cardiff University.

Natasha Barker, Exe Estuary Management Partnership.

David Carter, Department of Geography, University of Portsmouth.

James Coull, Department of Geography and Environment, University of Aberdeen.

Bob Earll, CMS Limited, Gloucestershire.

John Gibson, University of Cape Town, South Africa.

Carolyn Heeps, Environmental Policy Manager, The Crown Estate.

Duncan Huggett, Senior Policy Officer, Royal Society for the Protection of Birds.

David Johnson, Maritime Faculty, Southampton Institute.

Derek J. McGlashan, University of Dundee.

Ian R. Napier, North Atlantic Fisheries College, Scotland.

David Pinder, Department of Geographical Sciences, University of Plymouth.

Jonathan S. Potts, National Maritime Museum, London.

David Pugh, Visiting Professor, University of Liverpool (formerly Southampton Oceanography Centre).

Hance D. Smith, Department of Earth Sciences, Cardiff University.

Jane Taussik, Coastal Reseach, Consultancy and Training.

Acknowledgements

The book forms part of the National Maritime Museum's *Planet Ocean* initiative, which seeks to raise awareness of the legacy of the oceans and their importance now and in the future. To this end we are grateful to the Museum for supporting this project. Particular thanks goes to Dr Nigel Rigby and Rachel Giles for their support and encouraging comments.

Thanks are also due to the International Geographical Union Commission on Marine Geography for research support.

We are also indebted to Terry Clague at Routledge for his patience and understanding during the delivery of the typescript.

Finally, we would also like to thank all the contributors who have helped to ensure that this book has come to fruition.

Main
Book Title:
Introduction

Hance D. Smith and Jonathan S. Potts

The human activities on the coasts and seas of Europe are experiencing a period of unprecedented change. This is happening at a time when the eastern and western halves of the continent are gradually being re-united economically, socially and politically in the wake of the cataclysmic events of the twentieth century, beginning with the outbreak of the Great War in 1914 and ending with the fall of the Berlin Wall in 1989. At a global scale Europe is being increasingly perceived as a single economic entity, one of the largest in the world economy. In common with the other major concentrations of economic activity in North America and East Asia, Europe relies on maritime transport and communications and, to a lesser extent, marine resource development for sustaining its place in the world.

In this world of marine affairs, in the context of the spatial development of the marine economy international trade, shipping and port development continue on an expansionary track, while the great military divide which existed before 1989 has given way to a strategic European marine world focused on the activities of the North Atlantic Treaty Organization (NATO). In the sphere of marine resource development, the North Sea has reached the state of a mature hydrocarbon province, while exploration continues, especially to the north and west of the British Isles. The fisheries are in a state of severe crisis brought about by the long-term overfishing and the failure of fisheries management to cope with this, while coastal and marine aquaculture continues to grow in importance. The coastal environment in many parts of Europe – most notably in the Mediterranean – has in a real sense become the greatest marine resource through the development of the leisure and tourism industries. Meanwhile as far as the coastal and marine environment itself is concerned, considerable progress has been made in restricting and otherwise improving waste disposal both directly into the sea and from land-based sources, with much still to be done. Europe remains a leading region in the pursuit of marine science (Chapter 2) in the widest sense, conducted both with a view to develop the coastal and marine environment while at the same time aimed at mitigating environmental impacts of development, and simply improving understanding of the marine environment itself. Finally, much is also being done in the field of coastal and marine conservation on local, national and European scales.

The European maritime background provides the context for the central theme of this book – the management of Britain's marine and coastal environment. The primary focus is the coasts and seas surrounding Britain and Ireland, the two largest islands off the coast of north-west Europe. The book is primarily organized into offshore and coastal sections, with the first two chapters being concerned with aspects of the historical and cultural background. The offshore part of the book is in turn mainly based on key economic sectors; while the coastal section is concerned only partly with sectors, but with management, as it is the part of the overall environment which is by and large most intensely used, and in which novel approaches are being sought both to cope with this intensity and integrate the respective land and sea dimensions in the environmental management process.

So much for the structure of the book. This Introduction is, however, primarily concerned with a number of overarching themes which give form and substance to the opening remark concerning unprecedented change, themes which are interwoven through the contributions to this volume.

The first theme has to do with ideas. This book focuses on interrelationships between the coastal and marine environment on the one hand, and human activities on the other. For most of the past half-millennium, and especially since the onset of modern industrialization at the end of the eighteenth century, the dominant paradigm has been development in the broadest sense, although during the Enlightenment this involved the idea of 'improvement', especially among the landowning classes. Nowadays as the limitations of the environment to support human activities becomes ever clearer, the idea of sustainability – environmental, economic and social – is fast becoming the dominant paradigm (Chapter 14). Associated with it are a number of other ideas, notably the precautionary principle which, taken together denote a sea change in outlook reminiscent of a 'movement' as an historian might understand it. The attainment of a better balance between human activities and the marine environment around Britain and Ireland crucially depends upon application of these ideas in a sustained way over decades.

The second major theme is that of tradition – in this case the maritime traditions of the 'peoples of the sea' alluded to in Chapter 1, and again particularly apposite to the maritime heritage discussed especially in Chapter 7. It is axiomatic that Britain is regarded as a maritime nation. The sea has indeed been central to the development process throughout all of modern times, beginning in the late fifteenth century. Thus coastal settlements and communities have often as not been highly specialized and dependent on the sea – especially shipping and ports, naval activities, fisheries and leisure industries. Latterly offshore oil and gas has been added to this list. It is mainly upon these communities, and the national life as a whole, that the strong maritime traditions – and heritage – of Britain are built.

But what of the historical reality upon which these traditions rest? It is not difficult to perceive the central role played by economic and technological development of the maritime sectors (Chapters 1–8). Two further points are worth making. First, in the realm of ideas there is arguably a shift in emphasis from development per se to a more holistic view of the relationships between human activities and the environment. It may take decades for this to become fully evident; it represents a broad and deep-seated transformation of ideas, comparable in scale and complexity to the transition from medieval to modern times in European history. The second point concerns the technological and economic development of marine activities. Here the half-century or so evolutionary stages evident since the 'industrial revolution' of the late eighteenth–early nineteenth centuries are important. Presently a transition is arguably occurring from the late twentieth to the early twenty-first centuries stage, with accompanying considerable changes in the overall structure of the economic sectors of the marine economy.

A key indicator of development processes is the evolution of law. Much legal development, while deriving from a number of sources (Chapter 9), is sectorally based, with periodic major transformations in primary legislation. At the time of writing (March 2004) a political head of steam is developing to move the legal process forward to produce a 'marine act' which integrates at least some aspects of the hitherto primarily sectoral legislation, with emphasis on spatial planning, and taking into account an ecosystem-based approach to sea use management. A further dimension in the legal context is both the emergence of European law as the primary driver in the fields of living marine resource development and environmental management generally; and the emergence of more 'local' law beginning with the Zetland and Orkney County Council Acts, a process which may be further encouraged by the political devolution within the United Kingdom. As well as law, certain other professions also continue to play increasing roles in the management of the coastal and marine environment, notably marine science, education, surveying, engineering, accountancy and planning, reflecting the psychological, environmental, economic, social, political and risk factors which influence the interactions between human activities and the environment.

Discussion of the law in particular in turn focuses attention on the role of governance. This study has been completed at a time when changes are occurring in the respective roles of the three major sectors involved: the public or state sector, the private sector, and the voluntary sector. In the state and voluntary sectors, there has been a flurry of activities and related studies gathering pace throughout the 1990s and into the present decade on the management of the coastal and marine environment. The initiatives at the ideas level contributed by the voluntary sector in particular are worthy of note. Chapters 10 to 13 focus on the details of these, which may be regarded to a substantial degree as a theme of the changing role of organizations in coastal and marine development and management.

In conclusion we return to where we began in this short Introduction – the coastal and marine environment itself. In a management context it is possible to see the emergence of a hierarchy of integrated management regions over the next two or three decades. These will be specified at international, European, UK national, devolved UK government and local scales, and will involve further development of the law as well as relationships among the public, private and voluntary sectors. Aspects of all of these are discussed in the pages which follow.

Finally, in the spirit of philosophical development and integrated activity of this book, acknowledgement is made to the National Maritime Museum and the Commission for Marine Geography of the International Geographical Union. The joint initiative by these two organizations over the past four years has produced this study. As such the philosophy and approach of both towards the management of the coastal and marine environment are amply demonstrated.

Part I
The maritime world

1   Peoples of the sea

The British maritime world

Hance D. Smith and Jonathan S. Potts

Introduction

Why the sea? Especially when it has been said that, in terms of intensification of sea uses and related human activities, the sea is becoming increasingly like the land (King and Smith, 1986). In this sense, this book provides a contribution to an ongoing debate. It is undoubtedly true that the communities of people concerned with the development of sea trade and resources, and other human activities, have been in some senses separate and distinctive throughout long spans of human history. This separateness was, if anything, highlighted by the commercialization and industrialization of the global economy over the past half-millennium. Thus seafarers – commercial and naval, and fishermen – have remained in distinct communities such as seaports, naval bases and fishing villages for centuries, and have led lives that were relatively isolated from the land, inevitably leading to differences in traditions and outlook. More recently, especially in the second half of the twentieth century, other specialized maritime groups have appeared, notably in the leisure industries, offshore oil and gas, marine science and education, and marine conservation. These occupational groups have bequeathed a strong maritime heritage and tradition, which still endures to a remarkable extent, both in Britain and elsewhere, especially in the developed world, even although communities of people have in many senses been replaced by communities of interest (Smith, 2000a).

The purpose of this chapter is accordingly first to highlight key sequences of development of maritime activities and their contribution to the maritime heritage. This is followed by a brief evaluation of the maritime heritage in its contemporary manifestations, organized along the lines of major marine sectors. Finally, the implications of maritime development and the maritime heritage for the present and future of marine resource and environmental management are considered.

Sequences

The maritime heritage has been built up over a period that extends back to at least Mesolithic times, perhaps even beyond into the Palaeolithic. It is possible to distinguish at least three broad sets of traditional, or pre-industrial societies, namely, those extending from the Mesolithic to the early Iron Age, for which material remains provide the main lines of evidence for reconstruction; the Celtic and Roman societies of the later Iron Age, for which in addition to archaeological evidence, there is extensive linguistic evidence (including place names) and historical data; and those of the mis-named 'Dark Ages' down to the end of the medieval period around AD 1500. The next following early modern period witnessed the gradual transformation of the medieval society by large scale expansion of the economy, driven in large measure by the rise of commerce, in which maritime trade was perhaps the most important ingredient. Although there was a limited amount of industrialization during this period, the true onset of large scale industrialization dates from the end of the eighteenth century, and is now arguably drawing to a close. Beginning with the 'industrial revolution' from *c.* 1780–1830, the industrial period has been marked by a series of stages. The contemporary era now opening up has been termed 'post-industrial', but its outlines remain unclear. It is a remarkable fact that in the whole sequence described above the sea has played a central role (Padfield, 1999; Cunliffe, 2001).

In reconstructing the maritime dimensions of the early traditional societies, it should be remembered that, although there is necessarily reliance on material evidence, these societies are likely to have possessed sophisticated social organization, and advanced systems of thought commensurate with the economic and technological limitations of their respective periods. The Mesolithic society may have had the coast as the primary focus of settlement: not only was it possible to obtain reliable food supplies from the sea, but also coastal lands were often more amenable to settlement than forested and poorly drained inland areas. Coastal land and even inshore waters would similarly have been most suited to travel relative to inland areas.

The Neolithic and Bronze Age civilization which subsequently emerged was developed to a high degree, with extensive maritime links involving trade, movement of people and, above all, movement of ideas, extending from the western Mediterranean to Scandinavia. This society has left impressive material remains in the form of dolmens, and major buildings of composite age, such as Stonehenge, signifying advanced systems of thought and considerable knowledge of the natural environment. This society was built on much more advanced economic development, including agriculture and maritime trade links. Population would have been much higher than in the previous Mesolithic, with phases of extensive folk migration, and climatic conditions were generally more favourable for exploitation of both land and sea.

It is during the third phase of development of traditional society that a strong maritime heritage emerges very clearly. The principal element in this was the emergence of the Iron Age Celtic peoples who populated the region through migration from Central Europe, and settled extensively from Iberia, throughout western France and the British Isles. The Celts undoubtedly had a strong maritime tradition and were capable of voyaging long distances, certainly reaching Iceland, and probably even Greenland and North America (Bowen, 1977). Their social organization and systems of thought were very advanced, and the remnants of their civilization extend to the present day (Moffat, 2001), through for example, the place names of the still extant Celtic languages, and traditional boats – the curragh being the principal example. The later period of Celtic development took place during the expansion of the Roman Empire into the British Isles. Celtic civilization remained strong beyond the fringes of the empire, and was of course associated with the coming of Christianity after the Romans had left. At this time Ireland was the centre from which Christian influence spread eastwards into Wales and beyond into mainland Europe (Bowen, 1977).

The Romans of course also came by sea, initially in the form of an army of occupation, but later there was extensive settlement among the native population. While there is no evidence to suggest that the Romans relied on any but the shorter cross-Channel sea routes, the voyage of Pytheas perhaps beyond the fringes of the Arctic Circle bear testimony to the considerable maritime capability of the period in the waters around the British Isles (Cunliffe, 2002), which of course is more fully known with regard to the Mediterranean.

From a maritime perspective, as with the Celtic/Roman era which lasted for around a thousand years, the next millennium from the time the Romans left until the end of the Middle Ages is best regarded as a single period of evolution of yet another traditional society. As with the preceding period, the early centuries were marked by further large-scale folk movements into the region, this time mainly across the North Sea from the North European plain and the Scandinavian coastlands. The story of the coming of the Angles, Saxons, Jutes and Norsemen and the apparent displacement of the Celtic population needs no elaboration here. To the archaeological, historical and linguistic evidence can now be added more detailed and precise biological evidence based on analysis of mitochrondial DNA in the existing population, which demonstrates the sharp geographical division between the existing Celtic population and the incomers.

Of all the groups, the Vikings from western Norway were a quintessential maritime society. In early times they built up a network of sea routes linking Norway to the newly settled world of the northern and western British Isles (Small, 1968), Faroe, Iceland and Greenland, and they also settled North America for a short period. Their place names came to define the areas in which they settled, and the Norn language retained sway throughout the succeeding early modern period, evolving notably into modern Faroese and Icelandic. In the British Isles the Norse Scandinavian maritime culture is evidenced to the present day in place names (Wainwright, 1962), the design of traditional inshore boats (Brøgger and Shetelig, 1971), and numerous traditions, some of which were revived in the nineteenth century. Meanwhile, in the later part of the Middle Ages the rise of the Hanseatic trading network linked the eastern shores of the British Isles from Shetland to London closely to continental Europe. Of special note were the evolution of large decked sailing vessels (McGrail, 1981), and shore trading places, from the Steelyard in London to the Hanseatic booths in Shetland (Dollinger, 1970).

The next following early modern phase, from around 1500 until the early eighteenth century, was associated both with the rise of large-scale commercial maritime trade and expansion of distant water fisheries, and with the expansion of European maritime influence throughout the world. Again, there is no need to elaborate the well-known pattern here. Of special note, however, is the rise of England as one of the European maritime powers. This process began in the early sixteenth century under the Tudors, when England played a significant role in maritime exploration and trade, and in the Icelandic cod fisheries; it continued through the defeat of the Spanish Armada in 1588 and the Anglo-Dutch Wars between 1652 and 1674, after which England vied with France for maritime supremacy in Europe and, through that, the world – a process which did not reach a conclusion until the British victory at the Battle of Trafalgar in 1805. Associated with this process of naval expansion was that of mercantilist commercial expansion, led mainly by the Dutch for most of the period, who pioneered the trading, shipbuilding, finance, fisheries and whaling innovations upon which the all-important maritime dimension was based (Aymard, 1982). England participated in this process also, so that by the Union of the Parliaments of Scotland and England in 1707, Britain emerged as the leading maritime trading power (Smith, 1992a). The maritime heritage of the early modern period is impressive, not only in terms of historical sources, but in terms of material remains – including the World Heritage Site at Greenwich, and the oldest remnants of some of Britain's most important ports.

The sole remaining major stage in the sequence of maritime development is that of industrialization. Strictly speaking, this did not emerge fully until the last three decades of the eighteenth century, although the interplay of technological and economic factors prior to, say 1770, suggest a nascent process of expansion and contraction of the maritime economy along the lines of 'long waves' of around or just over half a century in length. Be that as it may, the industrialization of the British maritime – and global – economies has lasted from the end of the eighteenth century until now, when it is drawing to a close. It consists of four stages or 'long

waves' of approximately equal length, defined by combinations of technological advances and economic expansion and contraction. In a maritime
context, the principal features of the first stage (1780–1830) was expansion of trade, naval activity (for most of the time Britain was at war with
France) and fisheries. On land, textiles, iron-making, water power, canals
and turnpike roads were defining features. In the second phase from the
1830s until the 1870s, there was continued trade expansion, and expansion of distant water fisheries using decked vessels, ranging from cod to
whaling; although iron steamships were introduced, sail remained by far
the most important. From the 1870s until the 1930s, sail was replaced by
steam; this notably led to steam-powered fishing vessels and geographical
concentration of major fishing ports, together with serious overfishing.
The final phase, from the 1940s to the 1990s, witnessed major changes in
technology – from steam to motor vessels, new types of fishing gear, and
renewed economic expansion, contributing to serious overfishing. Other
major sea uses gained rapidly in importance, including marine aggregate
extraction, hydrocarbon exploitation, the marine leisure industries, and
increased pollution from both land and marine sources, while marine
science and conservation became major activities.

The contemporary era being entered at the millennium is the first,
arguably, in which the process of maritime industrialization is, in essence,
complete. However, further significant technological and economic
changes are either in train, or may be foreseen. From a technological
point of view, of special importance is the application of information
technology, continued improvement of fishing gear, automation of ships,
and other developments; economically, major changes can be foreseen in
continued concentration of fishing and trading ports, and continued
intensification of multiple sea uses. At this point it is useful to move on to
consideration of the nature of the maritime heritage bequeathed by the
sequence of development just outlined.

Heritage

The maritime heritage which has emerged from the several stages of the
long sequence of development as outlined above is both enormous and
diverse. It is useful at this stage to consider it in terms of three dimensions:
the material, the social and the mindsets of the traditions respectively. Each
of the dimensions can be in turn considered in relation to major groups of
sea uses. In the present discussion emphasis is placed upon the uses with the
longest history and therefore greatest strength and diversity of traditions,
including shipping and ports, naval activities, fisheries and marine science.

In a proper sense, navigation and shipping goes right back to the
beginning. Ports in a meaningful sense probably did not exist before
Roman times. Further, ports and shipping continue as a pivotal use of the
sea in so many ways: the past is to be found in the present of most of the

largest British ports, and in many smaller ones as well. In the largest ports (Bird, 1963), the early stages of development – one to four of the Anyport Model (Bird, 1971) have entered the realms of heritage conservation projects – the oldest docks, custom houses and warehouses fall into this category. Stage five areas of Anyport – roughly contemporaneous with the long wave of steam power from the 1870s to the 1930s – are the focus of large-scale urban renewal projects such as London Docklands, the Mersey Docks and Cardiff Bay, in all of which the port function is greatly reduced, and replaced by industrial and residential land uses.

The ports provide the primary location and focus of the country's maritime museums, and sometimes maritime displays in other museums. At the apex of the developing network of maritime museums is the National Maritime Museum at Greenwich, with other notable examples in Liverpool, Newcastle upon Tyne and elsewhere. An important adjunct to many museums is the nation's collection of historic ships, such as the *Cutty Sark* at Greenwich and the *Discovery* at Dundee. The final material element in the shipping heritage has been termed the 'underwater cultural heritage' (Couper, 1996; Drumgoole, 1999). This consists primarily of thousands of wrecks, most of which date from the 'industrial revolution' proper, which are located on the seabed within the Exclusive Fisheries Zone. As with the historic ships, but to a much greater extent, the wrecks provide an important source of information on the development of shipping technology and the growth of maritime trade.

Both by its very nature, and its role in the development of Britain as the world's first industrial nation, the shipping industry (Hope, 1990) gave rise to distinctive multinational communities of people living adjacent to the docklands, including not only seamen but most of the categories of workers engaged in the shipping and ports industries. Many seaward components of inner cities in Britain, such as the east end of London, Cardiff, Liverpool, Newcastle, Glasgow, Leith and others developed as sailortowns and communities of people working in the docks. The social realities of these communities are now largely consigned to history (Johnman and Johnston, 2001), but their physical form often remains. In a social sense employment in British shipping is now multinational, with many if not most of the crew non-resident in the U.K., while other categories of employees have joined the commuters of other industries, rather than living in close physical proximity.

In terms of the landward side of the shipping business, in the form of commodity exchanges, the Baltic Exchange, shipbroking, marine insurance and related activities (Cameron and Farndon, 1984), the City of London remains the centre, both in historical terms and present-day functions. By contrast, shipbuilding and marine engineering has largely disappeared from the major centres where these developed, particularly on the Clyde and Tyne. The remaining shipbuilders largely occupy specialist niches within this global industry.

The naval heritage (Pinder and Smith, 1999) replicates the commercial shipping heritage in considerable detail, albeit on a much smaller scale: port development, museums, historic ships, the underwater cultural heritage, naval dockyards and associated ordnance manufacturing, and former inner city communities in towns such as Portsmouth and Plymouth are all present. However, this heritage is geographically quite separate from commercial ports, and concentrated in a very few locations of varying ages on the strategic southern and eastern shores of mainland Britain: Pembroke Dock, Plymouth, Devonport, Portsmouth, Chatham, Deptford and Rosyth come to mind. A few of these of course remain active and conservation is limited, with the exception of Portsmouth, home to the *Mary Rose*, *Victory* and *Warrior*.

The heritage of the fisheries (Gray, 1978; Coull, 1996) is arguably even more extensive than mercantile shipping and the Navy, both temporally and certainly in geographical extent, where the eastern and southern coasts of the country in particular are characterized by innumerable small past and present fishing ports. It can be similarly classified in terms of material remains. However, also running through it is the major division into whaling (Jackson, 1978), herring and demersal fisheries (including especially cod); and the distinctions between coastal, inshore (March, 1970) and distant water fisheries (Warner, 1984).

In the case of the fisheries, it is particularly important to note that the past is perhaps more part of the present than certainly in the case of commercial shipping. Many historic fishing ports retain modern forms of their fishing industry, both on the catching and shore sides. Thus there remain active fishing communities which may be at least partly in the same location or close to it. This is particularly true in the fishing regions of North-East Scotland, Shetland and South-West England.

The theme of the past in the present is particularly true in the case of marine science, often not consciously regarded as part of the maritime heritage, but important nonetheless (Bailey and Parrish, 1987). The nature of the material heritage is somewhat different from the previous three; it really dates only from the second half of the nineteenth century in the main, and consists especially of the early marine laboratories set up either by the philanthropists, such as the Marine Biological Association; affiliated to university colleges, such as Millport, Port Erin and Dove; or associated with the early development of oceanography (Bidston) and fisheries science (Lowestoft, Torry). These remain as major marine science centres, though not always under the same management.

Of the remaining large-scale sea use groups, the exploitation of hydrocarbons is essentially contemporary, although no less valuable as potential heritage. Waste disposal and marine conservation share a common marine environmental orientation; the former has potential to destroy the heritage, while the latter strives to maintain at least the natural component (Defra, 2002). Marine leisure, recreation and tourism, as well as being economically and socially most important in many localities, is also the primary focus for the mediation of that heritage in the wider national life, as it were. It is largely through this group of industries and related activities that the economic value of the marine heritage is realized; and that public awareness and education is achieved. Because of this its importance is difficult to underestimate (Wallis, 1996). While there are old elements, such as the Victorian piers and some seaside holiday resort areas, it nonetheless remains primarily a contemporary phenomenon.

It has been remarked elsewhere that in the world of marine affairs, social communities of people in the same location have become in many cases communities of interest with people no longer located in the same place (Smith, 2000b). In this sense, the maritime world has become truly industrialized. But what of maritime traditions – the mindsets that underlie the stages of development and which still endure in certain respects at least? The central environmental, economic and cultural role of the sea in the evolution of all the traditional societies discussed above has been amply demonstrated by Cunliffe (2001) while Padfield (1999) demonstrates for the succeeding early modern period up to the foundation of the United States of America the continued role of the sea in influencing the commercial and naval prowess of the Anglo-American peoples in particular, as well as their overall outlook and its contribution to social evolution and political processes. For the truly industrial era that followed, a useful place to start is to examine the role of English literature, where the maritime heritage is enormous (Raban, 1993), while the language of the sea has become in part the language of the 'final frontier' of space.

Management

The word 'management' has to be treated with some care. In an environmental context it can have a wide variety of connotations covering both human actions and environmental consequences. In the present context it is defined as including both a series of technical and generally well defined measures governing physical interactions between human activities and the marine environment; and as having a general management dimension encompassing co-ordination of technical management measures, organizational decision-making, policy and strategic planning aspects (Smith, 1991). Here the material, social and traditional or mindset dimensions are discussed in turn. For material aspects the world management is often entirely appropriate. For the social, and especially mindset aspects, however, it is better to think rather in terms of the influence of thought processes, especially the practical areas involved in training, education and research.

The primary focus of management is the national heritage, outlined in the previous section. As a first approximation it is possible to consider the heritage in terms of the natural and built environments respectively. This underlines the dual nature of the heritage in comprising both physical and human components. However, as these interact continuously, in a management context it is more useful to adopt a geographical approach, distinguishing three elements defined in terms of use intensity, namely, the urban, rural and wilderness environments respectively (Smith, 1992b). This subdivision is familiar enough on land. It can also be applied to coastal waters and the open sea. In practice the wilderness environment more or less devoid of human activity hardly exists in a British context. The urban sea is real enough along all major urbanized coasts – mainly estuaries and firths, although it is largely confined to internal waters and the territorial sea as legally defined. The rest, and by far the greatest component, is the rural sea and coast, characterized primarily by resource extraction, coastal leisure, military exercise areas and a relatively small number of key shipping routes, together with mainly coastal conservation designations.

In the coastal and marine urban environment, the intensity of uses is greatest, with a corresponding concentration of management measures. Most of these coasts are urbanized to landward, and artificial – thus engineered with harbour works and coast protection schemes. Commercial navigation routes converge here on major ports; and there is a concentration of sea and land based maritime leisure, most notably the major holiday resorts on open coasts. Most of the waste disposal from the land is also concentrated here. Although land use planning generally stops at low water mark, less formal planning arrangements have become increasingly necessary. In a particularly British tradition this is supplanted by informal, rather than statutory management arrangements, in the form of coastal and estuary management initiatives spearheaded by English Nature, Scottish Natural Heritage and the Department of Environment in Northern Ireland. Ports play a major role through harbour acts and associated conservancy measures. The management situation continues to evolve, and the outcome remains unclear. One school of thought is to extend local authority planning powers to cover at least internal waters, redefining these where necessary to cover all 'urbanized' water areas.

In the rural environment, the nature of coastal and sea uses are such that the management characteristics and issues are primarily sectoral: navigation routes, military exercise areas, telecommunication cables, hydrocarbons, aggregates, fisheries, fish farming, yachting and cruising, and dumping grounds all present issues. While a good deal of informal co-ordination takes place, for example, in co-ordination of marine science (STWG, 1987), and at the behest of the oil industry through the UK Offshore Operators' Association (UKOOA), there is no integrated management system. It is important to recognize that the major industries – especially shipping and fisheries – have a legislative history extending over more than two centuries, which reflects to a considerable degree the long wave stages outlined above. The evolution of legislation should be seen in conjunction with current marine stewardship and marine act moves in the UK (Davison, 2000) and Europe (European Union, 2002); the North Sea ministerial conferences also promote an integrated approach to this off-shore rural sea (Ehlers, 1990).

At the level of the social heritage, a somewhat different view and practical approach is required. The issues here relate especially to communities based on specific industries. Of these the ports, oil and gas, fisheries, fish farming and holiday resorts are the most prominent. In the past half-century, the ports industry has become largely concentrated on a small number of east and south coast ports, with the remainder, including the large ports on the west coast, have declined greatly, leading to disappearance of port communities and large-scale urban renewal. Oil and gas communities are also concentrated on the east coast; by contrast these are very recent and still thriving on the whole, but with a lifetime largely limited to that of the North Sea oil province. Fishing communities are also mainly concentrated on the east coast, but are under severe strain due to declining fish stocks and competition from communities in mainland Europe; these can be expected to decline in many places. Fish farming is concentrated on the west coast of Scotland and in Shetland and, like oil and gas, is recent. If properly managed it can have a very long-term future. The holiday resorts have nineteenth-century roots, but have suffered severely through competition with the Mediterranean resorts since the advent of cheap air travel in the 1960s, and have had to reinvent themselves in a number of ways, with overall decline still a theme. All of this adds up to a social transformation, with the old communities consigned to history – or, more accurately, to the mindset of the British maritime tradition based on shipping and commercial ports, the Royal Navy and fisheries.

Apart from the material and social aspects discussed above, the British maritime tradition now resides at a mental level in museums and archives, in the increasing popularity of festivals of the sea involving restoration of traditional boats, and in folk traditions which have now largely disappeared into the realms of the literature. All this remains immensely important in educational and awareness terms. Even if it has become to some extent commodified (Wallis, 1996), together with current educational and recreational activities it is influential in interesting the younger generation in marine industries, affairs and careers (IACMST, 1998). It is they who are on the threshold of building a new maritime tradition based on modern industries.

Conclusion

In terms of sequences of development of the British maritime world, a succession of at least five sets of traditional societies followed by probably five industrial stages have been identified. Much research is needed to test the validity of this approach, and to determine the real nature and likely future of the post-industrial turning point which appears to have been reached in the first decade of the new millennium. It is particularly important to have an understanding of this broad historical sweep when approaching many of the marine management tasks noted above.

At both conceptual and practical levels, the maritime heritage is a record of the human use of the sea in all its diversity over a range of time scales represented by the sequence outlined above. However, it is much more: the natural environment and heritage is fundamental to the economic continuation of several of the major marine industries now developing as well as the traditional ones – especially fisheries. Further, the heritage itself has become a major economic and human resource, not only in what remains and continues to develop of specialist maritime communities, but also in the traditions enshrined in the museums, archives, restoration and elsewhere which forms the basis of so much of the educational and recreational fields.

The current preoccupation with marine stewardship and integrative legislative approaches is a sign that the time is now ripe for the consolidation of the management of the material heritage, both natural and human. This implies imaginative handling of community issues to promote the transition from old to new maritime traditions. Meanwhile, the partial commodification of maritime tradition remains an important ingredient in raising general public awareness and contributing to the education of the next generation who will go down to the sea, not only in ships, but in multifarious ways to further develop human activity in the marine environment around the British Isles.

References

Aymard, M. (ed.) (1982) *Dutch Capitalism, World Capitalism.* Cambridge: Cambridge University Press.

Bailey, R.S. and Parrish, B.B. (eds) (1987) *Developments in Fisheries Research in Scotland.* Farnham: Fishing News Books.

Bird, J.H. (1963) *The Major Seaports of the United Kingdom.* London: Hutchinson.

Bird, J.H. (1971) *Seaports and Seaport Terminals.* London: Hutchinson.

Bowen, E. (1977) *Saints, Seaways and Settlements.* Cardiff: University of Wales Press.

Brøgger, A.W. and Shetelig, H. (1971) *Viking Ships: their Ancestry and Evolution.* London: Hurst.

Cameron, A. and Farndon, R. (1984) *Scenes from Sea and City: Lloyd's List 1734–1984.* Colchester: Lloyd's of London Press.

Coull, J.R. (1996) *The Sea Fisheries of Scotland.* Edinburgh: John Donald.

Couper, A.D. (ed.) (1996) 'The protection of the underwater cultural heritage', *Marine Policy* 20: 4, 283–354.

Cunliffe, B. (2001) *Facing the Ocean: the Atlantic and its Peoples 8000 BC–AD 1500.* Oxford: Oxford University Press.

Cunliffe, B. (2002) *The Extraordinary Voyage of Pytheas the Greek.* London: Penguin.

Davison, A. (2000) 'An ocean act for the UK: progress and perspectives', in Cicin-Sain, B. and Rivera-Arriaga, E. (eds) *North American and European Perspectives on Ocean and Coastal Policy: Building Partnerships and Expanding the Technological Frontier.* Proceedings Vol. 1 International Conference on Coastal and Ocean Space Utilization, Cancun, 1–4 November 2000. Delaware, Center for the Study of Marine Policy: University of Delaware, pp. 75–9.

Department of Environment, Food and Rural Affairs (2002) *Safeguarding Our Seas.* London: HMSO.

Dollinger, P. (1970) *The Hansa.* London: Methuen.

Drumgoole, S. (ed.) (1999) *Legal Protection of the Underwater Cultural Heritage.* Dordrecht: Kluwer Law International.

Ehlers, P. (1990) 'The history of the international North Sea Conferences', *International Journal of Estuarine and Coastal Zone Law* 5: 1/2, 3–14.

European Union (2002) *Towards a Strategy to Protect and Conserve the Marine Environment.* COM (2002) 539 Final. Brussels, European Union.

Gray, M. (1978) *The Fishing Industries of Scotland, 1790–1914: a Study in Regional Adaptation.* Oxford: Oxford University Press.

Inter-Agency Committee on Marine Science and Technology (1998) *Education and Training Working Group Report No. 5.* London: IACMST.

Hope, R. (1990) *A New History of British Shipping.* London: John Murray.

Jackson, G. (1978) *The British Whaling Trade.* London: Adam & Charles Black.

Johnman, L. and Johnston, I. (2001) *Down the River.* London: Argyll Publishing.

King, J. and Smith, H.D. (1986) 'Marine resources: new opportunities for surveyors', *Land and Mineral Surveyor* 4: 9, 689–97.

March, E.J. (1970) *Inshore Craft of Britain in Days of Sail and Oar.* Newton Abbot: David & Charles.

McGrail, S. (1981) *Rafts, Boats and Ships: from Prehistoric Times to the Medieval Era.* London: HMSO.

Moffat, A. (2001) *The Sea Kingdoms: the Story of Celtic Britain and Ireland.* London: HarperCollins.

Padfield, P. (1999) *Maritime Supremacy and the Opening of the Western Mind.* London: John Murray.

Pinder, D. and Smith, H.D. (eds) (1999) 'Heritage resources and naval port regeneration', *Ocean and Coastal Management* 42: 10/11, 857–984.

Raban, J. (ed.) (1993) *The Oxford Book of the Sea.* Oxford: Oxford University Press.

Schlee, S. (1973) *A History of Oceanography: the Edge of an Unfamiliar World.* London: Hale.

Scientific and Technical Working Group (1987) *Quality Status of the North Sea.* London: Department of the Environment.

Small, A. (1968) 'The historical geography of the Norse Viking colonisation of the Scottish Highlands', *Norsk Geografisk Tidss* 22: 1–16.

Smith, H.D. (1991) 'The application of maritime geography: a technical and general management approach', in Smith, H.D. and Vallega, A. (eds) *The Development of Integrated Sea Use Management.* London: Routledge, pp. 7–16.

Smith, H.D. (1992a) 'The British Isles and the age of exploration – a maritime perspective', *GeoJournal* 26: 4, 483–7.

Smith, H.D. (1992b) 'Theory of ocean management', in Fabbri, P. (ed.) *Ocean Management in Global Change.* London: Elsevier Applied Science, pp. 19–38.

Smith, H.D. (2000a) 'The millennium and the peoples of the sea', *Ocean and Coastal Management* 43: 1, 6–8.

Smith, H.D. (2000b) 'The industrialisation of the world ocean', *Ocean and Coastal Management* 43: 1, 1–28.

Wainwright, F.T. (ed.) (1962) *The Northern Isles*. London.

Wallis, K. (1996) *Contrived Authenticity: Visitor Attractions and the Maritime Heritage of Great Britain*. Cardiff: University of Wales Ph.D. thesis (unpublished).

Warner, W.W. (1984) *Distant Water*. New York: Little Brown & Co./Atlantic Monthly Press.

2 UK marine science at the millennium

David Pugh

Introduction

Marine science, the systematic extension of our knowledge of the oceans, continues to prosper in UK laboratories and universities. Understanding the oceans and their processes is fundamental to the activities described elsewhere in this book. Here we look at the work of one UK scientist in a single year. This snapshot is interpreted in the wider context of the dynamic global marine science community, of which the UK is an important member. But the practical advantages of understanding and predicting marine processes have been known for many millennia.

Nearly two thousand years ago some fishermen on the Sea of Galilee who had caught nothing all night were advised to cast their nets on the other side of the boat. Suddenly they were rewarded with a full catch. There is always something new to learn about the sea and its behaviour, and although knowledge about the sea has always been valuable, this is especially true today, when our ability to use and abuse planet earth, which is 70 per cent covered by oceans, is so great, and yet our knowledge is still so small.

Human interest in the sea and its behaviour has a long history. From very early times those who worshipped the sun and moon thought of the sea's tides as some sort of terrestrial manifestation of their astronomical deities. In the time of Christ, knowledge about the seas was limited mainly to observed facts, though the Greek, Aristotle, had already asked challenging questions such as 'Why is the sea salty?' and 'What causes tides?' The small tides of the Mediterranean meant that Julius Caesar's fleet was ill prepared for the large regular changes of water levels and currents he found when he visited the coast of Britain in 55 BC, but he soon learned to plan accordingly.

Through the next thousand years very little advance was made in marine science. Exceptionally, the Christian monk, the Venerable Bede (AD 673–735) in writing about tides, especially those along the coast of his native Northumbria, noted that high tides occur at different times around the British coast. He also described how fresh river water spreads over the surface of the sea because it is lighter than the salt seawater.

Progress in marine and all other sciences has accelerated through the past

500 years, from the Renaissance (Deacon, 1997). In the past 50 years progress has been very rapid. Today we can measure, model and predict ocean behaviour with useful confidence and accuracy. Even so, these new skills, which have emerged only in the last few years, are still at an early stage of development. Marine science is still young, and there is much yet to learn.

Many people have asked: what is marine science? A simple, accurate response is impossible, but one rather glib answer is that 'marine science is what marine scientists do'. In preparing this account of British marine science at the millennium, we have been fortunate to have access to a diary kept by Sam, a working marine scientist at a large centre on the south coast of England, for a few months in the summer of the year 2000. Through Sam's experience we can learn a little about the day-to-day work, aspirations, frustrations and achievements of marine scientists in the United Kingdom today.

So first, something about Sam. After a first degree in physics, Sam studied for a marine Ph.D. at a major laboratory in North Wales, relating satellite images of the sea to actual sea-truth measurements. Ten years ago, after an enjoyable spell applying this expertise as a post-doctoral researcher on the west coast of Scotland, Sam joined the present centre as a Natural Environment Research Council employee. Since then, after two well-earned promotions and several critically acclaimed publications in international journals, Sam's present responsibilities have expanded to include leading a small team working on calculating biological production in the surface waters of the North Atlantic. The team includes a chemist, three biologists and a mathematician, as well as three research students and two European Fellows; together they try to make sense of the masses of observational data that they collect from satellites and ships, and from unmanned vehicles. The mathematician is especially good at fitting the data into computer models of the real ocean, which allows predictions and tests against further data.

Why marine science?

First an abstract from Sam's diary:

Monday 15 May
Arrived early this morning. It means making other arrangements for getting the children to school, but it avoids heavy traffic and we really must complete the abstract for the American Geophysical Union Meeting in San Francisco next December before their deadline. The data from the May 1999 cruise is now coming together, comparing the results of our samples taken at sea from the Discovery *with the satellite images seems to show a much broader spread than in other years. It seems that plankton growth is stronger and earlier, but can we relate this to the warm summer and mild winter of 1998? Working on the computer all morning editing satellite images.*

RRS *Discovery* is the main British research ship, owned and operated by the Natural Environment Research Council from Southampton. Although capable of working anywhere in the world, it mainly operates in the North Atlantic. *Discovery* can carry up to 28 scientists and has many specialized facilities including seven specialized wet and dry laboratories. She has a gross 2,536 tonnage, and a maximum endurance at sea of 55 days. The two other research ships that NERC operated in 2000 were the *Darwin* and the *Challenger*. A research ship costs around £10,000 for each day at sea, so making these measurements is not cheap. Because of the cost to scientific users, use of the three NERC vessels has declined steadily through the 1990s and soon the smallest of the three, *Challenger*, has now been sold.

It is quite normal for the analysis and preparation of the results from a research cruise to take two years or longer. Some preliminary laboratory analysis can be done on the ship while at sea, but precise work needs more elaborate shore-based equipment. Data from satellites also needs to be checked and calibrated, before the different types of information can be plotted on maps and used to test computer models and theory. This is a team effort, and while at sea the scientists work in shifts to keep the work going 24 hours a day. There is nothing like a large plate of sardine sandwiches and a couple of cans of beer, shared with a colleague on the midnight watch, to build lifelong scientific associations and personal friendships.

Working marine scientists come from several basic scientific disciplines (Deacon *et al.*, 2001). Many have studied for a first degree in physics, chemistry, biology, geology or mathematics. Marine scientists are sometimes split into sub-groups, and described as physical oceanographers, chemical oceanographers or marine biologists. Even as recently as 1995, the Institute of Oceanographic Sciences Laboratory at Wormley, Surrey (now incorporated in the Southampton Oceanography Centre) was organized into scientific divisions for physics, chemistry, biology and geology/geophysics.

Traditionally, physical oceanographers study waves, tides, currents and ocean circulation. The oceans play a vital role in stabilizing the earth's climate, absorbing heat in the tropics and transporting it to higher latitudes. As a very direct example of the importance of this transport for Britain, compare our climate with that of Labrador, which is on the same latitude, but does not enjoy the warming that the Gulf Stream and North Atlantic Drift bring to Northern Europe. Satellites are replacing ship observations as the main source of observation (Fu and Cazenave, 2001).

Chemical oceanographers map the variations in the salts dissolved in seawater and how they interact. In recent years there have been many studies of how carbon dioxide is absorbed, distributed and retained in the ocean. There are even proposals to artificially remove carbon dioxide from the atmosphere and deposit it in the oceans, a process called sequestration, which could reduce the increases of industrial outputs in the atmosphere, and hence combat global warming.

Many marine biologists focus on the plants and animals along the seashore, and the way in which they adapt and compete for the various layers or zones of exposure and submersion within the intertidal areas. Others look at the way in which animals live in the open ocean and the deep sea. Some of the most spectacular creatures on earth exist in the deep dark cold abyssal depths of the oceans. Many near-bottom fishes have large eyes, which can only be used for seeing the bioluminescence of other inhabitants. Below about 1,000 m depth (the average ocean depth is around 4,000 m) there is effectively no daylight (Herring, 2002).

Understanding geological processes at sea is fundamental for all geology. New understanding of plate tectonics, continental drift and the processes of sea floor spreading at the mid-ocean ridges has revolutionized the way geologists think about the earth in recent years. The earth's crust under the ocean is thinner, and much younger than under the continents, and is continually being regenerated at the mid-ocean ridges.

The life forms that inhabit the space around the hot and cold submarine 'volcanoes' of very salty water, which circulates in the rocks and then jets into the ocean at many places along the mid-ocean ridges, have confronted biologists with one of the most amazing challenges to conventional wisdom: that all life forms are sustained by solar energy and photosynthesis. These creatures form ecosystems, which are sustained by quite different chemical reactions.

This example shows why the traditional scientific discipline distinctions are breaking down, to be replaced by multidisciplinary studies (Summerhayes and Thorpe, 1996). Sam's team includes a mixture of scientists, to understand how phytoplankton, the basis of the marine food chain, converts light into life and supports the marine creatures at higher levels in the food chain. Integrated multidisciplinary projects are now the normal way of organizing marine scientists worldwide. Teams from all scientific aspects are more likely to be studying a general phenomenon like productivity or ridge vents. Integrated studies of coastal processes may also involve economists and social scientists, but these are still tentative associations.

People used to argue about the difference between marine science and oceanography, sometimes suggesting that oceanography excluded marine biology. Most now accept that the terms oceanography and marine science (note the singular) are synonymous and that an integrated scientific attack on understanding the seas is more important than arguing about how to label marine scientists. The new emphasis is on an integrating holistic approach; categorization and classification are out of fashion. The term *oceanology* is generally understood as technology in support of marine sciences, as opposed to marine technology that is much broader, covering the design of structures such as ships and oilrigs and pipelines to work at sea.

Today many students study directly for a first degree in marine science, perhaps attracted by the growing popular interest in the environment and how it is changing in response to human intervention and climate variability. There are many universities in the UK that teach specialized courses devoted to, or related to, some aspect of the sea. The three biggest are at Bangor, North Wales, and Southampton and Plymouth.

Marine science is an observational not experimental activity, a fact that is often not easily appreciated by the scientists who work in laboratories and wear white coats. The ocean is too big and there are too many factors that drive it for it to be subjected to the standard scientific experimental approach of testing hypotheses by changing one factor at a time, even if society would allow such interference. One recent exception has been the enhancement of phytoplankton growth by fertilizing a limited area of sea with dissolved iron.

Instead of controlled laboratory experiments, marine science has come to depend heavily on using vast computer models of the seas to test hypotheses. Basic theories and observations are incorporated into a model that seeks to reproduce the total behaviour of a particular sea. The model can be tested against new observations as they become available and, if the theory representing the scientific processes is valid, the model can be used for forecasting future conditions. Many complex global ocean/ atmosphere models have been developed for climate change studies, and to anticipate changes in ocean circulation and sea levels. The team that Sam leads is trying to develop methods of predicting how biologically productive the North Atlantic will be in future years.

Our ability to predict future seas, although still very limited, is improving. There is now clear evidence that human activity is influencing the seas, both directly through pollution and indirectly through enhanced greenhouse global warming. Larger, faster computers allow more realistic representation of the oceans. New instruments and systematic observations, especially from satellites contributing to the Global Ocean Observing System, provide real data to drive and constrain models. The big challenge is to understand the science that links all the complicated interacting factors which together determine how the sea will change. Globally this is important because the oceans store and transport vast quantities of heat which may then be exchanged with the more mobile atmosphere. As already explained, changes in ocean circulation can affect our climate, which is much warmer than normal for our latitudes.

The application of marine science in other areas is equally important and often more immediate. More locally, marine science contributes to the management of estuaries, the control of pollution, the design of flood defences, and can explain year-to-year variability in fish populations and help plan sustainable extraction of sand and gravel from shallow nearshore areas for the building industry.

As we shall see in the next section, UK scientists have played a leading role in developing many aspects of our understanding of the sea. Until recently, most of these people were not marine scientists in the modern sense, but academics who applied the scientific method to a wide range of problems and natural phenomenon, including the sea. Newton and Darwin are two outstanding examples.

The link between people who live and work by and on the sea who need to understand and predict, and marine scientists, has always been strong in Britain. The Navy and its hydrographers have enjoyed strong links with marine scientists, not only for predicting tides but for magnetic and other geophysical and geological discoveries. Hillaire Belloc in the *Cruise of the Nona* wrote provocatively of marine scientists, 'When they pontificate on tides it does no great harm, because the sailorman cares nothing for their theories, but goes by real knowledge...'. Belloc was wrong. Over the past 300 years there have been close productive links between marine scientists and the people who use the real knowledge they generate. In future these links will be even stronger.

Marine science: a history of ideas

Friday 26 May
At last we have finished the manuscript of our paper on plankton growth in 1998. Still a few changes to make but the worst is over. Writing up results for publication is always one of the hardest things to start and there are always excuses, one more calculation, a little more data . . . for leaving it for another week or so. Anyway, now it's done and things have come together very well. There are five authors, three from our group, Ian from Oban and Martine from Bordeaux. Had to press them for their final contributions . . . they have excuses too . . . which arrived on Monday by email, complete with diagrams.

Still a lot of discussion following Wednesday's seminar by a visiting speaker from Plymouth, about the Gaia hypothesis. Professor Lovelock proposes Mother Earth: biology, chemistry and geology are an integral part of a dynamic system. The hypothesis is that the life of earth operates as a single organism that defines and maintains conditions necessary for its survival. I think it might be relevant to work we are going to start soon, but some of the group are not convinced. John and some others think it's a non-testable hypothesis, and as such is non-scientific. I am more sympathetic. Anyway, it's livened up our coffee break and makes a change from talking about the rising price of petrol. No doubt the arguments will continue when we go for our weekly drink at the Grapes after work tonight.

Science makes progress by testing hypotheses and, if they prove sufficiently robust, adopting them as laws on which to build other theories and hypotheses. Mostly, marine science has taken scientific laws from other disciplines and applied them for its own purposes. For example, Newton's laws of motion applied to fluids on a rotating earth can predict the physical response of the sea to forcing by winds and air pressure, and by density differences. When Newton published the *Principia* in 1687, he almost incidentally produced an explanation of ocean tides, showing why there are two tides a day in terms of the gravitational attraction of the moon. His contemporary Halley, who paid for the publication from his own funds, wrote an account, initially for King James II, explaining why Newton's ideas were so important for understanding what caused the tides. Halley himself commanded what were probably the first marine science expeditions, for geomagnetic measurements in the Atlantic Ocean from 1699 to 1700, and then to map the tides of the English Channel in the summer of 1701.

The eighteenth- and nineteenth-century British explorers such as James Cook and James Ross included marine observations as part of their programmes, with the Royal Society and various committees advising and taking an active part in deciding what scientific data should be collected by naval expeditions. It was usual to include a scientist or naturalist on the ship's complement. The captain in command often welcomed a well-educated companion, but not always. Banks sailed with Cook, and Hooker made many important discoveries when he sailed with Ross to the Southern Ocean. However, without doubt the most famous attachment was the appointment of Charles Darwin to sail under Fitzroy on the voyage of the *Beagle* (1831–6). As well as formulating ideas on natural selection during the voyage, Darwin also developed a theory explaining the growth of coral islands and observed marine deposits at a high level in the Andes, proving vast vertical land movement over geological time. He also reported an eyewitness account of a tsunami approaching the coast of Chile 'in a fearful line of white breakers', following an earthquake in February 1835.

In these global expeditions, exploring the seas was less important than discovering and mapping new lands. The first expedition devoted to making discoveries about the global ocean itself was aboard HMS *Challenger* (1872–6). Under the naval command of Captain Nares and the scientific leadership of Wyville Thomson, and with the strong guidance of the Royal Society, biological, chemical and physical studies were made in a systematic way and eventually published in a 50-volume series.

More recently, major British contributions to twentieth-century marine science include George Deacon's 1930s investigations of the convergence and circulation of currents in the Antarctic, and the elegant proof that oceans are formed by sea floor spreading from mid-ocean ridges, by Fred Vine and Drummond Matthews in the early 1960s.

Scientists, in the same way as artists and writers, are stimulated and inspired by observing the oceans. Normally the scientific response is to apply general scientific principles to explain the particular behaviour of the oceans. Interestingly there is at least one example of the reverse, where explanations of particular ocean phenomena inspire a more general theory. When Thomas Young explained the behaviour of light in terms of wave theory he acknowledged that his ideas had been partly based on Newton's explanation of the daily tides in the Gulf of Tonkin, China.

UK marine science today

Thursday 15 June
Just back from Norwich where I am on the Steering Committee, making final plans for the Challenger Society Conference next September. We especially encourage research students to present their work. Two students from our group have had abstracts accepted and we will prepare three posters for display. Must make sure these are good, and rehearse the speakers beforehand. The standard has increased enormously since I gave my first scientific presentation to the same meeting twelve years ago. Now that there are prizes for the best presentations and posters, people take the competition very seriously and their laboratories get credit too. Good to meet colleagues from labs all round the country, who were also at the planning meeting. Marine science is quite a small field and so we get to know each other very well.

The Challenger Society for Marine Science, established in 1903 and named after the nineteenth-century expedition, is the natural focus for professional marine scientists in Britain. After some restructuring in the 1980s, it now has an active membership of around 450, an excellent journal, sub-groups and links with similar organizations in Europe. Unfortunately, it is still too small to employ permanent staff so its work depends very much on volunteers. The September 2000 conference in Norwich, like its predecessors, was a great success. Over one week, 250 people listened to and made presentations, took part in informal evening sessions to discuss posters and the future of marine science, and planned new science to conduct together.

Recently the former Institute of Marine Engineers has re-established itself as the Institute of Marine Engineering, Science and Technology (IMarEST). It plans to develop into an international professional membership body and learned society for all marine professionals. Through the Institute marine scientists can, through career development, apply to become Members (MIMarEST) and Fellows (FIMarEST). There is also an official qualification as a Chartered Marine Scientist. This is an exciting new development with which Sam will become involved.

In Britain marine scientists work in universities, in government laboratories and in the commercial sector. All of these interests were represented in Norwich. The main government laboratories are the Fisheries Research Services (FRS) Laboratory of the Scottish Executive in Aberdeen; the Centre for Environment, Fisheries and Aquaculture Science (CEFAS) in Lowestoft, with laboratories also at Weymouth and

Burnham; and specialist centres of expertise in the Environment Agency, Bath and the Meteorological Office, Bracknell. The Ministry of Defence has oceanographic interests (now privatized as QinetiQ) based in Dorset and Portsmouth.

The British commercial sector operates internationally and is especially strong in marine monitoring and assessment. There are also several small companies specializing in high-quality instruments for marine science. Marine scientific industries and consultants operate on quite a modest scale worldwide, and there are no major global market leaders. The UK companies are well respected and competitive in this market.

The two main university research centres are Bangor, North Wales, and Southampton. Bangor has just commissioned a new research vessel, named *Prince Madog* like its predecessor, for working in the Irish Sea and similar coastal and shelf waters. Many of the scientists in Southampton transferred from the NERC Institute of Oceanographic Sciences when the Southampton Oceanography Centre opened in 1995. Eventually all staff in Southampton will be employed by the university, as existing NERC employees retire. NERC maintains the Proudman Oceanographic Laboratory, soon to be moved to the Liverpool University campus. However, two former NERC laboratories, in Oban and Plymouth, now operate independently. Many other universities have specialist interests in marine science, often linked to excellent marine technical and professional training. These include Plymouth, Cardiff, Liverpool, Glasgow, Aberdeen, St Andrews, Newcastle, Hull and East Anglia.

The role of the key professional societies, especially the Challenger Society and IMarEST, in keeping an active network of people with similar interests is very important for the health of marine science in Britain. Meetings like that organized in Norwich are important for maintaining the links, as are others organized by NERC and the government Inter-Agency Committee on Marine Science and Technology.

Tuesday 27 June
A difficult day. The paper Martine and I sent to the Journal of Geophysical Research *in March has come back with referee's comments. Some good, some bad. We have to do more work on the data and justify our conclusions further before they will publish it. We have done most of the extra work demanded, but were planning a second publication. It looks as if we will have to merge the two publications into one bigger paper. Pity, because two publications looks better than one on the lists which are regularly produced to show progress: we are due to be externally reviewed in December! Still, we get extra credit for publishing with scientists in other countries.*

Even worse, my proposal to NERC for funding to start a new programme of regular Atlantic Ocean sections has been turned down. Although we got an alpha 3 rating this was not enough. Science Review Panels are often reluctant to fund long-term measuring programmes, although everyone agrees they are essential. Must talk to the people at the Sir Alister Hardy Foundation for Ocean Science in Plymouth who maintain long continuous plankton recorder sections and have some very exciting results from analysing data over decades.

All scientists know the problem of getting enough money to do their research: there is never enough available. For the younger scientists the success or failure of a proposal can make the difference between continuing a job in marine science, or leaving the field for other work. Competition can be fierce. Funding is allocated after external review on a competitive basis, mainly by the Natural Environment Research Council. NERC also provide partial support for the Scottish Association for Marine Science, based in Oban, and the Marine Biological Association in Plymouth. The government Inter-Agency Committee on Marine Science and Technology has made a study of employment and funding of marine science in Britain. Most scientists are more concerned about their project funding and their immediate work than about the overall health of funding marine science. Nevertheless, looking at the whole picture (Pugh and Skinner, 2002) makes interesting reading.

The estimated marine-related spend on research and development in 1999–2000 was £609 million, 1.4 per cent of the total marine-related contribution to Gross Domestic Product. In slightly different terms, marine-related research and development is 3.7 per cent of the total United Kingdom R&D, compared with the 4.9 per cent contribution of the marine-related sectors to GDP.

The main research and development was undertaken in government laboratories (£273 million), particularly in the defence sector. Government policy is to move public-sector research into the private commercial sector; the future transfer of defence research to a new commercial enterprise (QinetiQ) will involve about £200 million of marine R&D.

Commercial sector expenditure was around £220 million and university departments spent about £118 million on research and development. Between 1988–9 and 1994–5 there was an increase for marine-related university research in real terms of around 16 per cent, mainly in research council support, with a fall in direct government funding. A substantial increase in the money from the European Union led to a further increase of 10 per cent by 1999–2000, after adjusting for inflation.

The actual number of people involved in university research increased from around 1,924 to 2,450 between 1988 and 1995–6; in 1999–2000 the estimate was 2,238. There was a trend for these people to be concentrated in fewer universities. Academic staff numbers vary at around 550, but there has been a substantial increase in the number of postdoctoral researchers and postgraduate students, who together totalled more than 1,350 in 1999–2000.

For 1999–2000 the average funding for a research scientist was £22 k, compared with around £34 k for people working in marine technology research. However, the numbers of researchers directly involved in marine technology has fallen significantly in recent years, probably reflecting the fact that North Sea oil and gas operations are now technologically mature industries.

The most popular research topic in universities was the physiology of marine organisms, followed by basic biology of marine organisms. Coastal engineering and science and primary productivity, plankton and ecology were next. Not unexpectedly, industry research priorities were different: sensors, acoustic engineering, navigation and position fixing, followed by signal processing were the main research interests.

Sunday 9 July
Decided to stay in after lunch while the rest of the family went to the New Forest. I have to go through my notes for a talk at the local sixth-form college on Tuesday, about careers in marine science. I try to do two or three of these talks a year, and am probably seen as a role model by the science teachers. We try to respond to all invitations, as educating young people about the sea is the best way to ensure a sustainable future! Not just for the sea, but also for the university degree courses I help to run. Sometimes the postgraduate students go instead to the schools. Our Schools Liaison Officer tells me that these student talks get a very enthusiastic welcome, much more than for my talks (he explained this very tactfully), because school students relate much better to a younger speaker. O tempora. O mores!

Children are naturally enthusiastic about many things, including the mysteries of the sea. Those who choose to study in more detail often follow courses in marine biology: there are fewer takers for the mathematics, physics and chemistry courses. Yet surveys of job prospects in the marine commercial sector regularly show that skills in computing and modelling are at a premium.

For young people who want to learn more than is encompassed within the schools' national curriculum, local museums are worth visiting, particularly for those who can get to the National Maritime Museum in Greenwich. The NMM is moving into the new century with a complete refurbishment and an emphasis on environmental and global issues, rather than the traditional heralding of Britain's glorious maritime past.

Other ways of engaging with the sea include the Beach Watch programmes of the Marine Conservation Society, and the many local diving clubs, which welcome new enthusiastic members. In fact, Sam still dives around the Isle of Wight and in Poole Harbour when time, tide and family allow!

The wider seas

Wednesday 12 July

A good day. Heard this morning that Brussels has accepted our proposal for a three-year study comparing productivity in the coastal seas of the Mediter-ranean with those in the north-east Atlantic. This will cover 50 per cent of the costs for a group of scientists from France, Greece, Spain and Britain. One of my students will be completing his thesis soon and this will allow us to keep him on as a post-doctoral researcher, probably spending some time in Spain. The pay will not be very good, and he would do better moving to a different pro-fession, as some do, but he seems keen to stay and the work abroad will be an incentive.

Also, I have been invited by the Intergovernmental Oceanographic Commis-sion to join an Expert Group looking at the planning of ocean biological moni-toring in the north Atlantic. This plan will be part of the Global Ocean Observing System that is slowly being developed.

And another possible opportunity: we have just been told that NERC will be sending one of its ships (RRS Charles Darwin*) to the Indian Ocean next year. After the holidays I will work on a proposal to NERC for making measure-ments in the tropical waters of the Indian Ocean, or perhaps in the highly pro-ductive upwelling area off Oman.*

Writing an account of British marine science in isolation would be very difficult. The oceans pay no heed to human laws or to state boundaries. Sooner rather than later, scientists find themselves working together inter-nationally, exchanging data and ideas to build up a wide picture of how the oceans behave. This international flavour is what lifts a career in marine science into an exciting worldwide domain.

The global scientific approach is also increasingly being reflected in marine planning and legislation. The management of coastal seas, espe-cially around Britain, often involves many countries and administrations. The North Sea is an obvious example. Another is the Irish Sea, where the recent devolution of Scotland and Wales is making management more complicated, involving administrations in Edinburgh, London, Cardiff, Dublin and Belfast, and of course the Isle of Man.

Internationally, British scientists have a good standing and in many areas are among the world leaders. The World Ocean Circulation Experi-ment (WOCE, 1990–2002), a component of the World Climate Research Program (WCRP), has been the most ambitious oceanographic global experiment undertaken to date (Siedler *et al.*, 2001). The International Project Office for WOCE was at the Southampton Oceanography Centre. As well as observations by satellites, physical and chemical observations were made by nearly 30 nations in four of the world's oceans. At the same time global numerical ocean models have been developed to assimilate these measurements. The field phase of the project lasted from 1990–7.

This was followed by AIMS, the Analysis, Interpretation, Modelling and Synthesis activities. The success of WOCE AIMS will be important for future global marine programmes. The most immediate of these programmes are CLIVAR, a global study of ocean climate variability and predictability (also hosted in Southampton), and GODAE, the Global Ocean Data Assimilation Experiment that is building up to full operation in 2003–5.

Recognizing that the oceans contain some 50 times as much carbon dioxide as the atmosphere, and that small changes in the ocean carbon cycle can have large atmospheric consequences, Joint Global Ocean Flux Studies (JGOFS) was organized as a major global programme. Biological processes undoubtedly complicate the oceanic carbon cycle, although they probably do not affect the present uptake of additional carbon dioxide due to human activity. The goal of JGOFS has been to determine and understand on a global scale the processes controlling the time-varying fluxes of carbon and associated biological elements in the ocean, and to evaluate the related exchanges with the atmosphere, sea floor and continental boundaries.

WOCE and JGOFS have common interests, and have worked together to make best use of the limited scientific resources available, even on a global scale. The Global Ocean Observing System (GOOS), being developed by the Intergovernmental Oceanographic Commission of UNESCO and the World Meteorological Organization with scientific input from the International Council for Science, can help to organize global ocean measurements. Strong early British encouragement, and more recently effective British management of the GOOS Project Office in Paris, has helped steady development of GOOS, but there is still a long way to go. During 2000 several countries including Britain made commitments to deploy collectively around 3,000 ARGO floats throughout the oceans, which will measure vertical temperature and salinity profiles at regular intervals as they rise every ten days from a 'parking' depth of around 2,000 m. The data is transmitted by satellite to central data management and processing laboratories. Assimilating data from ARGO will be an essential part of GODAE (Global Ocean Data Assimilation Experiment).

Nearer home, a succession of framework programmes funded by the European Union has included marine science and technology as a major component in a series of MAST (Marine Science and Technology) programmes. Participants in European Union programmes must come from a group of countries in Europe. Ideally among these there should be a balance of countries between those that have high scientific expertise and those that are still developing their marine scientific skills. Although the Brussels-funded programmes will not pay for the full cost of proposed work, usually almost all of the additional costs are met. British marine scientists have looked for Brussels funding with enthusiasm and over a long period have enjoyed an above average success rate for their proposals. Britain has also been a leading contributor to the development of the European ocean observing system, EuroGOOS. The Marine Board of the European Science Foundation has prepared a new strategy for marine science in Europe which could mark a new beginning for a new millennium, and to which many British scientists contributed. This strategy looks both at the scientific opportunities, and the economic and social applications of better knowledge about the sea.

Scientists, especially at the government laboratories in Lowestoft and Aberdeen, also work internationally through the International Council for the Exploration of the Sea (ICES), one of the oldest intergovernmental marine organizations, which now has broader environmental interests than the original fisheries studies on which it first focused.

ICES also involves scientists in Canada and the USA. Given the common language and other cultural ties, it is not surprising that many British scientists spend time working in North America. Recently there has been a significant flux of several eminent North American scientists in the reverse direction to join the Southampton Oceanography Centre.

Management of the global oceans is still a distant prospect, but there is no doubt that human activity is beginning to have an impact and that we should recognize our power to change slowly even the vastness of the oceans. Legislators and governments are responding. One estimate suggests that there are now more than 500 international agreements of various kinds about the use of the oceans. There are at least 25 major international marine-related organizations in which Britain participates. Perhaps the most important of these is the United Nations Convention on the Law of the Sea, to which Britain has been a State Party since 1997. In response to UNCLOS, survey work on the sea bed and sediments to the west of Scotland was completed in 2000, as part of the preparation for a case for extending the British continental shelf beyond the normal 200 nautical miles. This case must be presented to the Commission on the Limits of the Continental Shelf within ten years.

Internationally and nationally many British government departments have some responsibility for the seas: fisheries, pollution, trade, shipping, defence, oil and gas extraction (Defra, 2002). Some countries, including Canada and the United States, now have a central Ocean Act, or legislation which seeks to bring the co-ordination of these responsibilities under one department. It could conceivably happen in Britain in the foreseeable future, and there would be advantages: experience elsewhere will be followed with interest.

Future seas for humankind

Throughout history it has been normal to assume that human waste and human activities were of no significance compared with the vastness of the total earth system. Perhaps a little late, but now without any doubt, we know that leaving the earth system to take care of itself, and assuming it can absorb the excesses of human activity without damage, is no longer an option. On land there are strong political pressures that are forcing social and economic responses, but for the 70 per cent of the earth's surface covered by seas these direct political processes are weak or absent. Yet the need for long-term care and planning for sustainable oceans is just as necessary. Inevitably, but perhaps slowly, we will have to embrace this responsibility over the next thousand years.

National boundaries mean nothing to the oceans. The challenge is to develop intergovernmental processes that work. The importance of the United Nations Convention on the Law of the Sea, established at the end of the twentieth century, will only be generally realized in a distant future. Global politics, intergovernmental agreements, and their enforcement on the high seas may seem remote and unconnected to the work of today's marine scientists, but this is changing. Recently the United Nations has started an annual series of ocean meetings in New York, called the Informal Consultative Process.

The British government funds and encourages scientific research, to 'create wealth and improve the quality of life'. Around the world other countries are making a similar investment. Especially for the oceans, political will, consensus planning, and even making sure people obey the laws that already exist, depends on a basic scientific understanding and an ability to predict consequences. Today's marine science will give us the means to respond to tomorrow's responsibilities. Over ten years it makes only a small difference, but over a thousand years that importance is impossible to estimate. For the future of Planet Earth the next thousand years is only the beginning: marine science today is not a small thing.

Epilogue

As the world changes, marine science is changing too. Fifty years ago oceanographers expected to be treated as bearded heroes just returned from sea. Sam, or Samantha as her mother still annoyingly insists on calling her, would not welcome that.

> *Saturday 22 July*
> *John has taken the children swimming.*

Today, Sam is not thinking about saving Planet Earth. There is packing to do before they drive tomorrow for a three-week camping holiday in France. It will be good to see Martine and her family again.

References

Deacon, M. (1997) *Scientists and the Sea, 1650–1900,* 2nd edn. Ashgate, 459pp.

Deacon, M., Rice, A. and Summerhayes, C.P. (2001) (eds) *Understanding the Oceans.* London: UCL Press, 300pp.

Department for Environment, Food and Rural Affairs (2002) *Safeguarding our Seas: a Strategy for the Conservation and Sustainable Development of our Marine Environment.* London: Defra Publications, 80pp.

Fu, L.L. and Cazenave, A. (2001) *Satellite Altimetry and Earth Sciences.* San Diego, CA: Academic Press, 463pp.

Herring, P.J. (2002) *The Biology of the Deep Ocean.* Oxford: Oxford University Press, 314pp.

Pugh, D.T. and Skinner, L.M. (2002) *A New Analysis of Marine-related Activities in the UK Economy with Supporting Science and Technology.* Inter-Agency Committee on Marine Science and Technology, IACMST Information Document No. 10.

Siedler, G., Church, J. and Gould, J. (2001) (eds) *Ocean Circulation and Climate.* Academic Press International Geophysics Series, 77, 736pp.

Summerhayes, C.P. and Thorpe, S.A. (1996) (eds) *Oceanography: an Illustrated Guide.* London: Manson Publishing, 352pp.

Part II

The open sea

3   Oil and gas from UK waters

Resources, technologies, corporate attitude and government

David Pinder

025   L7\
052   041
055

Introduction

Until the 1960s the economic significance of the British seas – in common with seas and oceans throughout most of the world – lay in the underpinning provided for two traditional activities: commercial fishing and maritime trade. Subsequently the trade dimension has gone from strength to strength, albeit with radical adjustments in the shipping and port systems. In contrast, from a resource exploitation viewpoint the spotlight has swung rapidly from fisheries to hydrocarbons as the UK continental shelf (UKCS) has become one of north-west Europe's two dominant oil producers and the leading source of natural gas.

Given this dramatic shift, no volume on the British seas would be complete if it failed to offer an overview of offshore oil and gas activity. But while one aim of this chapter is to provide this very necessary survey, the intention is to go substantially further by exploring aspects of offshore investment that are arguably neglected yet central to understanding the industry's achievements, problems and future prospects. Consequently, although we begin with a review of oil and gas developments over the last four decades, the majority of the chapter draws into the analysis three interrelated issues: rapid technological change as a facilitator of exploration and production; corporate attitude and the perception of investment opportunities; and the role of government in promoting sustained production.

Three further points are appropriate by way of introduction. First, the discussion deliberately avoids attempting to cover all aspects of the offshore industry and its impacts; such an ambition would require a book rather than a single chapter. It is by choice, therefore, that important potential themes – such as the industry's national economic significance, and its social and environmental consequences onshore – have not been addressed.

Second, exploitation of the UK's offshore oil and gas resources has naturally generated a large academic literature. Although reference is made in the text to elements of this literature, because of its scale no attempt at a comprehensive review is made here. Instead a sample bibliography – organized chronologically to enable the reader to judge shifts in research emphasis at various development stages – is provided in Appendix 1. Attention is also directed to the recently published collected writings of Peter Odell (2001; 2002a), both for the numerous papers covering the whole period of North Sea exploitation and for the bibliographies of the papers themselves.

Third, readers seeking detailed and comprehensive factual information on UK offshore activity should consult first the government's annual review, *Development of the Oil and Gas Resources of the United Kingdom.* Commonly known as the *Brown Book*, this formerly hard-copy publication is now available free on-line.[1] Also readily available, but much less comprehensive in terms of the range of information provided, are the field-by-field surveys published in Mager and Vieth's *European Oil and Gas Yearbook* and in industry journals such as *Offshore* and *Offshore Engineer.* Beyond this, certain private organizations hold invaluable information archives, both quantitative and qualitative. Of particular importance are the United Kingdom Offshore Operators' Association (UKOOA)[2] and the Energy Institute's Library and Information Service.[3] The latter maintains a particularly large collection of industry journals, many of which have been used extensively in this chapter.

Offshore hydrocarbons: four decades of development

Since the initial announcements in 1965, more than 450 hydrocarbon fields have been discovered on the UKCS. Four out of five lie in just three sectors – the southern, central and northern North Sea – with the large majority of the remainder concentrated in the Moray Firth (Figure 3.1). Significant finds elsewhere, such as the major Morecambe Bay gas deposits off north-west England, have been rare. While some fields are complex, containing combinations of oil, gas and gas condensates, these are a small minority. Most deposits are either oil or gas, with oil fields accounting for 48 per cent of all known reservoirs, and gas fields for 36 per cent. Echoing this bias towards oil-bearing structures, oil production in 2001 amounted to 117.9 million tonnes and gas production to 95.2 million tonnes of oil equivalent (mtoe).[4] In total this was equal to almost 95 per cent of UK primary energy consumption, although imports, exports and other power sources naturally complicated the actual usage picture, particularly with respect to oil.[5]

Knowledge of these resources has developed unevenly with time. Discoveries were most frequent between the early 1980s and the early 1990s, when the offshore industry identified, on average, 21 significant reservoirs a year. This high figure reflected three factors: the maturation of the industry; the attractions of developing North Sea oil fields following the oil crises of the 1970s; and opportunities to exploit rapid growth in UK

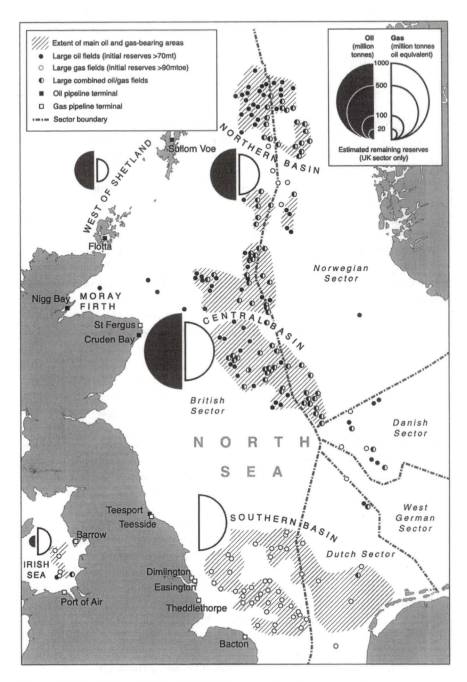

Figure 3.1 The UK continental shelf: sectors, production areas and resources.

natural gas demand in the final quarter of the twentieth century. Before and since this 1980s exploration heyday the discovery rate has averaged nine or ten fields per year and, as will be discussed later, since the mid-1990s has fallen to less than eight.

Although exploration began in the early 1960s in the relatively shallow waters of the southern North Sea, its subsequent history was not one of simple, steady migration northwards to deeper waters as technological advances took effect. The modal period for discoveries in the northern North Sea came as early as 1975–9, when 34 fields were found there. The equivalent peak period for the central North Sea was 1980–4 (28 significant finds). And, despite the fact that the southern North Sea was where UK offshore activity began in the 1960s, this sector's modal discovery period came as late as 1985–9 (39 new deposits).

Insights into this switch of emphasis from south to north and back once more can be gained by linking the distinction between oil and gas deposits with their distinctive geographies and energy market dynamics. Early exploration in the southern North Sea, inspired by the vast onshore gas discovery in the Dutch province of Groningen (Odell and Corelje, 2001), established that this sector of the UKCS continental shelf was almost entirely gas bearing. Throughout the southern sector's exploration history, all but two discoveries have been exclusively gas. When the 1970s oil crises rapidly raised interest in oil it was evident that the southern sector offered little prospect of oil discovery, and the balance of offshore exploration consequently swung northwards. The outcome was that 85 per cent of discoveries in the north, and 80 per cent in the central North Sea, found oil either alone or in association with gas or gas condensates (Figure 3.1). Then, as the 1980s progressed, strong demand growth for gas, coupled with generally sluggish oil prices, again raised gas up the agenda. While one strategic response by companies was to develop the gas resources recently discovered during the northward push, a second was for exploration to revisit – with considerable success – the gas-bearing southern North Sea.

The discovery of an oil or gas field, even if it is described as a significant deposit, is no guarantee that it will be developed (i.e. put into production). Within the financial context of oil and gas prices at a given time, and of government-imposed tax regimes, development decisions are particularly dependent on a field's size and location. Especially when prices are weak, small and relatively isolated deposits are unlikely to be developed because of the disproportionately high capital costs of production and transport infrastructures. Because the latter are dominantly – though not exclusively – pipeline systems, this has concentrated attention on reservoirs that can be attached, either directly or through 'tie-backs', to extensive and complex oil and gas networks serving the southern, central and northern North Sea (Figure 3.2). Discussion will return to pipeline tie-backs and networks later, in relation to technological advance.

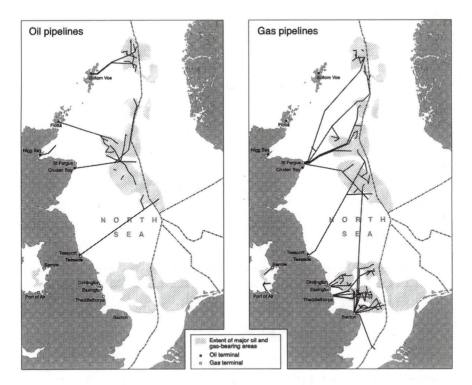

Figure 3.2 Oil and gas pipeline networks.

Over the offshore industry's history to date, these forces – field characteristics, costs and transport systems – have been mainly responsible for the fact that less than 60 per cent of all North Sea reservoirs have been developed. What this low figure does not reveal, however, is the full reality of the industry's growing reluctance to develop many fields. Because the average size of discoveries has fallen sharply over the decades, and because until recently the long-term trend in oil prices has been downwards,[6] the probability of new discoveries being put into production has declined. For example, more than 80 per cent of the late-1960s finds have subsequently been put into production, compared with only 40 per cent of fields discovered a quarter of a century later (DTI 2001, Appendix 5).[7] Increasingly, therefore, companies have held their less-attractive reservoirs in reserve. As we shall see, the future of UKCS oil and gas production is inextricably intertwined with the need to reverse this situation.

Despite companies' caution in relation to many discoveries, recent output expansion has been impressive. Oil production reached 91.6mt in 1990 but then escalated to approximately 130mt a year throughout the later 1990s (Figure 3.3). For natural gas output the upward trend has been even more striking: 40.6mtoe in 1990, rising to 58.9mtoe in 1994

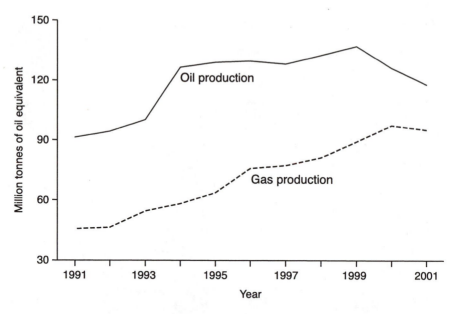

Figure 3.3 Oil and gas output since 1990.

and 97.3 mtoe in 2000. But what is also remarkable is that, despite these dramatically expanded production figures, the scale of proven reserves of both oil and gas has also increased significantly, to 669 mt and 681 mtoe respectively (Table 3.1). These data spotlight not simply recent success in exploring and exploiting North Sea oil and gas resources, but also the need to understand that success. How has the offshore industry achieved this remarkable rise in both production and reserves, especially in an era marked by growing assumptions – at least in many quarters – that the North Sea is a mature hydrocarbon province now heading inexorably into the end game of decline? (Skrebowski, 2001) On one level the answer to this is simple. Production has been boosted because it has been possible to slow the output decline of early fields whilst at the same time bringing

Table 3.1 Growth in proven reserves, 1990–2000

	Oil (mt)	*Gas (mtoe)*
Proven reserves 1990	513	503
Less production 1990–2000	1,288	739
Apparent reserve 'deficit' by 2000	−775	−236
Plus reserves declared 1990–2000	+1,444	+917
Remaining declared reserves, 2000	669	681

Source: Calculated from BP (2002).

many more reservoirs on stream. Between 1994 and 2000, for example, the number of producing fields doubled, from 77 to 145 (Read, 2002). But headline figures such as these leave unexplored the nature, scale and power of the processes underpinning these achievements. Consequently it is to these processes that we now turn.

Technological change, production and reserves

Technological change has been, and is still, a key force driving both production and knowledge of proven reserves. While the range of relevant technical advances is very extensive (Babusiaux and de la Tour, 1999; Pinder, 2001), an appropriate starting point for a review is the contribution made by a cluster of three technologies to the goal of maintaining output from oil and gas fields already in production.

Enhanced recovery

The first element in this cluster is *enhanced recovery* (Gregory, 2001). Output from North Sea oil fields, especially, peaks rapidly after they are brought into production because reservoir pressure falls. In most instances output would cease within a few years if enhanced recovery techniques were not applied. Like many technologies, these techniques have been subject to extensive development over the decades. However, the principles remain unchanged. Field pressure – and therefore production – can be maintained by drilling injection (rather than extraction) wells into a reservoir's periphery, and pumping down these wells liquids (normally water) or gases. Thus the Captain field, for example, not only has 16 production wells, but also five for injection and one to provide water for injection. Reflecting continuing technological progress, this water is combined with flow-enhancing polymers before injection. Gas injection, meanwhile, usually involves uneconomic quantities of natural gas that are produced in association with oil production. Much of it would at one time have been flared at source, generating significant greenhouse gas emissions. Thus enhanced recovery involving gas injection can have significant environmental benefits as well as output advantages.[8] In most instances injection is back into the reservoir from which the gas was produced, but companies are starting to devise more ambitious strategies, as the Foinavon field illustrates. Gas from this field – the first in the remote deep waters of the Atlantic frontier – is to be piped 185 km to Sullom Voe for enrichment with LPG before onward transmission a further 210 km to the Magnus oil field. There it will be injected to maintain reservoir pressure and extend reservoir life by several years (Potter, 2000; Anon, 2001a).

The effect of enhanced oil recovery naturally varies considerably from field to field, dependent on factors such as the geological structures, the porosity of reservoir rocks and the viscosity of the product. No clear-cut formulae apply. However, Gregory (2001) estimates that primary (i.e. unassisted) recovery from an oil field may yield 5–25 per cent of reserves. Secondary recovery by waterflooding may increase this to 15–65 per cent. And the technologically much more sophisticated third recovery stage – involving injection coupled with chemical, gaseous, thermal and microbial treatments – may achieve 30–80 per cent. This third stage was virtually unused in the North Sea in 1990 but is now increasingly widespread.

Directional drilling

Output has also been maintained through rapid advances in drilling technologies, and especially the emergence of *directional drilling*. This enables wells to be diverted from the vertical so that they can be driven into reservoirs at virtually any required angle and to any required position. This is again well illustrated by the Captain field, the drilling strategy for which entailed several horizontal sections up to 1,800 m in extent. By these means, new production wells in an established field can be positioned much more effectively to gather oil and gas from the hydrocarbon-bearing strata, while injection wells can similarly be placed at points calculated to maximize pressure maintenance. Although no specific data relating to the benefits of directional drilling in the UKCS have been released recently, the Statfjord field on the Norwegian-UK sector boundary amply exemplifies the potential. In this reservoir's Norwegian section the operator, Statoil, drills approximately 16 directional wells each year. At any given time a third of total output comes from wells completed in the previous 12 months. And Statoil intends establishing a rolling programme of new wells with the ultimate aim of maintaining the field in profitable production until 2020 (Warshaw, 2001).

Information technology

The third element in the technological cluster is advances in *information technology*. These have greatly increased the precision with which enhanced recovery and directional drilling technologies can be applied. One dimension of this has been progress towards the 'smart well', involving down-hole monitoring of a range of variables including the precise location of the drill bit in three dimensions. Another, now of crucial importance, is 3-D modelling of reservoirs and the location of oil and gas resources within them. This integrates major increases in data acquisition, made possible by progress with computer applications in seismic surveys, with advances in the computer processing of large data sets. The technique's on-screen visualization of structures greatly enhances understanding of hydrocarbon reservoirs, paving the way for related improvements in the design and implementation of enhanced recovery and directional drilling strategies. Now this approach is taking a further leap forward

through the development of 'immersive visualization' – the use of specialized rooms in which project planning teams can hold field development
discussions apparently inside computer-projected 3-D representations of
the structures in question (Fanchi, Pagano and Davis, 1999; McMillin,
1999; Eng, 2001). Targets of these strategies are frequently pockets of oil
or gas 'stranded' by earlier approaches to field exploitation. Moreover,
the improved speed and relatively low cost of 3-D surveys mean that repeat
analyses are now increasingly feasible, enabling the effectiveness of
enhanced recovery and directional drilling to be evaluated through time-
lapsed (4-D) surveys.

Since the early 1990s the trio of interrelated technologies discussed
above has increasingly been conceptualized as a key element in the UK
government's Improved Oil Recovery (IOR) strategy (Gregory, 2001), a
policy to which we return later. At this point, indications of the combined
impact of technologies such as these can be gained from data for the 11
oil fields put into production between 1975 and 1979. In the early years
their combined production totalled *c.* 85 mt, in part reflecting the fact that
they included the 'giant' fields of Forties, Brent and Ninian. In 2000,
almost one-quarter of a century later, these fields were still producing
12 mt a year or 11 per cent of total UK offshore oil.[9] Beyond this, however,
the significance of this technological cluster has by no means been limited
to extending the life of individual fields. On the contrary, the technologies in question have also been central in two other key arenas: the growth
of proven resources, and investment to bring additional oil and gas fields
into production.

Proven reserve growth

Proven reserve growth on the scale recorded in Table 3.1 is closely connected with the phenomenon of *resource appreciation*. In essence, this is the
increase in reserves declared by companies to be proved in, and technically recoverable from, known reservoirs.[10] Where these reservoirs are in
production, declared resources appreciate partly because of improved
understanding of reservoir structure and content (for example, through
3-D modelling) and also because enhanced recovery and drilling technologies increase significantly the volume of oil and/or gas that can probably be extracted. Where known reservoirs are not in production, and
consequently are unlikely to be subject to such intensive structural analysis, estimates of recoverable reserves can nonetheless be increased to
reflect the growing efficiency of drilling and recovery techniques.

Analysis of data relating to a random sample of 25 oil fields (i.e. 20 per
cent of the total) demonstrates the reality of resource appreciation after
1991 (Figure 3.4). It is true it was not a ubiquitous phenomenon: four
fields in the sample had lower declared reserves at the end of the period
than at the outset. But in 11 cases, despite continual production, declared

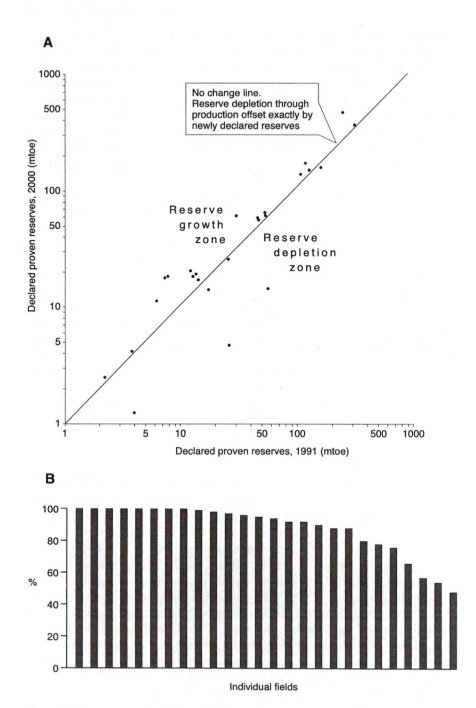

Figure 3.4 Resource appreciation for a random sample of 25 oil fields. A: Declared proven reserves 1991 vs 2000. B: Expected percentage depletion of fields excluding resources appreciation.

reserves grew by up to 10 per cent, and for a further ten fields appreciation was between 20 per cent and 78 per cent. Moreover, large-scale appreciation was associated with several major fields: Brent (reserves of 324.5 mt
in 2000, up 24 per cent); Magnus (129.9 mt, +21 per cent); Miller (61.4 mt,
+46 per cent); and Alba (61.4 mt, +21 per cent). Over the entire period,
growth in the sample's total declared reserves was equivalent to approximately 1.5 years' UKCS production at late-1990s levels. This suggests that,
for all North Sea oil fields, resource appreciation for the decade was
approximately equal to between five and seven years' production.

Reserves have also grown because of continuing exploration. In part
this has been the natural result of movement out from the established production areas. But to a great extent it reflects the fact that re-exploration
of these core production areas has brought to light new oil and gas fields
undiscovered by the technologies available in previous exploration phases.
In this connection the southern North Sea provides an outstanding
example (Table 3.2). Early gas finds in the late 1960s were made almost
exclusively in Permian deposits. Twenty years later substantial numbers of
discoveries were still being made in the Permian, and this trend continued
into the 1990s. By the late 1980s successes were also being recorded in
deeper Carboniferous strata, which two decades earlier had offered little
prospect of reward. Similarly, in the late 1990s discoveries at a depth of
5,000 m in the Triassic added 300 mtoe to the estimated recoverable
reserves in the cluster of gas fields around the Alwyn reservoir, taking its
declared reserve total to 1,000 mtoe (Anon, 1998a).

Output growth and maintenance

Very similar technology-based considerations have boosted UKCS output,
as opposed to known reserves, by bringing forward investment decisions to
put additional fields into production. Advances with enhanced recovery,
directional drilling and reservoir visualization have underpinned the reap-
praisal of modest reservoirs, and have also encouraged seismic re-survey as
the economics have appeared increasingly attractive (Crook, 2002b). In
this way some neglected deposits have undergone transition from the

Table 3.2 Gas discoveries by geological era and time period, southern North Sea

	1965–9	1985–9	1990–4
Tertiary	2	–	–
Cretaceous and Jurassic	–	–	–
Triassic	3	–	2
Permian	19	31	15
Carboniferous	–	8	11

Source: Compiled from DTI (2001).

clearly uneconomic category, towards marginal viability and ultimately into potential profitability. In order to understand this revaluation of economic viability more completely, however, other technologies – some related directly to those discussed above, but others quite independent of them – must be brought into the frame.

The first is multilateral well technology. This converts what is initially a single well into one that branches and can therefore gain access to several regions in a reservoir or to a number of scattered hydrocarbon deposits (Winton, 1999). Major economic advantages can be associated with this drilling technique, the clearest being its ability to reduce the total number of wells and well-head facilities required to put a field into production. This can dramatically reduce development costs, and consequently have a significant impact on marginality. Figure 3.5 shows, for the Tern marginal

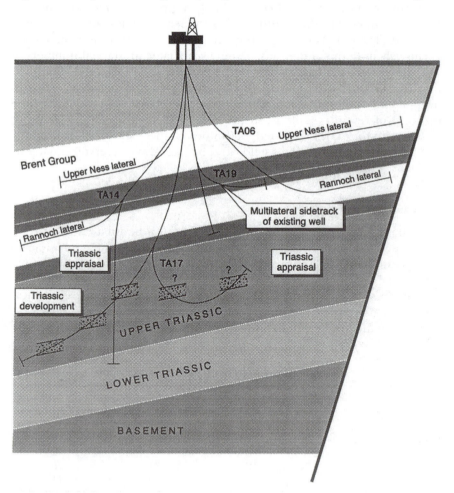

Figure 3.5 Multilateral drilling strategies applied to the Tern oil field.

oil field, how multilateral drilling has been used to develop the Upper Ness and Rannoch laterals in the upper reaches of the Brent Group; construct appraisal wells curving down to the Upper and Lower Triassic; and complete a deep development well passing accurately through a series of reservoirs in the Upper Triassic.

The process of overcoming the economic marginality of small and/or isolated reservoirs has also been closely linked with advances in production platform design. Large-scale steel structures fixed to the seabed and topped by impressive production facilities have been commonplace for clearly viable reservoirs, and to some extent continue to attract investment.[11] But because marginal or isolated deposits cannot support such costs, progress has demanded the development of far less traditional technological pathways.

Best known in this context, because the concept has been applied for many years, is the use of FPSOs (Floating Production, Storage and Offloading systems) for oil output. These were originally created by converting surplus crude oil tankers into floating production and storage facilities, moored at oil fields and emptied every few days by shuttle tankers. Subsequently, new-build FPSOs have become the norm because of the dwindling supply of sound hulls, increasing safety requirements and a trend towards more complex on-board processing equipment. This is very clearly demonstrated on the UKCS: ten of the 13 vessels currently in use were purpose-built after 1995, and the remaining three have all been updated since then. Although the new-build trend has undermined an early economic attraction – the use of cheap hulls that might otherwise go for scrap – FPSOs can still have appeal for fields too small to justify the cost of a traditional production platform. They are also viable in deepwater locations where depth would severely inflate the cost of installing a fixed structure. Two FPSOs on the UKCS are a response to this latter circumstance: the Schiehallion and Foinaven vessels in 395 m and 450 m of water on the Atlantic frontier. But the large majority tap what would otherwise be uneconomic small and medium-sized reservoirs, predominantly in the Central basin off eastern Scotland, and usually in depths of 150 m or less. Contrary to what might be assumed, there is no strong correlation between FPSO scale, on the one hand, and water depth or remoteness on the other. The two moored on the Atlantic frontier, for example, are among the largest and the smallest. Typically, however, North Sea FPSOs are between 80,000 and 120,000 dwt, with oil storage capacities between 70,000 and 80,000 tonnes (Fitzpatrick, 2002).

While every case is different, the potential economic advantages of FPSOs are highlighted by Table 3.3. Here the scenario is that of a North Sea marginal oil field, producing 25 million barrels of products in five years, located in 120 m of water and seeking a 12.5 per cent rate of return. Under these conditions, and given the oil prices prevailing in 1998, day-to-day operating costs are actually higher for the FPSO; but total production

Table 3.3 Comparative North Sea marginal field development costs

	Fixed platform ($/barrel)	FPSO ($/barrel)	Subsea production with riser to fixed platform ($/barrel)
Investment costs	14.2	3.4	8.3
Operating costs	6.5	7.8	6.0
Total costs	20.7	14.3	11.2

Source: Adapted from Babusiaux and de la Tour (1999).

costs are almost halved because of a 75 per cent reduction in investment costs achieved by dispensing with a fixed-platform.

FPSO technology is a well-recognized pathway to output profitability via cost reduction, but far less well-known investment in subsea production technologies must also be highlighted. The subsea 'completion' of wells allows automated production functions to be transferred from platforms to well-head facilities on the seabed. In the process, cost savings are made because companies are either able to employ simpler fixed production platforms or FPSOs, or it becomes possible to dispense with the use of local production platforms completely. In the latter case, subsea wells are 'tied back' by seabed pipelines either to trunk pipelines taking oil or gas to land, or to an existing but distant production platform or FPSO that has sufficient capacity and can be reached economically.

Subsea production began in the North Sea in the early 1980s in the Cormorant field, and this hydrocarbon province currently provides the world's largest subsea market (Westwood and Knight, 2002). Application of the concept was at first only feasible over short distances because of a range of problems, such as pipeline choking caused by hydrates, waxes and scale. However, technological breakthroughs – including insulated and heated pipelines – have significantly reduced such difficulties. Consequently the UK continental shelf now has well over 600 subsea well-head installations which together have brought more than 100 oil and gas fields into production. One recent prediction is that nearly 350 additional subsea wells will be completed by 2008 – a quarter of the number anticipated worldwide (Hillegeist, 2002; Anon, 2001b). In some instances the technology has been applied very intensively indeed: recent work towards the Atlantic margin to bring the Scott, Schiehallion and Foinavon fields on stream, and also limit investment in costly deepwater platforms, involved the completion of more than 80 subsea wells (Anon, 2001b). The longest tie-back envisaged so far is that for the Penguins cluster of fields in the northern North Sea, which together amount to the third-largest undeveloped accumulation of oil and gas on the UKCS. Output from here – oil, gas and condensate – will be piped 65 km south for processing on the currently under-utilized Brent 'C' platform before onward dispatch. On route to Brent 'C', products will pass through a 16-inch pipeline, itself encased in an insulated 22-inch carrier pipe (Beckman, 2002a; Crook, 2002a).

As with FPSOs, the cost advantages of subsea production systems vary from field to field. Moreover, subsea wells tend to perform less efficiently than those operated from traditional platforms because they are more difficult to maintain. This disadvantage can average around 25 per cent (Anon, 2001b). Even so, in the marginal field scenario set out in Table 3.3 the prediction is that subsea production can still save almost a third when compared with fixed-platform production. Moreover, Beckman (1999) has highlighted cases in which subsea systems are preferable to FPSOs. When this is coupled with the fact that subsea systems raise significantly the utilization rates of the pipelines and remote platforms to which they are tied back, it is scarcely surprising that there is enthusiastic talk of a subsea future (Olver, 2000), and that the large majority of new field developments are already subsea ventures (Table 3.4).

One final excursion into new technologies is appropriate. Reservoirs that in most circumstances would be uneconomic can on occasion be brought into production profitably through the development of 'minimal' platforms. Dating originally from the 1970s (Knott, 1998; Rosenblum, 1999) this concept continues to be refined and relies heavily on the principle that large-scale cost savings can be made by equipping platforms only with the facilities that are essential. The latest steps in this direction in the southern North Sea have been taken by Shell through the development of 'Trident', a prototype gas platform installed on the Skiff field and regarded by the company as the likely forerunner of many similar projects in these shallow waters. Trident's tubular legs economize by serving as conductors for its four wells. As a Normally Unmanned Installation (NUI) it requires no living quarters or helideck; visiting maintenance crews arrive by boat. Instrumentation is extremely restricted, and is in fact confined to the provision of basic well-performance data. Fire and gas detection equipment is restricted to portable units. Most importantly, designed

Table 3.4 Tie-back dominance of new field development, 2002–3

Production system	New fields
Tie-backs:	
– to remote fixed platform	20
– to FPSO	5
– unspecified	1
Traditional platforms	
– using extended-reach drilling	4
– other/unspecified	3
Total	32

Source: Compiled from *Petroleum Review*, September 2001, 14.

and built within 12 months, the platform's total cost was only £8 million, compared with individual price tags of more than £20 million for Shell's previous generation of minimal platforms in the southern North Sea (Strowlger, 2000). Similarly, in the Moray Firth a minimal platform, exporting 105 km to onland processing facilities at St Fergus, is central to a project to bring on stream in only two years gas previously stranded in the Goldeneye field (Beckman, 2002b).

Minimal platform designs such as Trident do not simply underline the role of cost reduction in the push to boost output by bringing minor reservoirs into production. They also illustrate the importance recently attached to corporate culture and collaborative working in efforts to maintain continued development of the North Sea as a whole. In the words of Trident's principal project engineer, key factors for that project were 'extensive organizational change ... that has enabled people to innovate and carry through ideas of their own', coupled with 'a very close working relationship between Shell and its contractor to replace a traditionally separatist culture' (Strowlger, 2000). Examination of the industry literature quickly indicates that this example is by no means isolated, and consequently points to the need to explore two questions in greater depth. What have been the problems of offshore corporate culture in the UKCS? And how has change in this culture contributed to the growth of known resources and output?

Resources, production and corporate cultural change

CRINE, LOGIC and the supply chain culture

In the early 1990s the UK government targeted a joint government-industry initiative – Cost Reduction in the New Era (CRINE) – at the North Sea. In 1999 this was translated into a successor programme: Leading Oil and Gas Industry Competitiveness (LOGIC). At the heart of both programmes has been the view that entrenched corporate attitudes and working practices, coupled with often poorly co-ordinated information, have raised field development costs substantially above those encountered in comparable offshore areas (Snieckus, 2000a). Well costs, for example, have been widely regarded as 30 per cent higher than in the Gulf of Mexico, with the margin for platforms often reaching 30–50 per cent. Thus the push has been to maintain exploration and production by reducing costs through changes in corporate culture (Potter, 1998).

The CRINE/LOGIC diagnosis is complex, but two key messages can be highlighted. The first is that companies have frequently adopted a 'silo' mentality (Ramm, 1994/5; Strowlger, 2000), isolating themselves from others working on the UKCS, shunning information exchange, relying internally on centralized top-down direction, rigidly dividing responsibilities for each facet of a project within the company, and adopting a confrontational stance in negotiations with suppliers. The analysis is that this mindset encourages various problems. In an industry in which information is so expensive that most companies will only be able to create for themselves a partial picture, unwillingness to exchange experiences and information can be counterproductive. The internal division of responsibilities extends planning times – and thus raises costs – because proposed projects must pass through an inflexible series of stages. These divided responsibilities also discourage team working and can lead to the loss of opportunities to find appropriate solutions through the interaction of complementary expertise. And a confrontational approach to suppliers is similarly unlikely to foster the corporate collaboration often required to deal effectively with cost-reduction problems whilst maintaining product quality.

Second, the critique is that companies have tended to embark on major schemes by turning to the drawing board and working *ab initio*. What they have commonly failed to do, therefore, has been to recognize that – while every field development is unique and requires its own solution – the careful selection and combination of standardized approaches to project design and equipment can deliver tailored solutions at relatively low cost. In 2001 this argument was articulated very explicitly by BP (Knott, 2001) in an analysis that portrayed the North Sea mindset as one which:

- all too often embarked on the design process with a blank sheet;
- aimed to optimize and innovate despite the risks of complication and unnecessary innovation;
- tended as a result to become lost in detail, in turn causing slow and often poor decision-making;
- and, not least because of these problems, was prepared to embark on fabrication while designs were still unfinished.

The consequences of all this were held to be an inevitable escalation of costs because of an emphasis on non-standard products, from platforms down to individual production modules. In sharp contrast, what was required in any project was:

- to start with an existing analogue, modifying it only after asking 'What do you want to change and why?';
- adopt the principle that the costs of innovation are only justifiable if a business case can be made for them;
- move on to simplify and standardize the design if at all possible, for example by using standard modules, fabricated elsewhere and delivered on sleds for rapid installation;
- focus on detail with the specific goal of lowering costs;
- and ensure through this 'wood-for-trees' approach that decision-making processes are clear and rapid so that the design stage can be completed before the timetable dictates the start of fabrication.

BP's ideal is close to the cultural model prevalent in design and fabrication for the Gulf of Mexico, and although allowance must be made for the fact that the company was at the time seeking to drive down UK contractors' costs for its Clair platform in the North Sea, the price discrepancies claimed are certainly in line with the 30–50 per cent range quoted at the start of this section.

Central to the CRINE/LOGIC vision of inter-firm relationships is the notion of alliances and partnerships. In some quarters the shift towards partnerships has provoked caution. For example, despite BP's enthusiasm for the new model, its alliance to develop an FPSO for its Schiehallion field was disbanded in favour of separate contracts for various aspects of the project. Reasons cited included unbridgeable cultural differences between alliance members; the impact of tight cost and time targets on profitability; contractors' relative inexperience in FPSO design and construction; and BP's failure to impose sufficient control over technical decisions at an early stage (Cassidy, 2001). More broadly, Kemp and Stephen (1999a) have investigated, through Monte Carlo simulation, the effects of partnership bonus and penalty schemes on the risk-reward relationship for contractors. Main conclusions were that typical bonus-penalty arrangements substantially increase the risks borne by contractors, and that their logical response should be to build in a higher expected rate of return when bidding for projects.

Higher rates of return, however, would not necessarily eliminate the gains to be made through alliances and partnerships. Moreover, as the earlier reference to Shell's Trident programme has already indicated, there is mounting evidence that significant shifts in corporate culture can lead to appreciable economies and profitable production from previously marginal reserves (Strowlger, 2000). Four further examples illustrate this point.

The first is provided by the development history of the Bittern, Guillemot West and Guillemot North West cluster of fields, in the Central basin 190 km south-east of Aberdeen (Cottrill, 1999; Potter, 1999). Bittern is an oil and gas reservoir with almost 20 mtoe of recoverable reserves, but the Guillemot deposits comprise a cluster of smaller accumulations dominated by gas. Exploitation has been complicated not simply by this fragmentation, but also by joint ownership of the Bittern reservoir by Amerada Hess and Shell. (This arose because of the field's position astride two licence blocks.) Soon after Bittern's discovery in 1996 it seemed possible that potential development costs would spiral as a consequence of the two companies' preference for separate and quite different production systems – an FPSO for Amerada Hess and subsea installations for Shell. But as early as March 1997 agreement was reached for much more economical joint development using an FPSO. Other companies with financial stakes in these fields (Esso, Enterprise, Paladin Resources and Veba Oil & Gas) then joined what was by then known as the Triton Project to pool expertise for the development. Shell and Veba formed a joint team to undertake all drilling. A highly sophisticated FPSO design was achieved partly by co-operation between the oil companies involved, and partly by the exchange of information with other FPSO operators and designers elsewhere. Finally, to reduce the unremunerative period before oil and gas could be produced and sold, the alliance broke with practice and undertook engineering designs while full appraisal of the fields was still in progress. The operators claim Triton collaboration provides 'a benchmark and model for future development', with first production achieved only three years after Bittern's discovery, total development costs below the sanctioned investment of £540 million, and annual operating costs estimated at only £36 million.

The benefits of a willingness to question standard practices are equally well demonstrated by Enterprise Oil's approach to the marginal Cook oil and gas field (recoverable reserves 3 mtoe) (Snieckus, 2000b). Having purchased this from Amoco in 1990 with a view to short-term exploitation, by the mid-1990s Enterprise had failed to devise a cost-effective development plan. But from 1996 onwards a rigorous strategy of streamlining was pursued. Water injection was abandoned and replaced by the decision to maintain reservoir pressure by limiting gas extraction. Metering costs were reduced by accepting standards offering 'sufficient', rather than near-perfect, accuracy. A degree of operational flexibility was sacrificed in exchange for the economies gained by planning a single flowline instead of two. Dedicated control and chemical-distribution systems were dropped in favour of 'piggy-back' systems run from the neighbouring Teal field. And contractors were encouraged to bid to provide what was functionally necessary, rather than what might be ideally prescribed. Enterprise estimated that economies such as these reduced total project costs from a prohibitive £87 million in 1996 to a much more affordable £60 million. Relating this gain to CRINE's twin priorities, the adoption of more flexible mindsets within the company accounted for approximately three-quarters of the improvement, with the remainder generated by partnership working with contractors. Yet even these gains did not guarantee the project: by 1998 Enterprise still lacked economic transport systems for the modest quantities of oil and gas to be produced. Corporate partnership proved crucial in this context. Finding itself with spare capacity on its *Anasuria* FPSO on the Teal field 12 km away, Shell created a win-win situation by agreeing to handle Cook's output via a seabed tie-back.

Enterprise Oil's experience in gaining the majority of savings through changed internal company attitudes is echoed by the Britannia gas field in the Moray Firth (Anon, 1998b). With reserves likely to exceed 100 mtoe, a reservoir stretching 40 km east–west and 10 km north–south, and a water depth of almost 150 m, Britannia was a major development demanding a large-scale platform. In their approach to this the joint developers – Chevron and Conoco – decided in 1994 to apply CRINE principles by aiming to invest significantly less than was typical for projects of the same size whilst at the same time maintaining quality. In terms of internal organization, two steps were fundamental. First, all functions were integrated into a single development team covering the full range of activity from geological and geophysical appraisal through to operation and commercial management. In this way the objectives of different interest groups could be pooled and reconciled. Second, the development was broken down into six sub-projects with investment ceilings of £100 million to £400 million. Creative thinking for each sub-project was encouraged by subjecting those involved to minimal central control and regulation. Despite the apparent risks involved in this hands-off strategy, the approach reduced the initial investment estimate of £1 billion by 30 per cent. Capital costs for the whole project were expected to amount to $22 per tonne of oil equivalent – probably the lowest figure for a project of this type in the North Sea. And anticipated operating costs in the first few years were similarly driven down by 20 per cent, to $6.4 per tonne of oil equivalent.

The fourth example is provided by the 'Finder' drilling strategy, launched towards the end of the CRINE programme as part of a 'Double the Value of Wells' initiative (Beckman, 2000a). In an era when multinationals look askance at proposals for exploratory 'wildcat' wells on the UKCS on the grounds that the investment is better committed to the Gulf of Mexico or West Africa, this procedure departs radically from tradition by adopting very limited objectives. The essential task of a finder well is literally to find: i.e. to establish whether hydrocarbons are present in significant quantities. Even detailed assessment of those quantities may not be a primary goal, and still less is the well intended to yield large volumes of data for geologists and reservoir engineers. Although in the past these data have been routinely collected during standard drilling programmes, it is argued that they are extremely expensive to gather because they extend significantly the drilling period, and also escalate the investment that must be made in well architecture in order to provide appropriate appraisal conditions. If justified, redrilling of successful finder wells to gain fuller data can be undertaken much more cheaply than if all wells are drilled to past standards. As one Amerada spokesman has observed, the North Sea is littered with dry (i.e. unproductive) holes on which investment has been lavished (Beckman, 2000a).

Experiences with finder wells in the North Sea have not always been smooth. Mobil, for example, has concluded that work on them in the Atlantic margin should be confined to the summer months. Even so, the company's prediction was that this would then cut well costs by up to 30 per cent. Confirming the validity of this target, a CRINE best-practice well drilled in the northern North Sea saved $1.1 million (37 per cent) through reduced drilling and evaluation time, less expenditure on drill casing and the elimination of coring and drill stem testing (Table 3.5).

Table 3.5 Best practice finder well versus conventional well, northern North Sea

	Finder well	*Conventional well*
Total drilling time (days)	15.9	25.5
Evaluation days	3	8
Casing strings (number)	2	3
Core taken?	No	Yes
Drill stem test?	No	Yes
Cost	$2.0 m	$3.1 m
Cost saving	37%	

Source: Williams and Foehn (1999).

Amerada Hess, meanwhile, has made two discoveries with the technique in the Outer Moray Firth and is now aiming for a 50 per cent cost reduction on wells. Similarly Conoco has two finder discoveries to its credit: the Vixen field, in the Southern basin off the Lincolnshire coast, has become a fast-track development being tied back as a satellite of the Viking B platform; and the Kappa reservoir in the Moray Firth may well be developed as a satellite of Conoco's neighbouring Britannia field (Beckman, 2000a). Although the finder strategy is in its infancy, therefore, it already appears to be identifying exploitable resources that might not have been drilled if companies had failed to challenge the prevailing drilling mindset, with all the costs that it entailed.

Picking up the PILOT: resource marginality and corporate cultural change

Work under the CRINE/LOGIC umbrella relates primarily to encouraging production through cost reduction in the supply chain. Parallel to this is a second stream of activity in which, in pursuit of the Improved Oil Recovery (IOR) strategy noted earlier, government again takes a catalytic role in stimulating the offshore industry. Originally driven by the Oil and Gas Industry Task Force, but since 2000 the responsibility of PILOT,[12] this thrust has two dominant goals for 2010: oil and gas production sustained at *c.*150 mtoe (compared with 213 mtoe in 2001) and annual offshore investment averaging £3 billion (Beckman, 2001a; Crook, 2002b; Skrebowski, 2002a). Achieving the latter target would maintain UKCS investment at roughly the 2000 level.

Table 3.6 is not entirely comprehensive, yet it distils the essence of PILOT, which already covers a wide and complex range of initiatives. Three lines of attack may be highlighted. One concentrates on technical action to encourage exploitation of neglected resources. This work relates partly to improved oil recovery from existing fields through SHARP, together with the expansion of known resources in 'brownfields' whose output is declining. But it is also closely concerned with the problem of

Table 3.6 Key PILOT measures relating to improved oil recovery (IOR)

Activity promotion	
Brownfields Workgroup	Brownfield definition: fields beyond their production plateau, but still producing. Workgroup aims to: – identify the distribution of potential reserves (target: 2 billion barrels of oil equivalent); – test potential reserves against company plans; – stimulate improved production; – maintain economic life of infrastructure. Organized by UKOOA (United Kingdom Offshore Operators' Association)
Sustainable Hydrocarbons Recovery Programme (SHARP)	Provides Department of Trade and Industry with technical support relating to maximum recovery techniques. Mounts dissemination events relating to Improved Oil Recovery.
Undeveloped Discoveries Workgroup	Aims to produce plans for selected undeveloped discoveries. Methods: Clusters fields on basis of geography or technical challenge; appoints 'champions' for clusters.
Satellite Accelerator Initiative	Invites – from industry as a whole – innovative solutions for technically marginal or commercially challenging discoveries. Encourages collaboration on solutions on a risk-share/reward basis. Organized by LOGIC.
Infrastructure Access Code of Practice	Supports Satellite Accelerator Initiative and Undeveloped Discoveries Workgroup by facilitating access to upstream third-party infrastructure, particularly pipelines.
IT Facilitation	
Licence Information and Trading (LIFT)	Oil and gas asset-trading website. Aims to accelerate asset exchange to speed development.
LIFT-Inspired Farm-in Event (LIFE)	Linked with LIFT. Encourages: – new partnerships for exploration in licence blocks not yet exploited fully; – innovative technologies and fresh ideas. New partners receive equity stake in return for work programmes or investment.
Digital Energy Atlas and Library (DEAL)	Information on location and availability of well and seismic data. Has map search facility. Aims at time and cost savings in location of data and contact names.
Well Operations Notification System (WONS)	Speeds drilling consent applications. Applicants able to monitor approval process.

Table 3.6 continued

Electronic Production Reporting	Aims to reduce red-tape and speed reporting. Step towards electronic infrastructure to collect, validate and publish information from internal databases.
Regulation *Fallow Blocks and Fallow Discoveries Measures*	Government statement of regulatory intent to review: (a) blocks awarded in First to Tenth Licensing Rounds on which no drilling has occurred for six years; (b) discoveries undeveloped for a similar period.

Source: Compiled from Department of Trade and Industry (2001).

how fallow reservoirs might be brought into production, not least by transforming them into satellites of existing fields and infrastructures. Figure 3.6 demonstrates how protracted the delay between discovery and production has often been. Central to thinking in this 'satellite accelerator' context is the fact that virtually all the 315 fallow reservoirs are within 35 km of platforms or pipelines, and thus theoretically susceptible to tie-back technology (Skrebowski, 2001).

Second, there is a cluster of initiatives made distinctive by the use of IT principles to promote investment. Many undeveloped reservoirs are in the hands of major companies whose investment priorities have swung towards other world regions. The LIFT asset-trading website aims to encourage the transfer of these reservoirs – as well as exploration blocks – to smaller, more adventurous, companies willing to take the development

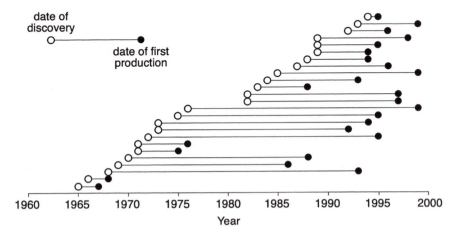

Figure 3.6 Production delays relative to field discovery, random sample of 25 fields.

initiative. LIFE similarly provides an electronic marketplace in which innovative businesses can bid for access to development partnerships. The
ambition of WONS is to encourage swifter, better-planned – and therefore
cheaper – drilling programmes facilitated by an on-line drilling consent
system. DEAL, meanwhile, makes available digital seismic and drilling data
relevant to LIFT and LIFE, but also to initiatives such as the Brownfield
and Undeveloped Discoveries Workgroups.

Third, while the main plank of government policy is facilitation and
encouragement, behind this is the threat of regulation. Particular targets
here are the 260 fallow licence blocks and the 300+ significant discoveries
lying fallow. Long-standing legislation gives government powers to review
company rights in this context, and in recent years it has been policy to
increase the attractions of voluntary activity by highlighting the possibility
of intervention. The government stance is that fallow fields have become
'a luxury we cannot afford at this stage in the UKCS life cycle' (Macalister,
2001). Specific threats have been made to review holdings from the first
ten licensing rounds wherever there has been a six-year absence of drilling
activity. While the intention is partly to kick-start investment by existing
companies, asset transfers from major corporations to more flexible
independent companies are also high on the agenda.

Assessment of PILOT's impact requires study beyond the scope of this
chapter, covering a period long enough to make detailed judgements on
progress towards the programme's individual initiatives as well as its over-
arching 2010 targets. However, data relating to the period covered by
PILOT's predecessor – the Oil and Gas Industry Task Force – underline
the importance of this policy thrust, especially for oil. For example, by
2000 the combined production of the 19 oil fields brought on stream in
1996 was almost 20 per cent above initial predictions, and these fields
were yielding almost a sixth of all UKCS oil output (Table 3.7). Similarly,

Table 3.7 Oil fields brought onstream in 1996: predicted[a] and actual output, 2000

	Output, 2000 (million tonnes)		
	Predicted	Actual	Difference
Fields performing above prediction[b]	8.2	14.2	+6.0
Fields performing below prediction[c]	9.4	6.8	−2.6
All 1996 fields	17.6	21.0	+3.4
Total UKCS oil production	–	126.2	–

Source: Calculated from DTI (2001).

Notes
a International Energy Agency prediction.
b Andrew, Columba B, Harding, Lennox, MacCulloch, Nevis, Pierce, Teal.
c Arkwright, Banff, Captain, Cyrus, Douglas, Fergus, Guillemot A, Magnus S, Pelican, South
  Teal, Thelma.

the role of new oil fields in cushioning the impact of the declining output of brownfield reservoirs was very evident: altogether they offset almost 40 per cent of the contraction from older fields. Maintaining a flow of newly commissioned fields is, therefore, a crucial objective to sustain production. For this reason, perhaps the most encouraging indicators from PILOT so far are those relating to asset exchange. Within a year of PILOT's creation, 38 fallow blocks had either been relinquished, or were about to be relinquished, to companies with plans to exploit them. Similarly, 15 fallow reservoirs had been sold or offered for sale. These figures compare quite favourably with PILOT's Satellite Accelerator Initiative, which by March 2002 could list only six projects (Crook, 2002c). In the near future the industry literature will no doubt detail numerous examples of the fruits of asset exchange. Meanwhile, takeover of the Heather field, east of Shetland, by the Norwegian company DNO provides a classic example of the capacity of independents to bring neglected resources into play (Beckman, 2000b).

Brought on stream in 1978 by Unocal, Heather met expectations only briefly because of various complexities. By the mid-1990s output had fallen 80 per cent since peak production, yet less than a quarter of the reserves had been recovered. With Unocal attracted by alternative investment opportunities in the Far East, abandonment seemed certain until in 1996 a new management team at DNO – one of the minority partners in the field – purchased Unocal's controlling interest. New 3-D seismic survey identified undiscovered satellite fields and revised upwards the estimate of oil-in-place in the main field. Maturing technologies – particularly horizontal drilling and subsea production methods – were deployed to bring into the frame three known satellite fields never exploited by Unocal because of their limited size, relatively remote location and geological complexity. With CRINE in mind, platform operating costs were cut by a third in a single year, and well-development costs were halved by a policy of redrilling existing bores instead of sinking new ones. In 1998 DNO acquired from Elf full control of a fallow oil field 15 km north of Heather, undeveloped by Elf because the company had no infrastructure in the vicinity. For the independent this was an opportunity to tie this reservoir back to Heather. Beyond this, having outstripped both Unocal and Elf in the adventure stakes, DNO then overcame the reluctance of two high-profile partners – British Gas and Texaco – to provide the finance necessary for further development wells. This was achieved by reminding the partners of the decommissioning bill they would face if the project ended early. Confronted with this potential unproductive outlay, they ceded their equity in the complex to DNO, the argument being that, if the latter maintained production, shutdown would be postponed until new technologies reduced substantially today's high decommissioning costs. The overall outcome of this wheeling, dealing and co-ordinated activity has been to enable DNO to establish a 2004/5 output target of

1.25 million tonnes per year for the cluster as a whole, five times Heather's production in 2000. This oil should be profitable with oil prices as low as $14 a barrel, 40 per cent below the average spot price for Brent crude in 2001 ($24.77).

Future prospects: towards the endgame?

Most of this chapter has sought primarily to raise awareness and understanding of how technological advances, and recent attempts to change corporate culture, have underpinned successful exploitation of oil and gas on the UKCS. The task of assessing the precise impact of these forces would be protracted and complex, but sufficient has been said to demonstrate their close links with the simultaneous processes of output growth and proven resource expansion which characterized the 1990s. Moreover, testimony to their significance has been provided by academic, industry and government sources alike (Kemp and Stephen, 1999b; Snieckus, 2000a; Anon, 2000); and Table 3.8 reveals a close association between a decline in unit cost trends and the period in which new approaches have been adopted.

While a retrospective review of these neglected forces is overdue, however, this chapter would be incomplete without consideration of possible futures. Given that the province's resources cannot last indefinitely – the EU (Commission of the European Communities, 2001) currently predicts that reserves will be exhausted within 25 years – how pressing is the prospect of decline? Are we indeed entering what Skrebowski (2001) has dubbed the endgame? In view of the offshore industry's contribution to the balance of payments (through oil exports and substitution for oil and gas imports) and also its direct and indirect employment, this is a key question on which to end.

A pessimistic scenario is not difficult to construct, and is in fact widely

Table 3.8 Date of development and field unit costs^a at 2002 prices

	Oil fields^b (£/barrel)	Gas fields (p/therm)
Fields starting production:		
before 1980	11	9
1980–5	16	23
1986–90	14	21
1991–5	9	14
1996–2000	9	14
All fields in production	11	13.5

Source: DTI (2001), Table 2.1

Notes
a Excluding tax, royalties and costs of abortive exploration.
b Including condensate fields and oil equivalent of associated gas.

used to argue that the end is in sight (Bentley *et al.*, 2000; Commission of the European Communities, 2001; DTI, 2001; Skrebowski, 2000, 2001). According to current official estimates, we have already consumed almost half the proven, probable and possible deposits of gas; for oil the equivalent proportion, nearly two-thirds, is even worse. Despite record output in the 1990s, oil production fell by no less than 14 per cent between 1999 and 2001; and between 2000 and 2001 the first decrease in gas production was reported, albeit of only 2.3 per cent. Using other measures, exploration is lacklustre. In 1990 224 exploration and appraisal wells were drilled, but by 1996 this figure had halved and by 1999 it was down by 84 per cent. Although drilling activity increased in 2000, even then the total number of wells completed was only 59. Moreover, the majority of these were appraisal wells designed to assess the potential of known fields; in sharp contrast, in 1990 70 per cent of the drilling was for exploration. As was indicated at the start of this chapter, this shift has fed through to a marked deterioration in the discovery rate for significant oil or gas deposits. After the mid-1990s this figure dropped to less than eight reservoirs per year, and early in this decade it fell still further to four or five, compared with an annual average of 21 throughout most of the 1980s. Pessimists can also point to UKCS reserve-production ratios. Although major additions to reserves were declared in the 1990s, production growth rates were even faster. Consequently, whereas in 1990 proved reserves were sufficient to sustain gas production for 12.3 years, by 2001 this had almost halved – to only 6.9 years. Because additional reserves are still being declared, this does not imply exhaustion by the end of the decade. But on average the reserve-production ratio for gas has been shrinking by five months a year, making it possible to suggest – through simple extrapolation – exhaustion within 16 or 17 years.

As other commentators have argued, however, reports of the impending death of North Sea oil and gas production may be grossly exaggerated (Brooks, 2000; Odell, 1995, 1996, 2001, 2002b; Olver, 2000; Snieckus, 2000a; Wood Mackenzie, 1999). Again there is a variety of reasons. Reserve-production ratios can be poor guides to the future. Worldwide, companies are constantly seeking to position themselves as advantageously as possible relative to governments, and the UK is no exception. Rarely is it in a company's interests to create the impression that resources are ample; much more advantageous is the perception that discovery and production are difficult, because this provides arguments to restrain governments' inclination to tax. In the UKCS, of course, there is truth in this perception, but high reserve-production ratios – such as that for gas in the early 1990s – may still be counterproductive from the offshore industry's bargaining viewpoint.

Several related observations are relevant at the micro- and macro-scales. At the micro-scale, despite the fact that decommissioning will assume growing significance (Terdre, 2001), only 14 fields have actually been shut

down to date.[13] In fact field-by-field analysis through time reveals a frequent alternative pattern: declared reserves for a reservoir often stay static
for a considerable period, only to be suddenly increased shortly before
they would be exhausted by current production levels. At the macro-scale,
the UKCS reserve-production ratio for oil has fluctuated over the last
decade, but has shown no clear downward trend paralleling that for gas.
In 2001 the ratio was 5.6 years – not a margin implying a comfortable situation, but exactly the same as in 1990. And comparative statistics for 2000
and 2001 identify a halt in the gas ratio's swift decline, perhaps indicating
that this too will now be held at a level intended to signal resource scarcity
but not imminent exhaustion.

Beyond this, there are signs of a halt to the decline in oil production
experienced in 2000 and 2001 (Skrebowski, 2002b). Linked with this, opti-
mists stress that technological advances, shifts in corporate culture, and
the rise of independent companies will continue to impact favourably on
the known scale and recoverability of UKCS oil and gas resources. The
crucial importance of technological change, so evident in the past, will
not suddenly wane (Babusiaux and de la Tour, 1999). New approaches
will become both possible and increasingly affordable as the refinement of
innovations drives down costs. While many of these approaches will be
highly relevant to the maintenance of existing producing areas, some will
also improve the feasibility of neglected prospects – partly in Atlantic
waters west of Shetland, but also in challenging geological conditions in
various parts of the North Sea (Clewes, 2000; Snieckus, 1999; Munns,
2002). In 2001 the discovery of the Buzzard field, with reserves probably
exceeding 50 mtoe, demonstrated that major new reservoirs are still to be
found – in this case south-east of the Moray Firth. Technological advances
will also start to make viable relatively large but previously extremely challenging reservoirs, as progress with the Erskine and Shearwater high-
pressure high-temperature fields has shown (Knott, 1999; Snieckus, 1999).
Thus the definition of what exists and is recoverable will continue to be
revised upwards. Moreover, having invested heavily in production infrastructures, companies are likely to keep them in commission as long as
possible to maximize their returns, and also to defer the unproductive
costs of decommissioning. Testimony to this is provided by the attitude,
noted earlier, of British Gas and Texaco to the prospect of decommissioning the Heather field, and more generally by the remarkably small
number of fields shut down to date.

Far-reaching shifts in corporate culture only began in the 1990s, and
still have much to achieve as they progress – particularly on the cost 'frontier'. And there is similar extensive scope for independent companies to
continue to take over assets from the major corporations as these giant
companies increasingly transfer their attention elsewhere in the world, to
new, challenging and potentially highly profitable frontier provinces.
Here the key point is that, particularly in the marginal field context, inde-

pendents operate at a scale that makes modest profits highly significant, whereas to an oil giant they may be trivial (Jones, 1999). Drawing together all these threads – technological and corporate – observers adopting optimistic views of the future of the UKCS are able to identify parallels with the recent trajectory of the US Gulf of Mexico. Seemingly unexciting and destined for decline as recently as the 1980s, this offshore province has subsequently experienced remarkable rejuvenation, largely through the drivers discussed above (Read, 2002; Snieckus, 2000a; Westwood and Knight, 2002).

Events will ultimately prove which analysis is correct, although there is much that is convincing in Odell's repeated assertion that, globally as well as in the UKCS, offshore resources are consistently underestimated. What should be highlighted, however, is that evidence from the marketplace now suggests that the bald distinction between the two opposing camps – pessimistic and optimistic – may mask a need for contrasted scenarios for oil and gas.

Data for 1991 and 2001 illustrate this effectively. Although oil consumption over this period grew dramatically in some European markets – notably by almost 50 per cent in Spain – this was not typical. Most other major continental consuming countries – Germany, Italy and France – showed little or no growth, and UK consumption actually fell by nearly 8 per cent. Making comparisons at the world scale, an overall increase in European oil usage of only 7 per cent was, from the industry's viewpoint, unattractive compared with a world average of 12 per cent, 17 per cent in the US, 42 per cent in Asia Pacific and no less than 60 per cent in Central and Latin America. For gas the data draw a dramatically different market picture. While global growth has still been impressive – up almost 20 per cent in the world as a whole, 61 per cent in Central and Latin America and 80 per cent in Asia Pacific – Europe has shared fully in the expansion. Consumption in Germany, France and Italy has risen by more than a third; Europe-wide the average increase has been 40 per cent; and in the UK it has been 68 per cent.

The significance of these market contrasts between oil and gas may well be fundamental. Mediocre European oil market conditions do not strengthen the case for companies to invest to maintain the UKCS as a significant oil producer, but this is certainly not true for gas. Strong market incentives exist to continue finding and exploiting this fuel (Beckman, 2001b). Over time, therefore, contrasting demand conditions may well prove to be a powerful force driving the industry towards a gas-based future – unless a dramatic event such as global conflict triggers a rapid rise in oil prices and consequent corporate re-evaluation of offshore Europe.

One final, and quite different, issue must also be brought into the equation. Although decommissioning has been held back by the costs involved and the need to keep investment productive as long as possible, it could soon exert a powerful influence on what is possible in the future. This is because marginal fields, on which strategies to maintain UKCS production must be heavily dependent, will in many cases need to be tapped into existing infrastructures if they are to be viable. Even with the application of improved technologies and new company practices, the profitability of modest reservoirs will often be highly questionable unless they can be tied back over relatively short distances to existing pipeline networks, platforms or FPSOs.

Two interrelated problems are now emerging in this context. The first is the growing expectation that decommissioning will remove platforms and – very importantly – pipelines that could handle output from marginal fields. In the central and northern North Sea, especially, decommissioning is currently predicted to accelerate rapidly after 2010. If that occurs, it is quite possible that by 2020 the tie-back option, which currently is at least theoretically available for virtually all known minor reservoirs, will have been reduced to a small part of the central basin, in the latitude of the Moray Firth and on the border with Norwegian waters (Skrebowski, 2001; Crook, 2002b). The second difficulty is that ownership of the infrastructures 'at risk' is overwhelmingly in the hands of the major corporations originally responsible for the development of the UKCS. As their decommissioning plans emerge they will be based on economic analyses that will be highly logical so far as the individual companies are concerned. But these plans will not, of course, be designed to meet the infrastructural needs of the smaller independent companies now considered so important to sustaining production from the North Sea. What is perfectly rational for one group of businesses could become a major obstacle for another, an obstacle with the capacity to hasten the end of production by leaving many reservoirs literally stranded. How government policy responds to this major challenge could be crucial to the North Sea's life expectancy.

Postscript

Since the completion of this chapter the geopolitical situation has changed significantly, a possibility envisaged on page 67. Following the Al-Qaida attack on New York's World Trade Center, and the invasion of Iraq by the 'Coalition of the Willing' led by the US and the UK, a new geopolitical uncertainty has prevailed. One effect of this has been to increase the significance attached to oil and gas resources in politically stable regions such as the North Sea. A second has been a substantial increase in oil prices, stimulated also by other forces such as uncertainty in parts of the Russian oil industry, and rapidly rising energy demand in Asia generally and China in particular. One school of thought argues that this price rise largely reflects the influence of speculators rather than the true long-term relationship of supply and demand, yet the fact is that the price of Brent crude oil has risen from less than $26 per barrel in May 2003, to almost $38 in May 2004 and $50 in October 2004. Many analysts are predicting that relatively high prices will be sustained, and there are growing signs that this is encouraging positive attitudes to North Sea development.

This is evidenced in part by recent production data. Oil output fell by almost 9 per cent between 2002 and 2003, in a weak-demand period when UK oil consumption also sank (by 2 per cent). However, the latest figures indicate that the downward production trend is ameliorating sharply: over the period May 2003 to April 2004, oil output was down by only 4.5 per cent relative to the previous 12 months. Similarly, although natural gas production experienced a plateau in 2002 and 2003, as the headlong rise in demand typical of the 1990s also eased, output of this fuel is now once more on an upward curve. When the May 2003 to April 2004 data are compared with the preceding twelve months, the rise was 2.2 per cent.

Other indicators also point in a positive direction. Asset trading, intended to open opportunities for smaller operators, is starting to be commonplace. In 2003 deals involved 27 commercial oil and gas fields worth £1.3 billion. The offshore industry's annual investment expenditure is currently around £400 billion, somewhat above the target set by PILOT. Likewise, it is expected that expenditure on the exploration and appraisal of oil and gas fields will rise by more than 12 per cent between 2003 and 2004. Although the trend for major oil companies to reduce their holdings has continued, for example through BP's sale of its stake in the Forties field, the rise in prices has seen the majors more prepared to consider the development of previously marginal fields. Also significant is the major companies' growing interest in fields that have long been regarded as technologically challenging. Now that the extremely complex high-temperature and high-pressure Clair field is about to come on stream, attention is starting to turn to other accumulations with similar challenging properties. These include the Rhum field, 380 km north-east of Aberdeen. By North Sea standards this is a significant reservoir, comprising at least 800 billion cubic feet of gas. But its remoteness and demanding reservoir properties have meant that almost 30 years elapsed between its discovery and the go-ahead for development in May 2003.

While major companies have continued with technological advances at the cutting edge, other technologies have continued to mature, become standard and thus affordable by smaller firms. Of particular significance in this context is continuing progress with the subsea completion of wells that are tied back to existing platforms and pipeline infrastructures. The fact that a high proportion of the petroliferous North Sea is now potentially accessible to tie-back systems (page 61) already offers the prospect of opening up at least 80 fields previously considered marginal. This effect can only be enhanced if the high price regime is maintained. Moreover, as increasing numbers of tie-backs are fed into pre-existing infrastructures, signs are emerging that the owners of these infrastructures are gaining benefits allowing their economic lifespans to be extended beyond their envisaged decommissioning dates. One clear indicator of tie-backs operating in this way is provided by the *Anasuria* FPSO (page 57). When Enterprise Oil entered into the agreement to pipe oil from the Cook field via this facility, the expectation was that Shell would withdraw the *Anasuria* in 2004. Recoverable reserves from Cook that could not be extracted by that date would therefore be lost. In the event the continued profitability of this FPSO has led Shell to cancel the vessel's planned removal.

One interpretation that could be placed on much of the above is that improved techniques will simply hasten the depletion of proven reserves, thus accelerating the industry's demise. In the new climate of global uncertainty, items on the North Sea's future have become commonplace in the press and the broadcast media, and typically they take this pessimistic view. As this chapter has been at pains to demonstrate, however, a fundamental consequence of technological advances is that they allow additions to be made to existing economically exploitable reserves, as well as facilitating their extraction. This emerges clearly from proven reserves data: for both oil and gas, the scale of exploitable UKCS reserves in 2003 was precisely the same as in 1993. It is, of course, prudent for the press, radio and television to prepare obituaries while their subjects are still alive, but premature publication is not good practice. Indeed, it could be argued that much of the effort invested in implying the imminent end of North Sea production would be better focused on other aspects of the UK's energy record, such as the weakness of its conservation policy and the low levels of research into genuinely innovative renewable energy technologies.

Bibliographic note: readers seeking easily accessible overviews of recent trends should consult Crook (2004) and Skrebowski (2004).

Notes

1 At the time of writing, on-line access to the Brown Book was most direct via http://www.dbd-data.co.uk/bb2001/. It is assumed that in future the final element in this address will change to reflect the year (bb2002/; bb2003/; etc). Access is also possible via http://www.og.dti.gov.uk. Click on Information and navigate from there. However, this is a more cumbersome route.

2 The current UKOOA website address is http://www.ukooa.co.uk but a replacement site (http://www.ukooa.com) is under development. The information email address is info@ukooa.co.uk.

3 The Energy Institute has recently been formed by the merger of two long-established professional bodies, the Institute of Petroleum and the Institute of Energy. The library and information services are based in the Institute of Petroleum's former headquarters at 61 New Cavendish Street, London W1G 7AR. Telephone +44 (0)20 7467 1000; fax +44 (0)20 7255 1472; email lis@petroleum.co.uk; website http://www.energyinst.org.uk

4 The calorific value of natural gas is commonly expressed in terms of oil equiva-

lence. The industry standard conversion factor is 1 billion cubic metres of natural gas to 0.9 million tonnes of oil.

5 The UK has recently exported nearly two-thirds of the oil produced; imports of crude have accounted for around 50 per cent of consumption. Natural gas was at one time imported in large quantities from Norway, equivalent to 20 per cent of consumption in the late 1980s. Although small quantities still come from that source, the expansion of UK output has led to self-sufficiency. A two-way 'interconnector' pipeline from Bacton to Zeebrugge has resulted in net gas exports to mainland Europe. A second interconnector (Johnstone-Ravenspurn) now carries gas from Scotland to the Irish Republic. In 2001 exports via these pipelines amounted to 15 per cent of production. Three-quarters of exports went to continental Europe, dominantly to the Netherlands.

6 Between 1980 and 1998 the dollar price of Brent crude, the reference oil for the North Sea, fluctuated but generally fell from \$36.98 per barrel to \$13.11 per barrel. Later recovery only raised it to an average \$24.77 per barrel in 2001.

7 The figures for recent finds are even lower (*c.* 20 per cent), but these are not comparable with those quoted because there has been insufficient time to plan field developments.

8 In the early 1980s flared gas was equivalent to *c.* 11 per cent of UKCS gas production. Ten years later the figure was down to *c.* 4 per cent and is now *c.* 2 per cent. It must be remembered, however, that output has increased sharply. When allowance is made for this, the early 1980s environmental impact of flaring has probably been halved. Altogether the offshore industry still accounts for 1 per cent of Britain's total CO_2 emissions.

9 For natural gas the picture is almost identical. Long-run figures for some fields are not available, but data for seven originally developed between 1965 and 1972 show that, despite an 80 per cent decrease in output by 2000, their combined production was still equivalent to 8 per cent of total UK output.

10 A widely accepted definition of proved reserves is that they are those quantities that geological and engineering information indicates with reasonable certainty can be recovered in the future from known reservoirs under existing economic and operating conditions (BP, 2002, 4).

11 For example, in March 2000 'the most complex topsides ever built' – weighing 11,700 tonnes – was lifted onto the Shearwater gas platform in the central North Sea. Several months later the Elgin gas platform – at 43,000 tonnes the largest steel structure ever put in place in a single operation – was installed in northern waters (Clewes, 2000; Knott, 2000).

12 Unlike LOGIC, PILOT is not an acronym but was instead chosen to reflect the function of the forum. The term is not used in the sense of a pilot (i.e. experimental) project.

13 Consequently more than 95 per cent of fields that have been developed are still in production. Moreover, the fields that have been closed by no means date from the North Sea's early development phases. Most abandoned deposits were discovered in the 1980s, and earlier cohorts of relatively large reservoirs have escaped almost unscathed. Life-cycle models applied at the macro-scale can, therefore, be extremely misleading at the field-by-field scale.

References

Anon. (1998a) 'Total to use technology, infrastructure to increase production from the North Sea', *Oil and Gas Journal* February 2: 21–8.

Anon. (1998b) 'Chevron/Conoco venture considers lessons of Britannia development', *Oil and Gas Journal* August 17, 92–3.

Anon. (2000) 'North Sea prospects looking good', *Petroleum Review* September: 24–5.

Anon. (2001a) 'Productivity shortfall puts deepwater exploration gains in perspective', *Offshore* April: 84, 170.

Anon. (2001b) 'Platform wells produce 25 per cent better than subsea because of routine interventions', *Offshore* June: 82.

Babusiaux, D. and de la Tour, X. (1999) 'Technology improvements in the petroleum industry and the impact on costs', *Energy Exploration and Exploitation* 17: 111–22.

Beckman, J. (1999) 'Operators re-visit subsea completions as option to costly FPSOs', *Offshore* August: 43–4, 185.

Beckman, J. (2000a) 'UK producers need to compete with lower well drilling costs', *Offshore* August: 38, 197.

Beckman, J. (2000b) 'Re-drilling ageing Heather rewards smaller producer', *Offshore* August: 40, 200.

Beckman, J. (2001a) 'UKOOA sets target production at 3 million BOE/D through 2010', *Offshore* March: 72–3, 118.

Beckman, J. (2001b) 'Future UK gas demand growth roiling waters for North Sea development', *Offshore* August: 44–6, 178.

Beckman, J. (2002a) 'Shell pushes ahead with Penguins development', *Offshore* August: 38–40.

Beckman, J. (2002b) 'Full welstream transfer to shore for 'stranded' Goldeneye development', *Offshore* August: 44–6.

Bentley, R.W. *et al.* (2000) 'Perspectives on the future of oil', *Energy Exploration and Exploitation* 18: 147–8.

British Petroleum (2002) *Statistical Review of World Energy*. London: BP.

Brooks, J. (2000) 'North Sea prospects looking good', *Petroleum Review* September: 24–5.

Cassidy, P. (2001) 'FPSOs: lessons to learn', *Petroleum Economist* 68, April: 15–16.

Clewes, B. (2000) 'Complex HP/HT development nears first gas in UK North Sea', *Offshore* August: 187–8.

Commission of the European Communities (2001) *Towards a European Strategy for the Security of Energy Supply*. Luxembourg: Office for Official Publications of the European Communities.

Cottrill, A. (1999) 'Triumph close for Triton triumvirate', *Offshore Engineer* December: 21.

Crook, J. (2002a) 'Long tie-back subsea projects', *Petroleum Review* January: 30–3.

Crook, J. (2002b) 'Meeting the challenge', *Petroleum Review* February: 19–20.

Crook, J. (2002c) 'Satellite Accelerator initiative opens window of opportunity', *Petroleum Review* March: 25–7.

Crook, J. (2004) 'UKCS need for innovative solutions', *Petroleum Review* September: 26–9.

Department of Trade and Industry (2001) *Development of the Oil and Gas Resources of the United Kingdom*. London: DTI.

Eng, R. (2001) 'New acquisition methods yield 3D seismic improvements', *Offshore* March: 48.

Fanchi, J.R., Pagano, T.A. and Davis, T.L. (1999) 'State of the art of 4D seismic monitoring: the technique, the record and the future', *Oil and Gas Journal* May 31: 38–43.

Fitzpatrick, P. (2002) 'Worldwide survey of floating production, storage and offloading (FPSO) units', *Offshore* August supplement.

Gregory, A. (2001) 'Enhanced oil recovery – ten years on', *Petroleum Review* August: 40–3.

Hillegeist, P. (2002) 'Subsea prospects looking good', *Petroleum Review* June: 42–5.

Jones, C. (1999) 'The UKCS: is there exploration life after crisis?' *Offshore* December: 46–8.

Kemp, A.G. and Stephen, L. (1999a) 'Price, cost and exploration sensitivities of prospective activity levels in the UKCS: an application of the Monte Carlo technique', *Energy Policy* 27: 801–10.

Kemp, A.G. and Stephen, L. (1999b) 'Risk:reward sharing contracts in the oil industry: the effects of bonus:penalty schemes' (sic), *Energy Policy* 27: 111–20.

Knott, D. (1998) 'Northwest Europe's offshore activity still brisk despite a mandated slowdown in Norway', *Oil and Gas Journal* August 17: 49–51.

Knott, D. (1999) 'Elf UK expands HP-HT expertise with Elgin/Franklin development', *Oil and Gas Journal* June 21: 18–22.

Knott, T. (2000) 'Top deck from Tyneside', *Offshore Engineer* April: 32–3.

Knott, T. (2001) 'UK suppliers face tough time on Clair', *Offshore Engineer* March: 11–12.

Macalister, T. (2001) 'Fallow oilfields "a luxury we can't afford"', the *Guardian* September 5.

Mager, H.-J. and Vieth, T. (eds) *European Oil and Gas Yearbook.* Hamburg: URBAN-VERLAGE.

McMillin, K. (1999) 'Visual immersion yielding more efficient well planning', *Offshore* July: 36–8.

Munns, J. (2002) 'Six UK plays hold potential opportunity', *Offshore* April: 48–50.

Odell, P.R. (1995) 'Europe's energy: panic over, opportunity knocks', *The World Today* 51, No. 10. October: 191–2, Royal Institute for International Affairs. Reprinted in Odell (2002a) 611–16.

Odell, P.R. (1996) 'North Sea oil and gas: the exploitation of Britain's resources, retrospect and prospect', in MacKerron, G. and Rearson, P. (eds) *The UK Energy Experience: a Model or a Warning?* London: Imperial College Press. Reprinted in Odell (2002a) 277–87.

Odell, P.R. (2001) *Oil and Gas: Crises and Controversies, Volume 1, Global Issues.* Brentwood: Multi-Science Publishing.

Odell, P.R. (2002a) *Oil and Gas: Crises and Controversies, Volume 2, Europe's Entanglement.* Brentwood: Multi-Science Publishing.

Odell, P.R. (2002b) 'European gas 2001: retrospect and prospects', in Odell, P.R. (2002a) 457–64. Text of keynote speech to the St Petersburg Forum, Bonn, 25 February 2002.

Odell, P.R. and Correlje, A.F. (2001) 'Four decades of Groningen gas production and pricing policies', *Netherlands Journal of Geosciences* 80: 137–44.

Olver, D. (2000) 'Setting sights on total subsea production', *Petroleum Review* September: 26–8.

Pinder, D. (2001) 'Offshore oil and gas: global resource knowledge and technological change', *Ocean and Coastal Management* 44: 579–600.

Potter, N. (1998) 'Driving well costs down', *Petroleum Review* December: 11–13.

Potter, N. (1999) 'How collaboration worked on the Triton development', *Offshore* August: 46–7.

Potter, N. (2000) 'BP Amoco development an indicator of Atlantic Margin prospectivity', *Offshore* August: 51–4, 202.

Ramm, T. (1994/5) 'Reducing both Capex and Opex cost by changing the "one-off" mindset', *Offshore International* Winter: 34–5.

Read, R. (2002) 'North Sea evolution to track Gulf of Mexico model', *Oil and Gas Journal* August 26: 40–3.

Rosenblum, R. (1999) 'Evolution of minimal platform concepts for marginal developments', *Offshore* April: 110, 116.

Skrebowski, C. (2000) 'North Sea – a province heading for decline?' *Petroleum Review* September: 12–15.

Skrebowski, C. (2001) 'North Sea – entering the end game', *Petroleum Review* 55, September: 13–17.

Skrebowski, C. (2002a) 'Straining every sinew to boost UKCS production', *Petroleum Review* March: 28–31.

Skrebowski, C. (2002b) 'Successfully squeezing the rocks', *Petroleum Review* September: 15–20.

Skrebowski, C. (2004) 'High prices spur development rush as North Sea production declines', *Petroleum Review* September: 12–13.

Snieckus, D. (1999) 'Elf harnesses an HPHT giant', *Offshore Engineer* August: 35–40.

Snieckus, D. (2000a) 'Putting sacred cows to pasture', *Offshore Engineer* April: 26–8.

Snieckus, D. (2000b) 'Cook finds the right recipe', *Offshore Engineer* April: 30–1.

Strowlger, P. (2000) 'Skiff puts both oars in', *Offshore Engineer* April: 34–7.

Terdre, N. (2001) 'Decommissioning high on the agenda', *Petroleum Review* October: 12–14.

Terdre, N. (2002) 'Dawn of the decommissioning era', *Petroleum Review* October: 19–20.

Warshaw, B. (2001) 'New drilling techniques raise hopes of big gains', *Petroleum Review* November: 24.

Westwood, J. and Knight, R. (2002) 'Looking at offshore Europe prospects in a global context', *Oil and Gas Journal* August 19: 22–5.

Williams, J.G. and Foehn, J.-P. (1999) 'Finding a new drilling concept', *Petroleum Review* June: 34–5.

Winton, J. (1999) 'Use of multi-lateral wells to access marginal reservoirs', *Offshore* February: 50–124.

Wood Mackenzie (1999) 'Pressure builds in the North Sea', *Offshore Engineer* August: 21–2.

Appendix 1: Chronological Bibliography

This appendix largely comprises a sample of major works by academics, industry experts, governments and agencies, rather than the more detailed industry literature on which the majority of the chapter is based. It does not aim to be comprehensive. Its chronological organization is chosen to provide a convenient cross-section indicating the evolution of North Sea studies through time.

(1963) Alexander, L.M., *Offshore Geography of Northwestern Europe: the Political and Economic Problems of Delimitation and Control.* Chicago: Rand McNally.

(1967) Jensen, W.G., *Energy in Europe, 1945–80.* London: Foulis Books.

(1967) Polyani, G., *What Price North Sea Gas?* London: Institute of Economic Affairs.

(1971) Odell, P.R., 'Europe and the oil and gas industries in the 1970s', *Petroleum Times* 1,929 and 1,930.

(1971) Manners, G., *Geography of Energy.* London: Hutchinson.

(1972) Casenove & Co., *North Sea Report.* London: Casenove & Co.

(1972) Odell, P.R., 'Europe's oil', *National Westminster Bank Quarterly Review* August: 6–21.

(1973) Francis, J. and Swan, N., *A Social and Environmental Assessment of the Impact of North Sea Oil and Gas on Communities in the North of Scotland.* Edinburgh: Church of Scotland.

(1973) International Management and Engineering Consultants, *Study of Potential Benefits to British Industry of Offshore Oil and Gas Developments.* London: HMSO.

(1973) Odell, P.R., 'Indigenous oil and gas developments and western Europe's energy policy options', *Energy Policy* 1: 47–64.

(1973) Odell, P.R., 'The geographic location component in oil and gas reserves' evaluation', in *Selected Papers of the International Oil Symposium.* London: Economist Intelligence Unit, pp. 25–41.

(1973) Posnan, M., *Fuel Policy: a Study in Applied Economics.* London: Macmillan.

(1974) Odell, P.R. and Rosing, K.E., *The North Sea Oil Province: a Simulation Model of its Exploration and Exploitation.* London: Kogan Page.

(1975) Mackay, D. and Mackay, G.A., *The Political Economy of North Sea Oil.* London: Martin Robertson and Co.

(1976) Chapman, K., *North Sea Oil and Gas: a Geographical Perspective.* Newton Abbott: David and Charles.

(1976) Odell, P.R., *The Western European Energy Economy.* Leiden: Stenfertkroese.

(1976) Odell, P.R. and Rosing, K.E., *Optional Development of North Sea Oil Fields: a Study in Divergent Government and Company Interests and their Reconciliation.* London: Kogan Page.

(1976) Ray, G.F., 'Impact of the oil crisis on the energy situation in Western Europe', in Rybczynski, T.M. (ed.) *The Economics of the Oil Crisis.* London: Macmillan for the Trade Policy Research Centre, pp. 94–130.

(1976) Saeter, M. and Smart, I. (eds) *The Political Implications of North Sea Oil and Gas.* Guildford: IPC Science and Technology Press.

(1977) Ion, D.C., 'The North Sea countries', in Mangone, G. (ed.) *Energy Policies of the World*, Vol. 2. New York and Amsterdam: Elsevier, pp. 121–6.

(1978) Arnold, G., *Britain's Oil.* London: Hamish Hamilton.

(1978) Brown, E.D., 'Rockall and the limits of national jurisdiction of the UK', *Maritime Policy* 2: 181.

(1978) Lewis, T.M. and McNicol, I.H., *North Sea Oil and Scotland's Economic Prospects.* London: Croom Helm.

(1978) Robinson, C. and Morgan, J., *North Sea Oil in the Future: Economic Analysis and Government Policy.* London: Macmillan for the Trade Policy Research Centre.

(1979) Odell, P.R., *British Oil Policy: a Radical Alternative.* London: Kogan Page.

(1979) Odell, P.R., *The Future Supply of Indigenous Oil and Gas in Western Europe.* Paris: International Energy Agency.

(1980) Noreng, O., *The Oil Industry and Government Strategy in the North Sea.* London: Croom Helm.

(1981) Davis, J., *High-cost Oil and Gas Resources*. London: Croom Helm.

(1982) Nicholson, J., *Future Oil and Gas Developments in the UK North Sea: Reserves of the Undeveloped Oil and Gas Discoveries and a Commentary on their Development Options*. Glasgow: Midland Valley Exploration Ltd.

(1984) Stern, J., *International Gas Trade in Europe: the Policies of Importing and Exporting Countries*. Aldershot: Gower.

(1985) Adamson, D.M., 'European gas and European security', *Energy Policy* 13: 13–26.

(1985) Hoffman, G., *The European Energy Challenge: East and West*. Durham, N.C.: Duke University Press.

(1985) Kemp, A.G. and Rose, D., 'The effects of petroleum taxation in the United Kingdom, Norway, Denmark and the Netherlands: a comparative study', *The Energy Journal* 6 (special tax issue): 109–24.

(1986) International Energy Agency, *Natural Gas Prospects*. Paris: OECD.

(1986) Odell, P.R., *Oil and World Power*, 8th edition. Harmondsworth: Penguin.

(1986) Weyman-Jones, T.C., *Energy in Europe: Issues and Policies*. London: Methuen.

(1987) Rowland, C. and Hann, D., *The Economics of North Sea Oil Taxation*. London: Macmillan.

(1988) Estrada, J. *et al.*, *Natural Gas in Europe: Markets, Organization and Politics*. London: Pinter Publishers.

(1988) Odell, P.R., 'The west European gas market: current position and economic prospects', *Energy Policy* 16: 480–93.

(1988) Robinson, C. and Morgan, J., *North Sea Oil in the Future: Economic Analysis and Government Policy*. London: Macmillan.

(1990) Odell, P.R., 'Energy: resources and choices', in Pinder, D.A. (ed.) *Western Europe: Challenge and Change*. London: Belhaven, pp. 19–36.

(1992) Anderson, S.S., *The Struggle Over North Sea Oil and Gas: Government Strategies in Denmark, Britain and Norway*. Oslo: Scandinavian University Press.

(1992) Kemp, A.G., 'Development and production prospects for UK oil and gas post-Gulf crisis: a financial simulation', *Energy Policy* 20: 20–9.

(1992) Williams, J.R., *Natural Gas Reserves and Production: the European Picture*. London: Shell International Gas.

(1993) UKOOA, *The CRINE Report*. London: United Kingdom Offshore Operators' Association.

(1994) Odell, P.R., 'World oil resources, reserves and production', *The Energy Journal* 15 (special issue): 89–114.

(1994) Odell, P.R., 'The geography of reserves development', *The Energy Journal* 15 (special issue on 'The Changing World Oil Market'): 96–105.

(1994) Stoppard, M., *The Resurgence of UK Gas Production*. Oxford: Oxford Institute for Energy Studies.

(1995) Estrada, J., Moe, A. and Martinsen, K.D., *The Development of European Gas Markets*. Chichester: J. Wiley and Sons.

(1996) Mackerron, G. and Pearson, P. (eds) *The UK Energy Experience: Model or Warning?* London: Imperial College Press.

(1996) Odell, P.R., 'The exploitation of the oil and gas resources of the North Sea: retrospect and prospect', in Mackerron, G. and Pearson, P. (eds) *The UK Energy Experience: Model or Warning?* London: Imperial College Press, pp. 123–33.

(1996) UKOOA, *Towards 2020: Future Oil and Gas Production in UK Waters*. London: United Kingdom Offshore Operators' Association.

(1998) Odell, P.R., 'Energy: resources and choices', in Pinder, D.A. (ed.) *The New Europe: Economy Society and Environment*. Chichester: Wiley, pp. 67–90.

(1999) Kemp, A.G. and Stephen, L., 'Price, cost and exploration sensitivities of prospective activity levels on the UKCS: an application of the Monte Carlo technique', *Energy Policy* 27: 801–10.

(1999) Kemp, A.G. and Stephen, L., 'Risk:reward sharing contracts in the oil industry: the effects of bonus:penalty schemes', *Energy Policy* 27: 111–20.

(1999) Odell, P.R., *Fossil Fuel Resources in the 21st Century*. London: Financial Times Energy.

(2001) Commission of the European Communities, *Towards a European Strategy for the Security of Energy Supply*. Luxembourg: Office for Official Publications of the European Communities.

(2001) Cox, P. and Gerrard, S., *The Environmental Assessment of Southern North Sea Pipeline Decommissioning*. Norwich: University of East Anglia Centre for Environmental Risk.

(2001) Northern Offshore Federation and the Department of Marine Technology, University of Newcastle upon Tyne, *Decommissioning the North Sea: Best Practice Guidance for Companies Entering the Decommissioning Market*. Washington, Tyne and Wear: Cameron Publishing.

(2001) Stern, J.P., *Traditionalists Versus the New Economy: Competing Agendas for European Gas Markets to 2000*, Briefing Paper, New Series No. 28. London: Royal Institute for International Affairs.

(2002) Scottish Grand Committee of the House of Commons, *The North Sea Oil and Gas Industry*. London: HMSO.

4   The race for offshore renewables

Meeting 2010

Carolyn Heeps

Introduction

The global response to climate change has become a significant driver in the establishment of national energy policies that shift the reliance away from carbon-based fuels towards energy from clean, renewable sources. Growing concerns over security of oil and gas supplies and the recognition that future energy sources will need to be imported from politically unstable areas also act as major drivers for change. As energy demands increase in developed countries, fluctuations in demand resulting in major disruption to the electricity supply could become a more frequent reality. Energy diversity is a critical component of energy reliability and security, and never before has so much attention been given to the potential for energy from marine renewable sources to become mainstream within the UK.

Historically, the industrial growth of the UK has been based on its indigenous fossil fuel resources, first coal and more recently North Sea oil and gas. However, as energy demand increases and economically recoverable reserves of hydrocarbons diminish, it is anticipated that by 2006 the UK will be a net importer of gas and 2010 for oil. The government forecasts that by 2010 the UK could be dependent on imported energy for 75 per cent of its total primary energy needs – mainly from Norway, Russia, North Africa, the Middle East and even Latin America (DTI, 2003a). Globally, future oil demand cannot keep pace with population growth and gas demand is growing even faster than oil (Douglas Westwood, 2002). In June 2003 the growing economic ties between the UK and Russia were strengthened through the ministerial signing of a memorandum of co-operation on a North European gas pipeline from Russia to the UK. The two countries also agreed to closer co-operation on tackling climate change (DTI, 2003b).

In Europe the environmental agenda has been a main driver for the renewable energy sector. The global framework is provided by the Kyoto Protocol 1997 (UN Framework Convention on Climate Change – UNFCCC) which established legally binding targets for reducing emissions. The Protocol is a coherent yet relatively flexible agreement, providing the conditions for change, but it is yet to become a fully global agreement; neither the USA nor Australia have become signatories. The Kyoto Protocol has set global targets to cut greenhouse gases by 5 per cent (on 1990 levels) by 2008 to 2012. The European (EU) level target under the Kyoto Protocol is an 8 per cent reduction against 1990 levels by 2008 to 2012. This EU target is being enacted through the Renewable Energy Directive (2002/358/EC) which requires 12 per cent of European energy supplies and 22.1 per cent of electricity to be sourced from renewable energy by 2010. For the UK, which contributes about 2 per cent of the global total of carbon emissions, the Directive stipulates an indicative target of 10 per cent. Data from the European Environment Agency recorded a rise in emissions in 2001, with levels at 2.3 per cent below 1990 levels compared to 1999 when emissions were 3.6 per cent lower (EWEA, 2003).

The emphasis on tackling climate change has brought significant environmental challenges linked to energy policy and the drive towards a low-carbon economy. The international commitment to reduce emissions by greenhouse gases has led to developed countries committing to reduce carbon emissions by 60 per cent on 1990 levels by 2050.

In 2000 the UK government announced its aim that renewable energy sources should supply 10 per cent of UK's electricity by 2010. At this time it also introduced economic instruments in the form of the Renewables Obligation (RO) and exempted renewables from the climate change levy. In the same year the Royal Commission on Environmental Pollution (RCEP) recommended that the UK should commit to the target 60 per cent reduction in carbon emissions by 2050. In 2002 the Performance Innovation Unit (PIU) conducted a major review of energy policy (The Energy Review) and set out a number of recommendations for development of a low carbon economy, including higher targets for renewable energy for 2020. The UK government responded in 2003 publishing its Energy White Paper, entitled *Our energy future: creating a low-carbon economy.* The White Paper set out the UK's long-term vision for the reduction in carbon emissions and even though it supported the proposals of the RCEP for a 60 per cent cut in 1990 levels of carbon pollution in UK as a whole by 2050, it did not adopt the PIU recommendations for setting higher targets of 20 per cent of energy derived from renewable sources by 2020. Instead it emphasized the aspirational ambition to the doubling of the 2010 target by 2020. The Paper indicated that regional delivery in meeting targets would be required and identified the need for substantial investment in energy efficiency. It also indicated that offshore wind energy would make a significant contribution to enable targets to be met and that the government would bring forward legislation as soon as possible to enable renewable energy generation to take place beyond the territorial sea on the UK continental shelf. Thus the White Paper set out a new energy policy for the UK, identifying the needs and challenges we face in the new millennium in light of climate change and reduced hydrocarbon production and reserves. It appeared that renewable energy was at last being given the political green light and as a consequence the marine renewable energy industry had an important role to play. This was strengthened further when the Secretary of State for Trade and Industry launched a cross-governmental and stakeholder group (the Sustainable Energy Policy Network) to help deliver the commitments of the Energy White Paper. However, the Institute of Civil Engineers in their State of the Nation 2003 report (ICE, 2003) were much more pessimistic, suggesting that the 10 per cent 2010 target will not be met and 20 per cent by 2020 target being completely out of the question without the right fiscal incentives. Despite the White Paper emphasis on no nuclear build for at least five years the ICE report argues that the nuclear option must be kept open as part of a truly sustainable solution – a view acknowledged by few.

The marine dimension

Wind energy is generally recognized as the fastest-growing renewable energy technology (WWF-UK *et al.*, 2001). Currently the UK renewable sector is dominated by onshore wind, except in Scotland where hydropower has been a significant source for many years. At present only 3 per cent of UK electricity comes from renewable sources. With onshore wind contributing only 500 MW in 2003 the offshore renewable sector, comprising offshore wind, wave and energy is expected to play a key role so that commitments to the Kyoto Protocol can be met. Considered to have the best wind resource in Europe, along with an excellent marine skills, technology and manufacturing base, the UK is well placed to take advantage of its natural marine resources. The British Wind Energy Association (BWEA) estimates that our present electricity needs could be met more than three times over by offshore wind energy (http://www.off-shorewindfarms.co.uk). As this new energy sector emerges there is already a raised expectation that the UK could become a world leader in electricity generation from offshore renewables, but this cannot be achieved without significant infrastructure requirements, rethinking and stiffening distribution networks and a change in public perception and awareness to gain widespread acceptance for large-scale offshore renewables projects. Even though non-governmental environmental and conservation organizations are supportive of the move towards renewable energy sources they are calling for a much slower approach to the 'dash to develop the oceans' (Birdlife International, 2003), with greater consideration being given to the potential impact on the marine environment and marine nature conservation. The ambitious targets for the exploitation of offshore renewable energy have renewed the call for marine spatial planning as a mechanism to resolve competing demands for sea and seabed space, not only within UK waters but also at a European seas level. Allocation of space and collaborative decision making for all forms of offshore renewables will become an increasingly important part of the process in order to optimize the socio-economic and environmental benefits and minimize impacts on the marine environment.

The global and European offshore windfarm sector

At present four EU countries have operational offshore windfarms: the UK, Denmark, Germany and the Netherlands. Germany has 20 windfarms proposed and an ambitious target of 3 GW by 2010 whilst the UK government hopes that as much as 5 to 7.5 GW will be installed by 2010. Other countries with proposals for offshore windfarms include Spain, Canada and the USA where 3.4 GW of offshore wind projects off the Massachusetts coast have been unveiled (Re-gen, p. 10, 2003). The next decade could see huge growth in the sector particularly as the technology develops to provide larger, more efficient turbines that have been developed and proven for use in the marine environment. Industry consideration for the development of deeper water technology through changing foundation design or turbines mounted on floating structures could see the limits pushed out to 50 m water depth. Globally there are currently 13 operational windfarms with a combined installed capacity of 336 MW and rapid interest in the industry has seen a growth in the number of projects from 95 projects and ten operational in 2002, to 173 projects and 13 operational in 2003 (Rowley and Westwood, 2003).

The construction of the 160 MW Horns Rev windfarm in Danish waters in 2003 provided a major milestone for offshore windfarm development in Europe. Prior to this the largest commercial offshore windfarm had been Middlegründen, installed in 2001 (40 MW). The UK has now established itself as a major contributor with the installation of two 60 MW windfarms: North Hoyle off North Wales which started producing electricity from 30 turbines in October 2003, and Scroby Sands off Great Yarmouth. Prior to these the UK could only boast a two-turbine, 4 MW 'demonstration' windfarm at Blyth off the Northumberland coast.

Round One UK offshore wind – a new industry emerges

In December 2000 the offshore wind energy industry took a major step forward with The Crown Estate's launch of the first round of site awards in UK waters. The Crown Estate, as landowner of the seabed out to the 12 nautical mile territorial limit plays an important role in the development of the offshore wind industry by leasing areas of the seabed for the installation of turbines and ancillary works such as cables and anemometry equipment. (The Crown Estate is also responsible for awarding leases for exclusive use of the seabed for activities within territorial waters such as pipelines, cables, moorings, dumping grounds, fish farms and marine aggregates dredging [excluding oil, gas and coal]. It also has rights to exploit natural resources on the continental shelf, excluding oil, gas and coal.) In April 2001, 18 developers pre-qualified for the award of sites on the basis of the financial and technological procedures set out by The Crown Estate (http://www.thecrownestate.co.uk). Since then only one developer has withdrawn from Round One. The 17 UK sites now account at present for almost 24 per cent of the world's projects (Figure 4.1). The sites were selected by potential developers, including some big-name companies and major utilities, primarily on the basis of bathymetry, grid connection and wind resource whilst taking into account the need to avoid selecting sites within areas designated for nature conservation under European legislation (the EU Habitats Directive). Developers also avoided areas of seabed where existing seabed activities and uses such as hydrocarbon extraction, pipelines, telecommunication cables, marine aggregate dredging and shipping lanes were potentially incompatible with offshore windfarm development. Even though turbine technology is making great advances the technology is still limited by the depth at which foundations can be placed, and the cost of grid connection is a major consideration in the economics of each project. Offshore projects are clearly up-front capital intensive; for example the anticipated cost of a 60-turbine site in the Solway Firth stands at £200 million (ReNews, 2003) with payback forecast to take 15 years.

Designed as a 'demonstration round' The Crown Estate awarded each pre-qualified developer an agreement for lease providing exclusivity to an area of seabed of no more than ten square kilometres. Sites had to be more than 5 km apart (unless developers agreed to collaborate on adjacent project developments) to protect the economic viability of the wind resource and no more than 30 turbines could be installed on each site. The agreement for lease from The Crown Estate allows developers to install anemometry equipment to measure the wind resource, conduct environmental and geotechnical surveys and gather data to apply to the government for statutory consents. Once all the necessary consents are obtained the developer is able to draw upon the full 22-year lease from The Crown Estate and commence construction and operation of the windfarm. The lease also sets out the schedule for rental payments to The Crown Estate once the windfarm is operational. The formula for rent was agreed between the industry (through the BWEA) and The Crown Estate and was calculated in 2000 and set on the basis of 2 per cent of the then prevailing electricity (4.4p per kilowatt/hour) indexed to the Retail Price Index over the next 20 years. This gives a rate of £0.088 per kWh which is then applied to the actual output of the windfarm in kWh. In 2002 the DTI requested that an additional site in the North-West should be awarded an option agreement for a novel co-generation project combining a gas platform and windfarm. In the same year the Department of Enterprise, Trade and Investment (DETI Northern Ireland), responsible

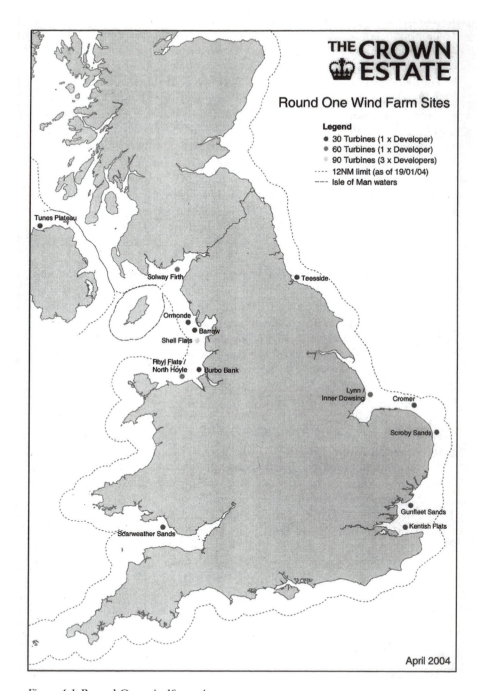

Figure 4.1 Round One windfarm sites.

for energy policy within Northern Ireland, expressed a desire to realize development potential off the north coast of Northern Ireland. A consortium of developers was awarded the site through competitive tender and has assessed the site through extensive environmental studies.

The role of The Crown Estate as landowner of the seabed around the UK is often confused with that of the UK government. The Crown Estate is a landowner, not a regulator. In England and Wales, energy policy is the responsibility of the Department of Trade and Industry (DTI). The DTI administers the provisions of the Electricity Act (1989) requiring developers to seek development consent for the construction, extension or operation of an offshore generating station of 1 MW and over. In Scotland similar development applications are dealt with by the Scottish Executive, and in Northern Ireland by the Department of Enterprise, Trade and Investment (DETI). The DTI have established an Offshore Licensing and Consents unit to act as a 'one-stop shop' for applications for offshore windfarm development in order to make the process of gaining consents from the different government departments more streamlined. Other government departments involved in consenting include the Department for the Environment, Food and Rural Affairs (Defra), with responsibility for fisheries, marine nature conservation and environmental protection. Defra give consent to works covered by the Food and Environment Protection Act (1985) Section 5 (FEPA). The Department for Transport (DfT) oversee navigation issues (sea and air) and consent works under the provision of the Coast Protection Act (1949) Section 34. The Transport and Works Act provides and alternative consenting routes applicable to offshore wind energy and details are issued by Defra's Marine Consents and Environment Unit (MCEU). In Welsh territorial waters some of these consents are administered by the Welsh Assembly Government. Other relevant government departments are consulted as part of the process. For example the Ministry of Defence have to be consulted about defence implications, particularly the potential impact on air defence radar.

By the end of 2003, 12 of the Round One UK projects were fully consented, with only one, North Hoyle, off the coast of north Wales fully operational and generating enough electricity for 50,000 average homes. In August 2004 Scroby Sands off Great Yarmouth became operational and construction work commenced on Kentish Flats with an anticipated completion date in spring 2005. In October 2004, following a Public Inquiry Scarweather Sands, off the coast of south Wales, received consent from the Welsh Assembly. Construction will commence on several other Round One projects in 2005 with possibly two more becoming operational by the end of that year. As a demonstration, Round One identified the significant level of interest from industry but also enabled them to assess the financial, technological and environmental constraints on development. It very clearly highlighted the urgent need for a more strategic and coherent approach to future rounds facilitated by a clear policy steer from government.

Economic costs, measures and incentives

Renewable energy projects are highly capital intensive. To aid development of the offshore wind energy industry the UK government has made subsidies available via a capital grant and research and development scheme administered by the DTI. The first 12 consented projects were all awarded a capital grant at around £10 million per project. Overall, the government has increased funding for renewables projects to £350 million over four years (ISES, 2003) including a research and development programme that provides funds for technological innovations, related mainly, but not restricted to, turbine and foundation design. Other forms of offshore renewable technology such as wave energy generators and tidal current turbines are also benefiting from this support mechanism.

The Renewable Obligation (RO) is the principal policy instrument for achieving the 10 per cent target in the UK and suppliers can use tradable renewable energy certificates to demonstrate compliance with their obligation. The Renewables Obligation Certificate (ROC) was introduced in 2002 requiring all licensed electricity suppliers in England and Wales to supply a specified proportion of their electricity sales (3 per cent in 2003 rising to 10.4 per cent in 2010) from a choice of eligible renewable sources. Each ROC is equal to 1 MWh of power generated and can be traded separately from the electricity, enabling each electricity supplier to meet the Renewables Obligation by purchasing ROCs for the proportion of the target they fail to meet. Suppliers are fined £30 indexed per MWh of generation for which they do not surrender valid ROCs. The money is put into a communal pot and is redistributed to the suppliers in proportion to the number of ROCs they have surrendered in the relevant compliance period – effectively a recycling payment. The true value of the ROC is derived from the £30 fine plus the amount of the recycling payment. Only ROC surrendered by suppliers are eligible for this payment (Re-gen, 2003). It is estimated that for every 1 GW of shortfall suppliers will have to find £50 million. In December 2003 the offshore wind industry was given additional financial incentives with the announcement that ROCs were being extended to 15 per cent by 2015. The announcement was welcomed by the industry and the financial institutions that had expressed concern about the nature of the ROC market beyond 2010.

Even though in terms of capital expenditure turbines represent about 4–45 per cent of the total cost of offshore wind, compared to 70 per cent for land-based turbines, capital costs of offshore wind are 30–50 per cent higher than on shore, mainly due to the installation, support, cable and distribution costs (Robb, 2003). For offshore projects economies of scale are becoming increasingly important and the increased revenue for better wind resource at sea (as much as 20 per cent higher in the nearshore and 40 per cent offshore) could outweigh the additional cable costs and transmission losses (Milborrow, 2003).

Distance from grid connection is a key economic factor, as any grid reinforcement is costly. The DTI initially indicated that it would consider extending the onshore electricity transmission system offshore to allow connection of windfarms at 'hub points' but a working solution will take some time to resolve. Licences could be issued to providers of high-voltage networks who will effectively be able to 'go out to meet' offshore projects rather than the present situation where offshore has to come ashore to meet the onshore transmission network. The issue is still being discussed at length. Who bears the cost will be an important factor in the final decision but the government has indicated that it will socialize the costs.

Round Two offshore windfarm provides opportunity for massive expansion

As soon as Round One sites were awarded developers were lobbying the government for rapid expansion of the sector through considerably larger-scale projects. This was set against criticism from environmental interests, particularly non-governmental and campaigning organizations who considered the 'mad dash for development' in Round One to be too much too soon. They called for a precautionary approach until potential environmental impacts had been given full consideration, and in some cases even called for a moratorium on development until studies and a full strategic environmental assessment had been completed. The government found itself in a position with intense pressure from the industry, the need to progress on 2010 targets and the need to work with the environmental sector to ensure impacts could be minimized. In November 2002, recognizing the need for a strategic approach, the DTI published a consultation report entitled *Future Offshore*. This report identified three strategic areas most suited to offshore windfarm development on account of bathymetry, grid connection and wind resource. The Greater Wash, the Thames Estuary and the North-West (Liverpool Bay) became the focus of attention and the DTI committed to carrying out a Strategic Environmental Assessment (SEA) on these areas, based upon the requirements of the EU SEA Directive. The SEA Directive became mandatory for government plans and programmes in August 2004, although the DTI had implemented an SEA programme for the licensing of oil and gas blocks in recent years.

The role of Strategic Environmental Assessment

Strategic Environmental Assessment (SEA) is used to support decision making at governmental level. The EU Directive 2001/42/EC on the Assessment of the Effects of Certain Plans and Programmes on the Environment became mandatory in August 2004. The UK government has already adopted the spirit of the Directive through oil and gas licensing in recent years. On this basis the DTI, as the government department responsible for all energy policy committed to the SEA approach to the second round of offshore windfarm development and in Future Offshore (2002), indicated an intention to take a strategic approach to future development, with environment at the heart of decision-making. This resulted in the identification of three strategic areas and the commencement of a SEA, culminating in an Environmental Report for consultation before the details of the second round competition could be issued. On the whole, environmental and other marine user organizations welcomed this approach as it provided for earlier consultation on a range of strategic issues.

The three strategic areas selected were the Thames Estuary, the Greater Wash and the North-West (Liverpool Bay), and all extended beyond the territorial waters onto the UK Continental Shelf recognizing the spatial and depth requirements of the industry. SEA focuses on strategic issues rather than site specific environmental issues which still need to be addressed through mandatory Environmental Impact Assessments (EIA). Consequently it considers alternatives as well as a comparative analysis of scenarios of development. In taking a strategic approach it assesses constraints, sensitivities and risks instead of detailed analysis of the characteristics of specific impacts (BMT-Cordah, 2003). A key characteristic of any SEA is that it should deal with potential cumulative impacts associated with development, not only on a sectoral basis (in this case offshore windfarm development) but also in combination with other marine activities and uses. The SEA for offshore windfarm development took less than six months and brought together existing information about the three areas under consideration. As this SEA was a desk-based study it did not include any new surveys or studies to fill known data gaps or uncertainties. This was a different approach to the oil and gas SEA programme where new data is collected to inform the SEA and subsequent decision-making. It is easy to see why environmental groups have criticized the lack of time available for compiling the offshore wind SEA and the very short consultation period.

The Environmental Report presented the conclusions of the SEA with only one month for stakeholder consultation. The SEA stated that there would inevitably be some environmental impacts of development at different locations within the three strategic areas. The responses to the consultation enabled the DTI to issue guidance to potential developers on the development restrictions that would be in place for Round Two. This included strong advice to developers that they should take into account the guidance provided by the DTI when submitting a tender application to The Crown Estate, along with consideration for a range of other activities, including hydrocarbon licensing, commercial fisheries, shipping and navigation, ports and Ministry of Defence issues.

As a precautionary measure the DTI identified a coastal exclusion strip within the three strategic areas where development would not take place in Round Two. The exclusion strip ranged between 8 and 13 km from the coast, depending upon the sensitivity of the coast (to take account of visual impact, potential impact on the marine environment, inshore fishery interests and other marine user groups). In addition, development was not to be allowed in water depths less than 10 m in the North-West strategic area due to the significance of these areas to the common scoter (*Melanitta nigra*), which overwinters in large numbers in the area. Figure 4.2 shows the strategic areas that were the focus of site development in Round Two (DTI, 2003c). The areas include areas on the UK Continental Shelf beyond the 12 nautical mile territorial sea limit.

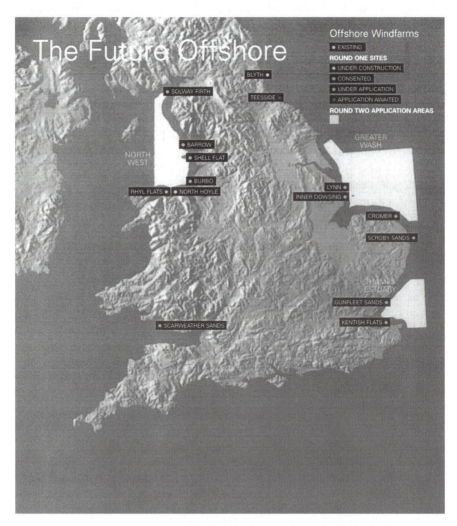

Figure 4.2 Offshore windfarms: existing and application sites (2003 status).

Beyond territorial water

The strategic areas include the UK Continental Shelf beyond the 12 nautical mile territorial sea limit. The DTI's *Future Offshore* consultation paper and the Energy White Paper indicated the government's intention to bring forward primary legislation to allow development of the UK Continental Shelf. To streamline the consenting process and provide a robust legislative framework for development on the UKCS the DTI put forward a new Energy Bill. The Energy Act received Royal Assent in July 2004. The Energy Act enables the UK government to establish a Renewable Energy Zone (REZ) on the UKCS and vests rights in The Crown Estate to provide licences for offshore renewable development in the REZ. The Crown Estate does not own the seabed beyond the territorial limits but does have the rights to exploit minerals excluding oil, gas and coal on the Continental Shelf. It exercises this right through the licensing of marine aggregates dredging. The Energy Act vests renewable energy rights on the Continental Shelf with The Crown Estate thereby providing a consistent leasing and licensing regime across the territorial limits.

The exploitation of the natural resources of wind, wave and tidal energy falls within the United Nations Convention on the Law of the Sea (UNCLOS) and the Energy Act enables the government to declare a Renewable Energy Zone (REZ) for the UK Continental Shelf, covering all forms of offshore renewable energy. This gives the government the ability to regulate the marine renewables industry. In addition to the provision to enable The Crown Estate to license sites in the REZ the Energy Act also extends certain provisions of the Electricity Act 1989 to establish a consenting framework for the generation, transmission and distribution of electricity in the REZ. Other provisions include the ability to create safety zones around renewable energy installations within both territorial water and REZ, to extinguish the public rights of navigation in relation to renewable energy installations and to set up a statutory regime for decommissioning projects.

Round Two announcement establishes UK as potential global leader

The SEA Environmental Report was circulated for consultation in May 2003 and the conclusions and responses to the consultation used by the DTI to define development guidance for the second round. On 14 July 2003 the DTI requested The Crown Estate to make available seabed within the three strategic areas for the purpose of offshore windfarm development. Government expressed a desire to see an additional four to 6 GW of installed capacity through Round Two, which combined with Round One would meet the target of six to 7.5 GW installed by 2010 providing a major boost to the offshore windpower industry. In addition, the DTI forecast that 6 GW would call for at least £6 billion of investment, creating over 20,000 jobs in offshore manufacturing, installation and maintenance and providing electricity for about 3.5 million homes. Due to the different arrangements required for Round Two, and the development guidance derived from the SEA, The Crown Estate launched a competitive tender on 15 July 2003. Arrangements for Round Two were designed to provide a framework for rapid and environmentally sensitive development of the offshore wind energy industry and the competitive tender aimed 'to award the largest most sought after sites to applicants most ready and best fitted to develop each site to its optimum capacity' (http://www. thecrownestate.co.uk). The tender closed on 15 October and the assessment process was completed in December 2003. The interest shown by the industry was evident through the 41 projects, totalling 27 GW of installed capacity, received by the close of the tender. Given the need for a scale of development required to meet government targets and the economies of scale to attract interest from the financial institutions to make projects economically viable, the tender received projects up to 1.5 GW in size. An important part of the assessment process included consultation with the relevant government departments and devolved administrations in order to gather high-level strategic input and identify key issues which were to be taken account of during the tender assessment. In December 2003 The Crown Estate and DTI (DTI, 2003c) announced the award of 15 new projects to 12 successful developers (Figure 4.3). Taking account of recommended capacity from the SEA these projects amounted to a potential 7.2 GW of installed capacity and were hailed as the biggest planned programme of offshore windfarm development in the world, calling for over £7 billion of investment.

Ambitious plans for each strategic area

Each successful developer signed an option agreement (Agreement for Lease) enabling them to undertake requirements of the statutory consenting process. As with Round One once all the necessary consents are granted by the government the developer is able to draw on the full term of The Crown Estate lease. For Round Two sites this is 40 years for projects up to 750 MW and 50 years for the largest projects. In accordance with the suggested capacity for the three strategic areas the largest projects will be developed in the Wash and the Thames Estuary (Table 4.1).

Four projects were awarded in the Thames Estuary and if developers' plans are implemented this strategic area will see 1,864 MW of new capacity, much of it within one project, the London Array. If the proposed programme keeps to time, construction could commence in 2006 with completion by 2010, resulting in a 1 GW development. Depending on turbine technology this could be between 200 and 300 turbines installed. Another proposed development lies 25 km offshore, straddling the territorial

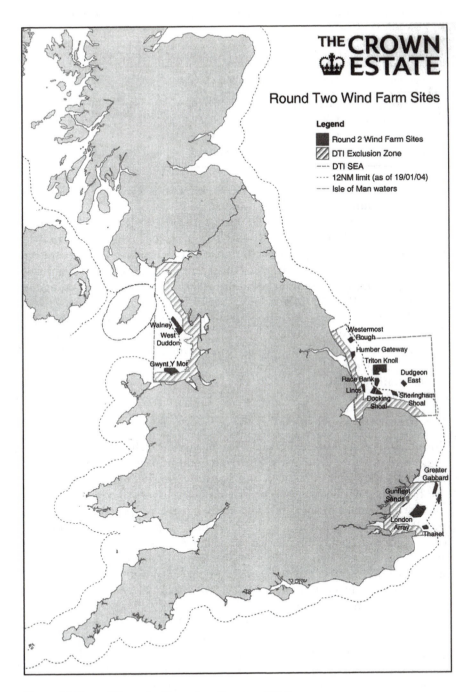

Figure 4.3 Round Two windfarm sites (January 2004).

Table 4.1 Round Two UK offshore windfarm projects installed capacity awarded in three strategic areas

Within territorial water		Beyond territorial waters (REZ)	Total
Strategic area	Installed capacity	Installed capacity	
Greater Wash	1,605 MW	2,000 MW	3,605 MW
Thames Estuary	1,664 MW	200 MW	1,864 MW
North-West	1,700 MW	None	1,700 MW
Total	4,969 MW	2,200 MW	7,169 MW

sea limit, whilst the smallest award of Round Two is a small extension to a consented Round One project, Gunfleet Sands.

The Greater Wash offers the greatest capacity for development, with a potential 3,605 MW from eight Round Two projects, including the world's largest proposed development with up to 1.2 GW installed capacity on the UKCS, at a distance of 30–40 km offshore. If consent is given it is unlikely that construction will commence before 2009. The other projects range in size from 240 MW to 500 MW.

In the North-West only three new sites were awarded, delivering a potential 1,700 MW of installed capacity. The largest scheme will be off the coast of North Wales seaward of the Round One North Hoyle scheme and to be developed by the same company. The other two projects will be of 450 MW and 500 MW.

Environmental concerns

Round One emphasized the need for more research into the potential impacts of offshore windfarms. Environmental Impact Assessments (EIAs) are a necessary requirement of the statutory consenting process (under the Electricity Act Section 36) and require developers to conduct a range of environmental investigations and studies at the proposed development site. Public consultation with all user and interest groups is also a vital part of the process. To aid the process, the Centre for Environment, Fisheries and Aquaculture Science (CEFAS) published a Guidance Note for Off-shore Windfarms for Environmental Impact Assessments to Food and Environmental Protection Act (FEPA) and Coast Protection Act (CPA) requirements (updated 2004).

Key concerns include potential impacts on bird populations (including collision, barrier effect to migration routes and displacement from benthic feeding habitats), the impact of underwater noise and vibration on marine mammals and fish, the impact of electromagnetic fields (EMF) from the seabed cables (particularly on elasmobranches), changes in benthic habitat, changes in sediment transport and coastal processes and visual impact. All theses issues need to be addressed in the EIA, along with an indication as to the mitigation measures to be put in place. The FEPA licence issued to a project will have conditions attached detailing the requirements for monitoring. The issues listed above are not exhaustive but need to be addressed within all project developments so they can be considered also at a generic level.

Recognizing the lack of information and data available to address these issues, through the Round One procedure, the Crown Estate established a research fund (called COWRIE – Collaborative Offshorewind Research into Environment) administered by a steering group drawn from the offshore wind industry and conservation agencies. The steering group has identified and prioritized environmental studies that have been commissioned to provide guidance or best practice (http://www.thecrownestate.co.uk). Research projects currently underway include an assessment of the impacts on fish of electromagnetic fields from cables, an investigation into the impacts of underwater noise and vibration during construction and operation phases, an assessment of bird survey methodologies and modelling the displacement of common scoter from benthic feeding habitats.

Successful Round Two developers were also required to pay an option fee to The Crown Estate for the purposes of establishing a fund along similar lines to COWRIE. The fund total of £2.4 million will be used for generic environmental research as well as data and information management and education. Data and information management is considered to be important under the conditions of the Agreement for Lease, and Lease developers will be required to submit data and metadata to The Crown Estate so that it can be made accessible for the benefit of the marine science community. This is seen as a significant contribution to widening access to data.

Beneficial environmental opportunities associated with offshore windfarms must not be overlooked. Developers frequently argue that the turbines will act as artificial reefs and in combination with restrictions on the use of mobile fishing gear within the windfarms this could provide some form of protected area. It is well documented that fish congregate around oil rigs and platforms so they could act as fish refugia. Research and monitoring will be required during the operation phase of the windfarms, but it may be some time before any benefits are evident. It has also been suggested that any scour protection around turbine foundations could provide suitable substrate for lobster hatchery programmes but this is yet to be investigated. Outside the UK, developers of two offshore windfarms are adopting a novel approach by integrating fish farming businesses into their business models (Martin and McGovern, 2003); in the Dutch sector one developer is planning to farm mussel seed on monopile foundation by hanging special nets between the piles. It is suggested that this could produce between 300–600,000 kg of mussel seed per annum. The nets will be hung in April and retrieved in September with the seed mussel being transferred to a mussel ground. Not only will this provide an additional income but it will also have environmental benefits, relieving pressure on the Waddensea and its important bird populations and mussel fishermen. This is being promoted as a good news story for the fishing industry who are otherwise very concerned about displacement from fishing grounds. In Spain offshore developers also want to combine fish farming and shell-fish bedding facilities with the windfarm. Underwater cages could be fitted around the turbines and leased out for fish breeding and rearing, although the plan is facing opposition from local fishing collectives.

As part of the EIA developers must also address other uses of the seabed. Commercial fishermen have voiced concern over the potential displacement from key fisheries due to the restrictions on navigation. For some Round One sites objections from the Ministry of Defence have also delayed progress, and it is likely that the MOD will have objections to Round Two sites, particularly in The Wash, and will need to work with the industry to identify technical solutions. In other areas visual impact has been the main concern for coastal communities. The message is very clear: developers need to engage with other marine user and interest groups at the earliest opportunity in the project. Increasingly, developers are using local coastal fora and estuary partnerships to act as the mechanism through which consultation can take place. This has enormous benefits in that coastal partnerships are best placed to provide opportunities for stakeholder dialogue and consultation with marine users and interest groups. For Round Two projects developers are collaborating on a regional basis for the purposes of environmental investigations such as bird surveys. It is only through improved co-ordination and pooling of resources that the industry can address cumulative and in-combination effects associated with their developments.

The call for spatial planning

The emergence of offshore windfarms as a new marine industry – with its large spatial demands competing and conflicting with other marine activities, users and stakeholders – has raised the intensity of the debate for the need for spatial planning in a marine context. Sea use planning is synonymous with marine spatial planning and for many implies the need for a more proactive, plan-led approach to decision-making for marine development and use.

In 2002 the UK government, through Defra as the lead body, published its marine stewardship report. Entitled *Safeguarding Our Seas* it set out the government's vision for the future management and protection of our seas. The report highlighted the need for management, the need for spatial analysis to accommodate multiple uses and the data requirements to undertake analysis for decision-making. Traditionally marine resources have been managed on a sectoral basis driven by single economic or political motivation and this has led to legislative fragmentation. Spatial analysis provides the opportunity to shape the future of marine resource management so as to accommodate multiple-use, minimize environmental impact, optimize environmental gain and protect the economic resource base. It requires better co-ordination and co-operation between sectoral interests and involves the location of activities and the allocation of space for a single use or variety of uses. The marine stewardship report emphasized the importance of spatial data, especially seabed biotopes in order that an ecosystem-based approach to management through better understanding between environmental features and human activities can be delivered. Non-governmental organizations in the UK have added to the discussion through the publication of a joint discussion paper which calls for the UK to adopt an effective spatial plan-led system for the marine environment (Wildlife, Countryside and Environment Link, 2002).

Offshore renewable energy needs to be developed within a coherent policy and marine resource management framework. As spatial planning involves a presumption for and against particular activities in particular areas the concept often meets resistance due to increased regulatory control and loss of traditional rights.

Commitments and obligations to spatial planning have been adopted at European level. At the fifth International Conference on the Protection of the North Sea in 2002 ministers agreed to strengthen co-operation in spatial planning processes as a component of the Bergen Declaration. They noted the importance of spatial planning in addressing cumulative effects of use and protection of the North Sea. At an OSPAR (the convention for the protection of the marine environment of the North-East Atlantic) meeting in June 2002 it was agreed that spatial planning should be taken forward to help meet the commitments under the Bergen Declaration. Further European commitment to spatial planning was expressed in October 2002 when the commission published *Towards a Strategy to Protect and Conserve the Marine Environment* which states 'the commission will address the integration of nature protection measures and the various sectoral activities impacting on the marine environment including spatial planning'.

Strategic environmental assessment is a step towards marine geospatial planning as long as it leaves behind the sectoral approach and becomes an integrated, multi-sectoral tool to guide the future location of activities to meet environmental, social and economic aims. Defra has committed to a pilot study on marine spatial planning, using the Irish Sea as a study area.

The potential for wave and tidal energy

Despite over 30 years of research and development programmes first started in the early 1980s the UK does not yet have any wave and tidal projects of a commercial scale. More recently it has been suggested that past estimates of the potential of wave and tidal energy capture have been greatly overplayed, even though these other forms of offshore renewable energy could potentially make a substantial contribution to the global energy demand. Grinsted (2003) calculated 0.1–0.2 TW of energy could be recoverable out of a total wave global energy resource of 10 TW. This compares with previous estimates of recoverable resource ranging between 1–10 TW and 2 TW (Re-News, 2003). For tidal energy Grinsted (op. cit.) considers 0.02–0.05 TW may be recoverable from a total estimated global resource of 2.5 TW, compared to previous generalizations of 1 TW recoverable from between 3–5 TW total resource. On the basis that about 1–2 per cent is recoverable from wave and tidal resource this would amount to 13 per cent of current world energy consumption.

With many more small demonstration and prototype projects coming forward in this sector of offshore renewables there is an increasing need for a better understanding of the nature and scale of the potential resource around the UK along with comparisons of engineering and technologies. This is necessary if a clear policy steer from government is to emerge as to the role this sector is expected to contribute to the energy mix beyond 2010.

In terms of potential energy, although tides are generally less well studied than waves, tidal energy is the most predictable of the marine renewable resource. Nonetheless it has been estimated that the theoretical potential from tidal energy in the UK as a whole is around 50 TWh per year and that the Pentland Firth in Scotland could alone account for 25 per cent of the tidal energy capability of the UK. Any assessment of the amount of energy available will also have to consider how much can be extracted, the technology required and the effect of energy extraction. For example in Yell Sound off Shetland a 10 per cent slowing anticipated at 120 MW at 2 ms. When comparing energy flow the energy from tides is very site specific and more intermittent and peakier than wind. Thus tides are no better than wind in energy density except in a few exceptional sites. The majority of annual collectable energy is at moderate range current speed of 1.5 ms not at the highest speeds associated with peak springs. As energy is extracted the tidal flow slows and this can cause up to 10 per cent energy reduction for 10 per cent extraction. Beyond a 10–20 per cent extraction there is a significant velocity decrease in a channel where there is no other route for water to escape. Devices placed around an island, for example have the potential to change flows within the surrounding area depending on the hydrography. It is also important to design technology for tidal energy at slower speeds as high tidal stream flow is available for only a limited time within the tidal cycle. For example 100 sites equal to Yell Sound would be required to equal one 1,200 MW power station. There are many headland and estuarine sites around the UK where the potential for tidal energy can be considered. As a consequence of a high tidal range several sites off Pembrokeshire, the Lleyn Peninsula, Menai Straits and the Severn Estuary have all been suggested in Wales as offering development potential (Ball, 2002) along with locations off the north Devon and Cornwall coasts.

Tidal projects range from tidal barrages to current turbines. Estuarine tidal barrages have been considered in the UK, from large-scale proposals such as the Severn Barrage to smaller barrages on several Welsh estuaries including the Conwy and the Loughor. The significant environmental consequences on estuarine ecosystems, especially of large-scale barrage projects coupled with major financial risks, have prevented these projects from coming forward. The range of marine current turbines currently under development and testing are often described as being analogous to underwater wind turbines. Most prototypes are a single rotor on a pile installation and produce about 100 kw. The commercial scale requirement is 5 MW and this can only be achieved through an array of current turbines. Development costs at present for prototypes are approximately £5,710 per KW but can and will have to be reduced for commercial delivery. Marine current turbines can work on both the ebb and the flood and many demonstration projects will lead to twin rotors for bi-directional operation.

Installation methods and attachment to the seabed are a major limiting factor to the potential for tidal energy. Gravity and anchoring systems are expensive, so developers are considering other innovative installation methods such as hydrofoils which use the down thrust from the tidal currents to hold the structure on the seabed, and have the potential to be utilized in both deep and shallow water sites.

Outside the UK a new tidal park known as Blue Concept is planned for the narrow strait of Kvalsundet in northern Norway, although financial problems due to higher than anticipated costs have delayed installation. The project will comprise 20 turbines which will produce 32 TWh per year. The location is ideal with a mean current velocity of 1.8 metres per second. The turbine system is able to continually adjust blade position in relation to tidal currents to maximize energy output. Each turbine will be mounted on a 30-metre-high foundation about 20 m below the sea surface. Environmental studies will be conducted to assess the impact of the project on the marine environment and to predict any adverse biological impacts on the installations such as reduced efficiency and corrosion due to fouling.

Onshore, shoreline wave energy is technically developed at a community scale, but offshore devices are at various stages of development. Many wave energy generators are based on oscillating water column devices as the proven concept and are often designed for deep water to take advantage of energetic wave spectra. Consequently, the mooring systems utilized need to be of robust construction and most have yet to demonstrate their long term reliability and effectiveness. Wave energy generators utilize horizontal component of wave motion in troughs and must be capable of capturing long lengths of wave crest. With an input power of 12 MW developers suggest it is realistic to expect 5 MW out, peaking at 20 MW for a 200 m-wide capture area. To capture this energy some devices under development have even been designed to focus waves and will be deployed in flotillas of 10–20 units.

As with tidal streams and flows there is a need to map wave power distribution around the UK. Most of the prototypes are being deployed in Scottish waters at present although Wales and the South-West offer suitable high-energy sites. The prospects for wave energy to contribute to 2010 renewable energy targets are largely constrained at present by the technological development costs, but wave energy may provide a longer-term prospect towards 2020. There is also considerable potential for islands and remote communities to benefit from community-based nearshore and shoreline schemes in the future.

The UK government is providing support for demonstration projects mainly through research and development funding. This includes funding for the European Marine Energy Test Centre at Stromness in Orkney, which provides facilities and cable connection for testing and certification of demonstration projects, research and development, as well as a sheltered location and good wave resource. The UK government has also identified work towards establishing a capital grants scheme to support wave and tidal projects, and in August 2004 announced that £50 million was to be made available to bring forward this new sector. Scotland has excellent marine energy resources and has emerged at the forefront of wave and tidal energy development although other regions such as the South-West of England also have aspirations to develop into test centres where offshore renewables could become an important part of the local economy.

Conclusions

The potential for renewable energy from UK marine waters is substantial and the government is optimistic that they can meet the target of 10 GW by 2010 with a mixture of at least 4.5–6 GW from offshore, 4 GW from onshore projects and the shortfall from biomass and other non-wind renewables. Offshore wind currently provides the best prospect but despite the expectations of the offshore wind sector, this industry is still in its infancy and there are many environmental and other obstacles to overcome before the UK can realize the benefits. These are challenging times for the government, the marine renewables industry, marine users and environmental organizations. With offshore wind most likely to deliver towards the 10 per cent target, 1,500 turbines would still need to be installed by 2010, along with grid strengthening, new infrastructure and a reliable supply chain. The first round of offshore wind promised around

1,000 MW of construction by 2005 but is more likely now to deliver less than 200 MW, mainly due to delayed timetables caused by financial uncertainty and plant delays. Offshore turbine technology is still untested even though new, larger turbines are being developed aimed specifically at the offshore market. At the outset of Round One a 2 MW turbine was considered to be at the forefront of technology and already some Round One sites will see 3 MW turbines, even 3.6 MW turbines installed. It is anticipated that 5 MW turbines will be standard for many of the Round Two sites, with some developers already considering 7 MW machines. The extension to ROCs to 2015 has given the industry and its financial backers renewed confidence and the government has indicated that it also review this economic instrument in 2005/6.

The more strategic approach to future rounds of development presents an opportunity to gain from regional development of manufacturing base and also sharing infrastructure. There will be additional local economic benefits due to the offshore wind industry such as the proximity of ports for dockside construction and pre-installation assembly and maintenance. Offshore projects will require new installation and lifting plant as well as dedicated new ships specially designed for turbine installation. Initiatives and support mechanisms such as RegenSW, Renewables NW and Eastern Renewables will play an increasing important role in co-ordinating activity and opportunity at a regional level whilst test centres such as that in Orkney and NaREC (New and Renewable Energy Centre) in Blyth, Northumberland are needed to provide opportunities for testing technology and concepts, skills development and greater exchange of information and expertise. Regional initiatives must also seize the opportunity to raise awareness about offshore renewables, to help inform the public and bring marine user groups together to resolve potential conflicts.

Environmental concerns will need to be addressed through increased attention to generic research and assessment of information provided through consents monitoring requirements. The SEA approach will go some way to addressing the data gaps and uncertainties in areas under consideration for offshore development as long as adequate resources are put in place and data management issues resolved. The move towards SEA that is multi-sectoral is encouraging and will be a key tool in delivering the government's intention to adopt spatial planning for the marine environment. Future SEAs will consider development for oil and gas licensing, offshore windpower and wave and tidal energy. To facilitate policy development the DTI has published an atlas of UK Marine Renewable Energy Resources (DTI, 2004).

There are many ideas being developed in the wave and tidal energy sector but the technology is still in the prototype demonstration phase so it is not clear as to which technology is best at a commercial level. Some projects are gradually moving towards deployment at a commercial scale but the first pre-commercial scale trials are unlikely before 2006/7, so major activity at a commercial scale is not expected until 2012 on current predictions. Wave and tidal is likely to contribute a relatively small percentage, maybe less than 2 per cent at global level. However, it is recognized that UK, due to its geographical position and coastal configuration, has suitable high-energy environments for wave power and suitable tidal streams around headlands and in estuaries associated with high tidal ranges. There are significant financial and technological risks associated with the early stages of any new industry and the variable forecasts as to availability of the wave and tidal energy resource and capability of the emerging technology need to be clarified as resource size and availability does matter.

At governmental level there is a need for a strong policy direction that embraces all forms of marine renewable energy, more investment in technological and environmental research and a combination of incentives and certainty beyond 2010. What is clear is that energy demand is growing and commitments to meet global targets in emission reductions need to be met in 2010 and 2015. Member states of the European Union are already showing wide differences in performance to meet emission targets under the Kyoto Protocol; only Sweden, UK and Germany are expected to meet national targets by 2010 (EWEA p. 14, 2004).

The marine renewables industry has political support and is gathering widespread attention. To see the full level of development required to meet government targets and international commitments some hurdles still need to be removed.

References

Ball, I. (2002) Turning the tide: power from the sea and protection for nature. AWWF-UK and The Wildlife Trusts. http://www.wwf.org.uk/filelibrary/pdf/turningthetide_full.pdf.

Birdlife International (2003) Ministers warned about wind problems. http://www.birdlife.net/news/pr/2003/06/wind_farm.html.

BMT Cordah (2003) Offshore Wind Energy Generation. Phase 1 proposals and environmental report. Report to DTI. http://www.og.dti.gov.uk/offshore-wind-sea/process/phase1_env_report.pdf.

CEFAS (2004) Offshore Windfarms Guidance Note for Environmental Impact Assessment in respect of FEPA and CPA requirements. Prepared on behalf of Marine Consents and Environment Units, Defra.

Department for Environment Food and Rural Affairs (2002) Safeguarding our seas: a strategy for the conservation and sustainable development of our marine environment. http://www.defra.gov.uk/environment/marine/stewardship/pdf/marine_stewardship.pdf.

Department of Trade and Industry (2002) Future Offshore – consultation paper. http://www.dti.gov.uk/energy/leg_and_reg/consents/future_offshore/Foreword.pdf.

Department of Trade and Industry (2003a) Energy White Paper: our energy future – creating a low carbon economy. London: HMSO.

Department of Trade and Industry (2003b) Press Notice: UK and Russia agree historic energy pact, 26 June 2003. http://www.dti.gov.uk/.

Department of Trade and Industry (2003c) Round Two offshore windfarms announcement. http://www.dti.gov.uk/.

Department of Trade and Industry (2004) Atlas of UK Marine Renewable Energy Resources. http://www.dti.gov.uk/energy/renewables/technologies/atlas.shtml.

Douglas Westwood Associates (2002) Renewable energy world market prospects. http://www.dw-1.com.

Douglas Westwood Associates (2003) Market opportunities becoming a reality. http://www.dw-1.com.

EWEA (2003) *Wind Directions* May/June: 12.

EWEA (2004) *Wind Directions* January/February: 14–15.

Grinsted, T. (2003) Resource Potential. Wind and Tidal Technology Seminar, NaREC, July (seminar proceedings). Renewable Power Association.

ICE (2003) State of the Nation Report 2003. An assessment of the state of the UK's infrastructure by the Institute of Civil Engineers: 13.

ISES (2003) *Re-Focus* May/June: 10.

Martin, N. and McGovern, M. (2003) *Windpower Monthly* April: 28.

Milborrow, D. (2003) Offshore wind rises to the challenge. *Wind Power Monthly* April: 51.

Re-gen (2003) Appleyard, D. (ed.) June/July: 90.

ReNews 27 (2003) Rigden, D. (ed.).

Rowley, W. and Westwood, A. (2003) Offshore wind energy, *Re-Focus* (ISES), May/June: 10.

Robb, D. (2003) Wind giants fuel growth. *Re-gen* June/July: 29.

The Crown Estate (2004) COWRIE. http://www.thecrownestate.co.uk.

Wildlife, Countryside and Environment Link (2002) A future for our seas. http://www.wcl.org.uk/downloads/2004/WCL05_MSP_BP2_19Apr041.pdf.

WWF-UK, English Nature, RSPB, BWEA (2001) Windfarm development and nature conservation: 16

5 Fisheries management at the millennium

Perspectives from an island community

Ian R. Napier

I believe that it may be affirmed with confidence that, in relation to our present modes of fishing, a number of the most important sea fisheries, such as the cod fishery, the herring fishery, and the mackerel fishery, are inexhaustible.

...the multitude of these fishes is so inconceivably great that the number we catch is relatively insignificant ... probably all the great sea fisheries, are inexhaustible ... nothing we do seriously affects the number of the fish.

Huxley (1883)

The world's fish stocks are in a state of crisis ... all over the world stocks of most species of fish are being severely depleted by over-fishing.

House of Lords (1996)

Developments in global fisheries

The twentieth century, and particularly its last few decades, saw a fundamental change in man's understanding of the effects of exploitation on marine fisheries and of the nature of marine resources. Man has exploited marine fish[1] for at least a million years (Fridman, 1998), but within the last few decades of the century fisheries that had once appeared limitless became severely depleted and in some cases collapsed completely. The cause of these declines was primarily a phenomenal increase in catches of marine fish, climbing to their highest recorded level at the turn of the century (FAO, 2002). Fuelled by increasing demand for fish from a growing world population and by rapid developments in man's ability to find and catch fish at sea, preserve it and transport it to markets, catches of marine fishes increased more than twenty-fold in the course of the twentieth century.

Huxley's comments in 1883 (quoted above) reflected a widespread belief that marine fish stocks were effectively limitless; that there were so many fish in the sea that nothing that man did could significantly affect their abundance. For most of the last million years this belief was largely correct; the available fish catching technology was so limited that its impact on fish stocks was negligible.

But the rate at which fish can reproduce and grow is limited by biological and environmental factors. So long as the rate at which fish are caught is less than the rate at which they can be replaced a fishery will be sustainable; it can continue indefinitely. But if the rate of removal exceeds the rate of replacement the yield from the fishery will decline. If this 'over-fishing' is sufficiently severe the abundance of fish may decline to such an extent that the fish stock collapses, because there are no longer sufficient mature fish to produce the next generation. A complicating factor is that fish also experience substantial natural changes in abundance as a result of changing environmental factors, and it can be difficult to distinguish the effects of over-fishing from natural fluctuations.

Throughout most of history catches of fish developed only very slowly, and by the mid-nineteenth century total world landings of marine fish are estimated to have reached only about two million tonnes per annum (Table 5.1). The industrial revolution, particularly the application of steam power to fishing vessels and the development of new catching methods such as the trawl net, provided a powerful boost to fishing intensity and landings had doubled to four million tonnes by 1900. By the late nineteenth century, fishing technology had developed to a stage where man was, for the first time, able to significantly reduce the abundance of fish. By the time Huxley gave his address there were already indications that some fisheries were being over-exploited, although there was considerable debate over this issue (Smith, 1994).

Fishing intensity, and evidence of over-fishing, accumulated through the twentieth century (although the over-fishing issue remained controversial for most of the century). The first decade saw the total world catch of marine fish grow by more than 10 per cent per annum on average (Table 5.1), with catches reaching 9.5 million tonnes by 1913. Despite the

Table 5.1 Total annual world landing of marine fish in selected years from 1850 to 2001, and average annual growth rate over each preceding period.

Year	Catch (mt)	Average annual growth rate (%)
1850	2.0	
1900	4.0	2.0
1913	9.5	10.6
1938	22.0	5.3
1950	16.8	6.4
1960	30.8	8.4
1970	58.2	8.9
1980	62.6	0.8
1990	79.1	2.6
2000	86.7	1.0
2001	83.7	−3.8

Sources: Coull, 1993; FAO, 2003.

massive dislocation to the fisheries industry caused by two world wars catches had reached 16.8 million tonnes by 1950.

The post-war decades saw a second industrialization of the fisheries industry (Cushing, 1988) with numerous technological developments, along with a general increase in the size and power of fishing vessels, further increasing fishing intensity. Of these, echo-sounders (used to locate shoals of fish), synthetic ropes and twines, and new types of fishing vessel such as factory stern trawlers and purse-seiners, are perhaps the most important.[2]

The intensification of fishing effort produced dramatic increases in landings of marine fish (Table 5.1, Figure 5.1) which more than trebled between 1950 and 1970, an average growth rate of almost 9 per cent per annum. The early 1970s, however, provided dramatic evidence of the finite nature of marine fish resources with the collapse of the Peruvian anchovetta fishery. Landings of Peruvian anchovetta had increased from 438 tonnes in 1950 to 12.3 million tonnes in 1970 (Sahrhage and Lundbeck, 1992), making it the world's largest single-species fishery, but fell to less than 5 million tonnes in 1972 (Coull, 1993). Largely as a result of the collapse of this fishery the rate of growth in global landings of marine fish declined abruptly during the 1970s. The rate of growth recovered somewhat in the 1980s, but slowed again in the 1990s, although landings reached a peak of about 86 million tonnes in 1996/97. Landings slumped

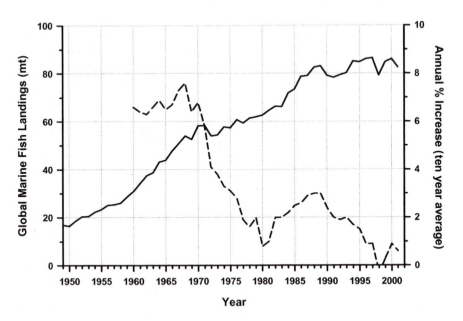

Figure 5.1 Total world landings of marine fish, 1950–2001 and running ten-year average of annual percentage increase in landings (data from FAO, 2003).

by 8 per cent in 1998, however, and although there has been some recovery since then landings have fluctuated between about 80 and 86 million tonnes per annum, with no sign of any continued overall growth.

The total catch of marine fish is actually much higher than figures for landings alone suggest. In 1994 it was estimated that an additional 27 million tonnes of fish (on average) were being caught and discarded each year (Alverson *et al.*, 1994), and illegal and unrecorded catches could be as high as 20 to 30 per cent of those officially recorded (Buckworth, 1998). Taking into account discards and illegal and unrecorded catches Pauly *et al.* (2002) estimated that the total world catch of marine fish had peaked at about 140 million tonnes in the late 1980s and had declined since then at a rate of about 0.7 million tonnes per annum.

The collapse of the Peruvian anchovetta fishery, together with collapses of other fisheries (including herring and cod) and the general slowing of the rate of increase in global marine fish landings fundamentally changed perceptions of marine fish resources. As evidence accumulated during the last three decades of the twentieth century the persistent belief in limitless marine fish resources increasingly gave way to a growing public awareness that these resources were in fact finite, and in many cases under severe strain.

Trends in global landings strongly suggest that marine fish production is close to (if not already beyond) its limits. Gulland (1971) estimated that the maximum potential harvest of traditionally exploited marine species was about 100 million tonnes per annum. Recorded landings of marine fish are currently not far short of this figure and estimates (Pauly *et al.*, 2002) suggest that the total catch is well beyond it. The growth of the 1960s and 1970s was largely supported by geographic expansion of fisheries, but with fisheries now taking place in virtually every corner of the world's oceans the potential for such expansion is now all but exhausted. Although the trend in landings continued upwards throughout the 1960s, 70s and 80s there was little (if any) further increase during the final decade of the century, by which time the rate of growth had fallen to near zero (Figure 5.1, Garcia and Newton, 1997).

The continued growth of world fish production in the latter part of the twentieth century actually masked much lower growth rates, and even declines, in many long-established 'traditional' fisheries (Arnason and Felt, 1995), including many of those in European waters. Much of the continued growth was only achieved by the development of new fisheries for a relatively small number of previously non-targeted species, many of which were small and of relatively low value. Global landings of species such as cod, haddock, hake and flatfish, for example, which are a key component of Northern European fisheries, have increased at a much lower rate than total landings of marine fish, and in some cases have actually declined (Figure 5.2).

At the beginning of the twenty-first century all of the evidence suggests

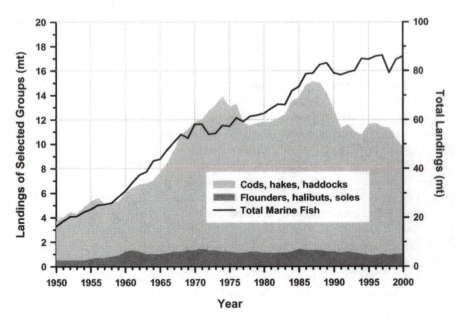

Figure 5.2 Total world landings of key whitefish groups (ISSCAAP groups) and total
world landings of all marine fish, 1950–2000 (data from FAO, 2003).

that the global harvest of marine fish has more or less reached (if not
exceeded) its sustainable limits. More seriously, the rapid development of
marine fisheries during the twentieth century has led to a situation where
most of the world's most valuable fish stocks are being, or have been, over-
exploited. Moreover much of the world's fisheries industry is severely, and
increasingly, over-capitalized, i.e. there is more fishing effort available
than is required to catch the available fish.

The slowdown in the growth of the total marine fish harvest, the
declines and collapses of many fish stocks, and the increasing overcapitalization of the fishing industry has given rise to an increasing public and
political perception of crisis in world fisheries. Numerous books, not just
scientific but also popular (e.g. McGoodwin, 1994; Crean and Symes,
1996; Hannesson, 1996; Harris, 1998; Kurlansky, 1998; Wigan, 1998)
describe and discuss every aspect of the problems facing marine fisheries.
Environmental organizations now target marine fisheries as they once did
whaling, and newspapers regularly report marine fisheries issues.

Shetland – an island community

Shetland is a group of about 15 inhabited islands lying some 160 km north
of the UK mainland and about 400 km west of Norway with a population of
about 22,500 people. Fish catching has a long tradition in Shetland, having

been practised on a commercial basis in the islands since at least the four-
teenth century, when German and northern European merchants first
visited the islands to barter for dried salt fish, and on a subsistence basis for
ten times as long. Following centuries of slow and hesitant progress the
twentieth century saw rapid advances in the islands' fish-catching industry,
and today Shetland has a modern and diverse fishing fleet.

The importance of fish catching to Shetland stems from the islands'
location at the heart of the rich northern European fishing grounds, but
historically the islanders were probably driven to exploit the seas around
them as much from necessity as from inclination. Shetland's generally
infertile soils and cool, wet and windy climate are not favourable to agriculture, but with the addition of the sea's resources it was possible to make
a modest living. This blending of two occupations, fishing and crofting
(small-scale subsistence farming), created the crofter-fisherman, who
dominated Shetland life until comparatively recently. Another important
factor in the islanders' exploitation of the waters around their islands has
been the long seafaring heritage handed down from the Norsemen who
ruled Shetland until the fifteenth century and whose influence dominates
the islands to this day.

At the turn of the millennium Shetland is perhaps best known to the
outside world for its association with North Sea oil and in particular as the
site of Europe's largest oil terminal at Sullom Voe, where oil brought
ashore through pipelines is shipped all over the world. Despite the high
profile of North Sea oil and the undoubted benefits it has brought the
islands, the fisheries industry continues to play a key role in the islands'
economy. In 1999 the fisheries industries had a turnover of nearly £190
million (of which about 20 per cent is accounted for by fish catching),
about one third of the total value of the Shetland economy (Table 5.2).

Table 5.2 The Shetland economy in 1999

	Turnover (million £)	*% of total turnover*
Fisheries industries	189.1	33.7
Fish catching	39.7	7.1
Fish processing	71.0	12.6
Aquaculture	78.4	14.0
Agriculture	11.8	2.1
Tourism	14.4	2.6
Knitwear	4.9	0.9
Oil industry	53.7	9.6
Services	175.0	31.2
Local government	112.7	20.1
Total	561.6	–

Source: SIC, 2001.

The importance of the fisheries industry to Shetland stems not just from its current contribution to the local economy but also from the fact that in these remote and resource poor islands it is perhaps the only industry that offers a realistic potential of making a substantial long-term contribution to the local economy.

Throughout the 1980s and 1990s the value of the fisheries sector grew steadily, while most other sectors of the economy either declined (e.g. the oil industry) or remained at a similar level (e.g. agriculture, knitwear and tourism). While fishing remained important in Shetland it declined in much of the rest of the UK with the result that Shetland has become one of the country's main fishing centres.

By the end of the twentieth century Shetland had a large, modern fishing fleet of some 200 vessels, ranging from shellfish fishing vessels less than five metres in length to pelagic trawlers of over 50 metres. In 1998 the Shetland fleet caught about 123,000 tonnes of fish, worth some £50 million (SIC, 1999; SOAEFD, 1999). Demersal species (cod, haddock, whiting, etc.) accounted for 20 per cent of the catch (by weight), while pelagic species (herring and mackerel) accounted for 60 per cent. Fifteen per cent of the catch comprised industrial species (blue whiting, sandeels, etc.) and the remaining 5 per cent was of shellfish (crabs, lobsters, scallops, etc.). In addition to the catch by the local fleet, an additional 55,000 tonnes of fish, worth some £11 million, was landed in Shetland by non-Shetland vessels in 1998.

The present crisis in world fisheries poses a serious threat to communities, like Shetland, that are dependent on fishing. The fisheries of the North Atlantic are amongst the worst affected; in European waters some 90 per cent of fish stocks are reported as being over-fished (Knauss, 1994). Declining fish stocks mean lower catches and lower earnings for fishermen, and potentially loss of employment. This has knock-on effects in the wider community. Many fisheries-dependent communities are located in remote areas with few alternative sources of employment or economic activity. The collapse of the northern cod fishery off Newfoundland provided a stark warning of what can happen to fisheries-dependent communities (Hannesson, 1996; Harris, 1998; Wigan, 1998).

The solution to the overexploitation of fish stocks appears to be simple in principle – catch less fish. More specifically, fisheries need to be more effectively managed to make sure that catches are in line with what the stocks can sustain. Overcapitalization also needs to be reduced to lessen pressure on fish stocks and to make the industry more profitable. A major concern for fisheries-dependent communities, however, is whether the cure might not be as bad as, if not worse than, the problem. Management measures intended to protect or to enhance the recovery of fish stocks, such as reductions in quota or fishing effort or fleet sizes, can also have serious economic impacts. At the start of the twenty-first century Shetland's demersal fishing fleet (along with much of the rest of the North Sea's fleet) is being severely affected by new European conservation measures intended to promote the recovery of North Sea cod stocks, which have dwindled to a fraction of their historical size and are believed to be in imminent danger of collapse.

Faced with these problems Shetland has taken a number of initiatives to try and safeguard the marine fish resources, and the fishing industry which depends on them, that make such an important contribution to the islands' economy.

Community ownership of fish quotas

Within the UK fish quotas are largely managed by a series of Producer Organizations through the 'Sectoral Quota' (SQ) system (Goodlad, 1998, 2001). Producer Organizations (POs) are established under the European Union's Common Fisheries Policy 'to encourage rational fishing and to improve conditions for sale of their members' products'. The main purpose of POs throughout Europe is to implement marketing regulations under the CFP. These cover issues such as the grading and freshness of fish, and the market support mechanism which guarantees fishermen minimum prices for their fish. Some POs have become involved in related activities such as the establishment of quality control systems, the marketing of fish and the establishment of fish processing plants, but it is only in the UK that they have come to play a central role in fisheries management. The UK has a total of 22 POs most (although not all) of which are regionally based.

Under the Sectoral Quota system each PO is allocated a share of the annual UK quota for each fishery – the UK quota is in turn agreed by the EU. The quota share allocated to each PO is calculated on the basis of the actual catches of member vessels during a three-year reference period; commonly referred to as their 'track record'. Since 1999 the reference period has been the years 1994, 1995 and 1996. Normally vessels can only join a PO if they already have a significant track record, on the basis of which the PO will receive a larger share of the UK quota.

Since 1992 track records, and thus quota allocations, have been attached to, and transferable with, fishing vessel licences, rather than to vessels themselves. However, standard legal agreements can separate the quota allocation from the licence and effectively allow it to be traded or rented. The last decade has seen an increasing amount of quota trading and a growing awareness amongst UK fishermen of the value of their quota allocations which acquired a significant and rapidly increasing value. Between 1993 and 1997, for example, the average value of demersal fish quota was £300 per tonne; it reached £1,000 per tonne in 1998, and £1,650 per tonne in 1999 (although values have fallen recently as a result of the decommissioning of fishing vessels placing more quota on the market). The quota allocation belonging to a fishing vessel may be worth almost as much as the vessel itself.

Despite the growing quota trade, UK fishermen do not have any legal title of ownership over their quota allocations, because under the CFP quotas are viewed as a 'common property resource' and thus cannot be the property of either member states, POs, or individual fishermen. The present UK system thus differs in important respects from the property-right based systems of fisheries management, such as ITQs, which have been implemented in other parts of the world. Although UK fishermen can buy and sell quota allocation they do not, strictly speaking, own it. The issue of property rights in fisheries management within the EU remains subject to considerable debate.

Although the development of the Sectoral Quota has brought benefits to UK fishermen, primarily in the form of greater flexibility, quota trading does pose a potentially serious threat to fisheries dependent communities such as Shetland. Shetland is particularly vulnerable because its fishing vessels are owned by individual shareholding members of their crews. The first threat is that quota allocation can be sold out of, and thus 'lost' to, the community. A fisheries-dependent community could thus lose the 'right' to fish.

The second threat is the obstacle to new entrants posed by the high cost of quota allocation. The future of the fishing industry depends on the continued entry of new, young fishermen to replace those who retire or otherwise leave the industry. Traditionally new entrants only had to raise the money to purchase a fishing vessel and a fishing licence; now they must also find sufficient money to purchase the necessary quota allocation (which may cost almost as much as the boat itself). Increasingly, the cost of quota is becoming an insurmountable obstacle to potential new entrants. Again the pattern of vessel ownership causes a particular problem in Shetland; the money for a new vessel (and quota) must be raised by individual, shareholding members of the crew. The high cost of quota also poses an obstacle to established fishermen who wish to expand their fishing opportunities by acquiring additional fishing rights.

The Shetland Fish Producers Organization recognized at an early stage the potential, as well as the potential problems, of quota trading (Goodlad, 2001). In 1993 the SFPO decided to make a substantial investment in purchasing quota allocation with the aim of holding this quota in common ownership for the benefit of current and future member vessels. Between 1993 and 1997 the SFPO invested some £850,000 in purchasing 2,386 tonnes of demersal fish quota, making it the only PO in the UK to become a quota holder in its own right. This investment enabled the SFPO to provide its member vessels with extra fishing opportunities, i.e. it allowed them to catch more fish, and the increase in the value of quota has also made the investment a financial success.

Given the importance of fishing to Shetland, and the potential threats of quota trading outlined above, the Shetland Islands Council (SIC; Shetland's local government) took the decision to invest in the purchase of further quota allocation to establish a pool of community-owned quota. This quota was to be held and administered by the SFPO. Between 1998 and 2001 a total of about £15 million was invested by the SIC's commercial investment agencies (using money earned through agreements with the oil industry) in the purchase of about 5,000 tonnes of demersal fish quota. Thus over 7,000 tonnes of demersal quota allocation is now held in community ownership in Shetland, roughly the same amount as is held privately by the Shetland fishing fleet.

This pool of community-owned quota has been used in a number of ways to benefit Shetland's fishing industry. First, it has been used to augment its member vessels' quota allocations to provide them with additional fishing opportunities. The rent paid generates a return on the investment, which has also appreciated in value. Second, some of the quota pool has been used to help new entrants, who cannot afford to purchase quota, to get started in the fishing industry. New fishing partnerships are able to join the SFPO (which they would not normally be able to do without their own quota allocation) by renting a share of the quota pool. In time, as these new partnerships become established they are able to purchase their own quota allocation and thus become less dependent on the community-owned pool which can then be used to assist further new entrants. Finally, quota for species in which the local fleet has little interest can be traded for additional quota for species, which the fleet does target, or can be leased out, generating income.

Shetland has pioneered a system of community ownership of quota allocation which secures access to the fish resources for a fisheries dependent community, and can be used to help young fishermen start their fishing careers. Responses to the initiative from other parts of the UK have been mixed, with some POs expressing interest in the concept which has been copied by some. Others, however, have seen it as a threat to their own members' interests, fearing that quota allocation purchased for Shetland will be lost to them.

With the current decline in the size of the local demersal fishing fleet (due to cod conservation measures) the community ownership of quota allocation is seen as being more important than ever. In the short term local fishing vessels are likely to be scrapped or sold out of the fleet, but in the longer term community ownership provides a means of ensuring that quota remains in the community and will thus be available to local fishermen when fish stocks have recovered and fishing opportunities are expanding. Without such a system the fear is that quota could be sold out of the local community, and may be difficult (if not impossible) to buy back in the future. It is not inconceivable that a (formerly) fisheries-dependent community like Shetland could be left without the right to fish in the surrounding waters.

Despite the success (from the Shetland perspective) of the community ownership of quota, questions were raised about its legality under European Union rules on state aid, competition and the free market. Following a two-year investigation the European Commission concluded in 2003 that the scheme was not compatible with the rules of the common market (EC, 2003). The Commission's objection was not to the community ownership of quota per se, but to the fact that the quota had been leased to local fishermen at below the market rate, thus conferring an unfair advantage. The Commission accepted that the parties involved had genuinely believed that the quota purchase scheme was compatible with the common market rules and therefore did not request repayment of the aid received. (The question revolved on the issue of whether the moneys used to purchase the quota should be regarded as private funds – the position of the SIC – or public funds – the position of the European Commission.) Given the benefits of the quota purchase scheme to the islands, efforts are being made to revise it to ensure that it does comply with the European rules on the common market.

Were the Commission to end the scheme it would inevitably be seen in Shetland as a serious blow to the efforts that this fisheries-dependent community has made to protect its fishing rights.

Co-operative management of fisheries

Recent years have seen fishermen coming under increasing scrutiny from the growing global environmental lobby. Coupled with the increasingly obvious evidence of widespread crisis in many of the world's fisheries, this has resulted in a shift in the public perception of the fisherman. Traditionally portrayed as a heroic toiler of the deep, labouring to fulfil the nation's demand for fresh fish, the fisherman is increasingly being portrayed as a rapacious despoiler of the oceans, indiscriminately pillaging fish stocks with no thought for tomorrow.

It would probably not be unfair to say that there are elements of truth in both stereotypes, and there are many legitimate concerns about the impact of fishing on the environment. Nevertheless, the increasing influence of conservation organizations over public opinion does give rise to concern in fisheries-dependent communities. Particular concern is caused by campaigns aimed at 'protecting' a particular species, usually one to which the general public are sympathetically inclined (seals, dolphins and whales are good examples), from the effects of fishing. Such campaigns can present a simplistic picture of what can, in reality, be a complex problem, and often fail to take account of wider biological, social and economic issues.

One of the most controversial European fisheries in recent years has been that for sandeels in the North Sea. The sandeel fishery is an 'industrial' fishery, meaning that the catch is used for purposes other than direct human consumption; usually for the production of fish meal and oil. Sandeels, predominantly *Ammodytes marinus* in the North Sea, are small eel-like fish that form an important component of the diets of many seabirds, fish and other marine animals. In recent years about a million tonnes of sandeels have been caught in the North Sea each year, giving rise to concerns that the fishery could result in the starvation of animals that depend on them.

Since 1974 Shetland has had a local sandeel fishery, distinct from the main North Sea fishery. Catches peaked at over 50,000 tonnes in 1982 but then declined rapidly through the remainder of the decade. Over the same period many important seabird populations in Shetland suffered disastrous breeding failures, apparently due to a shortage of the sandeels that they required to feed their chicks. The coincidence of the collapse of the fishery and the seabird breeding failures resulted in a bitter controversy in Shetland over whether or not overfishing had caused the decline in sandeel abundance and, consequently, the seabird breeding failures. The declining catches and the seabird breeding crisis eventually resulted in the government officially closing the Shetland sandeel fishery partway through the 1990 season, although the fishery had by then virtually ceased anyway (due to declining catches).

Subsequent research cast doubt on the link between fishing and the seabird breeding failures; it now appears that the fishery and the seabirds were both affected by natural changes in the abundance of sandeels around Shetland during the 1980s (although arguably closing the fishery was still a sensible precautionary measure). Following a recovery in sandeel abundance during the early 1990s the fishery was reopened in 1995 under a three-year management plan. Amongst other measures this management plan implemented an annual quota of 3,000 tonnes per annum, and the fishery was to close at the end of July.

Neither the fishermen nor the conservationists were happy with the new management plan. The fishermen wanted a higher quota and no closure of the fishery, but the Royal Society for the Protection of Birds (RSPB) wanted the fishery closed during the seabird breeding season (June–July). To try and resolve these differences prolonged negotiations were held between the Shetland Fishermen's Association (SFA; the representative body of Shetland's fishermen), the RSPB and Scottish Natural Heritage (SNH; the government agency with responsibility for natural heritage in Scotland). These negotiations led to agreement on a new management plan which was more acceptable to both sides. In return for the RSPB and SNH accepting a larger annual quota (7,000 tonnes) the SFA accepted that the fishery would be closed in June and July. The government accepted the new management plan and it was implemented in 1998. Initially implemented for three years, these new management arrangements have continued to the present.

As a result Shetland now has a sandeel fishery which is managed by a locally agreed management plan, negotiated by the various interested parties, rather than having a plan imposed by the national government. This management plan safeguards the interests of the seabirds whilst maintaining the sandeel fishery. Although the fishery concerned is small the Shetland experience has demonstrated that it is possible for fishermen and conservationists to work together to find mutually acceptable solutions where there are conflicts between fisheries and environmental interests. Although it is often portrayed as such, and not infrequently is, the relationship between fishermen and conservationists need not be one of conflict.

Local management of shellfish fisheries

Compared to the large demersal and pelagic sectors of the local fisheries industry, shellfish fishing in Shetland appears relatively insignificant, accounting for only about 5 per cent (by value) of total landings. However, shellfish fishing, primarily for crabs, lobsters and scallops, is an important activity for the smaller vessels which make up a large proportion of Shetland's fishing fleet. About 75 per cent of the fleet fishes mainly or wholly for shellfish, with the vast majority of these being under ten metres in length.

Within the UK, shellfish fisheries have been largely unregulated, particularly when compared to the demersal and pelagic sectors. In particular there are no limits on fishing effort or on catches, although there are minimum landings sizes for some species. In the absence of any such limits shellfish fishing developed rapidly in Shetland during the last few decades of the twentieth century, with catches doubling between 1989 and 1997, as a result of increases in both the number of shellfish fishing vessels, and the size and catching capacity of those vessels. The increase in catches of shellfish resulted in considerable concern in Shetland that if this trend were to continue the future viability of local shellfish fisheries could be threatened.

In the absence of national controls on shellfish fishing it was agreed in 1995 to seek a Regulated Fishery Order for Shetland. Such Orders, commonly known as 'Regulating Orders', can be granted within the UK to confer legal rights to manage shellfish fisheries to a local organization. Regulating Orders apply to the fisheries for specified shellfish species within a specified area and are intended to provide for the establishment, improvement, maintenance and/or regulation of shellfish fisheries. Although Regulating Orders had been available since the 1960s the range of species that could be covered had until fairly recently been very limited and only a few Orders had been granted, none of them in Scotland.

A new organization, the Shetland Shellfish Management Organization (SSMO), was established to apply for and implement a Regulating Order for Shetland. The SSMO was formed as a partnership between a variety of interested local organizations; Shetland Fishermen's Association, Shetland Islands Council, Shetland Association of Community Councils, Shetland Fish Processor's Association, North Atlantic Fisheries College and Scottish Natural Heritage. The primary aim of the organization was to manage Shetland's shellfish fisheries to ensure their long-term sustainability.

After five years of negotiations with the government, and a public inquiry, the Order – the Shetland Islands Regulated Fishery Order 2000 – was finally granted in January 2000. The Order covers the waters around Shetland between the low water mark and the six-mile limit, an area of about 6,000 km^2, and applies to all shellfish species that are, or might be, fished commercially (oysters, mussels, cockles, clams, lobsters, scallops, queen scallops, crabs, whelks and razorshells).

Under the Order the SSMO has implemented a local shellfish fisheries management plan, centred around a local licensing scheme aimed at controlling fishing effort. Certain restrictions on fishing gear and vessel sizes have also been introduced, along with minimum landing sizes for some species. Within the first year of operation some 160 fishing vessels were granted local shellfish fishing licences. The management plan is backed up by a programme of fisheries data collection and research being developed by the North Atlantic Fisheries College. This programme is intended to provide the SSMO with management advice and may result in additional regulations or controls being introduced in the future.

The Regulating Order is now in its fourth year of operation, but remains the only Order of its kind to have been granted in Scotland (although proposals for Orders for other areas are being developed). In general terms the Order can probably reasonably be considered as having been a success so far. Perhaps its most significant success is in achieving a relatively high level of compliance with its primary management measure – the local shellfish licensing scheme – at least amongst legitimate fishermen.

The Order is not without significant problems, however. Most significantly, perhaps, has been the chronic underfunding of the Shetland Shellfish Management Organization. Unlike most fisheries management schemes, which are generally government-funded, the SSMO has had to rely on the income from licence fees and on grants from various public bodies (especially the Shetland Islands Council). However, this funding has fallen far short of the level required to properly fund the activities that the organizations needs, or would like, to carry out (including enforcement, research and stock assessment). At the time of writing discussions are taking place with the Shetland Islands Council with a view to establishing a long-term package of financial and other support for the organization. In general it seems that if Regulating Orders are to prove as effective as a means of managing fisheries locally in Scotland, they will have to receive some measure of public financial support.

In the absence of adequate funding the SSMO has also found it more or less impossible to adequately and effectively enforce its regulations. Despite the generally high level of compliance there have been persistent problems with a relatively small number of fishermen who fish without licences, or breach other regulations. On a national basis the enforcement of fisheries regulations is a government responsibility (in Scotland through the Scottish Fisheries Protection Agency), but responsibility for enforcing regulations introduced under Regulating Orders lies with the grantee of the Order. The difficulty of enforcing its regulations inevitably threatens the credibility of the SSMO, as those fishermen who abide by the rules bitterly resent the organization's failure to take effective action against those who do not. More effective enforcement of its regulations is a high priority for the SSMO once a long-term funding package has been established. A very significant development occurred in May 2003 with the pledge by the newly elected Scottish government to give the Scottish Fisheries Protection Agency at least some responsibility for enforcing regulations introduced under Regulating Orders. Although the details remain to be worked out this extremely welcome move could provide substantial assistance and support to the grantees of Regulating Orders.

In terms of the Regulating Order's objectives of ensuring the sustainability of Shetland's shellfish fisheries, that is a long-term objective and it is too early to make a judgement as to whether or not the Order has been successful in these terms. What is certain is that meeting this objective will depend on both adequate funding of the SSMO's activities and effective enforcement of its regulations.

The Shetland Islands Regulated Fishery Order was the first of its kind to be granted in Scotland, and it represented the first time that a Scottish community had been granted local control of a local fishery. Other areas of Scotland have followed Shetland's experiences with interest and, as mentioned above, a number are developing plans for Regulating Orders for their own areas. Whilst the Shetland Shellfish Regulating Order has made significant achievements there is no doubt that significant challenges remain to be addressed, and the success of Regulating Orders as a tool for the long-term sustainable management of inshore fisheries remains to be proved.

Conclusions

At the turn of the millennium fisheries-dependent communities, such as Shetland, are coming under increasing pressure from two main sources. First, declines in fish stocks as a result of over-exploitation have a direct effect on these communities. Second, they are also affected by increasingly stringent regulations intended to reduce over-exploitation.

From the perspective of fisheries-dependent communities fisheries management measures are often implemented from far away; the decisions that affect Shetland's fishermen and communities are made in

Edinburgh, London or Brussels. If fisheries are to be successfully managed in the new millennium then fisheries-dependent communities need to play a much larger role in managing fisheries – it has been said that a fisherman's respect for regulations declines the further away from his home they are made.

The Shetland experience shows some ways in which a fisheries-dependent community has come to play a larger role in managing its fisheries, and shows that communities and fishermen need not be passive partners in the management process.

Notes

1 Throughout this chapter the term 'fish' is taken to include both finfish and shellfish, which in turn encompasses molluscs, crustaceans and other invertebrate species (but not mammals, reptiles, corals, etc.). In 2000 world marine landings of 'fish' consisted of 84.1 per cent finfish, 8.4 per cent molluscs, 6.8 per cent crustaceans and 0.7 per cent other groups (FAO, 2003).
2 For more detailed discussions of the technological developments that have occurred in the fishing industry see, e.g. Sahrhage and Lundbeck, 1992; Fridman, 1998.

References

Alverson, D.L., Freeberg, M.H., Murawsky, S.A. and Pope, J.G. (1994) *A Global Assessment of Fisheries Bycatch and Discards.* Food and Agriculture Organization of the United Nations. Fisheries Technical Paper 339. Rome: FAO.

Arnason, R. and Felt, L. (1995) 'Introduction: island fishing societies of the North Atlantic' in Arnason, R. and Felt, L. (eds) *The North Atlantic Fisheries: Successes, Failures and Challenges.* Charlottetown, Prince Edward Island: Institute of Island Studies, University of Prince Edward Island.

Buckworth, R.C. (1998) 'World fisheries are in crisis? We must respond!', in Pitcher, T.J., Hart, P.J. and Pauly, D. (eds) *Reinventing Fisheries Management.* London: Kluwer Academic Publishers.

Coull, J.R. (1993) *World Fisheries Resources.* London: Routledge.

Crean, K. and Symes, D. (eds) (1996) *Fisheries Management in Crisis.* Oxford: Fishing News Books.

Cushing, D.H. (1988) *The Provident Sea.* Cambridge: Cambridge University Press.

European Commission (2003) Commission decision of 3 June 2003 on Loans for the Purchase of Fishing Quotas in the Shetland Islands (United Kingdom). 2003/612/EC, Official Journal L211, 21 Aug. 2003: 63–77.

Food and Agriculture Organization of the United Nations (2002) *The State of World Fisheries and Aquaculture.* Rome: FAO. http://www.fao.org/docrep/005/y7300e/y7300e00.htm.

Food and Agriculture Organization of the United Nations (2003) *Fishstat Plus. v. 2.3: Capture Production 1950–2001.* Rome: FAO. http://www.fao.org/fi/statist/fisoft/fishplus.asp.

Fridman, A. (1998) *World Fisheries – What is to be Done?* Southbank, Australia: Baird Publications.

Garcia, S.M. and Newton, C. (1997) 'Current situation, trends, and prospects in world capture fisheries', in Pikitch, E.L., Huppert, D.D. and Sissenwine, M.P. (eds) *Global Trends: Fisheries Management*. American Fisheries Society Symposium 20. Bethesda, Maryland: American Fisheries Society.

Goodlad, J. (1998) 'Sectoral quota management: fisheries management by fish producers organizations', in Gray, T.S. (ed.) *The Politics of Fishing*. London: Macmillan Press.

Goodlad, J. (2001) 'Industry perspective on rights based management: the Shetland experience', in Shotton, R. (ed.) *Use of Property Rights in Fisheries Management*. Proceedings of the FishRights99 Conference, Freemantle, Western Australia. FAO Fisheries Technical Paper 404/1. Rome: Food and Agriculture Organization of the United Nations. http://www.fao.org/docrep/003/X7579E/x7579e00.htm.

Gulland, J.A. (ed.) (1971) *The Fish Resources of the Ocean*. London: Fishing News Books.

Hannesson, R. (1996) *Fisheries Mismanagement: The Case of the North Atlantic Cod*. Oxford: Fishing News Books.

Harris, M. (1998) *Lament for an Ocean*. Toronto: McClelland & Stewart Inc.

House of Lords (1996) *Fish Stock Conservation and Management*. Second Report of the House of Lords Select Committee on Science and Technology: Session 1995–96. London: HMSO.

Huxley, T.H. (1883) Address: Inaugural Meeting of the Fishery Congress. International Fisheries Exhibition (London 1883). http://aleph0.clarku.edu/huxley/SM5/fish.html.

Knaus, J.A. (1994) 'The state of the world's marine resources', in Voigtlander, C.W. (ed.) *The State of the World's Fisheries Resources*. Proceedings of the World Fisheries Congress, Plenary Sessions. New Delhi: Oxford & IBH Publishing Co. Pvt. Ltd.

Kurlansky, M. (1998) *Cod: A Biography of the Fish that Changed the World*. London: Jonathan Cape.

McGoodwin, J.R. (1994) *Crisis in the World's Fisheries*. Stanford, California: Stanford University Press.

Pauly, D., Christensen, V., Guénette, S., Pitcher, T.J., Sumaila, U.R., Walters, C.J., Watson, R. and Zeller, D. (2002) 'Towards sustainability in world fisheries', *Nature* 418: 689–95.

Sahrhage, D. and Lunbeck, J. (1992) *A History of Fishing*. Berlin: Soringer-Verlag.

Scottish Office Agriculture, Environment and Fisheries Department (1999) *Scottish Sea Fisheries Statistics, 1998*. Edinburgh: SOAEFD.

Shetland Islands Council (1999) *Shetland in Statistics, 1999*. Lerwick, Shetland: SIC.

Shetland Islands Council (2001) *Shetland in Statistics, 2001*. Lerwick, Shetland: SIC.

Smith, T.D. (1994) *Scaling Fisheries: the Science of Measuring the Effects of Fishing, 1855–1955*. Cambridge: Cambridge University Press.

Wigan, M. (1998) *The Last of the Hunter Gatherers*. London: Swan-Hill Press.

6 Ocean waste disposal

An acceptable option in the new millennium?

Martin V. Angel

053 054

058

(UK)

Introduction

A recent analysis of emerging environmental issues produced under the aegis of SCOPE (Munn *et al.*, 2000) concluded there are three sets of high-priority issues. There are the old issues that have grown and become transformed as scientific understanding and technical knowledge have increased. Public concern has intensified as socio-economic and cultural attitudes have shifted and environmental conditions have deteriorated, but its focus is unordered. These issues include the sustainable use of water, the impact of urbanization and the increase in the frequency and severity of natural disasters triggered by climate change and economic development. Second there are policy issues such as how to manage the growing water shortages in Africa and the implications of investment and change in world trade and aid patterns; their long-term implications for environmental management are yet to unfold. Third, there is the constant succession of unpleasant surprises in how ecosystems respond locally, regionally and globally to the changing environmental stresses and strains imposed by human activities. The realization is growing of how global ecology is strongly interconnected, so that actions taken to resolve one problem aggravate others. Dealing with the environmental problems is akin to the Greek myth about Hydra, a multi-headed monster that each time a head was cut off, sprouted several new ones from the severed stump. The SCOPE report cites a recent statement issued by the American Association for the Advancement of Science (Jasanoff *et al.*, 1997):

> *There has been a movement away from assigning simple causes to complex physical, biological and social phenomena. Feedbacks and synergies are now known to complicate causal stories that were once regarded as simple and linear. Dynamic cross-systematic explanations are sought where static and reductionist models once prevailed. Nowhere is this more clearly evident than in our understanding of the global environment, where the physical sustainability of the biosphere is now seen to be inseparably bound up with issues of economic development, social equality and international peace and security.*

Thus there is an increasing awareness of the limitations of our under-standing of the natural world. Our theories about ecosystems, on which we base the development of our management protocols, are constantly found to be inadequate. Ecosystem responses are often unpredictable, eroding public faith scientific evaluations and preventing us from keeping the impacts of our socio-economic activities within the bounds of sustain-ability. Scientific uncertainty leads to environmental groups and decision-makers adopting antagonistic attitudes. At one extreme scientific assessments are rejected, the opinions of scientists are derided and ridiculed, and there is strong advocacy to manage our activities according to passionately-held beliefs, often lent credibility by claims of their being ethical, which means they do not have to be defended by objective argu-ment. It also fosters a nostalgic and amnesiac belief that, because every-thing was better in the past, if we turn back the clock and revert to policies adopted when the human population was smaller, technologies were basic, and our accumulative environmental impacts were not threatening to overwhelm the global balances, all these problems will be resolved. In addition because there are considerable scientific uncertainties it is wise to take a fully precautionary approach. However, this leads to the irra-tional tenet that if a risk can be imagined, it must be real. An opposing and equally dangerous attitude is to have implicit faith that science will deliver and no remedial action is necessary until there is scientific cer-tainty about the implications. This attitude tends to be associated with a strong belief in market and economic forces providing the best way to manage human society and activity. This is the attitude that allows forests to be clear-felled, because in so doing there is greater short-term gain to the few who profit, since the money realized will grow faster if it is invested than if the trees are left to grow. However, this ignores the hidden and often unquantifiable costs of soil erosion, loss of water quality and natural diversity, and loss of pleasant environments to the community as a whole.

So environmental management has to walk a knife-edge between being *reasonably* cautious and not wasting limited resources on unnecessary or ineffective action. What is clear is that the growing population has to be kept reasonably healthy, housed, fed and occupied, otherwise social dissat-isfaction and poverty will foster social disruption. Social disruption inevitably leads to the neglect of environment. Damaging actions become justified as means to improve social fairness, to protest at national, reli-gious and racial discrimination, and, for the wealthy and militarily power-ful nations, to protect national security. These actions range from acts of terrorism to bombing and waging wars.

The difficulty of making rational choices is exacerbated by a mirage effect; our interpretations of the environment shift according to scale in time and space at which we view them, and also the context in which we address these problems (e.g. Angel, 2000). The apparent optimum solutions and the priorities given to solving issues vary depending on where you come from geographically, culturally and politically (e.g. Bewers, 1995). This chapter would have a very different content if it were to be written by an African, a South American or by a member of Greenpeace; it would also change if my gender, age or social status were different. This does not necessarily imply that I am right and that the others are either wrong or misguided. When you look at a landscape what you see changes as you move. It changes if you refocus your eyes or use binoculars. But it also changes if you are a birdwatcher or an artist, a city-dweller or a countryman. If such differences are not to compound the problems of decision-making, we have to be far clearer about what criteria should be used, what are we seeking to optimize and for whom, and who is to judge.

In this chapter the focus is on issues on a global scale and on some undeniable certainties, which simply cannot be ignored, and whose solutions may well involve uses of the ocean. There are three basic certainties facing the global environment (Vitousek, 1994): the rapid growth of the human population, the increases in atmospheric carbon dioxide concentrations and the nitrogen overload.

Human population

Human population is on course to double to 12 billion within the next century. Over two centuries ago Thomas Malthus (1798) pointed out that human population has the potential to grow geometrically and hence double every 25 years, whereas food production then tended to grow arithmetically. Thus human population has the potential rapidly to outstrip its resources, and so face internal stresses and strains (competition). In the short term, Malthus proved to be wrong. Since 1800, mankind's global population has increased sixfold without global food supplies becoming seriously limiting. Famines have occurred, but mostly as a result of local crop failures caused by droughts and wars, combined with an inability and/or unwillingness to supply food in from elsewhere (e.g. the potato famine in Ireland and the starvation suffered in the Netherlands immediately after the Second World War). Food resources have kept pace with the demands as a result of advances in plant breeding, the use of energy from fossil fuel in agriculture and the distribution of food, and the manufacture of synthetic fertilizers (Evans, 1998). During the post-war years human population doubled in 25 years, demonstrating Malthus was correct about human population growth. In 1965–70 it increased 2.1 per cent per annum (Cohen, 1995). Currently the rate of increase has slowed to around 1.6 per cent per annum (Horiuchi, 1992), but even at this rate, if unchecked the human population would reach 694 billion by 2150! During the last half of the twentieth century the population growth has been supported by a dramatic increases in agricultural productivity, achieved by increasing applications of nitrogenous fertilizers, chemical pest control and plant breeding, rather than by taking more land into agriculture. However, can further increases in productivity be achieved? Especially if further use of fertilizers and biocides is constrained by environmental feedbacks, and further improvements in crop productivity are inhibited both by antagonistic public attitudes towards genetic manipulation and the abuse of these novel techniques to generate higher profits for companies rather than greater crop production. Substantial improvements can be achieved in the efficiency with which we use food. For example, each year enough grain to feed 800 million people is used to feed animal stocks, so changing diet could make a substantial contribution to feeding the world. Social imbalances lead to obesity being a major health problem in some countries and malnutrition in others. If productivity per hectare cannot be increased, then food production will have to increase by taking more land into agriculture, not only placing greater demands on water resources and threatening global biodiversity, but also threatening the availability of suitable land. Each year a considerable area of productive land is lost – through urban sprawl, the building of infrastructure, houses, roads and industrial plants, through contamination of land with waste, through coastal erosion resulting from sea-level rise and climate change. The earth has a finite size (Table 6.1); at present population growth rates it will not be long before Malthus is proved right about resource limitation.

Carbon dioxide

The rise in atmospheric carbon dioxide levels resulting from the burning of fossil fuels and the removal of forest cover threatens to induce climate changes (Houghton *et al.*, 1996). These are changes that are linked to population growth, and it has been the availability of fossil energy that has temporarily de-coupled human ecology from the processes that would otherwise have held its growth in check. Changes to the global climate are likely to re-introduce some of these checks, by shifting the geographical regions in which basic crops can be grown, by increasing the frequency of natural disasters (storms, floods and droughts), by facilitating the spread of epidemics and by raising sea levels. Will climate change occur slowly enough for human societies to be able to adapt and keep pace with the changes? There is evidence emerging that climate can switch quite suddenly within a decade from one quasi-stable regime to another. Ice cores from the Greenland ice cap show dramatic flip-flops have occurred in the past (an effect also described as the oilcan effect) which have involved major changes in the thermohaline circulation of the oceans (Broecker, 1997). Already, smaller-scale regime shifts have been described from the North Pacific, for example in 1976, when there was a shift in the environmental equilibrium in the subpolar and boreal North Pacific (e.g. Beamish *et al.*, 1999). There have been major shifts in the ecology of the

Table 6.1 Areas (10⁹ hectares) of various biomes on earth with estimates of the relative values of their ecosystem services (from Constanza *et al.* 1997). These areas are also scaled according to the present global population of about 6 billion. A hypothetical future scenario of land use when the population reaches 10 billion is given. This is based on the assumption that the 'area per capita' for urban development and croplands is a constant, and that the additional area required will come from forest clearances and some drainage of wetlands. It has also been assumed that any expansion of range lands for grazing will be modest.

Population Biome	6 billion				10 billion	
	Area 10⁹ hectares	Area Per capita	Annual value $/hectares	Total annual value 10⁹$	Area 10⁹ hectares	Area Per capita
Forest, tropical	1.900	0.32	2,007	2.01	1.000	0.10
Forest, temperate	2.955	0.49	302	0.30	2.000	0.20
Range lands	3.898	0.65	232	0.23	4.129	0.41
Wetlands	0.330	0.06	14,785	14.79	0.300	0.03
Lakes/rivers	0.200	0.03	8,498	8.50	0.200	0.02
Desert	1.925	0.32	–	–	1.925	0.19
Tundra	0.743	0.12	–	–	0.743	0.07
Ice/rock	1.640	0.27	–	–	1.640	0.16
Croplands	1.400	0.23	92	0.09	2.333	0.23
Urban	0.332	0.06	–	–	0.553	0.06
Total land	15.323	–	–	–	15.323	–
Open ocean	33.200	5.53	252	8.38	33.200	3.320
Coastal, shelf	2.660	0.44	1,610	4.28	2.660	0.266
– estuaries	0.180	0.03	22,832	4.11	0.180	0.018
– coral reefs	0.062	0.01	6,075	0.37	0.062	0.006
– algal/seagrass	0.200	0.03	19,004	3.80	0.200	0.03
Total sea	36.302	–	–	–	–	–

north-east Atlantic (e.g. Beaugrand *et al.*, 2002), which may be related to the dramatic collapse of some of the fisheries. Moreover, the potential seriousness of climate changes has distracted attention away from the many other serious environmental impacts that these increases in atmospheric carbon dioxide will indubitably have (see for example, Field *et al.*, 1992; Bazzaz *et al.*, 1994; Coviella and Trumble, 1999; Angel, 2000).

Nitrogen overload

It is estimated that 60 per cent of nitrogen deposited annually on land is anthropogenic in origin (Vitousek *et al.*, 1997; Moffatt, 1998), and this has been highlighted by the Ecological Society of America as one of the most important emerging environmental issues (Munn *et al.*, 2000). Two of the main sources of this anthropogenic nitrogen are directly linked to agriculture – the fixation of atmospheric nitrogen by the Haber process in the manufacture of fertilizer and the cultivation of leguminous crops. The third major source comes from the NOXs emitted by internal combustion engines. In the short term there have been benefits. Without the increases in agricultural productivity achieved by application of fertilizers, far more land would have had to be taken into agriculture. Since the mid-1960s the area of land used for growing crops has remained the same – otherwise we would now be facing an even larger biodiversity crisis – but such benefits may be short lived. A growing proportion of the deposition on land comes from the atmosphere; such deposition is also occurring over the oceans. Much of the nitrogenous fertilizer applied to land finishes up in coastal seas via river outflows and the seepage of ground water. While there have been no detectable increases in the concentrations of nitrate in surface seawater, this may be because the phytoplankton rapidly utilizes the additional nitrogen. However, the enrichment is likely to be altering the population dynamics and composition of the phytoplankton, which will inevitably feed through into the dynamics of zooplankton and organisms higher in the food pyramid. There has been a major regime shift in the North Sea that has been linked to climate change (Reid *et al.*, 2001), and the increases in available nutrients may have played some role. Where exchanges of water are restricted the result is eutrophication and the stimulation harmful algal blooms (Anderson and Garrison, 1997; Paerl, 1997). Amongst the worst examples of eutrophication so far identified is in the Gulf of Mexico where on the seabed beneath the discharge plume of the Mississippi River a dead zone has developed over an area roughly the size of the state of Alabama (Christen, 1999). Eutrophication is mainly a problem in lakes, estuaries and shallow coastal seas where the circulation and turnover of water is limited. In the North Sea, it is an acute problem in the Waddensee and the German Bight, but elsewhere either tides keep the water well stirred, or stratification keeps productivity limited in summer outside the periods of the spring and autumn blooms.

Prioritization of biomes

It is the context of these global threats and the interconnectivity of global ecosystems that it is suggested that equivalent prioritization must be given to the conservation of the three major biomes of land, sea and atmosphere. Land suitable for agricultural use and supporting a diversity of natural ecosystems needs far greater protection from contamination and industrial development. Public perception seems to view conservation of the oceans being of higher priority than that of terrestrial ecosystems and the atmosphere. So in the developed world (e.g. IWCO, 1999) far more stringent regulations are placed on the use of the oceans (with the notable exception of fishing!) than on use of land and air. Disposal of waste into the ocean is deemed to be unsafe and unethical, whereas it is tolerated if dumped into landfill or incinerated into the atmosphere. Public opinion and policy-makers tend to consider that solutions are optimal in all contexts. For example, the discharge of exhaust fumes from incinerators into the atmosphere over land is considered acceptable, whereas their release at sea is not, leading to the ban on incineration at sea. States without ready access to the oceans and have no alternative but to manage waste streams on land, vigorously condemn proposals to use the oceans. Thus condemnation of the proposal to sink the *Brent Spar* in the Atlantic elicited violent public protest in Germany, a country without an offshore industry and without ready access to the oceans (Rice and Owen, 1999). Yet the discharges from the River Rhine add more metals and organic contaminants (many originating from Germany) each day than were contained in the *Spar*. The final solution of breaking-up the *Spar* and 'recycling' the structure as the basis of a roll-on/roll-off ferry terminal in Norway was certainly far more costly *environmentally* than the original proposal. However, such evaluations of cost are subjective and it was argued that dumping of the *Spar* in deep water was not only unethical but also created a precedent for further disposals. The ethical argument is not addressed implicitly here, but is a theme that underlies this whole chapter. Our stewardship of the earth must apply equally to all biomes.

The waste stream

All human activity produces waste. Individually, our normal every day physiological activity generates carbon dioxide, together with watery and solid wastes that become part of the sewage stream. Average domestic activity results in a stream of waste from food preparation, cleaning, refuse, the discarding of packaging, broken and redundant goods. Agriculture generates a variety of different types of waste, which range from straw to slurries of dung, to refuse from slaughterhouses. Such wastes have the potential to be recycled, but as demonstrated by the BSE crisis and various water pollution episodes, some of these 're-uses' carry serious risks to health, hygiene and the environment. Maintaining and running the network of infrastructure ranging from houses to transport and distribution of services takes space and generates waste. Commercial activity also generates considerable quantities of waste associated with packaging, which help to ensure goods reach the consumer in good order and transportation. Industrial processes generate wastes ranging from contaminated and heated water, to flue gases and active and inert chemical and mineral residues. Some of these need special treatment of detoxification, purification or containment before they can be safely disposed of, or recycled. The *Brent Spar* episode highlighted a significant problem of how best to deal with redundant plant and facilities that become redundant (Rice and Owen, 1999; Rose, 1998). It is a problem that is crucial to cleaning up any industrial plant, but tragically it distracted attention away from one fundamental issue – that it is cheap and easy to contaminate land and the coastal fringe, but not to bring such land back into safe productive use.

The optimum solution to any problem of waste has to be not to produce it in the first place. The whole process of manufacture can be stopped (e.g. the manufacture of PCBs and maybe ultimately CFCs). Improvements in efficiency can reduce the quantities produced and generate substantial cost savings; the design and construction of new plant has to be precautionary and to take into account the whole cycle from start to finish; what is acceptable now may well not be acceptable in the future. However, most waste policy is targeted at what to do with it once it is produced, to 'end-of-pipe' solutions. These included recycling, alternative uses, destruction and disposal. The cheapest and easiest short-term option is often to discard it into landfill, but not only is this unsustainable but it increases the inventory of contaminated land – land that in the near future may be urgently needed for agriculture or providing infrastructure. The production of some types of waste such as sewage is unavoidable. Its disposal exemplifies how other factors influence the choices made. Charges for sewage treatment are regarded as a community tax that may be levied either by increasing water charges or by reducing the profits of water companies. In a society dominated by economics there is a reluctance to limit profits. Second, human health in our increasingly urban society tends to be paramount, overriding any environmental consideration. The need to reduce health hazards to the community resulting from the spread of viral and bacteria pathogens may rule out certain types of re-use. In addition, in places the archaic infrastructure for collecting and processing the sewage stream results in its becoming mixed with industrial waste streams, and this reduces the range of options for its treatment and disposal.

For other domestic waste, there are several options; for example waste paper can be recycled, composted or incinerated to provide energy. Solutions often have to be tempered by pragmatism as recycling involves the cost of transporting the waste to a processing facility; it also requires public discipline in sorting wastes that may be lacking. Composting is only affordable if the product is subsidized by the community. Incineration plants are unpopular with local communities, who are fearful of the effects of fallout from the flue-gases. From this point of view, incineration at sea is undoubtedly a safer option, but was banned in European waters by international agreement in the 1980s. OSPAR is seeking to achieve zero discharges from ships, but there is no comparable target for land-based sources. Nor is OSPAR able to prevent contaminants entering the oceans via ground waters or via the atmosphere. It is putting pressure on industrialized coastal states to reduce their atmospheric inputs but it has no competence to demand similar reductions from land-locked states whose emissions fallout over land, or from countries outside the OSPAR area that are not signatories to the convention.

This difficulty is exemplified by nitrogen overloading in the North Sea – a problem highlighted by the disastrous bloom of *Chrysochromulina polylepis* in 1986, which was linked to spring applications of agricultural fertilizers being washed into coastal waters at a time when a period of calm, warm days reduced the turnover (Neilsen *et al.*, 1990). Estimates of the nitrogen imports and exports in the North Sea are provided by the recently published OSPAR Quality Status Report (OSPAR, 2000). They are dominated by ocean exchanges. Inputs from rivers (a mix of natural flux and agricultural run-off) are seven times those from sewage and double the atmospheric inputs, but those from diffuse source remain unquantified. These estimates suggest that, for the North Sea as an entire system, attempts to moderate riverine and atmospheric inputs are far more likely to be effective than trying to reduce inputs via sewage. However, there may still be areas where sewage inputs are locally significant.

There is a basic disagreement between scientists interpreting ecological evidence and the approach of many environmentalists (Bewers, 1995). There is clear ecological evidence that natural ecosystems do have a margin of tolerance towards low inputs of many toxic substances. Indeed, some metals normally assumed to be toxic are required in trace quantities for optimal growth (e.g. zinc, Sunda and Huntsman, 1992; copper, Manahan and Smith, 1973; and cadmium, Lee *et al.* 1995). This level of tolerance is the 'carrying capacity' of the ecosystem; the argument is that if inputs remained within the carrying capacity they are acceptable. If the substances are labile and subsequently are either decomposed or removed from the immediate environment by geochemical processes, then the continued inputs are sustainable (i.e. they become a component in the natural recycling budget). For biodegradable materials impact is generally reduced if the materials are diluted and dispersed; this became embodied in the derogatory catch phrase, 'dilution is the solution to pollution'. Contamination is then defined as the introduction of any substances (or energy) into environments in amounts that remain within the carrying capacity and so do not cause environmental damage. Pollution occurs once the inputs result in harm to ecosystems and/or individual species. These differences became incorporated in the definitions of pollution and contamination that were embodied in UNCLOS, the Law of the Sea Convention. Difficulties arise when trying to establish if damage to species or ecosystems has occurred, particularly because natural systems fluctuate. So unambiguously distinguishing between causes of change and determining whether they are predominantly natural or anthropogenic is a serious problem. The precautionary approach is to assume that any sign of physiological stress in individual species of communities, no matter how ephemeral, is the result of pollution. So the environmental movement rejects this distinction between contamination and pollution. Hence the addition of any substance, or energy, into the sea is regarded as pollution and so unethical and not to be tolerated. If such a rigorous definition of pollution were to be applied to terrestrial, freshwater and atmospheric systems, then all human activity would have to cease. The very act of breathing becomes unethical because some of the carbon dioxide we exhale is undoubtedly finding its way into the oceans, and is therefore causing pollution. If I pour a cup of freshwater into the sea, I am polluting it, but rain falling on it is a natural event. So any human activity is unnatural, and we are placed apart from the rest of nature.

Further to illustrate the illogicality of the arguments, one use of sewage sludge that has been strongly advocated by environmentalists is to 're-cycle' it by using it as a 'soil conditioner'. This is of course, what happens in China where 'night soil' is collected and spread untreated on the fields – a practice that would not be tolerated in Europe on human health grounds. However, a suggestion to 're-cycle' sewage sludges by discharging them over unproductive seamounts in the North Atlantic to create a new fishery has been roundly condemned. Yet, in essence, this is what was happening at the Garroch Head sewage sludge dump site in the Clyde. There the impacts of dumping a million tonnes of sludge a year was restricted geographically to within a few kilometres of the centre of the dump site. It supported a small local fishery (Pearson, 1986), which, following the ban on the dumping of sewage sludge in all European coastal seas, collapsed. Currently the solution to the perennial problem of what to do with sewage sludge in Britain is being solved in three ways: 1) by producing agricultural dressings for soils, for which there is no further capacity to increase; 2) by disposal into landfill, which is clearly unsustainable; and 3) by incineration, which hardly seems to be a sensible option when we are trying to reduce carbon dioxide emissions. Disposal with or without containment into the deep ocean is feasible (Angel and Rice, 1996; Valent and Young, 1998). There is a *prime facie* case that, although such disposal will inevitably have an environmental impact, this impact in a global context is likely to be far less serious to either human societies or the global environment than the other options currently considered to be acceptable. Note that ocean depths of 3,000–6,000 m cover 51 per cent of the earth's surface, and that the scale of benthic zoogeographical provinces is far greater than for terrestrial ecosystems (Ormond *et al.*, 1997). An industrial-scale experimental programme would be needed to confirm that these conclusions are correct (Thiel *et al.*, 1997). Objections to such a proposal are not based on refuting the scientific arguments, but on evoking either the precautionary principle because of the uncertainties of the scientific interpretations (hence the need for an appropriately scaled experimental programme), or on ethics, an attitude that seems to place greater value on marine rather than terrestrial ecosystems. There are a number of recent publications pleading the case for improving the conservation of oceanic environments (e.g. Earle, 1995; IWCO, 1998); these focus purely on marine issues and do not holistically evaluate natural resources at a global level.

Other legacies

In the last half of the twentieth century societies in the developed world have left a legacy of unresolved waste problems. These range from what to do about the stockpiled synthetic chemicals like PCBs that have proved to be accumulative, persistent and toxic, and how best to deal with large industrial structures and plant that are now coming to the end of their useful life (e.g. *Brent Spar*). Perhaps the most contentious of these issues is how to deal with radioactive waste, redundant nuclear plant and the stockpiles of equipment and weaponry assembled during the Cold War. The difficulties of dealing with some of these legacies are awesome, but must not be ignored. OECD Nuclear Energy Agency (1995) sends a clear ethical message that our intergenerational responsibility demands we clean up the wastes we have already generated, and that for any new plant the future liabilities are minimized by planning, at the initial design stage, for the whole cycle from construction, operational use and eventual decommissioning. It is clear that the needs for national defence are used as an excuse to ignore environmental restrictions, and that wars at any scale generate a legacy of major long-term environmental problems.

The concept of sustainability also demands that those who generate waste should shoulder the costs and the responsibility for dealing with it, and that no undue burdens are to be placed on future generations. The levels of environmental protection for the health of society and the environment must be commensurate between the present and the future. There is no basis, either ethical or environmental, whereby future health and risk of environmental damage can be currently discounted. No strategy for long-term waste management can be based upon the presumption that societal structure and organization will remain stable and permanently in place. We must bequeath an environment that will remain safe in the absence of active institutional controls. No development that ignores the resolution of major long-term threats to global society can be regarded as sustainable.

The first action must be to halt the proliferation of these problems. End-of-pipe solutions will not lead to prevention of the problems. The introduction of new synthetic chemicals, especially those designed to be persistent biocides, must be subject to far more stringent testing as to their potential long-term environmental impacts. Aspects of personal freedom and lifestyle currently enjoyed may have to be sacrificed (e.g. unrestricted personal use of motor vehicles or having various types of fresh food available at all times of year). During the last 50 years, technical, industrial and chemical developments have generated a vast and accumulating legacy of problems. These require solutions that are long-term and global. It makes no sense to store stockpiles of substances like PCBs, which can no longer be used; since their safe containment cannot be guaranteed forever, they must be destroyed. There may be environmental risks associated with their destruction, but even greater risks are taken by storing such materials, especially if the social fabric deteriorates. The same responsibilities apply to the safe management of radioactive waste (OECD Nuclear Energy Agency, 1995).

Radioactive waste

The drama of the tragic accident to the Russian nuclear submarine the *Kursk* reminds us that both the Russians and the Americans each have an ageing fleet of over 100 nuclear powered vessels, mostly submarines. In 1995 the cost of decommissioning just one nuclear-powered vessel was estimated to be around $2 billion (NATO, 1995), and would take at least a decade. Although the 'Polluter pays' principle is morally right and has been written into the OSPAR convention, in this case can the principle be enforced without disastrous side effects? Even if the USA can just afford the heavy economic burden of decommissioning their own vessels, who will pay for the decommissioning of the Russian nuclear fleet and weaponry? If the Russians are forced to pay (without asking how!) the country's economic and social stability might be put at risk, and with it the peace and stability of the whole world. Is such a risk worth taking?

So is the full and proper decommissioning of all these vessels either practical or affordable, and worth the political and social risks involved? The present approach seems to be to do nothing; the vessels are being left to deteriorate in shallow water where any leakage will contaminate the Arctic ecosystem and thence the whole of the northern hemisphere. So would it be both safe and affordable to entomb them and scuttle them in the deep ocean? If so, where? There are several sunken nuclear submarines scattered around the world's oceans, which are being monitored intermittently for the leakage of radioisotopes, but apparently not for their environmental impact. Similarly there has been almost no monitoring of the NEA dump site in the north-east Atlantic since the cessation of dumping in 1982. These sites represent experiments, albeit poorly controlled, whereby the environmental impact of such disposal can be evaluated at least in the medium-term. What limited monitoring that has been carried out has shown slight but detectable leakage, but no attempts have been made to assess whether or not the canisters have induced any changes in the deep communities other than those resulting from the introduction of hard substrates (OSPAR, 2000). The vast majority of radioactive contamination of the oceans has resulted from weapons testing, particularly in the atmosphere. Weapons testing introduced about 5–10 metric tonnes of plutonium into the oceans, and reprocessing and dumping have added a further 300–500 kg. Yet the sum total of all anthropogenic radioactivity has increased natural background levels of radiation by less than 1 per cent.

There are three basic approaches to managing radioactive wastes (OECD, Nuclear Energy Agency, 1995); none of which are entirely satisfactory:

1 Dilution and dispersion. This will require strict controls and will be subject to unexpected effects such as global climate change, and cannot be an appropriate option for long-lived and accumulative isotopes.
2 Storage and monitoring. This passes on a heavy responsibility for action to future generations. So is it ethical? Will future generations continue to have the ability and willingness to carry out the safety checks and institutional security measures that will be required?
3 Containment and isolation. This has to be either in repositories in geology, either on land or under the ocean. The latter provides an additional barrier to any leakage contaminating human environments. The technology exists whereby the risks posed by such disposal can probably be kept at an acceptable level and will not pass major liabilities on to future generations. However, the level of risk needs to be assessed by studying existing dump and accident sites. However, achieving public acceptability of any containment solution, particularly one involving marine disposal will be a major problem.

Ocean disposal of carbon dioxide

Compared with the radioactive waste problem, the issues of population control, depletion of natural resources and the dispersal/disposal of chemical by-products such as carbon dioxide, sulphur oxides and nitrogen oxides have far greater potential consequences globally. As world population doubles, emissions of carbon dioxide per capita will have to be halved to keep emissions at current levels, and will have to be reduced by 60–70 per cent if the worst effects of climate change and other environmental effects are to be avoided. However, the trend is for per capita emission to increase. There seems to be a remarkable lack of any sense of urgency by both governments and the newly emerging globalized companies and financial organizations to take responsibility for the global environment, and in particular to develop sources of energy without generating carbon dioxide emissions. What has emerged is the concept of trading in emissions, which is a way of allowing the wealthy offenders to carry on, so long as they pay for others not offending or to take actions (like growing trees) that will take up the carbon dioxide they emit. It is a short-term measure that does little to resolve the fundamental problem. The sequestration of carbon dioxide in either deep geology or in the deep ocean is a more medium-term approach. It can be justified as an interim measure that will allow time for human societies to adapt to either alternative energy sources or much lower availability of energy or probably both. Estimates suggest that if we are to merely peg emissions to present levels, by 2050 as much energy will need to be generated from renewable, non-CO_2 emitting sources as is currently generated; i.e. about 10 Tw (10×10^{24} watts), and this will need an immediate financial commitment similar to that given to the Manhattan Project or the Apollo Space Program (Hoffert *et al.*, 1998). The cost of the capture and disposal of carbon dioxide is high and it will reduce the efficiency of fuel utilization by about a third (Ormerod, 1997). In Western Europe the Utsira sandstone deposit that underlies the North Sea is believed to have the capacity to sequester about 200 Gt of carbon (i.e. 700 Gt of carbon dioxide) (Holloway *et al.*, 1996), which is sufficient to take up Western Europe's total emissions for several centuries. Experience is already being gained in the process of re-injecting carbon dioxide into deep geology by the Norwegian company Statoil. This company needs to reduce the carbon dioxide content of the natural gas it extracts from some of its fields before the gas can be supplied to customers. Rather than vent it (legitimately) to the atmosphere, the company has chosen to re-inject the million tonnes of carbon dioxide a year it is extracting into a geological strata 800 m beneath West Sleipner field in the North Sea (Baklid and Korbøl, 1996). Recently the British government Panel on Sustainable Development (1999) has recommended that the geological option is preferable to deep ocean disposal. While this may be an appropriate preference for Britain and Europe, it may not be appropriate for countries that lack potential geological deposits. The argument advanced in support of deep ocean disposal is that it has an enormous potential capacity (about 2,000 GT) to sequester carbon dioxide without venting it in substantial quantities back to the atmosphere. However, since the discharge of industrial wastes into the ocean or the 'subsoil' of the ocean bed is now banned under international conventions, it appears that the two best potential options for ameliorating the problems in the medium term may be prohibited.

Criteria of acceptability

If the oceans are to be utilized as a component of a global waste management strategy, then research programmes need to be specifically targeted
at evaluating any uses and at winning public acceptance (Thiel *et al.*,
1997). There is no doubt that such use will involve environmental penal-
ties, but these may be appreciably lower than the other options currently
considered to be acceptable. Any selected option should satisfy a number
of criteria of acceptability. These can be can be categorized into anthropocentric and environmental criteria. They include:

Anthropocentric criteria
1   Amenity must be maintained.
2   Exploitation of resources (living and non-living) must not be disad-
    vantaged.
3   There must be no significant associated health hazards (e.g. transmis-
    sion of pathogens and viruses or effects of toxic materials).
4   It must be affordable economically and in terms of the energy
    required.

Environmental criteria
1   It must not cause significant loss of biodiversity.
2   It must not cause significant habitat degradation.
3   It must not cause significant impact on ecological processes.
4   It must take into account synergistic interactions.

If tested against such criteria, many currently accepted waste management
options would fail, although how the significance of the impacts is determined will have a large effect on the assessments. I would suggest that if
the precautionary principle were to be applied to presently accepted activities as rigorously as it is applied to marine options, they too would also be
rejected. I would also further suggest that ethical considerations such as
concepts of intergenerational responsibility and stewardship are extremely
important especially if public acceptance of solutions is to be gained.
However, they should be global and holistic, and not weighted against
future uses of the oceans.

References

Anderson, D.M. and Garrison, D.J. (eds) (1997) 'The ecology and oceanography
    of harmful algal blooms', *Limnology and Oceanography* 42: 1009–305.
Angel, M.V. (2000) 'The Buckland lecture 1998: the rational use of ocean
    resources', *Buckland Occasional Papers* 5: 35.
Angel, M.V. and Rice, A.L. (1996) 'The ecology of the deep sea and its relevance
    to global waste management', *Journal of Applied Ecology* 33: 754–72.
Baklid, A. and Korbøl, R. (1996) 'Sleipner Vest CO_2 disposal, CO_2 injection into a

shallow underground aquifer', *SPE 366M*. Richardson, Texas, USA: Society of Petroleum Engineers.

Bazzaz, F.A., Miao, S.L. and Wayne, P.M. (1994) 'CO_2-induced enhancements of co-occurring tree species decline at different rates', *Oecologia* 96: 478–82.

Beamish, R.J., Kim, S., Terazaki, M. and Wooster, W.S. (eds) (1999) 'Ecosystem dynamics in the eastern and western gyres of the subarctic Pacific', *Progress in Oceanography* 43: 157–487.

Beaugrand, G., Reid, P.C., Ibanez, F., Lindley, J.A. and Edwards, M. (2002) 'Reorganization of North Atlantic marine copepod biodiversity and climate', *Science* 296: 1992–4.

Bewers, J.M. (1995) 'The declining influence of science on marine environmental policy', *Chemical Ecology* 10: 9–23.

British Government Panel on Sustainable Development (1999) http://www.sustainable-development.gov.uk.

Broecker, W.S. (1997) 'Thermohaline circulation, the Achilles heel of our climate system: will man-made CO_2 upset the current balance?', *Science* 278: 1582–8.

Christen, K. (1999) 'Gulf dead zone grows, perplexes scientists', *Environmental Science and Technology* 33: 396A–7A.

Cohen, J.E. (1995) 'Population growth and the Earth's human carrying capacity', *Science* 269: 341–6.

Constanza, R., d'Arge, R., de Groot, R., Farber, S., Grasso, M., Hannon, B., Limburg, K., Naeem, S., O'Neill, R.V., Paruelo, J., Raskin, R.G., Sutton, P. and van den Belt, M. (1997) 'The value of the world's ecosystem services and natural capital', *Nature* 387: 253–60.

Coviella, C.E. and Trumble, J.T. (1999) 'Effects of elevated atmospheric carbon dioxide on insect-plant interactions', *Conservation Biology* 13: 700–12.

Earle, S. (1995) *Sea Change: a Message of the Oceans*. New York: G.P. Putnam's Sons.

Evans, L.T. (1998) *Feeding the Ten Billion: Plants and Population Growth*. Cambridge: Cambridge University Press.

Feldt, W., Kanisch, G. and Vobach, M. (1989) 'Deep-sea biota of the Northeast Atlantic and their radioactivity', in *Interim Oceanographic Description of the Northeast Atlantic Site for the Disposal of Low-level Radioactive Waste*. 3, Vienna: OECD Nuclear Energy Authority, Vienna, pp. 178–204.

Field, C.B., Chapin, F.S., Matson, P.A. and Mooney, H.A. (1992) 'Responses of terrestrial ecosystems to the changing atmosphere: a resource-based approach', *Annual Review of Ecology and Systematics* 23: 201–36.

Hoffert, M.I., Caldeira, K., Jain, A.K., Haites, E.F., Danny Harvey, L.D., Potter, S.D., Schlesinger, M.E., Schneider, S.H., Watts, R.G., Wigley, T.M.L. and Wuebbles, D.J. (1998) 'Energy implication of future stabilization of atmospheric CO_2 content', *Nature* 395: 881–4.

Holloway, S., Heederik, J.P., van der Meer, L.G.H., Czernichowski-Lauriol, I., Harrison, R., Lindeberg, E., Summerfield, I.R., Rochelle, C., Schwarzkopf, T., Kaarstad, O. and Berger, B. (1996) 'The underground disposal of carbon dioxide: summary report', CEC Non-Nuclear Energy R&D Programme JOULE II. Keyworth, Nottingham: British Geological Survey, p. 24.

Horiuchi, S. (1992) 'Stagnation in the decline of the world population growth rate during the 1980s', *Science* 257: 761–5.

Houghton, J.T., Filho, L.G.M., Callander, B.A., Harris, N., Kattenberg, A. and

Maskell, K. (1996) 'Climate change 1995: the science of climate change. Contribution of Working Group I to the Second Assessment Report of the Intergovernmental Panel on Climate Change', Cambridge: Cambridge University Press.

Independent World Commission on the Oceans (IWCO) (1998) *The Ocean, Our Future.* Cambridge: Cambridge University Press.

Jasanoff, S. *et al.* (1997) 'Conversations with the community: AAAS at the millennium', *Science* 278: 2066–7.

Lee, J.G., Roberts, S.B. and Morel, F.M.M. (1995) 'Cadmium: a nutrient for the marine diatom *Thalassiosira weissflogii*', *Limnology and Oceanography* 40: 1056–63.

Manahan, S.E. and Smith, M.J. (1973) 'Copper micronutrient requirement for algae', *Environmental Science Technology* 7: 829–33.

Moffatt, A.S. (1998) 'Global nitrogen overload grows critical', *Science* 279: 988–9.

Munn, R.E., Whyte, A. and Timmerman, P. (2000) 'Emerging environmental issues for the 21st century: a study for GEO-2000', *Environmental Information and Assessment Technical Report.* UNEP/DEIA&EW/TR. 99–5, 27pp.

NATO (1995) 'Cross-border environmental problems emanating from defence-related installations and activities, Final Report II Chemical contamination', NATO Report 205.

Nielsen, T.G., Kiorboe, T. and Bjornsen, T. (1990) 'Effects of a *Chrysochromulina polylepis* subsurface bloom on the planktonic community', *Marine Ecology Progress Series* 62: 21–35.

OECD Nuclear Energy Agency (1995) 'The environmental and ethical basis of geological disposal: a collective opinion of the NEA Radioactive Waste Management Committee', Paris: OECD.

Ormerod, B. (ed.) (1997) *Ocean Storage of Carbon Dioxide Workshop 4: Practical and Experimental Approaches.* Cheltenham: IEA Greenhouse Gas R&D Programme.

Ormond, R.F., Gage, J.D. and Angel, M.V. (eds) (1997) *Marine Biodiversity: Patterns and Processes.* Cambridge: Cambridge University Press.

OSPAR Commission (2000) *Quality Status Report for Region II: the North Sea.* London: OSPAR.

Paerl, H.W. (1997) 'Coastal eutrophication and harmful algal blooms: importance of atmospheric deposition and groundwater as "new" nitrogen and other nutrient sources', *Limnology and Oceanography* 42: 1154–65.

Pearson, T.H. (1986) 'Disposal of sewage in dispersive and non-dispersive areas: contrasting case histories British coastal waters', in Kullenberg, G. (ed.) *Scientific Basis for the Roles of the Oceans as a Waste Disposal Option.* Dordrecht: D. Reidel, pp. 577–95.

Pimentel, D., Herdendorf, M., Eisenfeld, S., Olander, L., Carroquino, M., Corson, C., McDade, J., Chung, Y., Cannon, W., Roberts, J., Bluman, L. and Gregg, J. (1994) 'Achieving a secure energy future: environmental and economic issues', *Ecological Economics* 9: 201–19.

Reid, P.C., Borges, M.F. and Svendsen, E. (2001) 'A regime shift in the North Sea *c.*1988 linked to changes in the North Sea horse mackerel fishery', *Fisheries Research* 50: 163–71.

Rice, T. and Owen, P. (1999). *Decommissioning the Brent Spar.* London: Routledge.

Rose, C. (1998) *The Turning of the Spar.* London: Greenpeace.

Sunda, W.G. and Huntsman, S.A. (1992) 'Feedback interactions between zinc and phytoplankton in seawater', *Limnology and Oceanography* 37: 25–40.

Thiel, H., Angel, M.V., Foell, E.J. and Rice, A.L. (1997) *Environmental Risks from*

Large-scale Ecological Research in the Deep Sea: a Desk Study. Bremerhaven: Commission of the European Communities, Contract MAS2-CT94-0086.

Valent, P.J. and Young, D.K. (1998) 'Abyssal seafloor waste isolation: a technical, economical and environmental assessment of a waste management option', *Journal of Marine Systems* 14: 201–398.

Vitousek, P.M. (1994) 'Beyond global warming: ecology and global change', *Ecology* 75: 1861–76.

Vitousek, P.M., Mooney, H.A., Lubchenco, J. and Melillo, J.M. (1997) 'Human domination of Earth's ecosystems', *Science* 277: 494–9.

Part III

The coast

7 The development of fishing communities with special reference to Scotland

James Coull

Introduction

There is something of a common ethos in fishing communities in different parts of the world: this has been forged against the background of uncertainty, hardship and danger which is their common lot. Fish has been an important food source to human groups from remote prehistory; and it has in many situations been a significant – and in not a few cases a dominant – source of protein in the diet. For the great part of history and prehistory fish have been caught by communities who get the main part of their food supply from farming; but local ecological situations have been such that fish from fresh water or the sea have often supplied an essential diet component. In some extreme cases, of which Indian communities on the West Coast of Canada are a prime example, fish have been the main food resource. In the modern world, fishing communities may be divided into two main classes. In the first place are traditional communities (now mainly in the Third World) in which fishing or fishing-related activities are virtually the only occupations, in which son follows father, and productivity measured by economic criteria is low. By contrast are the communities of the developed world, in which characteristically only a minor part of the employment is in fishing but in which productivity is notably higher, where there is employment in various services, and in which members of fishing families can move relatively freely into other occupations.

Inevitably fishing communities have now been affected by modernization – a process that began over two centuries ago in Scotland, and was related to economic take-off in Britain; and this subsequently spread and in the present century has become worldwide. This has produced many-sided changes, of which developments in fishing itself have only been one small part. It has entailed that not a few fishing communities (like others) have been able to enjoy raised living standards; but it has also involved far-reaching adjustments or dislocations that have often been difficult and painful, and have to an extent been de-stabilizing in community terms.

Literature on fishing communities is not wanting, although much of it is less than scholarly. Probably most common are studies in local history, in which folk memory is united with varying amounts of documentary material. The main other type of study has been that of sociologists and social anthropologists: the fact that a distinctive character of community in the fishing context is now often associated with problems has proved an attraction to a significant number of these scholars.

In any event, Scotland's fishing communities have developed over many centuries, and provide illustrations of many of the characteristics and developments found in the wider world.

Historical development before the nineteenth century

While specialized fishing communities are known to have existed for centuries, and possibly for thousands of years, it is a basic principle that these can only exist with the development of trade and of commercial networks. It was this that allowed some communities to concentrate on fish production, and to secure their other food and material requirements by exchange. Although for centuries specialized fishing communities have been known in rural situations like the coasts of Norway, Newfoundland and Scotland, it is probable that the first specialized fishing communities developed in urban situations where there was a relatively big market in the immediate vicinity. Places of the size of towns or cities on coasts or on major rivers gave such opportunities. Fish is known to have been important in the diet of early civilizations in Egypt and Mesopotamia, and has for centuries been a major source of food protein for thousands of years to millions in China. The first fishing communities appear to have been in cities in these parts of the world, and later there is evidence for comparable provision in the coastal cities of the Classical Mediterranean. The practice of curing fish for out-of-season use and for transport are of unknown antiquity, but there is some evidence for trade in fish over distances to supply demand: the rich fish stocks of the Sea of Azov, for example, helped supply cities in ancient Greece.

While it is much later before there is evidence for specialized fishing communities in Scotland, there were fishing quarters in such main coastal towns as Aberdeen and Ayr from medieval times (Coull, 1996). At a later stage, but before modern developments in transport, such towns also drew part of their fish supplies from fishing villages within walking distance.

For centuries too there has been fishing from places of town status on Scotland's two major firths – those of the Forth and Clyde, which are at either end of the Central Belt, which has always been the most densely populated part of the country. Towns here, often as part of wider maritime activity, were involved in fishing that was important in regional food supplies, and which could produce surpluses for export.

An element of specialized fishing may well have developed as part of the economy of feudal estates, especially where such estates fronted the coast. While evidence is fragmentary it appears that many of the Scottish villages started as communities of small-holders who produced part of their own food supply from the land, but who also engaged in fishing. Such dual dependence is well attested in later times in the Scottish Highlands and Islands, in Norway, Newfoundland and elsewhere. A pattern in which fishermen started as people with insufficient land to maintain a family, or were indeed landless, is known on the coasts of various countries. Also, when new villages were founded this was often done by getting fishing families to move from existing settlements to the new foundations.

In the siting of fishing villages, as a rule the most basic requirement was a landing beach on which boats could be pulled up out of the water; most often this was a shingle (as opposed to a sand) beach (e.g. Figure 7.1). Such shore-side sites are still commonplace in the Third World and are the most usual on the world scale for fishing settlements. As well as giving a relatively firm surface on which to beach the boats, they also gave a freely drained surface on which fish could be spread to cure. From an early date it was usual that part of the catch would be prepared in this way for out-of-season use and for trade. So important was a site by a landing beach that even very restricted sites at the foot of steep banks or even cliffs were used (e.g. Figure 7.2). Much of the work of line baiting and splitting and cleaning of fish was done around or in the houses; and it is on record that the older houses had earth floors that could be sprinkled with sand –

Figure 7.1 Cairnbulg, Aberdeenshire. This village is known to have been in existence for around four centuries, and is an example of the basic situation beside a shingle landing beach, on which boats could be pulled up and fish spread to cure. While still a place of residence for active fishermen, the fishermen now commute to the harbour of nearby Fraserburgh.

Figure 7.2 Sandend, Banffshire. The village is on a restricted site beside a rock cove and beneath a steep bank. The piers are late additions. As shown here, sand coasts were very largely avoided in the siting of villages. As well as sand being inadequate for foundations, it was also preferred to draw boats up on shingle beaches.

as this became fouled it could be swept up and thrown out and clean sand sprinkled in its place.

There are parts of the Scottish coast, however, where there could be suitable landing coves beside which there was insufficient a space to build houses. In a fair number of cases this resulted in the building of villages on a clifftop (e.g. Figure 7.3), although this entailed considerable inconvenience for the work relating to fishing; the boats had to be reached by steep paths which could be slippery and fish and baited lines would have to be carried up and down the paths.

When studied in detail, fishing in traditional subsistence communities is integrated into a regular but flexible pattern of activities that varies with the seasons. While the work of fishing has traditionally largely been a male task, women have been involved in a variety of ancillary tasks like line baiting and fish curing; and with the development of commercial economies they have often been involved in fish selling.

The early development of fishing villages in Scotland, which can be traced from at least the sixteenth century, is much associated with the development of exchange (including by barter) at the local level, whereby coastal villages supplied fish to local hinterlands and got in exchange such

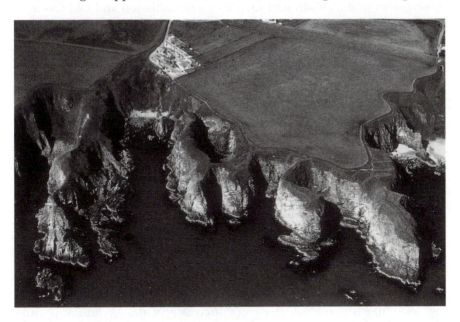

Figure 7.3 Bullers of Buchan, Aberdeenshire. Here the houses were built at the top of a cliff well over 100 ft. high as there was inadequate space by the landing beach below. Access to the boats had to be via a path up the steep slope. This village is unusual in that it failed to expand much in the nineteenth century and consequently it illustrates the small size that was typical of earlier times. (Photograph by courtesy of Prof. I.B.M. Ralston.)

farm products as meal and cheese. The manner in which this fitted into the earlier feudal economy is instanced in North-East Scotland, where virtually every coastal estate had at least one such village (Summers, 1988). This is also linked to the emergence of one of the best-known figures of traditional Scottish life – the fishwife. Women from fishing villages burdened with their fish creels might cover many kilometres in a day's walk among the rural farms. Since in Scotland as a whole the main concentrations of population have always been within 20 or 30 kilometres of the coast, this type of complementary exchange was particularly feasible. It was also known on the coasts of Holland, Denmark and elsewhere.

The main activity of Scottish villages was to supply their hinterlands with white fish, of which the most common was haddock. The women of fishing communities, with some help from the children, were much involved in this with the gathering and shelling of mussels to bait the lines. With hooks being at intervals of rather over a metre, and boats shooting literally kilometres of line, this was work that took many hours daily. A graphic illustration of the family involvement in this is shown in the way that in the Aberdeenshire parish of Slains in the 1790s, attendance at the school in the main fishing season decreased due to the involvement of the children of the villages of Collieston and Old Castle in line baiting (O.S.A. V, 284). Haddock, whiting and other fish were available at all seasons on inshore grounds; in the spring especially there was a tendency to fish further off at distances of ten miles or more for bigger fish of which the cod was most important. As well as supplying fresh fish to their hinterlands, there was also some curing by salting, and there was also some development of smoking which also gave a variation in taste as well as acting as a short-term preservative. After the fish were landed, the women had a big role in dealing with them in gutting, cleaning and curing.

In the longer term the multiplication and expansion of specialized fishing communities came with economic development: increasing trade and rising living standards encouraged concentration on full-time fishing and more investment in boats and gear. In the seventeenth and eighteenth centuries there was a general increase in number of the Scottish villages. To this day the predominance of three or four family names in each of these settlements points to there having been a handful of households at their origins, although in the nineteenth century many of them expanded to have populations numbered in hundreds. As well as supplying local needs some villages were increasingly drawn into supplying places at a distance with cured fish. This sector of trade was largely the work of specialized merchants, and the most prominent feature here was the provision of cured fish to the main towns on the Firth of Forth with fish from the North-East.

The Shetland Islands had a distinctive development of their own in the eighteenth century with the expansion of the export-oriented 'haaf' fishery, which supplied cured ling and cod to the Continent, especially Spain. At this stage the Shetlanders were almost universally crofter-fishers, and the division of work in households and communities (Smith, 1984) illustrates the integration of farming and fishing that has occurred in many communities in different countries and continents. Although men concentrated at the main haaf stations during the summer fishing season, they reverted to their homes in crofting townships for the remainder of the year. They could take part in the spring work of cultivation before the haaf season and in the harvest after it, but the women participated in much of the croft work, and were aided by the older men and the children while the men were fishing. Shetland has been noted for the truck system under which this operated: this entailed control by landlords and merchants, and engagement in fishing for the landlord was a condition for the tenanting of house and land (Smith, 1984). Crofter-fishing and truck systems also persisted in Norway, Newfoundland and other outlying fishing-dependent societies into the nineteenth and even the twentieth centuries, and meant that communities were put in a situation of subjection to merchants in situations in which competition at the producers' end was effectively inhibited. The second half of the twentieth century saw the persistence of such settlements in various outlying locations in the developed world: Figure 7.4 is an example of a Newfoundland fishing

Figure 7.4 Bay de Verde, Avalon Peninsula, Newfoundland. Despite being in Canada, the predominant feature here is the great number of small boats still used in commercial fishing in the 1970s. The 'flakes' (wooden stages) in the background are used for the spreading of cod fish to cure. With its summer cod fishery, Newfoundland was able to find a market for its sun cured fish well into the second half of the twentieth century.

settlement that well into the second half of the twentieth century concentrated on the production of salt-cured fish for the Spanish market. Comparable situations are also known in the modern Third World.

Crofter-fishing has persisted in Shetland and in much of the rest of the Highlands and Islands of Scotland into the twentieth century, although from the later nineteenth century the rise of the separately organized herring fishery played a big part in the elimination of truck relationships. Even so, it has only been in the most recent decades in these outlying communities has there been more concentration on full-time fishing.

Fish are essentially a mobile resource and they vary much in seasonal availability. One of the consequences of this is that there have been long-standing elements of seasonal mobility associated even with some traditional fisheries, and this has had social consequences with the periodic splitting of communities. Prominent here was the concentration of effort in the Lofoten cod fishery in Norway in the early months of the year; and mobility and seasonal concentration of effort has also been known from medieval times in European herring fisheries. In the modern period with power-driven boats, mobility has been rendered easier and operation away from the home base has become a frequent part of fishing activity.

Developments in the nineteenth century

The far-reaching social and economic changes that accompanied the full emergence of the industrial economy also affected fishing communities in Scotland and elsewhere, and gave new challenges and opportunities. Associated with these changes were expanding markets and an enhanced ability to reach them through much improved transport; and a main motivation was the opportunity to raise living standards in fishing communities in parallel with those in society generally. While this was general for fishing communities in Western Europe and North America, arguably developments at this stage in Scotland were more far-reaching than anywhere. The greater detail of information available in the national census from the early nineteenth century shows that many fishing settlements expanded vigorously. This could be associated with considerable building on a grid plan where sites allowed, but expansion was not always inhibited on more difficult sites (Figure 7.5).

Expanding markets in industrializing Britain saw a vigorous increase in the line fisheries for whitefish, and this got to a point at the latter end of the century that there was a great shortage in Scottish supplies of mussel bait. Mussels were transported and traded to a large extent around the coasts, and there was a big increase in the production of fish for the market, with much use of rail transport.

In the later part of the century this expanded traditional fishery was effectively cut short by one of the major modern developments – that of bottom trawling from power-driven boats. This, as well as disrupting the

Figure 7.5 Gardenstown, Banffshire. Here the original village was a row of cottages built by the shore from 1720. However, it has been one of the most successful of Scottish fishing communities, and in later times it spread upslope on a difficult site and, as shown, the latest building is on the more even land at the top of the slope. Harbours were built at several villages (including here) in the nineteenth century, but the long-term forces of centralization of operation to the bigger ports have rendered these harbours of minor consequence.

efforts of the traditional line fishermen, came to dominate the expanding market. This was also to cause major disruptions and readjustments in the communities in which the fishermen lived. (The full effects of this are considered below.)

Although developments in the white fishery were extensive, the dominant development of the nineteenth century was actually the growth of the herring fishery. This was the fulfilment of a long-standing Scottish ambition, and entailed great changes in fishing communities. There was a new degree of concentration of operation at main harbours, and in the longer term resulted in an unprecedented degree of mobility as the personnel employed in the fishery moved to different bases at different seasons. Herring fisheries in other European countries, like Norway, Sweden and Holland have also been prominent in inducing such seasonal mobility. For the most part the herring fishery was operated from the same communities that were involved in the line fisheries, and in the early part of the nineteenth century it was achieved mainly through diversion of a large part of the fishing effort during a two-month summer season. From an early date it involved the use of bigger boats for which harbours were desirable, in contrast to the landing beaches on which the boats for the white fishery were drawn up. This resulted in some seasonal splitting of communities as the men concentrated for the season at the harbours, although there was also movement of women to the same places for work in herring curing yards. The women also had work in the making of nets; and when nets became factory-made from *c.*1830 onwards, there was still a big task for them to mend nets that were torn in use. This work expanded much after about 1860 with the replacement of linen nets by the lighter cotton, which resulted in boats enhancing their catching power by increasing the numbers of nets they carried (Coull, 1996). The growth of the herring fishery also meant an increase in the number of fish curers and in coopers for making the barrels for the herring.

The development of the herring fishery in the first half of the nineteenth century were mainly on the east coast, but with success in the fishery and increased investment in boats and gear, it became desirable to extend the two-month east coast season, which was from early July to early September. This could be done by engaging in the early summer fishery in the Hebrides, and from the middle of the nineteenth century it became usual for fishermen from east coast communities to go to the Hebrides in May and June. This involved a seasonal split in their personnel: the women stayed at home, and curers and coopers generally accompanied the fishermen, with much of the female labour for gutting and packing recruited in the islands. Various other bases in Britain in time became used for the herring fishery at different seasons: the most important of these were East Anglia and Shetland. The former was the venue for the autumn season from October to December: this began in the 1860s and became of major-scale at the end of the century (Coull, 1992); and Shetland became the main seat of the early summer fishing from the 1880s (Coull, 1988). When the herring fishery was at its peak in the closing years of the nineteenth century and the opening years of the twentieth, both of these involved the seasonal movement of over 1,000 boat crews and upwards of 10,000 fishermen from Scottish fishing communities; they also involved the movement of thousands of women gutters and other shore personnel. An important factor which stimulated this mobility was the rapid displacement of the sailboat by the steam drifter from 1900 as the main catching unit. As well as making mobility itself easier, the steam drifter entailed a big increase in investment, which needed expanded catching effort to justify it.

The increase in size of herring boats which culminated in the advent of the steam drifter had social effects in fishing communities with the acceleration of the trend whereby boat ownership became concentrated in fewer hands, and a bigger proportion of crews became hired men without a share in boat or gear. Nonetheless, throughout the development of the herring fishery, there remained in Scotland a firm tradition of independent share fishermen with family-owned boats.

As the herring fishery came to dominate the year for many fishermen, a significant number of them moved, with their families, from their old homes in villages to towns like Peterhead (Figure 7.6), Fraserburgh and Wick which were main home harbours for the fleets, and these towns acquired expanded fishing quarters.

In the pattern of migrant seasonal labour, the crofting communities of the West Highlands and Islands became main exporters of both male and female labour. With the shortage of capital in the region for investment in up-to-date boats, many of the men went as part crews on east coast boats and women worked in the curing yards.

A consequence of this large-scale movement around the coasts was that both men and women from different fishing communities intermingled to an unprecedented extent in the different fishing ports. An outcome was considerably more intermarriage between communities, especially among

Figure 7.6 Peterhead, Aberdeenshire. The original site of this burgh was by what became the north harbour to the right of the picture. On a coast which is notably short of natural harbours, two small offshore islands aided the development of the port through a series of phases. This settlement gained greatly from the centralization of operation of the herring fishery in the nineteenth century, and continued as a main port with the switch to white (demersal) fishing in the latter half of the twentieth century. (Photograph by courtesy of Aberdeen Journals Ltd.)

places on the east coast: and after marriage members of both sexes became domiciled in host communities. While there was also some inter-marriage between east and west coast communities, this was much rarer. This was at least partly because of the prevalent language barrier, with the seasonal migrants from the west coast being Gaelic speakers. There were also occasional instances of intermarriage between communities on the east coast on the one hand, and East Anglia or Shetland on the other, which were the result of contacts made during seasonal migration.

Offshore and distant-water fisheries

Through most of history fishing communities have normally been less subject than other seafaring communities to the problems and social strains of having their menfolk away for protracted periods. In traditional fishing communities men may work odd and irregular hours in response to weather, tides and known fish behaviour, but fishing is usually in the vicinity of home, and they are seldom away beyond the span of one or two working days. In contrast distant-water fishing can entail fishermen being away for weeks or months. Although distant-water fishing has been more frequent in the past century than previously, it was known to an extent from the medieval period in Western Europe. Very generally it has involved bigger vessels, greater elements of business organization, and a considerably greater scale of capital investment. This has produced a dif-ferent type of fishing community, especially in the main base ports of the vessels. While systems of remuneration of crew members have generally retained a high degree of dependence on catch results, crews have been bigger and there has been a more pronounced hierarchy in them.

The earliest distant-water fisheries of which there is any clear evidence appear to have consisted of trips in big decked craft from Western Euro-pean countries to Iceland and other northern waters to fish or trade for cod. From the fifteenth century these fisheries developed to a greater extent on the Grand Banks with vessels from Spain, Portugal, France and Britain crossing the Atlantic for the summer cod season. It was basic to such fisheries that voyages lasted for months and that catches were salt-cured.

Although herring, as an oily fish, were more difficult to cure satisfactor-ily than cod, salt-curing them in barrels was mastered by the Dutch, who with their busses developed their profitable North Sea herring fishery, which also entailed crews being away for weeks or months. While there were attempts to copy this in Scotland and elsewhere, these at first were on a much smaller scale. With the help of the incentive of government tonnage bounties, this did develop on a considerable scale in Scotland in the second half of the eighteenth century, with at one time over 300 busses and over 3,000 men in their crews. The majority of the busses were based on the Clyde; they were away from base for up to three months at a time, although there is very little information on how their crews were recruited, let alone their social or family situations.

Since the nineteenth century, business organization has become more prominent in the main fisheries, and mobility has also been enhanced by the leading developments in fishing for more than a century having employed power-driven vessels. A substantial component of these modern developments have been in distant-water fisheries. Included have been many vessels of a large size capable of staying at sea for protracted periods; and in a number of cases big ships have operated in fleets accompanied by various ancillary vessels like factory ships and tankers. Most important here have been trawlers, although various types of catching methods and fishing gear have also been used.

Not a few of such developments have greatly altered fishing communities or indeed forged new ones. They have been concentrated in bigger ports with the facilities for selling the fish and servicing the fleets. The pioneer development of these was in England with the nineteenth-century expansion of whitefish trawling to satisfy the markets in burgeoning industrial cities. The earlier stages of this was with sailing trawlers; with these boats in the 'fleeter' system the crews could be at sea for weeks while their catches were trans-shipped and taken to market by sailing cutters. The recruitment of labour for the trawlers was not without measures of coercion (Robinson, 1996), with many boys recruited on indenture, including many from orphanages. This created obvious problems in maintaining a stable and dependable labour force, but it did contribute to the expansion of the fishing communities in the trawling ports, especially in Hull and Grimsby. There were moves to improve working and social conditions, and with the advent of steam trawling from the 1880s there was a general move to 'single-boating' as opposed to fleeter operation which had the general effect of reducing time at sea for the crews. However, this type of fishery was always arduous, and well into the twentieth century men might only have two or three days on shore between trips which lasted up to three weeks.

Scotland too developed a trawling sector, although this was initially largely an offshoot of the English industry as their trawlers pushed northwards in the North Sea in quest of more grounds to exploit. In Scotland this resulted in a new level of capital investment and in company, as opposed to family, ownership, and in a new and distinctive type of fishing community – especially in Aberdeen, but also to an extent in Granton on the Forth. Trawling was a boom industry in Aberdeen for a period from the 1880s and from the start of the twentieth century. It was the city's leading industry until after World War II, with direct employment on boats at the peak exceeding 3,000, and with over 6,000 also in directly related ancillary activities like fish processing and marine engineering. Many of the early trawl skippers, engineers and some deckhands came from England.

Trawling had an adverse effect on the traditional line fishing, both by thinning out the fish on inshore grounds and by interfering with the operations of the line men. One result was that men from Scottish fishing villages came, for a variety of motives, to take berths on the trawlers. Although they did make a good deal more money than they had done at lining, they had lost independence and status and largely became hired hands. As well as having to spend much more time away from home, conditions aboard the trawlers were again often particularly arduous. The system of remuneration on the trawlers also made a big distinction between skippers and mates on the one hand and deckhands on the other.

Distant-water trawling was also developed to an extent by other Western European nations, especially Germany in the early twentieth century; at the same time Japan established itself as the world's leading fishing nation, which also entailed a distant-water component in the Pacific. Between World War II and the 1970s there was an unprecedented expansion in world fishing as modern methods and fishing aids were developed at an accelerated rate and diffused around the world. Distant-water fishing became large-scale, especially on the part of the two leading fishing nations of Japan and the Soviet Union, but also in other countries of Eastern Europe, and in Asiatic countries like Korea and Taiwan. In the case of the USSR expansion of the distant-water fleet to be able to work in all oceans was a main element in the policy of food provision, and by 1972 the USSR had a bigger fleet of ocean-going vessels of 1,000 g.r.t. or over than the rest of the world combined (OECD, 1973). This involved the building up of a labour force of many thousands from a population with little ocean-going experience, and involved substantial recruitment incentives. Cities like Murmansk in the west and Nahodka in the east became largely domiciles for thousands of fishermen and their families. While there was some recruitment to crews of women for galley and other duties, the crews were dominantly male, and families had to adapt to men being away for months at a time. Although the USA was not a leading power in fishing, the tuna fleets bases in California in the twentieth century also developed a large range in the Pacific.

The large-scale development of capital-intensive fisheries has also had a big impact on traditional fishing communities, comparable to the earlier experience in Scotland and elsewhere around the North Sea. It has had a large impact on markets, and has been accompanied by accelerated exploitation rates on fish stocks. As a consequence traditional fishermen have often found themselves faced with much better-equipped competition, and have often felt that they have been roughly shouldered aside. Inevitably reaction and opposition have been provoked in the traditional communities.

This happened first around the North Sea with the development of trawling in England, and spread into the North Atlantic in the early twentieth century. After World War II development accelerated, and big modern boats have been more mobile and have been able to fish on grounds worldwide. The effects of this have inevitably been felt by traditional fishermen and fishing communities, and in many cases and in different parts of the world trawling was made illegal in inshore waters. While the problem of conflict between traditional and modern methods has generally decreased in developed countries with the run-down of traditional fishing and with the imposition of 200-mile national fishing limits, it has persisted to a much greater degree in developing countries with the persistence of many thousands of small operators among whom there is a high incidence of poverty. Yet even in the Third World there has been sufficient advantage and impetus for the use of modern methods to be deployed and the control of the trawl method has become a matter of major concern. For example, in Malaysia, where by the 1970s the trawl method had become dominant and which had at the same time provoked a major conservation problem. The difficulty in the Third World of finding resources for adequate enforcement of regulations within 200-mile zones aggravates the situation.

Figure 7.7 Pulau Ketam, West Malaysia. This settlement is on the coast near Kuala Lumpur, and was developed from the nineteenth century by immigrant fishermen from China. From the 1960s, the trawl was adopted as the main fishing method, and the boats shown here are trawlers. Although seldom as much as 40 feet in length, they are power-driven; however, the increase in catching power has produced a conservation problem – which is all too typical of the modern situation in fishing throughout most of the world.

Twentieth century trends in Scotland

Even in the developed world, in many countries numbers of fishermen continued to increase and fishing communities continued to expand into the early decades of the twentieth century, and with rising populations in the Third World these trends are continuing. However, the modernization of fishing had been earlier in the world's first industrial nations, and in Scotland numbers of fishermen started on the downward path at the beginning of the twentieth century, although in many fishing communities new employment opportunities were scarce till after World War II, if indeed they arrived at all.

In Scotland there has in fact been an accelerating readjustment in employment patterns in fishing communities for the whole of the twentieth century. With fishing itself more and more dominated by bigger boats, there has been a run-down in fishing manpower, accompanied by movement of some members of fishing families into other employment; related to this there has been significant migration to other places both in Britain and abroad. Since 1900 recorded numbers of fishermen have gone down from over 40,000 to under 8,000. Numbers in ancillary employment cannot be stated with the same precision, but the decrease in fish processing employment has been less dramatic, if substantial. On the other hand the more sophisticated modern fleet with its hydraulic and electronic equipment has generated new needs, although these are partly catered for by firms which also deal with other shipping. Mobility has continued to be a basic characteristic with boats prepared to go hundreds of miles for fish, although in the post-1970s world of international 200-mile fishing limits, distant-water operation has been much scaled down. Since World War II especially there been entry of members from fishing families into a variety of employments for which advanced education is necessary, and these have included the professions. Less commonly, with the more flexible modern labour market there has been some recruitment to fishing of men with no family fishing background.

Fishermen are still substantially concentrated in main ports, but near-universal modern car ownership has enabled many fishermen to remain domiciled in traditional villages while berthing their boats in town harbours. Although there has been a general run-down in fishing, there are still communities which are emphatically fishing-dominated. Probably the best examples in Scotland are the village of Gardenstown in Banffshire and the island of Whalsay in Shetland.

The latest phases have witnessed aggravated problems of conservation, and the whitefish fleet, which has now been for over half a century the main component of Scottish fishing, is currently involved in a painful process of contraction by decommissioning.

Conclusion

Despite the prevalent forces of modernization, there are to be found today in many parts of the Third World fishing communities which still operate largely in traditional labour-intensive modes, with the majority of their people still directly fishing-dependent. However these modes are tending to change with the pressures of development: it is not now uncommon to find the installation of motors in traditional boats, the use of gear made of synthetic rather than natural fibres, and the use of ice to preserve fish to reach the consumer in better condition.

In developed countries too fishing communities still have a tendency to be distinctive and although modern fishing is largely a matter of applied science, it has often a high proportion of small operators and small units of production compared with other economic sectors. Despite this, much of the effective catching power is very often relatively capital-intensive and concentrated in big boats, and a variety of specialized functions now have to be provided for the fleets; in general terms it is only the bigger fishing settlements that can provide these. With the scale and range of ancillary functions, characteristically only a minority of the labour force in a community is directly employed in fishing. Modernization has been most problematical for communities when traditional small operators have been faced with the direct competition of fishermen using more productive capital-intensive methods. Modernization has also had other impacts in fishing (as in other communities) in opening up new opportunities in employment, education and social contacts for members of both sexes. The fact that traditional fishing communities are often sited in outlying locations has often entailed that participation in these new opportunities has been more difficult and has meant leaving the parent community.

In the case of Scotland, fishing communities have developed over many centuries, and their history is much linked to the growth of commerce. In this context towns played an important role in the beginning of fishing communities, although for centuries the majority of them were a specialized type of rural settlement; and with the more powerful focusing of modern life on towns, the much more developed modern fishing has become town-based and concentrated on relatively few harbours, but linked to more mobility and commuting. In the later phases there has been a big decline in the number of fishermen in most fishing settlements. Fishing villages now commonly have various incomers living in them, while in bigger places it has become common for fishing families to move from the old fishing quarters and mix in the modern parts of towns.

Effective conservation of the resource base is now a very general concern to fishing communities throughout the world, but the dangers of over-fishing are generally greater in developed countries with the availability of vastly enhanced capital-intensive catching methods. This has been accompanied by the politicizing of fishing to an unprecedented extent, with the demands of various sectional interest groups for an adequate share of resources and for a voice in resource allocation and conservation policy. Fishing has long been politically important in societies like those of Atlantic Canada and Norway, and modern management concerns have enhanced its importance at the grass roots in these and other countries.

In conclusion, despite manifold changes fishing continues to be one of the most distinctive occupations in our modern world of mass production, computers and information technology; despite manifold changes fishing communities still carry a distinctive stamp and fishing still has the inescapable hardships and dangers of the heaving deck.

References

Coull, J.R. (1988) 'The boom in the herring fishery in the Shetland Islands', *Northern Scotland* 8: 25–38.

Coull, J.R. (1989) 'The fisherfolk and fishing settlements of the Grampian region', in Smith, J.S. and Stevenson, D. (eds) *Fermfolk and Fisherfolk*. Centre for Scottish Studies: University of Aberdeen, pp. 26–49.

Coull, J.R. (1992) 'Seasonal fisheries migration: the case of migration from Scotland to the East Anglian herring fishery', in Fischer, L.R., Hamre, H., Holm, P. and Bruijn, J.R. (eds) *The North Sea: Twelve Essays on the History of Maritime Labour*. Stavanger Maritime Museum, pp. 127–47.

Coull, J.R. (1996) *The Sea Fisheries of Scotland: a Historical Geography*. Edinburgh: John Donald.

Farquhar, Rev. A. (1791) in Sinclair, Sir J., *The Statistical Account of Scotland, Vol. V: The Parish of Slains*. Edinburgh: William Creech, p. 284.

Organisation for European Co-operation and Development (OECD) (1973) *Review of Fishing in OECD Member Countries, 1972*. Paris: OECD.

Robinson, R. (1996) *Trawling. The Rise and Fall of the British Trawl Fishery*. Exeter: University of Exeter Press.

Smith, H.D. (1984) *Shetland Life and Trade 1550–1914*. Edinburgh: John Donald.

Summers, D.W. (1988) *Fishing off the Knuckle – the Fishing Villages of Buchan*. Aberdeen: Centre for Scottish Studies, University of Aberdeen.

8 Challenges and opportunities for coastal recreation and tourism in the twenty-first century

David Johnson

Introduction

Hall and Page (1999) state that tourism, recreation and leisure are generally seen as a set of interrelated and overlapping concepts. The motivation to participate in these activities at the coast has changed little over the last century and the same factors are likely to persuade us to continue to want to enjoy the coast during our free time in the twenty-first century. Coastal locations offer us an opportunity to feel healthier, have fun, be free, learn, explore, experience new as well as familiar places, test ourselves, say 'we were there', collect memories, be alone or be together. Collectively and individually we value the coast aesthetically and materially.

As a consequence a major trend is that attractive accessible parts of the coast often become overcrowded. This is a global issue, with some destinations attracting huge numbers of visitors whilst others are despoiled or in decline. In the UK regeneration of seaside resorts has become a strategic priority, as has the interpretation of maritime heritage and the conservation of 'unspoilt' rural coasts. Ironically, by contrast, the oceans remain relatively inaccessible, unexplored and unused for leisure and recreation. Water sports participation is moving from organized seasonal club activities to more individualistic hi-tech, all-conditions, all-year pursuits. Time, cost and opportunity constraints favour water-based activities that can provide a 'fast fix' adrenaline rush. At the same time a more affluent, older society is demanding more passive shore-based recreation activities. Users are also demanding a clean, safe and well managed coastal environment.

Challenges include finding a fair means to 'ration' the coast. Currently, despite the universal right of navigation, lack of physical access points represents the biggest constraint to coastal water-based recreation participation. Safety is a major worry as the potential for conflict between activities increases. The density of craft on the water is much higher than in the past and, with some of these craft becoming so much faster, the time to avert problems is reduced. The need to fund infrastructure provision and ensure environmental quality will also increasingly tax maritime leisure managers.

Thus key questions, which are likely to determine future directions for coastal recreation, are:

1   In the new millennium where will the coast stop? Can we ease the pressure by extending or creating new coastlines using virtual playgrounds, artificial islands, floating resorts; and by popularizing underwater as well as above water recreation?
2   How will we police recreational activities in the most popular locations to ensure that everyone and all activities have their fair share of coastline and water space without injuring themselves and each other?
3   Which new technologies will capture our imagination and how can they be incorporated sensibly and safely in areas that are already overused?
4   Are we strong enough as a society to insist on sustainable leisure solutions that respect carrying capacity and promote intergenerational and intrasocietal equity?

Background

Leisure is a legitimate and important use of the coastal zone, and it includes both terrestrial and water-based recreational activities. In Britain the 'seaside' holiday became popular in the nineteenth century as a result of rail access to the coast. British seaside resorts developed rapidly from the mid-1830s. Pursuits were largely passive, focusing on beaches, sea bathing, piers, pleasure steamers, public entertainment and catered accommodation. A century later, individuals' economic circumstances, mobility, preferences and pursuits have radically changed. Far more people can now participate in water-based leisure activities. Active sports are popular and society's expectations of coastal locations are changing.

In many ways factors that persuade us to participate in coastal recreation are constant. A new British obsession, however, is risk-taking for pleasure, also termed 'soft adventure' or 'extreme sports' (*Guardian*, 1999). Factors that enable and encourage participation in a wide range of leisure activities include economic growth, demography, socio-economic change and technology. In this respect, ways in which government shapes public policy, for example the release of former Ministry of Defence property such as Portland Harbour in Dorset and reductions in public subsidy for local authority recreation provision, are influential. The potential introduction of a five-term school year could have far-reaching implications for leisure attractions in the immediate future. A consequence of this changing environmental, economic and social equation is increasing competition for leisure time. In Britain at the twenty-first century longer working hours and increased job insecurity are likely to set traditional leisure pursuits (arts, sport and enjoyment of open spaces) against a fast-fix technological revolution.

Coastal recreation managers need to make value judgements to determine both the balance of recreation with other uses and an acceptable mix of leisure activities (Goodhead and Johnson, 1996). At the strategic level coastal recreation has been examined on a regional basis. Coastal resort regeneration, estuary and harbour recreation management plans have been developed. To implement these, a number of tried and tested management tools continue to be used to create appropriate space for formal and informal recreational pursuits. Environmental impact assessment is required to obtain permission for formal developments such as coastal golf courses, marinas and offshore artificial surf reefs. Bylaws impose speed limits on water-based craft within harbours. Charging, permits or licences attempt to regulate sports such as wildfowling and fishing, and maintain carrying capacities by, for example, restricting numbers of boat moorings or controlling the numbers of visitors to sensitive sites. Management of some of the most popular activities, however, relies upon the voluntary co-operation of participants, albeit often influenced by club controlled access. Walking is confined to coastal rights of way but managed indirectly using countryside interpretation techniques. Surfers and swimmers often share bathing waters within determined safety limits. Many water sports, such as diving, are governed by voluntary codes of conduct. The present position is an uneasy balance. Undoubtedly as demand increases, water space and environmental quality in the most favoured locations will be at a premium. Established cultural perceptions will continue to be challenged. Within the next 20 years a new mix of regulatory, socio-economic and technological solutions for managing coastal recreation is likely to evolve.

The Royal Institute of Chartered Surveyors Research Foundation *20:20 Vision for the future of leisure* (RICS, 2000) set out three possible scenarios as follows:

1   Continuation of current trends (tension between the free market and sustainability) with an emphasis on development of brownfield or contaminated land sites and controls on cars.
2   'The American Dream' – reduced government intervention and greater economic growth. This scenario envisaged social polarization; increasing disposable income/social exclusion; increasing demand for high quality 24-hour private facilities; and an affluent older generation of those able to retire early.
3   Greater government intervention and environmental priorities based on the promotion of healthier lifestyles; the growth of active pursuits and importance of local provision.

Whilst these scenarios were intended to inform and provide decision-makers with 'food for thought', elements of all of them can be recognized in coastal recreation. It is therefore timely to consider where coastal recreation currently stands and what might change. This chapter aims to give an overview of present coastal recreation trends; to critically evaluate problems which may arise or will become apparent as a result of these trends; and having analysed potential, to suggest some future directions.

Current trends in UK coastal recreation

The popularity of the British coast for people who want to spend their free time besides, in or on the water continues to grow (Ratcliffe, 1992). In 1998 the Institute of Leisure and Amenity Management (ILAM) estimated that leisure accounted for £38 billion per year to the UK economy, some five per cent of GDP, and this figure included 241 million day-visits to the coast. The demand for coastal tourism contrasts with the relative unknown nature of the oceans, of which we have explored and regularly utilize less than one per cent.

For land-based activities, wind and wave-dominated coasts with beaches continue to be the most popular locations. In addition to seafront entertainment and beach recreation, popular activities include walking, golf, horse riding, sea angling, bird watching, rock climbing, mountain biking, fossil collecting, beach combing and metal detecting. Associated infrastructure includes hotel and guest accommodation, car parks, camping and caravan sites, beach huts, golf courses, public rights of way and visitor centres.

In terms of water sports participation, however, it would appear that the absolute number of people involved has levelled off, although changes in types of activities and the time and location they take place in are evident. The Environment Agency estimates calculate that some seven million British people currently participate in water sports each year. Different activities have established focal centres such as surfing in Newquay, sailing in Cowes, diving in Orkney and gig racing on the Isles of Scilly. Social changes such as health awareness, the influence of fashion and green consumer choices have been influential in determining participation trends. Most recently, changing working patterns, resulting in longer hours spent at work, make finding large blocks of time more difficult, which in turn is popularizing short spontaneous breaks. Traditional water sports are time consuming and a discernible trend is the increasing demand for access to short breaks and exhilarating activities such as parascending.

Such activities are made possible by rapid advances in water sports technology (Orams, 1999). Advances such as self-furling sails and large-scale water-ski tows make activities easier and 'more available' to participants. Better clothing, such as breathable foul weather gear, has encouraged year-round access. Technological improvements in equipment mean that a range of sports is better able to cope with adverse wind and sea states. Sailing dinghies can cope with heavier conditions. As a result, within sailing, the emergence of one-design sports boats is a major trend. Asymmetric dinghies provide a fast-fix adrenaline rush and have become the new Olympic boat: easy to use, very quick and able to function in light winds. Similar technology for windsurfing has prompted the development of big, wide boards, which are easy to use in light winds, being able to plane at 6–7 knots. Global positioning satellite (GPS) navigation aids, fishfinders and advances in hull design and engine technology have all allowed vessels to be more self-sufficient and cruise further in less time carrying more passengers (Orams, 1999). The Professional Association of Diving Instructors (PADI) has opened up recreational scuba diving to a whole new audience. Highly mobile leisure platforms – shallow draft vessels equipped with 15 sets of scuba gear and an on-board compressor – allow instant and continuous diving anywhere.

Throughout the UK the predominance of power craft remains at an estimated ratio of 4:1. The instant gratification provided by such craft (i.e. get in and go, similar to a car) is the most likely explanation for their continued popularity. A recent National Youth Water Sports Audit suggested that this trend is set to continue (Anderson *et al.*, 1996). In this research young people expressed a preference for the instant thrill of power boating and personal watercraft rather than what they perceived as 'old fashioned' sailing clubs. Advances in technology have also partly prompted a new safety culture. Evidence of this is the development of licensing legislation, aimed at both experts and novices, and the requirements for licensing of the adventure activity industry, providing facilities for under 18s, operated by Activity Centres (Young Persons' Safety Act 1995 and Adventure Activities Licensing Regulations 1996).

Coastal resource managers have responded to these new demands by introducing multiple-use marine areas for popular locations. The implementation of Poole Harbour Aquatic Management Plan, for example, has used combinations of legislation, economic regulation, education and consensus building. More attention is being paid to the quality of the environment for coastal recreation, with an emphasis on good water quality and higher standards of amenity facilities.

Having stated that coastal recreation in the UK is buoyant, it should also be noted that, in terms of the global tourism market, Britain is increasingly less popular than warmer, sunnier, more exotic locations overseas. Contributory factors are the decreasing cost of foreign travel and the fashion for experiencing different cultures, with cult movies such as *The Beach* establishing mass trends for international youth. Cruise tourism, dominated by the aggressive marketing of three (latterly two) main corporations, has also become the fastest growing and most profitable sector of the world leisure business during the late 1990s. This business is centred on the Caribbean although the UK provides a niche market, with specialist cruise companies promoting holidays enjoying spectacular coastal landscapes such as the Western Isles of Scotland. Overseas there has been growth in bespoke water-based discovery and adventure holidays, with companies such as Island Discovery operating 40 ft catamarans amongst the British and US Virgin Islands, Windward and Leeward Islands of the Caribbean offering sailing, kneeboarding and diving packages. Furthermore, individuals with a strong engagement with their water sport are now prepared to go long-haul rather than spend time in Britain or the Mediterranean. Popular locations for competitive sailing are now the Caribbean, USA, South Pacific and Australia/New Zealand. One consequence of growth in recreational chartering overseas is a decline in UK chartering. In January 2000 two UK charter companies, Britannia Sailing and Neptune's School of Yachting, both ceased trading (*Sailing Today*, 2000).

The expansion and success of coastal and marine tourism abroad has finally prompted action in the UK. Regeneration of seaside resorts, recognized to be in long-term decline due to under-investment, failing attractions and inadequate marketing, has become a government priority (Lane, 2000; Hampson, 2000; Agarwal, 2002). This initiative features strongly in 'Tomorrow's Tourism', part of the National Tourism Strategy (DCMS, 1999). New ways of marketing Britain's coastal resorts are developing. Cleethorpes in Lincolnshire, for example, claims to attract 20,000 visitors from around the world to its kite festival. Conference tourism, in resorts such as Bournemouth, Brighton and Torquay, takes advantage of available accommodation stock either side of a relatively short summer season. Long overdue investment is being encouraged in coastal infrastructure and former seaside attractions. Brighton's West Pier Trust, for example, hopes to invest £30 million, of which £14.5 million has been promised by the Heritage Lottery Fund (Geographical, 2000), on restoring the pier and associated enabling works. Key issues are higher customer expectations in terms of amenities and accommodation and, with an ageing society, a more active retirement sector. Increasingly maritime local authorities in the UK are also turning to maritime heritage to rekindle interest in the urban waterfront. Examples are Portsmouth Harbour, Liverpool Docks, Chatham Docks, Bristol Waterfront and Port Leith in Edinburgh. Much of this regeneration centres on what Pinder and Smith (1999) termed 'animating the environment', using a mix of vessels, heritage and waterfront competition.

Challenges now facing UK coastal recreation

A number of challenges, which will demand the attention of coastal recreation managers in the foreseeable future, can be identified as a consequence of the trends described above. These are overcrowding due to access limitations; conflicts of interest associated with multiple users resulting in safety concerns; and issues related to new technology; environmental integrity; climate change and future funding.

A result of the popularity of specific coastal locations is seasonal over-crowding. Depending on weather and water conditions, visitor numbers can exceed physical and perceptual carrying capacity. This causes congestion, resulting in travel delays, crowded beaches, restricted access to the water and at peak times too many people on and in the water. Participation trends and activity preferences are set to exacerbate this problem. The demand for access is also making some recreational activities increasingly exclusive. For example, on the south coast a planning presumption against the expansion of marina facilities has resulted in a shortfall of supply against demand. Typically in the popular estuaries there are currently eight-year waiting lists for moorings and prices reflect the level of demand. The challenge is therefore to create better access and more opportunities for coastal recreation, while at the same time warding off concerns about the intensity of leisure activities damaging the physical and social environment (Clark *et al.*, 1994).

Crowding can also lead to conflict between activities. New sports often give rise to new problems and, in particular, safety is a major concern for coastal recreation (May, 1996). An important ingredient of water-based recreation is 'freedom of activity', but a combination of competition for space and new technology is raising the potential for conflict, whilst the time available to avert problems is being reduced. The relatively new sport of kite boarding (or kite surfing), for example, where participants are using kites operated by up to 30 metres of high tensile string, cannot be zoned. Kite board lines trail downwind and have the potential to bruise arms and slice ears. Furthermore participants are moving at up to 20 knots, performing jumps and stunts! Typically new technology is making it easier for more people to go quicker on the water, but many inexperienced participants are on the edge of 'out of control'.

The House of Commons Environment Committee review of the impacts of leisure activities on the environment (HM Government, 1995) also recognized that certain new activities challenge cultural perceptions of how the natural environment should be enjoyed. Personal watercraft, for example, currently present a particular management challenge. They are intrusive, potentially dangerous to other activities and their use in the UK is currently largely unrestricted. Arguments have been presented for maintaining freedom for individuals and counter-arguments that favour compulsory training, licensing and selective bans (Johnson and Anderson, 1998). The water sports industry is keen to broker voluntary solutions. To be successful, coastal zone managers must fully understand the requirements of developing high-tech recreational activities, such as personal watercraft, which are perceived to threaten the existing status quo.

French (1997) highlighted the pollution of seas in coastal areas, caused by large influxes of people, as a key challenge posed by coastal tourism and recreation. In turn environmental integrity has an impact on participation and choice of location for recreation. Failure to comply with environmental standards will increasingly influence participants' choice of recreation location. Best practice in beach management, improving bathing water and access for the disabled were the major issues under discussion at the year 2000 Blue Flag Beach Management Conference. Of these recreational water quality is perhaps the most contentious. Pressure groups, such as Surfers Against Sewage, continue to draw attention to the need for improvement. Campaigners would like managers to look beyond compliance with water quality standards to consider how public health is protected. In this respect, requiring coastal local authorities to provide reliable, real-time, water quality information at beaches used for recreation is a key challenge associated with the revision of the EC Bathing Waters Directive. Historically, poorly managed coastal tourism has exceeded environmental carrying capacity as a result of unsustainable practices, such as poor waste disposal, resulting in despoliation of destinations. Adverse impacts of coastal recreation include noise, wildlife disturbance, collection of curios and parts of wrecks, leakage of hydrocarbons, sewage discharge, damage by irresponsible divers, litter and traffic fumes. Despite action and raised awareness problems persist. Thus, whilst over half of UK beaches were included in the 2003 Good Beach Guide, the Marine Conservation Society (MCS) tenth annual Beachwatch report, based on 2002 data, indicated a significant and disturbing long-term increase in beach litter volumes (http://www.mcsuk.org).

Another major consideration, which will affect all aspects of coastal management in the UK, is relative sea-level rise and the associated effects of global warming. These phenomena will benefit some recreational activities but restrict others. Relative sea-level rise will disproportionately affect the south and south-east of England, where the combination of isostatic uplift and eustatic sea-level rise are predicted to result in an increased frequency of extremely high sea-levels (Bray *et al.*, 1997). The concern in terms of coastal recreation is for low-lying clubs, beaches that will become steeper and narrower, and erosion of paths and access to the foreshore. The predicted increased frequency of high winds and stormy seas may benefit extreme sports, but other more established activities will need to reassess their position. For example, beaches in exposed areas are likely to become less stable, requiring additional and more frequent beach nourishment or sediment replacement. Some local authorities and landowners are already investing in defending coastal golf course facilities and the future effects of climate change on coastal courses was a key element of a recent conference hosted by the Royal and Ancient Golf Club of St Andrews (Barratt, 2000).

Finally, competition for limited funding is likely to bedevil regeneration of British seaside resorts and thus the ambitions of individual resorts to attract visitors. Inevitably the best-located and managed attractions will win out. There are signs in some areas that the renaissance of maritime heritage in already in trouble. A number of ambitious plans are on hold.

Local government is looking to 'best value', which cynically might be rein-terpreted as 'a smaller cake, more slices' syndrome.

Opportunities and directions

A combination of demand, economic incentives and new technology has the ability to increase opportunities for access to coastal leisure opportun-ities, as can be illustrated by the following three potential areas of develop-ment. The first is the proactive development of 'brown coast/sea' sites, involving encouragement for cleaning up and making use of despoiled areas combined with ecological restoration. This has been achieved with spectacular success in other parts of the world. For example, Heron Island, part of the Great Barrier Reef, has been transformed from a turtle cannery to an exclusive playground. In other words, we have the ability to create the right conditions for leisure where they do not currently exist. Such developments must be fully integrated with coastal processes unlike previous attempts to construct beaches or deep-water facilities, which have often been at the expense of coastal instability. An example of future developments of this nature is the UK's first artificial offshore reef struc-ture designed as a coastal recreation benefit, proposed by Bournemouth Borough Council in 1999/2000. The proposal, which will create calm lagoon-like conditions in the summer and surf conditions from October to April, has been subject to public consultation and appropriate scrutiny by independent coastal engineers.

Second, access can be improved by bringing marine interest to land-based visitors. The following examples illustrate ways in which this can be achieved:

- In the United States hazard free, man-made inland beaches have been constructed miles away from the coast. Incorporating wave pools, imported sand, palm trees and infrared heat, facilities such as The Island Kingdom in Denver, located in a former warehouse, allow vis-itors the opportunity to surf and tan well away from the ocean! Typhoon Lagoon in Disney World, Orlando features snorkelling expe-ditions among small sharks and stingrays providing safe thrills. This concept, also using an optical illusion that magnifies specimens, is under consideration by Center Parcs for their holiday village complex at Longleat in Wiltshire. The introduction of standing waves, uphill flume rides and thrill inducing swirling plunges, as installed in Bas-ingstoke's leisure pool, have responded to young people's lust for 'perceived danger' (Ives, 2003);
- Virtual experiences such as IMAX screening of whales, surfing a tube, or being at the scene of a sea battle offer tremendous potential to inspire and involve large audiences;
- Interactive computer techniques allow individuals access to specialist

marine environments such as the opportunity to investigate one of the 30,000 wrecks around the English coast; and

- Marine aquaria are increasingly providing education and interpretation, capturing their visitors' imagination, as part of a recreational experience.

Third, there is the option of moving coastal recreation and tourism offshore. The continued growth of cruise tourism, with ships equipped as floating hotels offering more amenities and more choice, will offer a leisure experience in which the ship becomes the destination. Accommodating large numbers in a confined, strictly controlled, water-based environment is arguably a highly sustainable option (Johnson, 2002a). Cruise ships dedicated exclusively to health and fitness are currently being built and the 'America World City Project' envisages a huge ship with a complement of 8,600 passengers and crew. A more futuristic but entirely plausible concept is the development of floating ocean 'villages' or resorts. Such resorts would offer accommodation above and below the water. They would also provide every conceivable leisure bolt-on including micro submarines. Imagine sending the children to kids' club while you set off before lunch in a highly manoeuvrable one-person submarine, capable of exploring depths to 1,000 metres!

In order to reduce and avoid conflict between coastal recreation activities, studies are needed to determine recreational capacities for individual locations. New technology, however, is requiring more dedicated space. For example, competitive windsurfing courses demand 3 km reach top and bottom, 1,500 m beat and run, and the windsurfers themselves adopt a 50–55 degree angle of attack reaching speeds of over 30 knots. Coastal recreation managers must establish new safety margins. Thus, for example, Chichester Harbour has recently produced a Navigational Safety Guidance Note, which states 'high speed sailing dinghies should have due regard for slow moving vessels which may be unable to respond in sufficient time to keep clear'. Strict spatial and temporal management (Kenchington, 1993) is likely to remain the most effective solution, with high levels of policing and charging in order to maintain standards of safety and environmental quality. This will also require clear and unambiguous information, advice and professional support. The Exe Estuary Partnership, for example, responding to safety concerns, has drawn up a Kite Boarding Code of Conduct and Risk Assessment (http://www.exe-estuary. org). In many ways the future estuary could operate like a contemporary leisure centre with a restricted booking system for water-based activities. It is ironic, given acceptance of 'right to roam' in the UK on land, that the universal right of navigation may have to be tempered.

In the twenty-first century water sports will continue to embrace new technology and materials. Use of carbon fibre, which is light and strong, is likely to transfer from the elite to the everyday equipment. Personal watercraft are perhaps the start of a future direction, away from clubs to personal access and mobility. Increasingly participants want controlled risks, equivalent to a marine fairground ride – the wetter the better and on film! This mix of thrill-seeking and exploration is perceived as offering a sense of immediate achievement. It represents a change of pace from sedentary lifestyles and a new relationship with natural world. As part of 'coasteering' in Pembrokeshire, for example, participants explore headlands and bays the alternative way, traversing cliffs and jumping into the sea.

Future opportunities for coastal recreation are also inextricably linked to sustainable management of coastal resources. This will involve partnerships and co-operation between a wide range of stakeholders. The twenty-first century will continue to witness increasing consumer consciousness regarding environmental issues. Studies into beach user preferences, for example, have shown strong links to environmental factors (Young *et al.*, 1996), and the Blue Flag eco-label is in great demand from beach operators and is well recognized (although not necessarily fully understood) by beach users. The total of 105 UK Blue Flag awards won in 2003 was almost double the awards given out in 2000. Increasingly marine environmental improvements and sustainable solutions are being demanded. Thus, for example, since 1998 there has been a legal requirement for all UK ports, including harbours and marinas, to implement waste management planning (Ball, 1999). In 2000 the British Marine Industries Federation (BMIF) produced a revised and updated Environmental Code of Practice, and resistance from industry to the introduction of more stringent controls, such as improvements to noise and exhaust emissions from recreational craft (MBM, 2000), is, in the author's opinion, putting off the inevitable. The popularity of ecotourism activities, such as visits to the seabird colonies of the Farne Islands, is also set to grow (Johnson, 2002b).

Finally the Energy Change Unit at Oxford University predicts a sunnier summer Mediterranean climate for the UK with attendant lifestyle change. Whilst the challenges associated with unpredictable winter weather and relative sea-level rise have already been discussed, a technical report into the impacts of climate change in the South-East in the twenty-first century (Wade *et al.*, 1999) also identified opportunities. Potential benefits are associated with regeneration of resorts on the basis of a more favourable and predictable 'British summer'. Beaches and water sports would become even more popular. For an ageing society this could also prompt a renaissance of more passive holidays and the sort of café society currently associated with Southern Europe. Alternatively, if melt waters from the Arctic ice cap stall the Gulf Stream as some predict (Alley, 2000), temperatures in Britain could drop dramatically and we could be racing skidoos across the North Sea!

Conclusions

On the basis of the discussion above the following conclusions are presented by way of answers to the questions posed in the introduction to this chapter. They draw on basic sustainability concepts including the need for long-term planning, social equity, environmental value and quality of life.

First, coastal recreation will demand new space, created by regulatory, socio-economic and technological solutions, in which land and ocean attractions both have a part to play. Potential answers can be found in forms of coastal recreation, which although they currently seem novel, are already being pioneered in other parts of the world. The emphasis of this discussion has been on extending physical access, but social access to coastal recreation for ethnic minorities, those with disabilities and different social groups also needs more thought. The challenges identified, particularly relative sea-level rise, are likely to encourage leisure investment for mass participation in lower risk, more predictable environments. These may be largely self-contained and increasingly remote from the real world of coast and ocean. Taking large numbers away from the coast, however, will allow traditional activities to continue.

Sound management, including strict spatial and temporal zoning, will be required to meet safety standards for active water-based coastal recreation. Purchasing of 'exclusive', 'private' facilities in the most desirable locations, as currently practised by a number of hotel chains and cruise companies, suggests that equity of coastal recreation provision is a future issue that will need to be addressed. The twenty-first century is likely therefore to witness increasing tensions between the private and public sectors.

Increasingly young participants will be involved in fun, fast-fix, 'frightening' activities involving 'controlled risk'. This preference partly explains the enduring pre-eminence of Blackpool as Britain's most popular and enduring seaside resort, with its selection of white-knuckle roller coaster rides – in addition to the ever popular illuminations, ballroom dancing and fish and chips! Hi-tech water sports offering similar experiences on and in the water must be similarly integrated with existing, more traditional activities. Coastal recreation managers will have to meet the increasingly diverse demands of both young and old.

Finally a new forward-planning agenda, which places the environment first and which recognizes the need to anticipate climate change, will be needed to redevelop existing coastal recreation facilities. This will be driven by public demand but ultimately it must also respect and incorporate natural coastal processes, harness new technologies, incorporate the range of established leisure activities and continue to satisfy our desires to enjoy being beside, on, in and under the sea.

References

Agarwal, S. (2002) 'Restructuring seaside tourism – the resort lifecycle', *Annals of Tourism Research* 29: 1, 25–55.

Alley, R.B. (2000) *The Two-mile Time Machine: Ice Cores, Abrupt Climate Change and Our Future*. Princeton, New Jersey: Princeton University Press.

Anderson, J., Savill, T., Andrews, R., Edwards, C. and Harris, I. (1996) *National Youth Watersports Audit*. BMIF/Southampton Institute.

Ball, I. (1999) 'Port waste reception facilities in UK Ports', *Marine Policy* 23, 4–5: 307–27.

Barratt, M.F. (ed.) (2000) *On Course for Change: Tackling the Challenges Facing Golf in the First Decades of the New Millennium*. Report of a conference held in February 2000 at the Royal and Ancient Golf Club of St Andrews, Scotland.

Bray, M.J., Hooke, J.M. and Carter, D.J. (1997) 'Planning for sea-level rise on the south coast of England: advising the decision-makers', *Transactions of the Institute of British Geographers* NS, 22: 13–30.

Clark, G., Darral, J., Grove-White, R., Macnaghtoen, P. and Urry, J. (1994) *Leisure, Culture and the English Countryside: Challenges and Conflicts*. Lancaster University/CPRE.

Department for Culture, Media and Sport Tourism Division (1999) *Tomorrow's Tourism: a Growth Industry for the New Millennium*. London: DCMS.

Department of Environment, Transport and the Regions (1999) *Code of Practice on Conservation, Access and Recreation: Consultation Draft*. Department of the Environment, Transport and the Regions, April 1999.

French, P.W. (1997) *Coastal and Estuarine Management*. London: Routledge.

Geographical (2000) 'Pier pressures', *Geographical Magazine* 2000: 14–22.

Goodhead, T.J. and Johnson, D.E. (eds) (1996) *Coastal Recreation Management: the Sustainable Development of Maritime Leisure*. London: E & FN Spon.

Guardian (1999) 'Call of the wild', the *Guardian*, 9 June 1999.

Hall, C.M. and Page, S.J. (1999) *The Geography of Tourism and Recreation: Environment, Place and Space*. London: Routledge.

Hampson, P. (2000) 'UK seaside resorts – behind the façade', *Inland, Coastal, Estuarine Waters* 4: June/July, 6–7.

HM Government (1995) *The Environmental Impact of Leisure Activities*. House of Commons Environment Committee Session 1994–95 HC246-1. London: HMSO.

Ives, J. (2003) 'Pools: design trend "what next for leisure water?"', *Leisure Manager* 21: 3, 22–4.

Johnson, D.E. (2002a) 'Environmentally sustainable cruise tourism: a reality check', *Marine Policy* 26: 261–70.

Johnson, D.E. (2002b) 'Towards sustainability: a critical evaluation of coastal tourism in the UK', in Harris, R., Griffin, T. and Williams, P. (eds) *Sustainable Tourism: A Global Perspective*. Butterworth Heinemann: 167–79.

Johnson, D.E. and Anderson, J. (1998) 'Conflict resolution in the coastal zone: a review of the UK personal watercraft problem', in Monso de Prat (ed.) *Sustainable Waterfront and Coastal Developments in Europe*. Littoral 98 Eurocoast Spain: 43–9.

Kenchington, R. (1993) 'Tourism in coastal and marine environments – a recreational perspective', *Ocean and Coastal Management* 19: 1–16.

Lane, P. (2000) 'Tourism and resort action plans – identifying a methodology', in

Fleming, C.A. (ed.) *Coastal Management: Integrating Science, Engineering and Management.* London: Thomas Telford, pp. 219–27.

May, V. (1996) 'Marine recreation: innovations and impacts and their implications for coastal management', in Taussik, J. and Mitchell, J. (eds) *Partnership in Coastal Zone Management.* Cardigan: Samara Publishing, pp. 251–7.

MBM (2000) 'Emissions impossible', *Motor Boat Monthly* October: 50–2.

Orams, M. (1999) *Marine Tourism: Development, Impacts and Management.* London: Routledge.

Pinder, D. and Smith, H. (1999) 'Animating the environment: vessels, heritage and waterfront competition', *Ocean and Coastal Management* 42: 861–89.

Ratcliffe, T. (1992) 'Responsibility for water sports management development', *Ocean and Coastal Management* 18: 259–68.

Royal Institution of Chartered Surveyors (2000) *20:20 Vision for the Future.* London: RICS.

Sailing Today (2000) 'Two UK charter firms sink', *Sailing Today* April: 22.

Young, C., Barugh, A., Morgan, R. and Williams, A.T. (1996) 'Beach user perceptions and priorities at the Pembrokeshire Coast National Park, Wales, UK', in Taussik, J. and Mitchell, J. (eds) *Partnership in Coastal Zone Management.* Cardigan: Samara Publishing, pp. 111–18.

Wade, S., Hossell, J., Hough, M. and Fenn, C. (eds) (1999) *The Impacts of Climate Change in the South-East: Technical Report.* Epsom: WS Atkins.

9   Coastal zone law in the UK

Lessons for the new millennium

John Gibson

Introduction

The process of coastal management inevitably raises questions of law. Law provides the statutory powers and duties of the various authorities and agencies involved in the administration of the coast, and it defines the legal rights and responsibilities of the stakeholders who use that area. However, law is neither the sole nor a sufficient determiner of human activity, and its role in coastal management is a complementary one. The influence of law may also be both positive and negative; although ideally it should support the implementation of policy and prevent the occurrence of unwanted events, it also possesses a potential to produce the opposite result. Unless the nature and role of law in the coastal zone are properly understood, and its strengths and limitations appreciated, it may become an impediment rather than an instrument of progress.

A decade has now passed since the House of Commons Environment Committee urged the United Kingdom government to improve the protection and planning of British coastal zones (House of Commons Environment Committee, 1992). The intervening years have witnessed a steady stream of non-statutory measures in the form of consultation papers, reviews, strategies, plans and guidance. Yet in this sea of policy initiatives, law has remained a remote and largely unchanging feature, whose omnipresence in the background is more often seen as a hazard to be avoided than a welcome port of call. The purpose of this chapter is to assess the validity of that perception. It examines the impact of law on the effectiveness of coastal management in the United Kingdom, and considers what lessons may be learned from past experience in order to harness the benefits and avoid the pitfalls of law in the new millennium.

The problematic legal framework

It is important at the outset to recognize that most of the laws which apply to the coastal zone of the United Kingdom were originally created for purposes that have nothing to do with the ideals of integrated management.

They are also derived from a wide variety of sources that compounds their characteristic diversity. It is, indeed, a fiction to refer to 'coastal zone law' as if it constituted a coherent and self-contained body of legal principles; instead, it is composed of elements drawn from common law, statute, local and subordinate legislation, European Community law and international legal instruments.

The legacy of property

At the foundations of the legal framework lie traditional rules of common law dealing with the ownership of land and the existence of public and private rights, which originated in the medieval period and reflect the legacy of the feudal system. Thus, the UK coastal zone is sub-divided by tidal property boundaries that are based on the historic extent of the Crown's title to the foreshore and sea bed. The Norman conquest of England in the eleventh century vested land in the king, which was subsequently distributed to subjects through feudal tenure, with the result that any land not granted in this way remained Crown property. Soil that was permanently or intermittently submerged by the sea lacked agricultural value, and so was less likely to be included in medieval grants of feudal manors. This has enabled the Crown since the sixteenth century to assert claims to residual ownership of the inter-tidal foreshore, which became valuable with the growth of land reclamation and subsequently of submarine mining for coal and tin. The assertion of these property rights was intensified in the nineteenth century when the hereditary estates of the sovereign were transferred the management of the Commissioners of Woods, Forests and Land Revenues by the Crown Lands Acts 1810 and 1829. The Crown Estate Commissioners, who are the modern successors to this body, still own approximately half of all the foreshore of the United Kingdom.

The identification of the legal boundary between Crown foreshore and private land above high water mark inevitably gave rise to disputes, which the courts resolved in a compromise that applies the criterion of an average tide line.[1] Unfortunately, a desire to provide equity between competing claimants has resulted in an arbitrary, invisible and somewhat impractical boundary that divides rather than integrates the ownership of the coast. The situation is also complicated by the decision of the Scottish courts to adopt a different standard in Scotland based on mean spring tides.[2] There has been less litigation about the ownership of the territorial sea bed beyond low water mark, but the Scottish Court of Session has ruled that it is also Crown property, although the basis for this is sovereignty rather than feudal tenure.[3] In March 2003, the Scottish Law Commission recommended that the present extent of the Crown's title to the foreshore and sea bed in Scotland should be defined by statute, and published a draft bill to achieve this, although it has not yet been implemented (Scottish Law Commission, 2003).

The presumption of Crown property in the foreshore has not prevented the recognition of extensive claims by private landowners, whose title is derived from feudal grants; in other places, particular beaches are also owned by local authorities, port authorities or the National Trust. The Crown Estate Commissioners have statutory powers to transfer Crown land under the Crown Estate Act 1961, although they normally create leases and licences rather than permanently dispose of the foreshore. However, the Crown Estate Act has an essentially land-based focus, and it does not make separate provision for the coastal and marine estate. Further complications arise in the Duchy of Cornwall, where the heir to the throne is *prima facie* owner of the foreshore, and in the Duchy of Lancaster, where it belongs to the sovereign. The ownership of the sea bed beyond low water mark is generally simpler, but the Crown's title is occasionally displaced in estuaries, including the Thames and parts of the Severn.

A peculiar feature of Crown foreshore and sea bed in England and Wales has been its exclusion in the past from the system of registration of title, since, for historical reasons, land held in demesne by the Crown as ultimate feudal overlord could not be registered. This made such land particularly vulnerable to encroachments by squatters, who were able to acquire title to it by occupation, despite the Crown's ignorance of their presence. Following recommendations by the Law Commission (Law Commission, 2001), this anomaly has recently been addressed in the Land Registration Act 2002,[4] which will enable the Crown in future to grant itself a registrable freehold estate in demesne land, including the intertidal foreshore and some parts of the sea bed under internal waters. Squatters will be required to apply to the Land Registry in order to register claims based on 60 years' adverse possession of those areas; the Crown Estate Commissioners or the relevant Duchy will then be notified, and will have two more years in which to recover their property.[5] In such piecemeal ways, some of the historical anomalies associated with Crown property in the foreshore and sea bed are gradually being addressed, but the fundamental principles remain largely unchanged.

Public and private rights

Irrespective of the ownership of the coastal zone, members of the public engage in activities there for recreational or commercial purposes, which are popularly assumed to reflect a legal entitlement. The common law confers general public rights to navigate and fish in tidal waters, and although their exercise may be restricted by legislation, regulatory measures need legal justification. Navigation and fishery are historic rights of economic necessity, and are clearly supported by case law. However, other popular activities, such as sea bathing and beachcombing, lack legal authority because they do not have the same original basis.

The common law, which is expressed in the decisions of judges, has a dynamic capacity to adapt in order to meet new situations, but it can only do so if an issue is disputed in the courts. Consequently, the common law is reactive, and is replete with gaps and uncertainties. For example, it was not until 1993 that the High Court decided that bait-digging for personal use is included in the public right of fishing.[6] Likewise, it was belatedly held in 1997 that the right to collect shellfish on the submerged foreshore continues to exist when tide is out.[7] More recently, the ability of a foreshore owner to charge yachtsmen for fixed moorings has been found to be displaced if it is inconsistent with the statutory power of a port authority to regulate mooring in the same place.[8] Sometimes, however, judicial decisions may generate new problems in the process of solving existing ones. Thus, in a case concerning compensation for an injured jet-skier, it was legally determined that personal water craft are not vessels, and that navigation requires planned movement from one place to another for the purpose of transporting persons or cargo; although it was not the intention behind the particular judgment, one might now question the compatibility of some recreational boating with the public right of navigation.[9] The common law also supports the legality of private rights of fishing in particular places, which supersede the public right, but the courts have held that they must be proved or presumed to have been created by the Crown before the year 1189.[10] The modern relevance of this archaic principle is clearly limited, but a number of such rights nevertheless continue to exist in relation to salmon and shellfish.

In view of the uncertain nature of common law public rights over the foreshore and sea bed, the Scottish Law Commission has now recommended that they should be abolished in Scotland, and replaced by more extensive statutory public rights, which would include most recreational activities and would also apply to the shore above high water mark (Scottish Law Commission, 2003: Part 3). However, this would produce some overlap with the new system of statutory public access rights created by the Land Reform (Scotland) Act 2003, which covers most open land, including the foreshore, but not the sea or its bed. No corresponding reform of the common law has yet been officially proposed in England and Wales, where the Countryside and Rights of Way Act 2000 excludes the foreshore and adjacent coastal land from statutory public rights of access, although it provides for the possibility of their inclusion in the future.[11] The legal distinctions between the treatment of these issues in different parts of the United Kingdom are thus being compounded.

The limits of planning law

Although legislation is usually more recent than the common law doctrines discussed above, one regularly finds legal principles transplanted from a context in which they once made sense, and then expected to do another job for which they are quite unsuited. One of the most criticized examples is the geographical extent of statutory planning control in the UK coastal zone. In England and Wales, land-use planning law generally ends at the mean low water mark; in Scotland the limit is mean low water springs, and in Northern Ireland it is the mean high water mark. Successive governments have declared their satisfaction with these diverse rules. And yet, the invisible tidal boundaries, which are seen only in the pictorial world created by map-makers, were never consciously chosen by Parliament as the logical frontiers of the planning realm, and are not even mentioned in planning legislation. Instead, they have arisen by an historical process of coincidence and accident. As has already been explained, the tidelines in question were first selected by judges in the nineteenth century to settle property disputes about the ownership of coastal land. They were then adopted for local government purposes in order to levy financial rates on private property, and so they also became the boundaries of local government areas. When planning control was introduced in the twentieth century, it was made a local authority function, and thus it automatically applied within the same jurisdictional limits. However, nobody thought about coastal boundaries at the time, or questioned whether they were suitable for this new purpose (Gibson, 1993).

When the law imposes such artificial constraints, it also inevitably stimulates people to search for ways of overcoming them. Although planning control stops at the land's end on the open coast, there is still the possibility that it may apply beyond low water mark in estuaries and other parts of the sea that are associated with the land and included in local government areas. That option, admittedly, was ruled out in Scotland by the Court of Session in 1976,[12] but the case was never appealed, and the reasoning is open to question. By contrast, in England and Wales, the government has stated on several occasions that local authority planning powers can be exercised anywhere inside local government boundaries.

The trouble is that estuarial boundaries and the few seaward extensions of local government areas have again not been chosen with planning in mind, and they vary dramatically in extent from place to place. It is also surprising how little use has been made of the opportunity to take advantage of them by local planning authorities, although there is a notable example of the former Avon County Council granting planning permission in 1993 for aggregate dredging in the middle of the Severn estuary.

Another obvious difficulty is that the planning system has been devised with land in mind rather than water, and to apply it to developments in the sea involves straining some of its basic concepts. In 1997, the Court of Appeal managed to hold that a floating helicopter pad in the tidal Thames, which was not attached to the riverbed, nevertheless involved development of the land under the water, and so needed planning permission.[13] In the same year, the Secretary of State for the Environment was faced with a proposal to station a prison ship, *Weir*, in the port of Portland.

As the ship was beyond low water mark, it was legally outside planning control, and the only development that needed his approval was some minor ancillary work on the shore. Nevertheless, the Secretary of State decided that the impact of the prison ship on the local area was still a factor which he was entitled to take into account when deciding whether to approve a fence and an office, and so indirectly he was making a planning decision about the acceptability of the ship itself. In such curious ways, developments beyond low water mark can sometimes become subject to planning procedures. However, subtleties of this kind only serve to disguise the unsuitability of the existing law, and they are no substitute for its reform. It is to be hoped that the current Review of Development in Coastal and Marine Waters, which was initiated by the Department for Transport in 2002, may at last confront such issues.

Statutory constraints

One of the most important, but invisible, legal influences on the process of integrated coastal management is the principle known to lawyers as *ultra vires*. This is a doctrine designed to prevent the abuse of power by public authorities, by rendering illegal any actions that exceed what they are expressly or impliedly authorized to do. Whereas private individuals can generally do anything they like unless there is a law to prohibit it, statutory bodies can do nothing at all unless there is a law expressly or impliedly to permit it. Effective coastal management depends on the co-operative involvement of stakeholders, including all the sectoral authorities with statutory responsibilities in the coastal zone; unfortunately, the safeguard of the *ultra vires* rule can sometime frustrate the ability of such bodies to work together for the public good in ways that were not envisaged when their legislation was drafted.

It was, for example, this principle that initially prevented sea fisheries committees from contributing to the protection of marine nature reserves in the early 1980s, because their statutory functions were defined in terms of promoting commercial fisheries (Gibson, 1988). Since then there have been selective amendments to legislation that have ameliorated the problem to some extent. Thus, the Environment Act 1995[14] empowers fishery ministers and local sea fisheries committees to make orders or by-laws for marine environmental purposes, and this has been used to benefit seabirds by banning dredging for razorshells in the Wash.[15] Likewise, harbour authorities and sewerage undertakers now have statutory duties to take account of environmental factors when deciding how to exercise their powers,[16] and so they can lawfully subordinate their primary interests in order to protect the environment. These, however, are essentially passive obligations that confer considerable discretion. Harbour authorities have also been given the positive opportunity to obtain by-law-making powers for nature conservation purposes,[17] but this too is elective, and few have chosen to take advantage of it; there are honourable exceptions at Langstone Harbour,[18] and also at Rum where Scottish Natural Heritage is the harbour authority,[19] but these are not typical commercial undertakings.

Another problematic area where reform is needed is the ability of local authorities to make by-laws regulating public recreational activities on coastal land and water. In England and Wales, this is still based on restrictive public health acts,[20] where the range of activities that can be controlled is limited, and the purpose of the by-laws must be to prevent nuisance or annoyance to other people; the government proposed the introduction of new legislation in 1998 to widen the scope of future by-laws, but nothing has been done so far done to implement this (DETR, 1998). In contrast, local authority by-laws in Scotland can already restrict public recreation for environmental as well as safety reasons,[21] and the Scottish Law Commission has recommended additional measures to regulate new statutory rights over the foreshore and sea bed in the future (Scottish Law Commission, 2003: 3.31–4). The powers and responsibilities of public authorities depend ultimately on law, and only legislative solutions can resolve many of their inherent deficiencies.

Lessons for the new millennium

The coastal zone is a dynamic environment, and the law concerning it must develop and adapt to meet new circumstances and needs. The complex range of issues with which the law must deal in this area inevitably leads to legal as well as practical difficulties, and it is easier to be critical than constructive about them. However, in addition to problems, there are also emerging trends that offer some positive encouragement and prospective opportunities for the future role of law in coastal management. Significantly, many of these have emerged at levels above or below that of national government.

The impact of European Community law

The obligations owed by the United Kingdom as a Member State of the European Union have an inevitable impact on domestic law, because they often require a legal response. In order to demonstrate formal compliance with EC directives, it is generally necessary to enact national legislation. European law also places new powers in the hands of stakeholders to police its implementation by governments through complaints to the European Commission and challenges in the courts. There are already many EC directives affecting the coastal environment, which exert a significant influence on the management of that area. These include sectoral measures on water quality, such as the Bathing Waters Directive 76/160/EEC, the Urban Waste Water Treatment Directive 91/271/EEC and the Nitrates Directive 91/676/EEC. The new Water Framework Directive 2000/60/EC is particularly relevant, since it requires the preparation of river basin management plans, which must cover estuaries and coastal waters up to one nautical mile from the baseline of the territorial sea. In addition, the Integrated Pollution Prevention and Control Directive 96/61/EC applies a holistic approach to the regulation of industrial activities that may pollute water, land and air.

Two European measures that have been especially influential are the Environmental Impact Assessment Directive 85/337/EEC and the Habitats Directive 92/43/EEC, both of which have prompted the UK government to transcend the legal as well as the physical divide between land and sea. National measures that were originally confined to land areas have gradually been extended to the sea in response to pressure from the European Commission and non-governmental organizations. Reluctantly and often belatedly, the United Kingdom has been compelled to introduce statutory environmental impact assessments for marine fish farming, offshore petroleum development and (prospectively) aggregate dredging, where previously non-statutory or informal methods have been preferred. In addition, the new Strategic Environmental Assessment Directive 2001/42/EC should enlarge this process to include environmental assessment of coastal plans and programmes, instead of concentrating exclusively on individual developments.

The implementation of the Habitats Directive was initially limited to areas inside the 12-mile limit of the territorial sea, but litigation by Greenpeace in the High Court successfully demonstrated that the Directive itself is equally applicable to the continental shelf.[22] As a result, the Department of Trade and Industry has now made the Offshore Petroleum Activities (Conservation of Habitats) Regulations 2001,[23] which apply the requirements of both the Habitats Directive and the Birds Directive 79/409/EEC to oil and gas development on the UK continental shelf; the government is also contemplating the designation of special areas of conservation there, which should increase the scope of protection to embrace any potentially damaging activities. Without the catalyst of European obligations, progress would have been markedly slower: a Private Member's Bill[24] to establish marine sites of special interest in the territorial sea around England and Wales was lost in 2002 through lack of parliamentary time, and the possibility of government legislation on this issue depends on the outcome of the Review of Marine Nature Conservation, which the Department for Environment, Food and Rural Affairs conducted between 1999 and 2004.

Although directives are the principal form of European legislation used for environmental purposes, other instruments are also employed. Thus, regulations are generally used to support the Common Fisheries Policy and the Common Agricultural Policy. Regulations have the advantage that they are directly applicable in Member States without being transposed in national legislation, although supplementary measures may be required to administer and enforce them. Another less common type of legal instrument that has recently been enlisted for ICZM is the EC recommendation. On 30 May 2002, the European Parliament and the Council of the European Union adopted Recommendation 2002/413/EC Concerning the Implementation of Integrated Coastal Zone Management in Europe. Despite its statutory character, a recommendation does not bind Member States, and only has advisory status. Nevertheless, Member States are expected to follow such formal advice, and the UK government has already begun the first stage of implementation.

The preamble to the ICZM Recommendation cites the diversity of national legal and institutional frameworks within Europe as a justification for guidance rather than binding legislation at community level. Chapter three urges Member States to conduct a national stocktaking exercise to analyse the major actors, laws and institutions that influence the management of their coastal zones. They should then develop national strategies under chapter four, in order to implement the principles of integrated management described in chapter two, and they should report on their experience by February 2006. The Recommendation does not seek to dictate the mechanisms to be adopted at national level, and it recognizes the need for a combination of instruments. However, law is clearly included among the available options, and the Recommendation suggests that land purchase, declarations of public domain and contractual agreements with coastal zone users should all be considered. It also advises that national, regional and local legislation should address both terrestrial and marine areas together, and it emphasizes the importance of full and co-ordinated implementation of relevant Community laws. In addition, the Recommendation advocates the use of international conventions between neighbouring countries to deal with cross-border issues.

The choice of an EC recommendation rather than a binding directive was a controversial decision, and the resulting text is inevitably a compromise between the concerns and ambitions of the Council and the European Parliament. It is too soon to judge the effectiveness of the measure, but it has at least stimulated a process of review. More worrying, perhaps, is the fact that Member States will be responsible for evaluating their own performance, and there is a risk that the traditional self-satisfaction of the UK government with its non-statutory approach to coastal management may encourage complacency and a reluctance to contemplate legislative reform. In its first Marine Stewardship Report published in 2002, the Department for Environment, Food and Rural Affairs maintained that the principles in the ICZM Recommendation were already part of the UK's approach to coastal policy (Defra, 2002a: 3.11), and the subsequent consultation paper on delivering its marine environmental strategy shows little enthusiasm for the option of new primary legislation (Defra, 2002b: 1.9–12).

The opportunities of devolution

The devolution of government in Scotland, Wales and Northern Ireland during the last six years has also created both opportunities and constraints for the process of coastal management in the United Kingdom. On the one hand, the constitutional and administrative structure has become more complex and fragmented; on the other, it has enabled new initiatives to be introduced on a regional basis with greater speed and originality than might have been achieved at national level.

Devolution requires boundaries to be drawn between sea areas that were previously attributed to the United Kingdom as a whole. Thus, the Scotland Act 1998,[25] the Government of Wales Act 1998[26] and the Northern Ireland Act 1998[27] all provide for these to be defined by Orders in Council. The Scottish Adjacent Waters Boundaries Order 1999[28] and the Adjacent Waters Boundaries (Northern Ireland) Order 2002[29] each divide both the 12-mile territorial sea and the 200-mile British fishery limits, and the allocation of fishing zones to England, Scotland and Northern Ireland has inevitably been controversial, since it concerns access to natural resources. In contrast, the National Assembly for Wales (Transfer of Functions) Order 1999[30] only defines common boundaries between England and Wales in the territorial sea. However, the method of delimitation, which is based on the model of international boundaries between sovereign states, has produced the anomalous result that part of England in the Severn estuary has inadvertently been awarded to Wales: a median line has been drawn between the islands of Steep Holm and Flat Holm in the middle of the estuary, which ignores the fact that this area is already inside the English local government boundaries of Bristol.

The borders between the constituent countries of the United Kingdom are located in the middle of estuaries, which need holistic management, but the process of devolution has instead reinforced their fragmented legal status. While this problem may be overcome by co-ordinated administrative policies, constitutional law is not itself contributing to that solution. The only legal provision for shared estuary management in the devolution measures is the creation of the Loughs Agency, which was established in 1999 under the Belfast Agreement, and is responsible for fisheries and marine resources in the Foyle and Carlingford areas of Northern Ireland and the Irish Republic. This, however, relates to the external rather than the internal relations of the United Kingdom.

Within the United Kingdom, the transfer of central government functions to devolved institutions has not been uniform, but there is greater similarity between Scotland and Northern Ireland, where all matters are transferred unless they are expressly excepted or reserved. Reserved matters include offshore oil and gas in Scotland and the foreshore and sea bed in Northern Ireland. In Wales, a reverse approach applies, whereby functions must be specifically transferred by Order in Council. The Welsh

Assembly has been given the previous statutory responsibilities of the Secretary of State for Wales; it has no powers to enact primary legislation, and may only make statutory instruments under Acts of the UK Parliament. Moreover, with the exception of a few matters relating to the abandonment of offshore installations, none of its functions are applicable beyond the 12-mile limit.

The devolved governments are also responsible for implementing some European Community legislation, particularly in relation to environmental protection and fisheries. However, this has led to increased delay in the fulfilment of European Community obligations compared with previous combined responses by the United Kingdom as a whole. In practice, the lead is often taken by government departments in England, with the other components of the United Kingdom following suit at a later date. Nevertheless, the situation now seems to be improving, and it is noteworthy that the Scottish Parliament was the first to implement the Water Framework Directive 2000/60/EC by enacting the Water Environment and Water Services (Scotland) Act 2003.

Perhaps the most positive aspect of devolution is the freedom that it offers for experimental initiatives to be pursued at a regional level without the need for central government approval. The Scottish Parliament and Executive have shown particular activity in this respect. For instance, the National Parks (Scotland) Act 2000[31] provides a statutory framework, which has no counterpart elsewhere in the United Kingdom, for the future designation of national parks in marine areas, although this opportunity has not yet been used. Another imaginative example is the Shetland Islands Regulated Fishery (Scotland) Order 1999,[32] which utilizes current statutory powers under the Sea Fisheries (Shellfish) Act 1967,[33] but applies them to a new context. Legal procedures for obtaining exclusive rights to manage shellfish beds have existed since the nineteenth century, but regulating orders have normally been sought by established authorities such as sea fisheries committees. This time, however, a special company – the Shetland Shellfish Management Organization – which represents a range of community interests including fishermen, local councils and Scottish Natural Heritage, was created specifically to promote an order empowering it to control fishing for shellfish within six miles of Shetland. This demonstrates how existing legal mechanisms may sometimes be used creatively for new purposes of coastal management, although the scope and flexibility of such opportunities are inevitably limited.

Devolved assemblies may also be able to circumvent the pressures on parliamentary time that often impede legislation at Westminster. An illustration is the Sea Fisheries (Shellfish) Amendment (Scotland) Act 2000, which enables compatible fishing methods for different species to be used within protected shellfish beds in Scotland, whereas a Bill to achieve the same result throughout Great Britain failed to be enacted by the UK

Parliament in 1999. On the other hand, legislative delay is not confined to central government, and a 1997 proposal to give Scottish local planning authorities statutory responsibility for overseeing the environmental impact assessment of fish farms beyond low water mark has yet to be implemented,[34] although the Orkney and Shetland Islands Councils have been given equivalent powers under the Environmental Impact Assessment (Fish Farming in Marine Waters) Regulations 1999.[35] The delay is regrettable, since this reform would constitute the first large-scale example of local planning jurisdiction in the sea, albeit a selective one; if the principle is conceded in this way, it should be harder to resist pressure for a more comprehensive role in the future.

The wind of change

One context in which the UK government as a whole has already acknowledged the need for legislative change is the development of offshore renewable energy, where an inadequate legal framework may otherwise impede the exploitation of those resources (DTI, 2002). Although the United Kingdom has claimed a continental shelf in accordance with international law since 1964,[36] it has not exercised its entitlement under Part V of the UN Convention on the Law of the Sea to a 200-mile exclusive economic zone, but has limited itself to an exclusive fishery zone instead. However, the sovereign rights of a state over its continental shelf relate only to the sea bed and subsoil, and so they exclude the natural resources of the water column and air space, including wind, wave and tidal power. In order to assert jurisdiction over renewable energy beyond the 12-mile territorial sea, the United Kingdom will need to enact primary legislation declaring either an exclusive economic zone (which would include all living and non-living natural resources) or a more restricted 200-mile renewable energy production zone.

The statutory regime that currently governs offshore windfarms inside the 12-mile limit was not designed for that purpose, and reforms are needed to rationalize complex and overlapping procedures. There are several different ways in which windfarms may be authorized, but the basic method involves consents under the Electricity Act 1989 and the Coast Protection Act 1949. However, these do not protect a developer against potential actions for public nuisance arising from interference with the rights of navigation and fishing,[37] and so alternatively a statutory order may be sought under the Transport and Works Act 1992. Another approach is to promote a Private Parliamentary Bill authorizing the obstruction of public rights, such as the Robin Rigg Offshore Windfarm (Navigation and Fishing) (Scotland) Bill, which was passed by the Scottish Parliament in June 2003. In all cases, a lease of the sea bed is also required, together with a licence under the Food and Environment Protection Act 1985, and other permissions will be necessary in some situations. In an attempt to simplify applications, a Marine Consents and Environment Unit was established in April 2001, in order to provide a single point of contact for multiple offshore consents in England and Wales. Although this only co-ordinates procedures administered by the Department for Environment, Food and Rural Affairs and the Department for Transport, it also provides advice about other authorizations. Nevertheless, it addresses the symptoms of a problem, rather than the cause, which is rooted in the inherent inadequacy of the law. Only legislation can remove such defects, and provide a coherent regulatory system for both the territorial sea and a 200-mile zone.[38]

Conclusion

This chapter has examined some of the ways in which law influences the management of the coastal zone in the United Kingdom. It is clear that irrespective of whether one supports a statutory or non-statutory approach to coastal management, law is an element that will always have to be taken into account. The current administrative system depends on a complex framework of independent legal provisions, which have accrued over a long period, yet are now expected to operate harmoniously in support of new policy objectives. This inevitably places a considerable strain on the capacity of law to adapt dynamically in response to changing circumstances. Common law principles of Crown property and public rights, which originated in the Middle Ages, still determine ownership and access in the coastal zone. They have been supplemented by layers of sectoral legislation that reflect rather than replace the historic concepts of the common law, and entrench the jurisdictional dichotomy between land and sea. Such legislation also erects barriers between the functions of statutory authorities, which can create impediments to co-operation and efficient administration. These problems have so far been approached in an *ad hoc* manner rather than in a comprehensive way, and so new examples inevitably continue to emerge.

A popular perception of law is that it is primarily concerned with regulation and compulsion. However, law can also be an instrument of facilitation with the power to support initiatives as well as the capacity to hinder them. If its strengths and weaknesses are appreciated, there are opportunities to use law as a positive force for coastal management. The UK government, however, still remains wary of legislative reforms in the coastal zone. At the moment, the best examples of the creative use of law are emerging not within central government, but at the opposite extremes of supranational European Community law and the regional legislation of the devolved institutions.

Notes

1 Attorney-General v. Chambers (1854) 43 *English Reports* 486.
2 Fisherrow Harbour Commissioners v. Musselburgh Real Estate Co. Ltd (1903) 5 *Fraser* 387.
3 Shetland Salmon Farmers v. Crown Estate Commissioners (1991) *Scots Law Times* 166.
4 Section 79.
5 Land Registration Act 2002, Sch. 6, para. 13.
6 Anderson v. Alnwick District Council (1993) 3 *All England Reports* 613.
7 Adair v. National Trust (1998) *Northern Ireland Law Reports* 33.
8 Ipswich Borough Council v. Moore, *Times Law Report*, 25 October 2001.
9 Steedman v. Scofield (1992) 2 *Lloyd's Law Reports* 163.
10 Malcomson v. O'Dea (1863) 11 *English Reports* 1155.
11 Countryside and Rights of Way Act 2000, s. 3.
12 Argyll and Bute District Council v. Secretary of State for Scotland (1976) *Session Cases* 248.
13 Thames Heliport plc v. Tower Hamlets London Borough Council (1997) *Journal of Planning and Environment Law* 448.
14 Sections 102–3.
15 Razor Shells, Trough Shells and Carpet Shells (Specified Sea Area) (Prohibition of Fishing) Order 1998, S.I. 1998/1276.
16 Harbours Act 1964, s. 48A; Water Industry Act 1991, s. 3.
17 Harbours Act 1964, Sch. 2, para 16A.
18 Langstone Harbour Revision Order 1999, S.I. 1999/266.
19 Scottish Natural Heritage (Rum) Harbour Empowerment Order 1999, S.S.I. 1999/202.
20 Public Health Acts Amendment Act 1907, s. 82; Public Health Act 1936, s. 231; Public Health Act 1961, s. 76.
21 Civic Government (Scotland) Act 1982, s. 121; Land Reform (Scotland) Act 2003, s. 12.
22 R. v. Secretary of State for Trade and Industry, ex parte Greenpeace Ltd (2000) *Environmental Law Reports* 221.
23 S.I. 2001/1754.
24 Marine Wildlife Conservation Bill.
25 Section 126(2).
26 Section 155(2).
27 Section 98(8).
28 S.I. 1999/1126.
29 S.I. 2002/791.
30 S.I. 1999/672.
31 Section 31.
32 S.S.I. 1999/194.
33 Section 1.
34 The Water Environment and Water Services (Scotland) Act 2003, s. 24, provides for the extension of local authority planning control over fish farms up to the 3-mile limit, but this is not yet in force.
35 S.I. 1999/367.
36 Continental Shelf Act 1964.
37 Walford v. Crown Estate Commissioners (1988) *Scots Law Times* 377.
38 Since this chapter was written, the Energy Act 2004, Part 2, has introduced a new regime for renewable energy sources beyond the territorial sea.

References

Department for Environment, Food and Rural Affairs (2002a) *Safeguarding Our Seas*. London: Defra.

Department for Environment, Food and Rural Affairs (2002b) *Seas of Change: the Government's Consultation Paper to Help Deliver Our Vision for the Marine Environment*. London: Defra.

Department of the Environment, Transport and the Regions (1998) *Review of Bye-law Powers for the Coast: Report of the Inter-Departmental Working Group*. London: DETR.

Department of Trade and Industry (2002) *Future Offshore: a Strategic Framework for the Offshore Wind Industry*. London: DTI.

Gibson, J. (1988) 'Marine nature reserves in the United Kingdom', *International Journal of Estuarine and Coastal Law* 2: 328–39.

Gibson, J. (1993) 'Coastal zone planning law: role of law in the management of the coastal zone in England and Wales', *Marine Policy* 17: 118–29.

House of Commons Environment Committee (1992) *Coastal Zone Protection and Planning*, HC (1991–2) 17. London: HMSO.

Law Commission (2001) *Land Registration for the Twenty-first Century: a Conveyancing Revolution*. Law Commission 271. London: The Stationery Office.

Scottish Law Commission (2003) *Report on Law of the Foreshore and Sea Bed*. Scottish Law Commission 190. Edinburgh: The Stationery Office.

10 A sea change at the coast

The contemporary context and future prospects of integrated coastal management in the UK

Rhoda C. Ballinger

Introduction

Although the coast of the United Kingdom (UK) has been actively managed since Roman times for sea defence purposes, it is only in the last century that a range of additional priorities have forced a wider view of the coastal management process. Today, the coast of Great Britain and Northern Ireland is not only one of the most densely populated, but also one of the most diverse coasts in Europe. It ranges from the low-lying, sub-siding soft rock coasts of South-East England, where most of the urban development and associated infrastructure occur, to the highly indented and rocky shores of parts of western Britain, generally of a more rural character (Ballinger, 2002). This diversity presents a significant challenge to integrated coastal management (ICM). It necessitates a range of management approaches, from the maintenance of the conservation interests of a wide range of habitats, to the need to ensure that the huge development pressures within the major urbanized and industrialized estuaries, are dealt with in a sustainable manner and in the context of potential sea level change predictions. Further variations in the socio-economic, cultural heritage and political geography of the UK coasts add to the complexity of the ICM process in the UK.

After brief consideration of UK definitions of the coastal zone, the chapter outlines the legal and policy context for ICM development in the UK, focusing on both international and supranational as well as national influences. A summary of the evolution of ICM over the last century follows. Developments since the 1992 House of Commons Environment Select Committee Report *Coastal Zone Protection and Planning* (House of Commons Select Committee on the Environment: HOCESC, 1992) are explored in detail, updating and expanding the previous paper by this author on the evolution of ICM in England and Wales (Ballinger, 1999). The subsequent discussion of coastal management efforts considers the contrasting development and approaches of national, constituent home country, regional and local administrations as well as those of the private and voluntary sectors. With emphasis on the implications of the recent devolutionary process and the new institutional and administrative systems within the home countries, as well as on local level non-statutory partnership approaches, this chapter complements the previous paper by Ballinger (2002). In the final conclusion, the stage, status and future of ICM in the UK are discussed along with a brief evaluation of the extent to which UK ICM addresses European ICM principles.

Defining the UK coastal zone

Although there is no legal definition of the coastal zone, the UK has claimed a 12-nautical mile territorial sea and a 200-nautical mile exclusive fishing zone (Gibson, 2001a). Figure 10.1 shows the complexity of coastal jurisdictions, which mitigate against a clear coastal zone boundary. However, there are several generic definitions of the coastal zone in non-statutory guidance, including national guidance for the preparation of statutory development plans, as well as in many local coastal and estuary management programmes. Planning guidance definitions are restricted though by the seaward boundary of local authority jurisdiction, generally low water. As a result the extension of local authority powers, particularly for planning purposes, has been the subject of considerable debate over the last decade, especially in Scotland. Issues surrounding the impact and local accountability of offshore projects, including wind generation developments, the need for better integration between regulatory processes in territorial waters, and a desire for a more holistic approach to offshore

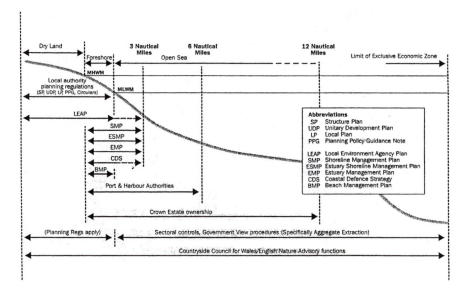

Figure 10.1 The onshore and offshore boundaries of coastal planning in England and Wales (modified from Countryside Council for Wales, 1996).

nature conservation, particularly following the implementation of the EU Habitats Directive, have fuelled such debate.

Legal and policy context

International and supranational law and policy

The law governing the administration and use of the UK coast is complex, derived from many legal sources at different jurisdictional levels (Gibson, 2001b). The UK is a signatory to many international legal and non-legal agreements, including some relating to general environmental and pollution matters in addition to others which are specifically marine (Table 10.1). At a 'regional sea' level, the UK is also party to a range of agreements relating to marine environmental protection, fisheries management, marine science, fisheries and ports, including the OSPAR Convention for the Protection of the Marine Environment of the Northeast Atlantic. European Community law and policy have, and will continue to have, a major influence on the state and management of the UK coast (EC, 1996 – XI/79/96). There is now a vast array of EC policy and legal instruments relating to pollution control, environmental protection and many coastal activities, including agriculture and most notably, fisheries. Within this, the influence of the 'Habitats' Directive (92/43/EEC) on coastal and particularly nearshore management cannot be underestimated, since it requires a more strategic overview of impacts of activities for many estuary and nearshore areas than previously undertaken. It also has forced many formerly unlikely 'bedfellows' to come together to participate in 'coastal' management for marine Special Areas of Conservation. In addition, the Strategic Environmental Assessment Directive (2001/42/EC) and the Water Framework Directive (2000/60/EC) will further enhance coastal environmental management. Meanwhile, a European Marine Strategy is being developed, focusing on marine biodiversity, fisheries, environmental protection and pollution control amongst other things.

Although coastal management had been on the European political agenda for at least 25 years (since the Council of Europe in 1973), a Recommendation on implementing integrated coastal zone management (ICZM) in Europe was only recently adopted by the European Union (on 30 May, 2002). Though not legally binding, this is likely to be an important catalyst for UK ICM development. It suggests that Member States should conduct or update an overall stocktaking to 'analyse which major actors, laws and institutions influence the management of their coastal zones', which then informs the development of a national strategy or strategies to implement integrated management of coastal areas in accordance with the EC's ICZM principles.

Table 10.1 International and supranational law and policy relating to ICM in the UK

International agreements of relevance
Non-marine/coastal specific agreements, include:
• The Convention of Biological Diversity (1992)
• The UN Framework Convention on Climate Change (1992)
• The Bonn Convention on the Conservation of Migratory Species of Wild Animals the Bern Convention on the Conservation of European Wildlife and Natural Habitats (1979)
• The Ramsar Convention on Wetlands (1971)
• Chapter 17 of Agenda 21 (1992: non-legal)

Marine specific conventions, include:
• The UN Convention on the Law of the Sea defines a comprehensive jurisdictional framework for oceans and seas
• London Convention on the Prevention of Marine Pollution by Dumping of Wastes and other Matter 1972 (including 1996 protocol)
• International Convention for the Prevention of Pollution from Ships (MARPOL) 1973/8
• International Convention on Oil Pollution Preparedness, Response and Co-operation (OPRC) 1990

Regional Sea agreements and international conferences of relevance
• OSPAR Convention for the Protection of the Marine Environment of the Northeast Atlantic
• The International Council for the Exploration of the Sea co-ordinating fisheries research in the North Atlantic
• The Paris Memorandum on Port State Control 1982
• International Conferences on the Protection of the North Sea (1984–)
• Irish Sea Conferences (1990 and 2000)

EC directives of relevance include:
• Environmental Impact Assessment Directives (85/337/EEC and 91/11/EEC)
• Freedom of Access to Information on the Environment Directive (90/313/EEC)
• Bathing Water Directive (76/160/EEC)
• Birds Directive (79/409/EEC)
• Dangerous Substances Directive (76/464/EEC)
• Habitats (and Species) Directive (92/43/EEC)
• Integrated Pollution Prevention and Control Directives (96/61/EC)
• Nitrates Directive (91/676/EEC)
• Shellfish Waters Directive (79/923/EEC)
• Urban Waste Water Treatment Directive (91/271/EEC)
• Strategic Environmental Assessment Directive (2001/42/EC)
• Water Framework Directive (2000/60/EC)

National legal and policy framework

The complexity and sectoral nature of UK primary legislation, which provides the statutory basis of the administration of coastal activities is well recognized (Gibson, 2001b). The report of the House of Commons Environment Select Committee report (HOCESC, 1992) noted over 80 Acts of Parliament relating to coastal matters in England and Wales alone.

Although there is no legal framework for ICM, *Policy Guidelines for the Coast* (DOE, 1995) has collated existing guidance developed under sectoral legislation for the English coast, and in Scotland the Scottish Coastal Forum has recently published a detailed overview of legislation relating to foreshore and seabed development (Cox, 2001a). Reference should also be made to Smith (2000) for a description of the roles and responsibilities of those national bodies involved in coastal and maritime affairs.

Some aspects of the administrative framework for coastal areas, dating back centuries and embedded in the UK's informal constitution, impede integrated management. These include the traditional property rights of the Crown, indirectly perpetuating a land/sea divide in coastal administration, and the long-standing *ultra vires* principle, requiring that statutory bodies only undertake matters expressly or implicitly authorized by the legislation under which they operate (Gibson, 1993). Significant changes to the UK constitution came about as a result of major reforms in the 1990s. These devolved many central government functions to the regional governments in Scotland, Northern Ireland and Wales (the Scottish Executive, Northern Ireland Assembly and the National Assembly for Wales). In coastal management terms, however, administrative devolution has been relatively limited and comparatively land-oriented at central government level. For example, UK central government departments, such as the Department of Trade and Industry, remain responsible for most marine affairs (particularly shipping and ports, defence, and oil and gas development) beyond territorial waters. Cox (2001b), Smith *et al.* (2001) and the Northern Ireland Executive (2001) provide a useful discussion of excepted and reserved matters from the devolved assemblies.

Evolution of ICM

The evolution of coastal management in the UK can be subdivided into several phases over the last century. Key events and developments are listed in Table 10.2, but for a detailed discussion of ICM development reference should be made to Ballinger (1999).

In the immediate post-WWII period institutional reform and restructuring provided visionary and long-standing national systems for development planning, nature conservation, landscape protection and access to the countryside (Sheail, 1976; Ballinger, 1999), profoundly influencing the planning and management of coastal areas. Further environmental despoliation of the coast led to the establishment of pioneering, but predominantly land-based nature conservation and landscape protection programmes, which over the last few decades have successfully protected much of the character of the UK's rural, open and rocky coasts. Of especial note are coastal land acquisition programmes of the National Trust, *Enterprise Neptune* (now called the *Neptune Coastline Campaign*), and the non-statutory heritage coast programme in England and Wales (Country-

Table 10.2 Selected key events in the development of coastal management in the
UK (1940s–2003)

Year	UK events
1940s	Surveys of the coasts of England and Wales undertaken by Professor J. Steers
1952	Only entirely coastal national park designated (Pembrokeshire Coast National Park)
1956	First Area of Outstanding Beauty designated (Gower)
1963	Government Circular to Local Authorities *Coastal Preservation and Development* (56/63)
1965	The National Trust's *Enterprise Neptune* campaign launched
1966	Government Circular *The coast* (7/66)
1968	*Torrey Canyon* incident
1970	*The Coastal Heritage and The Planning of the Coastline* (Countryside Commission)
1972	Government Circular *The planning of the undeveloped coast* (12/72)
1973	First Voluntary Marine Conservation Area established (Lundy)
	First Heritage Coast in England and Wales designated (Glamorgan)
	Coastal Planning Guidelines published for Scotland
	Zetland County Council Act and Orkney County Council Act
1982	*An evaluation of the Heritage Coast system in England and Wales* (Countryside Commission)
1984	1st North Sea Inter-Ministerial Conference (Bremen)
1986	1st Marine Nature Reserve declared (Lundy)
1987	2nd North Sea Inter-Ministerial Conference (London)
1989	Heritage Coast Forum established in England and Wales
	Sefton Conference: *Planning & Management of the Coastal Heritage*
	Scapa Flow Management Strategy published, one of the first UK ICM initiatives
1990	3rd North Sea Inter-Ministerial Conference (The Hague)
	1st International conference on the Irish Sea and establishment of the Irish Sea Forum
	Government publish *This Common Inheritance: Britain's Environmental Strategy*
	National Coasts and Estuaries Advisory Group (NCEAG) established
	A future for the coast? Proposals for a UK coastal zone management plan (Marine Conservation Society)
	Turning the tide: a future for estuaries (Royal Society for the Protection of Birds: RSPB)
1991	Coastal Defence Forum established by Welsh Office and Ministry of Agriculture Fisheries and Food
1992	*Coastal Zone Protection and Planning* (House of Commons Environment Select Committee Report)
	Coastal Planning (Planning Policy Guidance Note 20) Department of the Environment/Welsh Office
	English Nature launched its *Estuaries Initiative* as part of its *Campaign for the Living Coast*
	The National Trust's *Enterprise Neptune* campaign relaunched (*Coastline in Crisis*)

continued

Table 10.2 Continued

Year	UK events
1993	*Managing the coast: a review of coastal management plans in England and Wales and the powers supporting them* (Consultation paper) Department of the Environment/Welsh Office *Development Below Low Water Mark. A Review of Regulation in England and Wales* (Consultation paper) Department of the Environment/Welsh Office *Coastal planning and management: a review* (A report to the Department of the Environment; DoE) 1st annual national Coastal Management for Sustainability *Review and Future Trends Conference* *A good practice guide to coastal planning and management* (NCEAG) *A shore future. RSPB vision for the coast – The RSPB Save our Shoreline Campaign* Strategy for Flood and Coastal Defence in England and Wales/1st Shoreline Management Plan produced Scottish Natural Heritage launched its *Firths Programme*
1994	1st national coastal forum. The Coastal Forum (for England) established *Directory of coastal planning and management initiatives in England* (NCEAG)
1995	4th North Sea Inter-Ministerial Conference (Esbjerg) UK Government issued list of possible sites (including marine) for consideration as *Special Areas of Conservation Policy Guidelines for the Coast* (DoE) – for England 1st of regional *Coastal Directories* launched by the Joint Nature Conservation Committee Local Government Management Board produce guidance *Action on the coast*
1996	*Towards Best Practice Guidelines on CZM* (DoE) Byelaws Discussion Paper (DoE) Launch of CoastNET Scottish Coastal Forum launched *Seas, shores and coasts* CCW's Maritime Policy
1997	United Kingdom ratified United Nations Convention on Law of Sea on 25 July 1997 National Planning Policy Guidance 12 *Coastal Planning* NPPG13 published by Scottish Office Welsh Coastal Forum launched
1998	Report *'Cleaner Seas'* published by Defra Revision of procedures for licensing offshore aggregate dredging Scottish Office publishes *'Classifying the coast for planning purposes'* Planning Advice Note 53 *Review of byelaw powers for the coast* (Inter-departmental Group) House of Commons Select Committee on Agriculture report *Flood and Coastal Defence* Technical Advice Note (Wales) 14 *Coastal Planning* issued by the Welsh Office Report *Coastal management in Wales; looking to the future* published by CCW
1999	Thematic reports from the European Commission's demonstration projects on ICZM (European Commission, 1996–9) Towards sustainable estuary management (English Nature) *State of the environment of England and Wales*: coasts published (Environment Agency)

Table 10.2 Continued

Year	UK events
2000	Communication from the Commission to the Council and the European Parliament on *ICZM: a Strategy for Europe* A Review of Marine and Coastal Environmental Protection Legislation (The Wildlife Trusts and WWF-UK, 2000)
	A National Coastal Zone Management Strategy (Wildlife and Countryside Link)
	On the Edge – the coastal strategy (LGA)
	Review of Shoreline Management Plans 1996–9, Final Report (DETR)
	Coastal Strategy sub-group of the Scottish Coastal Forum set up to undertake preparation of a Scottish Coastal Strategy
	Scottish Coastal Forum website launched (September)
	North West Coastal Forum established
	Department for Transport publishes ports policy *'Modern ports: a UK policy'*
2001	*Review of Marine Nature Conservation Interim Report* (DETR)
	Shoreline Management Plans: a guide for coastal defence authorities (Defra)
	Regional Development Strategy *Shaping our Future* for Northern Ireland published (includes coastal reference)
	Role of Scottish Local Initiatives in Implementing the Principles of ICZM (Scottish Executive Report)
	Marine Consents and Environment Unit (Defra/Department for Transport)
2002	Fifth North Sea Inter-Ministerial Conference (Bergen)
	EC Recommendation on the implementation of ICZM (EC/2002/413/EC)
	EC Communication *Towards a strategy to protect and conserve the marine environment* (COM (2002) 539 final)
	Safeguarding Our Seas: the Government's Marine Stewardship report (Defra)
	Seas of change: the Government's consultation paper to help deliver our vision for the marine environment (Defra)
	Defra Conference *Marine stewardship and Integrated Coastal Zone Management* report of conference (14 November)
	Review of Development in Coastal and Marine Waters announced
	Irish Sea Pilot study commences (May 2002–March 2004)
	Quality Status Report of the Marine and Coastal Areas of the Irish Sea and Bristol Channel (Defra)
	Future Coast study predicts coastal change in England and Wales over the next 100 years
	Second round of shoreline management plans commences
	Coastal Futures (*Scotland*) first annual, Scottish conference on the coastal management
	State of Maritime Nature Report (English Nature)
	English Heritage's *Initial policy for the management of maritime archaeology in England*
	Wales Coastal and Maritime Partnership launched
2003	Work commences on UK ICZM National Stocktake
	CoastNET organizes workshop *Partnership approaches to ICZM: a vision and action plan* and publishes action plan
	Wildlife and Countryside Link publishes *Marine Spatial Planning for the UK*

Source: Ballinger, 1999.

side Commission, 1970). Concerns about offshore development, notably associated with the rise of the North Sea offshore hydrocarbon industry, also prompted ICM-related activity in Scotland, including *Coastal Planning Guidelines*, which provided a framework for the consideration of oil and gas-related onshore developments (Gubbay, 2001).

Alongside rapid urbanization and the associated littoralization of the population throughout the following decades there was increasing environmental awareness and a gradual adoption of modern environmental management principles by the government (Secretaries of State for the Environment and the Foreign and Commonwealth Office *et al.*, 1990). Such change was partly the result of the campaigns of an emerging and vociferous non-government organization (NGO) sector and, in the early years, by media coverage of events, such as the *Torrey Canyon* incident. With a gradual shift to a 'greener', more proactive and holistic view of environmental management, significant reorganization of administrative arrangements and organizational procedures has accompanied an overhaul of primary legislation (Ballinger, 1999), facilitating a more integrated approach to environmental, and in particular, pollution matters (Ballinger, 2002). These have included the formation of a new Department for Environment, Food and Rural Affairs (Defra), incorporating many responsibilities of the long-standing Ministry of Agriculture, Fisheries and Food with the former Department of the Environment, Transport and the Regions (DETR).

During the last two decades there has been a rekindling of both interest and practice in coastal management as it has moved away from a bias towards conservation and open, rocky cliffs to a more holistic approach covering a wider range of coastal, including estuary and shores, that is more in line with emerging ICM philosophy (Cicin-Sain and Knecht, 1998). Academics, local practitioners and NGOs have promoted a comprehensive and integrated approach (Halliday, 1986; Smith, 1991). Through a series of influential reports and the landmark 1989 Sefton Conference (Houston and Jones, 1990), these have questioned the adequacy of organizational arrangements for dealing with coastal affairs, highlighting the particular plight of estuarine areas (Rothwell and Housden, 1990; Gubbay, 1990; Royal Society for the Protection of Birds, 1993).

Over the last decade the government has shown much more interest and commitment to action on coastal affairs as witnessed by the initiation of English Nature's *Estuaries Initiative*, Scottish Natural Heritage's *Firths Initiative* and the issuing of Planning Policy Guidance Note 20, *Coastal Planning* (DOE and Welsh Office, 1992). The former initiated locally based non-statutory estuary management projects around the English coast, enhancing the already growing network of independent, non-statutory collaborative coastal fora (Fletcher, 2003a) and providing a more holistic approach to coastal issues through the active involvement of key agencies and stakeholders (Heeps, 1992; Burbridge, 2001). *Coastal Plan-*

ning was important, being the first piece of planning guidance relating specifically to development planning in coastal areas. At more or less the same time, inadequacies in the organizational, policy and planning frameworks relating to coastal affairs were expounded in the highly influential report of the House of Commons Environment Select Committee (HOCESC, 1992). The report included far-reaching recommendations, including the need for the government to adopt an integrated approach to coastal management as well as to rationalize legislative and institutional arrangements relating to coastal affairs. In response, the government confirmed its recognition of a coastal zone and its commitment to effective coastal protection and planning. Subsequently, it has produced various consultation papers reviewing elements of the organizational and regulatory framework for coastal affairs as well as instigating a number of initiatives and institutional changes to improve the situation (Holgate-Pollard, 1996). However, the government has continued to reject the statutory approach to coastal management (Gubbay, 1996; Huggett, 1997; Ballinger, 1999), remaining adamant that the voluntary process is effective (DOE, 1992).

At the current time there are a many factors within several sectors and policy areas, which are influencing the development of integrated coastal management in the UK (Table 10.3). Within these the increasing marine policy and marine stewardship dimension is particularly noteworthy as is the increasing regional sea focus of many policy developments. Of all the influences, however, the role of the European Commission and in particular the Recommendation on ICZM, referred to earlier, is likely to become the most important driver for the ICM process. The UK government has taken a positive and proactive approach to implementing this Recommendation. Defra, leading the UK's response, has already initiated an extensive national debate on possible changes needed to deliver a more integrated approach to the management of coastal areas (Defra, 2003). It has also completed its national stocktaking exercise and is taking an influential role in the Commission's European ICZM expert group, supporting the implementation of the Recommendation.

An evaluation of current ICM efforts

National dimension: statutory framework

At a national level there is no overall authority responsible for the coastal zone. Instead, administration is subdivided among central departments and agencies in which marine and coastal affairs are dealt with alongside cognate land matters (Smith, 2000; Ballinger, 2002). Such a framework, which has evolved over decades to address sectoral concerns, has frequently been criticized because of its failure to provide the integration and particularly the inter-agency co-ordination required for effective ICM

Table 10.3 Current influences on the development of ICM in the UK

INTERNATIONAL AND SUPRANATIONAL INFLUENCES
- Law and policy (see Table 10.1):
  EC Recommendation on ICZM
- EC funding:
  e.g. INTERREG and LIFE funding streams

UK SECTORAL POLICY AND PRACTICE
- Development of shoreline management (2nd round of Shoreline Management Plans) and flood management initiatives and plans (e.g. estuary and coastal development capacity studies; Catchment Flood Management Plans and Sustainable Urban Drainage Systems)
- Archaeological heritage coming onto ICM agenda (English Heritage and Cadw)
- Planning reforms
    Introduction of spatial planning (terrestrial and consideration of marine spatial planning)
    Reforms to statutory development planning system
    Consideration of offshore development control
- Marine conservation
    Marine Conservation Review
    Irish Sea Pilot Study – Regional Seas and ecosystem approach to management being trialled developments in relation to Natura 2000, including the Habitats Regulations and proposed coastal habitat management plans for European marine sites
- General advances in sectoral management
    - Technological advances and innovation
    - More open decision-making processes

MARINE INITIATIVES
- Development of the EC Marine Strategy
- UK Government's marine stewardship initiative
- Marine Consents and Environment Unit (Defra/Department for Transport)
- Review of development in marine and coastal waters (Department for Transport: England and Wales)
- Consideration of Marine spatial planning/Irish Sea Pilot Study
- UK Marine Conservation Review

UK GOVERNANCE INITIATIVES
- Marine environment: marine stewardship initiative (*Safeguarding our seas; seas of change*, November 2002 Defra conference)
- The emergence of regionalization and the devolved administrations
- *Modernizing Government* initiative
- New ways of operation of Local Government including the emergence of community plans

ICM INITIATIVES
- Home country initiatives – including coastal forums
- National ICM networks – e.g. CoastNET, LGA's Coastal Special Interest Group
- Local coastal and estuary partnerships – issues relating to their future, security, status and interaction with other plans
- Integrated mapping project by Hydrographic Office, Ordnance Survey, British Geological Survey

---

Table 10.3 Continued

NGO AND COASTAL NETWORK LOBBYING/PROMOTION OF ICM
- National ICM networks (see above)
- NGOs particularly Marine Task Force of the Wildlife and Countryside Link

INCREASING PUBLIC INVOLVEMENT AND ENVIRONMENTAL AWARENESS
- Media coverage of selected coastal issues – e.g. Bathing water quality; Climate change
- Involvement in local partnerships (including coastal/estuary), community; Local Agenda 21 and beach cleaning initiatives
- Increasing profile of some local coastal partnerships

PRESSURES ON COASTAL ENVIRONMENT
- Continuing pressures and conflicts within intensely used urban coasts and associated waters
- Growth of offshore renewable energy generation
- Offshore aggregate extraction in nearshore waters
- Land claim for significant increases in housing development in estuary areas
- Continued inappropriate siting of coastal development with respect to coastal processes
- Maintenance of extensive conservation interest – coastal squeeze of habitats
- Demise of UK fisheries and implications for rural communities
- Redevelopment: coastal resort regeneration and industrial restructuring
- Pollution issues, particularly marine debris and implications for coastal tourism
- Continued postglacial isostatic uplift and downwarping
- The scale and implications of climate change

(Gubbay, 1990; WWF, 1994). For example, there are problems associated with the historic, sectoral division of responsibilities between coast protection (protection of land from erosion or encroachment by the sea), sea defence (prevention of flooding of land) and development planning (House of Commons Select Committee on Agriculture, 1998; Carter *et al.*, 1999; LGA, 2000) which perpetuate narrow, sectoral, technocentric approaches to coastal risk management (Ballinger *et al.*, 2002). Even coastal and sea defence are administered under separate legislation. However, the rationalization of policy and administration that is frequently called for (House of Commons Select Committee on Agriculture, 1998) is not necessarily always the solution, sometimes merely transferring the problem. Hiving off coastal defence policy from inland flood defence policy for example would merely create another artificial boundary between coastal and inland flood defence (Gibson, 2001b).

There have been some significant improvements to the co-ordination of coastal affairs at a national level over the last decade following the House of Commons Environment Select Committee report (HOCESC, 1992). These have included the establishment of a small Coastal Policy Unit within Defra, the establishment of an Inter-Departmental Group (IDG) on Coastal Policy and the production of a six-monthly newsletter, *Wavelength*, which reports on cross-cutting government initiatives in the coastal and marine environment across the UK. The coastal unit is the UK's formal focus for ICZM, supporting the IDG and production of *Wavelength*, as well as leading, alongside the devolved administrations, UK action in response to the EC. Over the last decade it has commissioned a range of useful research reports and produced a variety of consultation papers, advocating a more democratic, consensus-building approach to coastal management (DOE, 1996). Concerns that coastal matters could become sidelined within this unit in the government (Ballinger, 1999) appear somewhat unfounded as the recent impetus from the ICZM Recommendation has resulted in considerable ICZM-related activity over recent months, although whether this increased activity can be sustained in the long run remains to be seen. The IDG, made up of representatives from relevant central government departments and from the devolved administrations, exchanges information on new policies and initiatives affecting coasts. Concerns over the accountability, role and functioning of the group, which largely came about because of a lack of public records of meetings (Ballinger, 1999), are beginning to fade as the group's bulletin, reporting on the group's meetings, is made available to a wider external audience. Although the exchange of policy information is laudable, it remains questionable whether an IDG, which only meets every six months, can really influence 'joined-up' decision-making between such diverse Whitehall departments. Nor is the incorporation of the *Bulletin of the IDG on Coastal Policy* within *Wavelength* a substitute for minutes of meetings, although the breadth of information on coastal initiatives in recent issues has made *Wavelength* a most useful publication for a wide range of stakeholders. The recent establishment of the Marine Consents and Environment Unit, an alliance of the Marine Environment Branch of Defra and Ports Division of the Department for Transport, is also noteworthy. This unit provides a central facility for the receipt and administration of applications for certain developments in tidal waters and at sea, so facilitating a co-ordinated and streamlined approach to certain aspects of offshore regulation.

Non-statutory efforts

In addition to these central government-led initiatives, various informal national coastal fora, networks and dedicated coastal management websites, such as the recently relaunched http://www.theukcoastalzone.com site, have been established to enhance knowledge and understanding of coastal issues and activities. They also promote the exchange of information on coastal matters, including new initiatives and best practice. Fora include the Special Interest Group on Coastal Issues of the Local Government Association (LGA), which has promoted a more integrated approach to ICM and a major overhaul of the coastal planning system in *On the Edge: the coastal strategy* (LGA, 2000) and its recent update. In its follow-up to its strategy the LGA has commissioned research on the inter-face between shoreline management and the statutory planning system in England and Wales (Ballinger *et al.*, 2002b). Voluntary networks also include CoastNET. With a UK-wide membership representing all coastal sectors and a wide range of disciplines, this network promotes exchange of ideas and experience on ICM through a newsletter and regular semi-nars on topical coastal issues. However as Ballinger (2002) notes, this and other national coastal networks have been in a continuous state of flux over recent years. At this stage of ICM development, the non-statutory status and the uncertainty surrounding the role and funding of such fora, hinders the commitment of organizations required to make such networks successful (Ballinger and Brown, 2000).

ICM in the home countries of the UK

Differences in coastal policy and management practice are emerging within the devolved administrations of the UK. As Table 10.4 shows, there are many factors that have influenced and continue to influence the development and divergence of coastal management policy and practice within the home countries. Some aspects, such as their contrasting coastal physical and human geography, necessitate different approaches, irrespec-tive of political and devolutionary processes. In Wales and Northern Ireland, for example, the focus on coastal conservation management has resulted from the need to manage extensive stretches of rural coasts of high conservation status. By contrast, developments in the Scottish oil industry, sea fisheries and fish farming have led to many innovative sec-toral management approaches. Certain aspects of coastal areas, however, transcend administrative boundaries and so demand trans-boundary, bilat-eral or even multilateral approaches. For example, the management of economic development along the north-east and south-east coasts of Wales needs to be considered within the context of economic forces outside the principality. In these areas east–west axes of development centre around the trans-national economic 'cores' of Merseyside and Bristol and their associated east–west strategic communications.

Sectoral policy divergence

Some coastal policy divergence between the home countries pre-dates the administrative devolution of the late 1990s. For example, the Environ-mental Protection Act 1990 gave rise to the establishment of separate countryside agencies for each home country. This in turn resulted in dif-ferent approaches to both coastal conservation and wider coastal manage-ment in the respective countries. For example in England and Scotland, English Nature and Scottish Natural Heritage (SNH) have had a marked influence on ICM practice through pioneering and pump-priming the

Table 10.4 Devolutionary impact on ICM development in the UK

FACTORS INFLUENCING DIVERGENCE OF COASTAL AGENDAS
Contrasting coastal issues and priorities
• Contrasting home country coast characteristics
• Contrasting home country development opportunities and constraints

Diverging institutions
• Separate home country institutions, including:

  • devolved administrations (with various level of legal competence, administering various devolved matters)
  • national coastal forums (Scottish Coastal Forum; Wales Coastal and Maritime Partnership; Coastal Forum for England)
  • conservation agencies (English Nature; Scottish Natural Heritage; Countryside Council for Wales) and their associated policy and practical initiatives related to ICM, particularly EN's *Estuaries Initiative* and SNH's *Firths Initiative*
  • countryside and development agencies
  • other bodies e.g. LGA

• Result in divergence of approach, research and funding for ICM

Diverging planning structures and policies
• Planning policy divergence (since early 1990s) between home countries (see text)
• Variations in structure of development planning between home countries (e.g. only unitary development plans in Wales)
• Different commitments to regional planning guidance and its coastal content both within and between home countries
• Proposed reforms to statutory development plan process

FACTORS INFLUENCING CONVERGENCE OF COASTAL AGENDAS
• Supranational 'umbrella' framework, including EC Recommendation driving ICM development
• National co-ordination:

  • offshore management regime administered by central government (reserved matters)
  • Inter-Departmental Group on Coastal Affairs

• Organizations with trans-boundary remit

  • e.g. English/Welsh organizations (Environment Agency)
  • Joint Nature Conservation Committee

• Trans-boundary coastal (physical and socio-economic) processes
• Cross-border estuary and firth strategies and programmes

OPPORTUNITIES PROVIDED BY DEVOLUTION FOR ICM DEVELOPMENT
• More transparent and accountable
• More participatory decision-making
• Management more likely to be flexible and to suit local circumstances

CONSTRAINTS PROVIDED BY DEVOLUTION FOR ICM DEVELOPMENT
• Strategic, natural level eroded
• Fragmented and parochial agendas especially for research
• Cross-border issues and anomalies causing practical management issues

---

development of estuary and firth management. In contrast, the Country-side Council for Wales has been unable to support an equivalent estuary programme, although it has contributed to the debate on ICM through policy documents (Countryside Council for Wales, 1996) and related research (Ballinger *et al.*, 1997; Ballinger, 1999; Smith *et al.*, 2001).

Divergence in planning policy guidance relating to coastal develop-ment under the Town and Country planning system also commenced prior to the establishment of the devolved administrations and has con-tinued apace. Currently, such national guidance is set out in Planning Policy Guidance 20 for England (DOE and Welsh Office, 1992), National Planning Policy Guidance 13 for Scotland (Scottish Office, 1997), Plan-ning Policy Wales and Technical Advice Note 14 for Wales (Welsh Office, 1998) and the Regional Development Strategy *Shaping our Future* for Northern Ireland (Department for Regional Development, 2001). Although these documents only address development landward of low water, with the exception of the document for Northern Ireland, they all clearly refer to the need to consider links between land and inshore activ-ities, issues and impacts (Gubbay, 2002). Despite there being little substan-tive difference in policy direction between these documents, there are differences of detail of relevance to ICM. The Welsh guidance, for example, makes a much stronger and explicit requirement for local authorities to consider relevant coastal zone management plans (Gubbay, 2002; Welsh Office, 1998).

Coastal national fora

However, these minor policy variations will soon be overshadowed by major planning system reforms arising from the need for a more relevant and modern planning system, which is transparent, efficient, inclusive and streamlined. Pressures to move towards larger-scale planning frameworks, partly prompted by the European Spatial Development Perspective, have also resulted in decisions to produce spatial strategies for Northern Ireland and Wales (NAW, 2002a) as well as to include a more spatial planning perspective through regional strategies in England and through NPPGs in Scotland. Following extensive policy development and consultation, includ-ing separate Green Papers on the future of planning in England (Depart-ment of Transport, Local Government and the Regions, 2001) and Wales (National Assembly for Wales, 2002b), the Planning and Compulsory Pur-chase Bill is set to transform the respective planning systems. Whereas in England, local and unitary development plans are to be replaced by regional spatial strategies and Local Development Schemes, in Wales the fundamental structure of the current system will remain. In Wales, though, there will be changes in the delivery of the planning system, including an update of the Assembly's secondary legislation, policy, technical and pro-cedural advice (National Assembly for Wales, 2002a).

In addition to the sectoral initiatives described above, the separate establishment of national coastal fora in England, Scotland and Wales paves the way for further divergence of coastal policy and practice. Even though at different stages of development, they all provide an opportunity for networking, keeping up-to-date, exchanging issues and raising issues at a national level (Gubbay, 2002). Although the Coastal Forum for England was the first to be established (in 1994), it has had the most chequered history (Gubbay, 2002). Whilst initial meetings were well attended and fairly frequent, there has been no activity for well over a year and its current status is unclear (Gubbay, 2002). Concerns have been expressed over its lack of focus and work programme and the fact that it has become little more than a 'talking shop' (Ballinger, 2002). Conversely, the Scottish Coastal Forum, established two years later, is now the most advanced and active of the 'national' fora, although it still lacks permanent long-term funding arrangements (Gubbay, 2002). This forum, supported by a Coastal Officer and a Secretariat, operates through an independent chair with members of the Scottish Executive attending as observers. It has the widest remit, acting as the national focus for coastal issues, co-ordinating the dissemination of best practice and distributing information on coastal management to a wide audience through its newsletter and technical publications. It also advises the government on the development of Scottish coastal policies (Scottish Coastal Forum, 2003a) as well as responding to relevant government consultations. A sub-group commenced work on a national coastal strategy in 2002, predating current government action under the EC ICZM recommendation.

Whilst the Wales Coastal and Maritime Partnership is a more recent development, its predecessor, the Wales Coastal Forum, was set up in 1997. The Wales Coastal and Maritime Partnership, which includes representatives from public, private and voluntary sectors relevant to Wales, is less well resourced than its Scottish counterpart, with only a part-time officer. However, it does have links to the government, through the Countryside and Coastal Policy Branch, Countryside Division in the Welsh Assembly Government and a structured work programme. In 2002/2003 these links included a review of the Assembly's approach to a range of matters, including renewable energy, flood and coastal defence funding and sustainability indicators as well as a priority item relating to the implementation of the EU ICZM Recommendation in Wales.

Despite a proposal to establish a national coastal forum for Northern Ireland back in 1995 to advise the government on the development of a Coastal Zone Strategy (Ballinger, 2002), and considerable pressure from NGOs and politicians to establish such a forum (Dalzell, 2001), none, as yet, exists due to an apparent lack of funding. However, a recent scoping study, commissioned by the Environment Policy Division in the Department of the Environment Northern Ireland, investigated the value and potential scope of such a forum (Dalzell, 2001) and, more recently, the

Northern Ireland Biodiversity Strategy has recommended the establishment of such a forum (Gubbay, 2002).

Competence of the devolved administrations

The establishment of the devolved administrations has opened up further possibilities for the delivery of coastal zone policy and planning (Gubbay, 2002). The varying levels of competence of the devolved bodies, however, limit such possibilities. For example the Scotland Act 1998, whilst setting out the role, powers and functions of the Scottish Executive, allows for a directly elected legislation. Devolved matters for Scottish domestic consideration include various elements of relevance to ICM: environment, fishing, ports and harbours. In contrast, the Government of Wales Act 1998, which established the powers and functions of the National Assembly for Wales, does not allow for a separate primary legislature although the Assembly has the powers to administer and implement certain aspects of legislation and to create secondary legislation. However, unique within the EU, the National Assembly for Wales has a duty to promote sustainable development through section 121 of the Government of Wales Act. This is potentially an important lever for ICM development and already has resulted in a sustainability action plan and development of sustainability indicators for the marine and coastal environment.

Regional dimension

Within parts of the UK, particularly England and Northern Ireland, there has been a strengthening of regional institutions and opportunities for elected regional government. Such regional institutions include the Department for Regional Development in Northern Ireland as well as eight coastal regional Government Offices (GOs), Regional Development Agencies (RDAs) and regional chambers in England. These bodies have an important role to play in ICM development as they promote economic regeneration and sustainable development within their respective regions (Gubbay, 2002). The RDAs, for example, focus on co-ordinating regional economic development and regeneration and are supported by regional chambers, representing the interests of the region. However, work on ICM has been very variable and generally limited in scope, having 'failed to recognize the potential of ICM to harness the value of coastal and marine economies for the regions' (Gubbay, 2002). Even the GOs, which bring together the activities and interests of different government departments within a single organization and, as such, are uniquely placed to deliver 'joined-up' policies, have tended to deal with coastal issues on a sectoral basis. The GO for the North-West, however, has been in the forefront, having actively promoted and supported ICM, commissioning research (DETR, 2000a) and establishing a North-West Coastal Forum to develop a coastal strategy for the region (North-West Coastal Forum, 2003; Baker, 2002). Such efforts reflect the prominence of coastal initiatives in the region where there has been a networking group of estuary projects for some time (Partnership of Irish Sea Coastal and Estuary Strategies, 2001).

Alongside the strengthening of regional institutions, there has been an associated major revival in regional planning and management. This corresponds with the increasing importance of regional and sub-regional spatial frameworks within the rest of Europe and the distribution of EU regional development funds (Ballinger *et al.*, 2000). Such regional initiatives include the Regional Development Strategy for Northern Ireland (Department for Regional Development, 2001) along with the regional planning guidance and regional economic strategies in England and their associated regional sustainable development frameworks. Such initiatives, however, tend to focus on terrestrial spatial development issues and are very variable in the extent to which they provide a framework for coastal policy development. Regional economic strategies, a recent initiative linked to the formation of the RDAs, have not really addressed coastal issues explicitly or adequately enough, despite the coastal zone's relevance to most UK regional economies (Gubbay, 2002). In contrast, most of the regional sustainable development frameworks, designed to enhance co-ordination between regional initiatives and place them within the context of high-level regional sustainable development frameworks (DETR, 2001), make reference to various coastal or marine issues, and some consider aspects of ICM. The North-West regional sustainable development framework, for instance, mentions the role of coastal fora and the importance of ICM (Gubbay, 2002). Despite guidance on regional planning in England suggesting that regional planning guidance should identify key coastal characteristics and should consider the scope for integrated coastal planning, it has not, as yet, resulted in a consistent approach to coastal matters in such documents (PPG 11: DETR, 2000b). Consideration of coastal matters ranges from the very sectoral approach of the North-East to the North-West, where ICM is promoted and given a high profile (Gubbay, 2002).

In addition to the regional devolution outlined above, a widespread and strong regional tier has developed within the non-statutory approach to coastal defence. This has been in existence since the mid-1980s in England and Wales, but is a more recent development in Scotland. Coastal Groups in England and Wales, based on littoral cells, have been particularly important in the move towards a more sustainable and co-ordinated approach (O'Riordan and Ward, 1997; Leafe *et al.*, 1998; Potts, 1999; 2000a; 2000b), having played a vital role in preparing shoreline management plans and shaping national shoreline management plan policy (Oakes, 1995; Hooke and Bray, 1995). Using a co-operative, multi-agency approach, they have also promoted liaison and co-ordination between stakeholders (Potts, 1999) on matters relating to coast protection and sea defence over 18 littoral regions across England and Wales. The chapter by Potts and Carter in this book discusses this important element of coastal management further.

Local dimension

Statutory bodies

A range of statutory organizations, including local government bodies, harbour authorities and sea fisheries committees, design and implement policies relating to coastal matters at local levels. Local government is particularly important, because of its democratic status and range of coastal-related functions, including responsibilities relating to land use planning, coast protection, environmental health, leisure and recreation. Despite recent calls for it to play a central role in ICM development and practice (LGA, 2000; Smith *et al.*, 2001), its involvement and interest has been somewhat variable. Inevitably, perhaps, where responsibilities are split amongst departments and vary from council to council (Ballinger *et al.*, 1995) liaison has been generally poor. Departmental isolation has also been perpetuated by the disparate training and discipline-basis of staff, along with the peripheralization of ICM per se in countryside divisions (Ballinger, 2002). Only in a few locations, where there has been a history of interest in coastal management (such as along the south coast of England) or where specific legislation has given local councils special off-shore powers (such as in Shetland and Orkney) has coastal management really permeated onto the local government agenda. The Zetland County Council and the Orkney County Acts of the early 1970s are of special note. Although designed principally for use in relation to the oil industry, they resulted in Shetland Islands Council having the potential to plan and manage the near-shore coastal area as well as Orkney Islands Council becoming, *inter alia*, the harbour authority for Scapa Flow. This in turn led to the production of the Scapa Flow Management Strategy in 1989, one of the first UK ICM initiatives (Gubbay, 2001).

Ballinger *et al.* (2002b) have recently singled out the inadequate level of co-ordination between shoreline management and development planning at local levels and within local government. They stress the need for an integrated approach to coastal risk management, because of potential increased vulnerability of coastal locations resulting from climate change (Halcrow Group Ltd. *et al.*, 2001) and the continued demand for new housing (National Statistics, 2001). This can only be realized through suitable collaborative mechanisms to ensure adequate dialogue and interchange of expertise and information between planners and engineers. However, because of the traditional and divergent attitudes, perspectives and backgrounds of the key decision-makers lying deeply embedded within the 'system', this is likely to be a lengthy process (Ballinger *et al.*, 2002b). However, various national efforts, designed to improve collaboration and partnership, have already sought to bridge this divide (Environment Agency, 1997; Environment Agency and LGA, 2000).

Plans and programmes

Until recently programmes and plans addressing the conservation of extensive stretches of coast of historical landscape and ecological value dominated coastal planning at local levels. However, over the last ten years, many additional, non-statutory plans and programmes have attempted to complement and bridge sectoral mechanisms at this level, as well as trying to address additional coastal issues. These range from multi-sectoral strategies, covering extensive stretches of coast or estuary and a wide variety of issues, to more detailed programmes, dealing with the management and planning of fewer sectors within more limited geographical areas (Figure 10.2). As Ballinger (2002) notes, most are essentially land-by-sea approaches and many, even some of the ones based on conservation designations, are confined within administrative rather than natural boundaries. With the exception of certain multi-sectoral strategies, few programmes provide a strategic and offshore perspective for local plan development and action.

This gradual proliferation of coastal plans and programmes has become one of the main impediments to integration at local levels, sometimes even exacerbating existing confusion between coastal bodies (Ballinger, 2002). Even co-ordination between different plans emanating from within the same organization is frequently inadequate, often relying more on individual personalities, vision and determination than formal commitments. There have, however, been some joint-planning programmes for some coastal and estuary areas, such as the *Joint Issues Document for the Severn* between the Severn Estuary Strategy and the Severn Local Environment Agency Plan (Severn Estuary Strategy and Environment Agency, 1998), which illustrate the benefits of collaboration, notably increased efficiency and consistency. Additionally, multi-sectoral strategies attempt to co-ordinate such activities, though in practice this can be difficult, even where there are special Protocols and Memoranda of Understanding between organizations (Ballinger and Brown, 2000).

Local coastal partnerships/multi-sectoral approaches

No discussion of the local dimension of ICM would be complete without further consideration of the recent, voluntary partnership approach to coastal management (Ballinger, 1999; Burbridge, 2001). There are currently over 40 estuary and firth partnerships as well as a range of other partnerships. Those of relevance to the Welsh coast are illustrated in

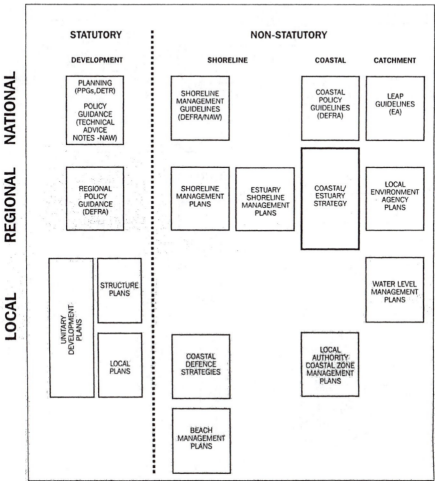

Figure 10.2 Coastal plans and programmes in England and Wales (2002).

Figure 10.3. These action-centred networks (Masters, 1995) promote a multi-sectoral approach and emphasize local partnership and consensus building, encouraging public participation in programme initiation, development and implementation through involvement of public, private and voluntary sectors. Consequently, such partnerships allow those affected by management outcomes to be involved in the management process, facilitating the inclusion of anecdotal and community-held information, formerly overlooked (Edwards *et al.*, 1997). With no statutory authority, these partnerships, relying on 'consensus and agreement for

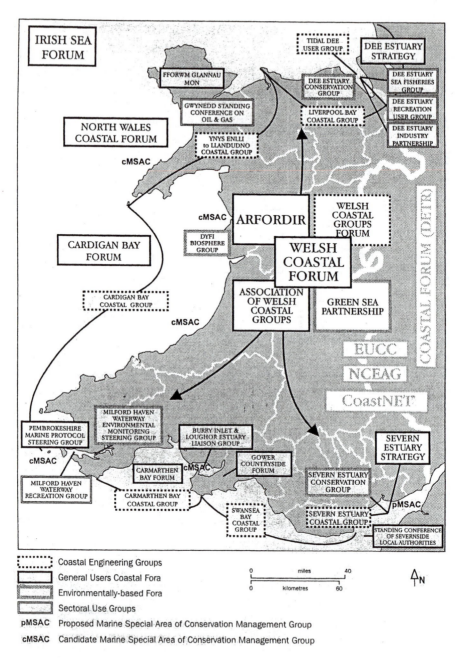

Figure 10.3 Coastal groups and fora in Wales (2002).

voluntary actions and the powers of participating authorities' (English Nature, 1993), have been perceived as a flexible and cost-efficient way of managing local coastal and estuary areas. More recently, a national workshop on coastal partnerships demonstrated the 'added value' of such partnerships, highlighting a wide range of positive outputs and outcomes from such groups (CoastNET, 2003).

With a perceived coastal policy vacuum at a national level (Jewell *et al.*, 1999), coastal partnerships have been seen as a vital mechanism for delivering ICM at local levels and for promoting sustainable development on the coast. Support for such bottom-up initiatives has come from many sources, including the EC Recommendation (EC, 2002), the non-government organization Wildlife and Countryside Link (Wildlife and Countryside Link, 2002), Defra (Defra, 2002) and a wide range of delegates at a recent CoastNET workshop (CoastNET, 2003). Former government documents have also suggested that plans emerging from such processes should 'build on, support and inform the existing planning and management structures operating on estuaries', and have called on parties to 'involve themselves actively in the plan process to the fullest practical (and where relevant, statutory) extent of their respective responsibilities' (DOE, 1995). To some extent this has happened, although progress has been hampered by a number of internal and external constraints relating to the coastal partnership working. These include the insecure funding, lack of status and low profile of these groups as well as issues surrounding the representativeness of stakeholders and accountability (Burbridge, 2001; Smith *et al.*, 2001; Ballinger and Brown, 2000; Fletcher, 2001; 2003a) of the partnerships. These factors also undermine the value of the partnerships' outputs (Fletcher, 2001; 2003b). As a result of such concerns, and as part of the ongoing national stocktake process, the value and role of such groups is currently under considerable scrutiny. It remains to be seen what the future of such partnerships will be, although CoastNET, recognizing its potential as a national and neutral facilitator, has recently produced a vision and action plan to take forward and promote the partnership approach based on its workshop findings (CoastNET, 2003).

Private and voluntary sectors

The private sector has rarely become actively involved in ICM apart from the port sector, which has played a major role in coastal conservation, recreation and waste management over the last decade (Ballinger, 2002). The port sector has made a significant contribution to the debate on and implementation of Schemes of Management for Special Areas of Conservation under the 'Habitats' Directive, and has rapidly developed capacity in environmental and waste management over the last few years (Wooldridge *et al.*, 1998). Although other coastal heavy industries, such as steel production and oil refining, are involved in environmental

management, as yet their active involvement with ICM, like many small-
and medium-sized enterprises, remains limited and is of concern
(Ballinger, 2002). It is hoped that the ICZM National strategy development will realize its intention to engage these stakeholders in the debate
on the future of ICZM in the UK.

In contrast, the voluntary sector continues its traditional, centre-stage
role, lobbying for change at national, regional and local levels as well as
commissioning research on a range of related topics (Ballinger, 2002).
Many national non-government organizations, with well-qualified and
established workforces, have gradually gained acceptance over the last few
decades and now have representatives sitting on a range of national
coastal fora and advisory groups. Indeed, the Chair of the Wales Coastal
and Maritime Partnership is from such a background. As with previous
coastal campaigns, these organizations not only raise public awareness of
issues, but also formulate ideas, priorities and policies of relevance. The
most recent WWF Oceans Recovery Campaign for example, is arguing for
a UK Marine Act amongst other things (WWF-UK, 2003). Local offices
and campaigns of these as well as other specialist groups, societies and
grass roots conservation organizations, including archaeological and natu-
ralists' trusts, also play important roles, raising public awareness of coastal
issues and involving local people in practical field projects (Ballinger,
2002). However, the increasing co-ordination of many of the most influential environmental marine and coastal voluntary organizations in the
UK through the Marine Task Force of the Wildlife and Countryside Link
has been one of the most significant developments of recent years. This
link has increased the efficiency and effectiveness of the NGO sector,
bringing together relevant environmental voluntary organizations to
exchange information, develop and promote policies. Recently, it has co-
ordinated NGO input to the government's Review of Marine Nature Conservation and the Irish Sea regional pilot sea project as well as promoting
issues such as marine spatial planning (Wildlife and Countryside Link,
2003).

Conclusions and the way forward for ICM in the UK

Over the last half century coastal management policy and practice has
been dominated by the continuation and strengthening of sectoral initiatives, resulting in a reasonably strong and coherent, but largely terrestri-
ally-based environmental management framework for coastal areas,
particularly in relation to landscape, species and habitat protection, and
pollution control. However, these improvements, and in particular those
associated with the strong conservation tradition, may have led to complacency in the quest for more integrated, multi-sectoral coastal management
(Ballinger, 1999). However, in response to continuing calls for ICM development from a wide range of bodies, there has been something of a sea

change in attitude and approach over the last decade as the UK has moved into an emergent phase of ICM development. To the benefit of ICM significant organizational restructuring and legislative reform have taken place alongside the formation and development of non-statutory estuary and coastal multi-stakeholder partnerships. These have provided a new vision and approach, including commitment to inclusion and community involvement.

There is still much improvement to be made in the extent to which UK coastal management is integrated and conforms to EU principles. There is no formal mechanism to co-ordinate the management activities of all the actors involved in coastal affairs, and the institutional framework still fails to deliver an integrated or systems-based approach. The land-by-sea approaches dominating coastal and conservation management have exacerbated inadequate integration across the land/sea boundary, resulting from contrasting administrations on either side of the shoreline. Few management efforts, apart from those relating to the shoreline management process and the pilot scheme for the Irish Sea, are based on natural system boundaries. Weak inter-disciplinary collaboration and training relating to coastal matters and a lack of inter-disciplinary vision and training also perpetuate the top-down and inflexible management structures associated with traditional sectoral management. Considerable progress is required to ensure that coastal management in the UK adopts a more adaptive, precautionary and holistic perspective, although the efforts of coastal partnerships and the environmental management sectors referred to above have begun to address these matters. As noted, the former add a particularly new and important dimension to coastal management. They involve relevant administrative bodies, employ participatory planning processes and reflect local characteristics. However, their lack of a long-term focus, resulting from their insecure funding base, and their limited use of a combination of instruments, resulting from their relatively weak status, detract from their performance and likely future impact when measured against EU principles.

This paper has attempted to assess ICM effort in the UK. However, any evaluation is currently fraught by the difficulties arising from a lack of specific outcome-related information (Ballinger, 2002). With the exception of some recent evaluations and quantitative estimates of the impacts of the Scottish firth programme (including Gubbay, 2001; ITAD Ltd and BMT Cordah Ltd, 2002; Firn, J.R. and McGlashan, D.J., 2001; Burbridge, 2001) and the recent qualitative findings of the CoastNET coastal partnership conference (CoastNET, 2003), there is little information to help estimate the 'added value' of ICM initiatives per se. As Ballinger (2002) notes, where information exists, it tends to refer to process-related goals rather than substantive, on-the-ground outcomes. There are further problems in isolating benefits from coastal management initiatives, particularly coastal partnerships. Alongside partnerships there are many other programmes and initiatives for coastal areas (Figure 10.2), many of which have inter-related or overlapping objectives and actions. Indeed, the rationalization of plans, as well as the strengthening and establishment of clearer links between plans, is a priority for ICM.

Looking to the future, it is likely that the wide range of factors illustrated in Table 10.3 will continue to determine the development of ICM in the UK. Technological advances and more open decision-making processes in sectoral management, along with increasing knowledge and awareness of critical socio-economic and environmental issues, particularly relating to climate change and associated sea level rise, are likely to stimulate development. However, whilst coastal management is 'non-essential' and non-statutory, interest and involvement in ICM will remain peripheral (Ballinger, 2002). In the medium-term, the potential of the new regional bodies and the devolved administrations cannot be overlooked. Although these add another level of administration, policy development and decision-making, they have the potential to secure additional enthusiasm commitment and support for ICM. Indeed, the current level of increased activity in Scotland is already clearly apparent. In the short term, though, the EC Recommendation and the development of new legislation for the marine environment are likely to be the main drivers. It is likely then that, despite the current sea change of approach and attitude towards ICM across many sectors and levels of governance, ICM will continue to develop incrementally, relying on gradual improvements in sectoral and environmental management regimes as well as from the impact of local, voluntary multi-stakeholder ICM efforts.

References

Baker, M. (2002) 'Developing institutional capacity at the regional level: the development of a coastal forum in the North-West of England', *Journal of Environmental Planning and Management* 45: 5, 681–713.

Ballinger, R.C. (1999) 'The evolving organisational framework for Integrated Coastal Management in England and Wales', *Marine Policy* 23: 4/5, 501–23.

Ballinger, R.C. (2002) 'An evaluation of integrated coastal management in the United Kingdom', in Cicin-Sain, B., Kornhauser, A. and Belfiore, S. (eds) *An Evaluation of Progress in Coastal Policies at the National Level: a Transatlantic and Euro-Mediterranean Perspective.* Proceedings of a NATO Advanced Research Workshop: Kluwer Academic Publishers.

Ballinger, R.C. and Brown, J. (2000) 'Coping with the undercurrents of national and subnational institutional reform: lessons from a UK non-statutory estuary management programme', *Periodicum Biologorum* 102: 1, 625–31.

Ballinger, R.C., Havard, M.S.H., Pettit, S.J. and Smith, H.D. (1995) *A Review of Coastal Management in Wales.* Report to the Countryside Council for Wales.

Ballinger, R.C., Havard, M.S.H. and Potts, J.S. (1997) *Coastal Management in Wales: Looking Towards the Future.* Report to the Countryside Council for Wales. Bangor: CCW.

Ballinger, R.C., Taussik, J. and Potts, J.S. (2002) *Managing Coastal Risk: Making the Shared Coastal Responsibility Work; Coastal Planning and SM: a Review of Legislation and Guidance.* Report for the LGA's Special Interest Group on Coastal Issues.

Burbridge, P.R. (2001) *Lessons Learnt from Local Coastal Management Partnerships: a Report to the Scottish Coastal Forum, the Scottish Executive and Scottish Natural Heritage.* Scottish Coastal Forum Research Report 3, Edinburgh.

Carter, D., Bray, M., Hooke, J., Taussik, J., Clifton, J. and Mitchell, J. (1999) *A Critique of the Past: a Strategy for the Future.* Isle of Wight: Standing Conference on Problems Associated with the Coastline (SCOPAC).

Cicin-Sain, B. and Knecht, R. (1998) *Integrated Coastal and Ocean Management: Concepts and Practice.* Washington, D.C.: Island Press.

CoastNET (2003) *Partnership Approaches to ICZM: a Vision and Action Plan.* Colchester: CoastNET.

Countryside Commission (1970) *The Planning of the Coastline.* Cheltenham: Countryside Commission.

Countryside Council for Wales (1996) *Sea, Shores and Coasts.* Bangor: CCW.

Cox, M. (2001a) *Coastline Scotland* 11: September. Edinburgh: Scottish Coastal Forum.

Cox, M. (2001b) Devolution in Scotland: the effect on coastal policy. Paper presented to Coastal Management for Sustainability – review and trends – Conference, January: http://www.scotland.gov.uk/environment/coastalforum/outputs reports.asp.

Dalzell, R. (2001) Department of the Environment, Northern Ireland, *pers. comm.*

Department for Environment Food and Rural Affairs (2002) *Seas of Change: the Government's Consultation Paper to Help Deliver Our Vision for the Marine Environment.* London: Defra Publications.

Department for Environment Food and Rural Affairs (2003) *Marine Stewardship and Integrated Coastal Zone Management.* Report of conference, 14 November 2002. London: Defra Publications.

Department of Environment, Transport and the Regions (1998) *Index of Local Deprivation.* London: HMSO.

Department of Environment, Transport and the Regions (2000a) *Research into Integrated Coastal Planning in the NorthWest Region.* Government Office for the NorthWest and University of Liverpool.

Department of Environment, Transport and the Regions (2000b) *Good Practice Guide on Sustainability Appraisal of Regional Planning Guidance.* London: DETR.

Department of Environment, Transport and the Regions (2001) *Guidance on Preparing Regional Sustainable Development Frameworks.* London: DETR.

Department for Regional Development (2001) *Shaping Our Future: Regional Development Strategy for Northern Ireland.* http://www.drdni.gov.uk/shapingourfuture.

Department of the Environment (1992) 'The Government's response to the second report of the House of Commons Select Committee on the Environment', *Coastal Zone Protection and Planning.* Presented to Parliament by the Secretary of State for the Environment by Command of Her Majesty, July. London: HMSO.

Department of the Environment (1995) *Policy Guidelines for the Coast.* London: DOE.

Department of the Environment (1996) *Coastal Zone Management: Towards Best Practice.* London: HMSO.

Department of the Environment and Welsh Office (1992) *Planning Policy Guidance Note 20.* London: HMSO.

Department of Transport, Local Government and the Regions (2001) *Planning: Delivering a Fundamental Change.* London: DTLR.

Edwards, S.D., Jones, P.J.S. and Nowell, D.E. (1997) 'Participation in coastal zone management initiatives: review and analysis of examples from the UK', *Ocean and Coastal Management* 36: 1–3, 143–65.

English Nature (1993) *Towards Sustainable Estuary Management.* Peterborough: English Nature.

Environment Agency (1997) *Liaison with Local Planning Authorities.* Bristol: Environment Agency.

Environment Agency and Local Government Association (2000) *Working Better Together.* London: Local Government Association; Bristol: Environment Agency.

European Commission (2002) *Recommendation of the European Parliament and of the Council of 30 May 2002 Concerning the Implementation of Integrated Coastal Zone Management in Europe.* EC/2002/413/EC. Brussels: European Commission. http://www.europa.eu.int/comm/environment/iczm/home.htm.

Firn, J.R. and McGlashan, D.J. (2001) An initial assessment of the socio-economic benefits from ICZM in Scotland. A report to the Scottish Coastal Forum. http://www.scotland.gov.uk/environment/coastalforum/outputs-reports.asp.

Fletcher, S. (2001) *Inherent Problems with 'Inclusive and Democratic' Coastal Planning and Management in the UK.* Paper presented to the Royal Geographic Society at the Institute of British Geographers' Annual Conference, Plymouth, 3–5, January.

Fletcher, S. (2003a) *Stakeholder Involvement in Coastal Partnerships: Towards Secure Representation.* A thesis submitted in part fulfilment of the requirements of the Nottingham Trent University and Southampton Institute for the degree of Doctor of Philosophy, June.

Fletcher, S. (2003b) 'Stakeholder representation and the democratic basis of coastal partnerships in the UK', *Marine Policy* 27: 3, 229–40.

Gibson, J. (1993) 'Coastal zone planning law. The role of law in management of the coastal zone in England and Wales', *Marine Policy* 17: 118–29.

Gibson, J. (2001a) The coastal zone website: http://www.cf.ac.uk/claws/gibson/.

Gibson, J. (2001b) 'Legal jurisdiction in the territorial sea adjacent to Wales, Chapter 3', in Smith, H.D., Ballinger, R.C., Gibson, J. and Taussik, J. (eds) *Analysis of Options for Improving the Planning and Management of Wales' Territorial Sea.* Report to the Countryside Council for Wales, Contract No. FC-73-02-163. Cardiff University.

Gubbay, S. (1990) *A Future for the Coast? Proposals for a UK Coastal Zone Management Plan.* Report for the World Wide Fund for Nature (UK) from the Marine Conservation Society. Ross-on-Wye: Marine Conservation Society.

Gubbay, S. (1996) *How Far Have We Come? The Need for a New Agenda.* Presentation to the National Coasts and Estuaries Advisory Group Conference, *CZM: the New Agenda,* 4 November 1996, London.

Gubbay, S. (2001) *The Role of Scottish Local Initiatives in Implementing the Principles of Integrated Coastal Zone Management.* Edinburgh: Scottish Executive Central Research Unit.

Gubbay, S. (2002) *Just Coasting: an Assessment of the Commitment of the Devolved Administrations and the English Regions to Integrated Coastal Management.* Report from the Wildlife Trusts and WWF.

Halcrow Group Ltd., H.R. Wallingford and John Chatterton Associates (2001) National appraisal of assets at risk from flooding and coastal erosion, including the potential impact of climate change. Report produced for Defra.

Halliday, J.E. (1986) *Coastal Zone Management in England and Wales: a Study of Area,*

Organisation and Attitude. Cardiff: University of Wales. Unpublished Ph.D. Thesis.

Heeps, C. (1992) *Caring for Your Coast: the Coastal Forum Approach.* Ross-on-Wye: Marine Conservation Society.

Holgate-Pollard, D. (1996) 'Coastal management: the policy context', *Marine Environmental Management Review of 1995 and Future Trends.* Gloucester: Coastal management for Sustainability, pp. 27–30.

Hooke, J.M. and Bray, M.J. (1995) 'Coastal groups, littoral cells, policies and plans in the UK', *Area* 27: 4, 358–68.

House of Commons Select Committee on Agriculture (1998) *Flood and Coastal Defence.* Vol. I. London: HMSO, p. 54.

House of Commons Select Committee on the Environment (1992) *Coastal Zone Protection and Planning.* Second Report. London: HMSO.

Houston, J.A. and Jones, C.R. (1990) *Planning and Management of the Coastal Heritage.* Sefton, Southport: Symposium Proceedings.

Huggett, D. (1997) *A Review of Progress Since the House of Commons Environment Select Committee Report 'Coastal Zone Protection and Planning'.* Sandy: RSPB.

ITAD Ltd and BMT Cordah Ltd (2002) *Assessment of the Effectiveness of Local Coastal Management Partnerships as a Delivery Mechanism for Integrated Coastal Zone Management.* Report to the Scottish Coastal Forum.

Jewell, S., Roberts, H. and McInnes, R. (2000) 'Does coastal management require a European Directive? The advantages and disadvantages of a non-statutory approach', in Fleming, C.A. (ed.) *Coastal Management: Integrating Science, Engineering and Management,* London: Thomas Telford, pp. 209–18.

Leafe, R., Pethick, J. and Townend, I. (1998) 'Realising the benefits of shoreline management', *The Geographical Journal* 164: 3, 282–91.

Local Government Association (2000) *On the Edge: the Coastal Strategy.* London: LGA.

Masters, D. (1995) 'Action centred networks: the key to decision-making in coastal zone management', in Healy, M.G. and Doody, J.P. (eds) *Directions in European Coastal Management.* Cardigan: Samara Publishing Limited.

National Assembly for Wales (2002a) *Wales Spatial Plan: Pathway to Sustainable Development.* Cardiff: NAW.

National Assembly for Wales (2002b) *Consultation Document Planning: Delivering for Wales.* Cardiff: NAW.

National Statistics (2001) *The Official UK Statistics.* http://www.statistics.gov.uk/.

North West Coastal Forum (2003) website: http://www.nwcoastalforum.co.uk.

Oakes, T.A. (1995) 'The role of regional coastal groups in planning coastal defence', Paper presented at *Littoral '94, Eurocoast Conference.* A multi-disciplinary symposium on coastal zone research, management and planning, 26–29 September, Lisbon, Portugal, 63–76.

O'Riordan, T. and Ward, R. (1997) 'Building trust in shoreline management: creating participatory consultation in Shoreline Management Plans', *Land Use Policy* 14: 4, 257–76.

Partnership of Irish Sea Coastal and Estuary Strategies (PISCES) (2001) website http://www.northwestcoast.org.uk/pisces.htm.

Potts, J.S. (1999) 'The non-statutory approach to coastal defence in England and Wales: Coastal Defence Groups and Shoreline Management Plans', *Marine Policy* 23: 4/5, 479–501.

Potts, J.S. (2000a) 'Coastal defence groups in England and Wales: benefits, shortcomings and future requirements', *Periodicum Biologorum* 102: 1, 13–21.

Potts, J.S. (2000b) 'Towards an improved shoreline management process in England and Wales', *Planning for the Natural and Built Environment.* Journal of the Royal Town Planning Institute: 14–15.

Rothwell, P.I. and Housden, S.D. (1990) *Turning the Tide: a Future for Estuaries.* Sandy: RSPB.

Royal Society for the Protection of Birds (1993) *A Shore Future: RSPB Vision for the Coast – the RSPB Save our Shoreline Campaign.* Sandy: RSPB.

Scottish Coastal Forum (2003a) http://www.scotland.gov.uk/environment/coastalforum/default.asp.

Scottish Coastal Forum (2003b) http://www.scotland.gov.uk/environment/coastalforum/newsletters.asp.

Scottish Office (1997) National Planning Policy Guidance 13: *Coastal Planning.* Edinburgh: Scottish Office.

Secretaries of State for the Environment and the Foreign and Commonwealth Office, the Chancellor of the Exchequer, the President of the Board of Trade, the Secretaries of State for Transport and Defence, the Minister for Agriculture, Fisheries and Food, the Secretary of State for Wales, the Chancellor of the Duchy of Lancaster, the Secretaries of State for Scotland, National Heritage, Northern Ireland, Education, Health and Employment and the Minister for Overseas Development by Command of Her Majesty (1990) *This Common Inheritance: the Government's Environmental Strategy.* Cmnd. 1655. London: HMSO.

Severn Estuary Strategy and Environment Agency (1998) *Joint Issues Document for the Severn.* http://www.severnestuary.net/sep/pubs.html.

Sheail, J. (1976) 'Coastal planning in Great Britain before 1950', *Geographical Journal* 142: 2, 257–73.

Smith, H.D. (2000) 'Coast and ocean management in the UK: a present and future evaluation', in Cicin-Sain, B. and Rivera-Arriaga, E. (eds) *North American and European Perspectives on Ocean and Coastal Policy: Building Partnerships and Expanding the Technological Frontier.* International Conference on Coastal and Ocean Space Utilisation, Proceedings Vol. 1. Nov 1–4, Cancun, Mexico, 69–73.

Smith, H.D., Ballinger, R.C., Gibson, J. and Taussik, J. (2001) *Analysis of Options for Improving the Planning and Management of Wales' Territorial Sea.* Report to the Countryside Council for Wales, Contract No. FC-73-02-163. Cardiff University.

Welsh Office (1998) Technical Advice Note (Wales) 14: *Coastal Planning.* Cardiff: Welsh Office.

Wildlife and Countryside Link (2002) *EC Recommendation on ICZM: Joint Wildlife, Countryside and Environmental Links Discussion Paper on the Structures and Tools Necessary for Implementation in the UK.* London: Wildlife and Countryside Link.

Wooldridge, C.F., Tselentis, B.S. and Whitehead, D. (1998) 'Environmental management of port operations – the ports sector's response to the European dimension', in Sciutto, G. and Brebbia, C.A. (eds) *Maritime Engineering and Ports.* WIT Press, pp. 227–42.

WWF-UK (1994) 'Local authorities and integrated coastal zone management plans', *Marine Update* 18. Godalming: WWF-UK.

WWF-UK (2003) *Oceans Recovery Campaign.* http://www.wwf-uk.org/orca/.

11 The partnership approach to integrated coastal management in Britain

(UK)

Derek J. McGlashan and Natasha Barker

Q24 Q25

Q28 Q58

Introduction

Britain's coast is often dynamic and is certainly diverse. From the Shetland Isles to the Isles of Scilly, the geomorphology and human use of the coast and estuaries varies considerably. Britain is an island; there are no land connections to the continental landmass of Europe. As a result, nowhere in Britain is far from the coast. The coast of Britain is also very long and, in places, deeply indented. This makes estimating its length quite challenging (Rees, 1998; McGlashan and Firn, 2003), but it is probably in the region of 18–24,000 km (given that the Scottish coast is considered to be *c.* 16,600 km long: Norman, 2001).

In the far north of Scotland there are vertical hard rock cliffs (e.g. Duncansby Head or Dunnet Head – the most northerly point on the British mainland); often large sandy bays with extensive dune systems lie adjacent (e.g. Sinclairs Bay and Dunnet Bay). There are deep-water coastal inlets used by the oil industry near Invergordon and extensive shingle beaches at Spey Bay on the Moray Firth. A fjordic landscape on the north-west coast of Scotland may be contrasted with the large funnel-shaped estuaries on the east (e.g. the Forth and the Tay).

Further south there are the rapidly eroding cliffs of the Holderness coast in North-East England. Much of East Anglia is also subject to erosion. On the south coast of England there is a mix of high chalk cliffs (e.g. the Dover cliffs or Beachy Head) and large depositional forms (e.g. Chesil Beach and Dungeness).

Beyond the geomorphology and value of the natural coastal environment, there are many and diverse uses of the coastal 'zone'. From busy ports to popular tourist resorts and proposals for offshore windfarms, the coast and its resources are important to the national economy and society as a whole. International shipping lanes, major ports (e.g. Dover, Southampton, Grimsby, Grangemouth) and plans to expand or build new ports (e.g. Dibden Bay, Hunterston, Scapa Flow) are challenging the concepts of integrated and sustainable management of coastal resources. The coast is an important place for industry, often needing cooling water, or good links to sea transport; indeed, in 1999 22.5 per cent of all enterprise and 17.9 per cent of all employment in Scotland was within one kilometre of the coast (Scottish Coastal Forum, 2002). Much of the UK military capability is also based on the coast – not just naval bases, but many army bombing and firing ranges and Royal Air Force bases are also built on coastal land. With the encouragement of government, offshore wind energy, tidal stream power and wave power are likely to become increasingly popular ways to generate electricity.

The coast has always been popular with tourists; although generally holidaymakers now head for foreign shores, many coastal towns have populations that expand dramatically during the holiday season (e.g. Rhyl in North Wales, Burnham-on-Sea in Somerset). Many coastal towns have, however, seen a substantial drop in the numbers of holidaymakers (see Johnson, this book and Box 11.1).

Many of Britain's key towns and cities are built on the coast, or by an estuary. The most obvious example of this is London. It is often forgotten that this is a coastal city, situated near the head of the Thames Estuary, protected from storm surges by the Thames Barrier (Penrose, 2000). Often the most desirable residential property in a town or city has coastal views. Massive new development has, over the last few decades, taken place on former dockland in many of Britain's cities (e.g. London, Liverpool, Edinburgh). With all these competing development interests, not to mention conservation and global sea level rise affecting much of the British coast, management of the coastal environment is an important issue.

Despite various calls for coastal areas to be treated as an integrated unit (see Ballinger, this book; 2002), the planning system was not developed for coastal areas or the sea. The current planning systems in Scotland, England and Wales are land use planning systems; their use if extended to the sea would be questionable at best (Cox, 2002). It is beyond the scope of this chapter to review the development of coastal management in the UK; the reader is referred to Ballinger (this book; 1999; 2002; Ducrotoy and Pullen, 1999; McGlashan, 2002a). Despite Great Britain consisting of

---

Box 11.1 Tourism on the Clyde

An example of the change in tourist visits to the British coast can be found on the Clyde. Only a generation or two ago, large numbers of visitors would sail 'doon the waater' to visit locations like Dunoon, Rothesay, Helensburgh and Largs from Glasgow on steam ships. However, they are now only a short drive or train journey from Glasgow, therefore, a sunny day can see large numbers of day visitors, but the week or fortnight stay appears to be rare now.

three countries (Scotland, England and Wales) and three legal systems (English, applying to England and Wales, Scots, applying to Scotland, and udal, applying to parts of Orkney and Shetland; McGlashan, 2002b), the approach to coastal management can be considered similar: 'The way forward must be integrated management to achieve common goals delivered locally through voluntary partnerships' (Department of the Environment, 1996). At present there are over 40 coastal partnerships (CoastNET, 2003) that exist on sections of the British coast, which can be split into seven broad types (Box 11.2). However, only small sections of the British coast are covered by coastal partnerships.

The partnership approach to coastal management

The partnership approach to coastal management as used in Britain involves the various coastal stakeholders in an area coming together to form a partnership or forum. There are a number of different types of coastal partnership that can be recognized (Box 11.2). The set-up of these partnerships is highly variable depending on the relevant issues: maturity, funding and engagement. Coastal partnerships generally formed first in the major estuaries, often as part of either the English Nature *Estuaries Initiative*, or the Scottish Natural Heritage *Focus on Firths* project in the early 1990s. Over the intervening years new coastal partnerships have emerged, either on the back of similar initiatives (e.g. The European Commission Demonstration Programme on Integrated Coastal Zone Management) or where there has been a local need, or wish for action (Box 11.3). It is beyond the scope of this chapter to review individual coastal partnerships, for published information on individual partnerships, see Table 11.1 and Annex 11.1.

The partnerships that were formed through the *Estuaries Initiative* or the *Focus on Firths* initiative had a conservation agency (e.g. Scottish Natural Heritage or English Nature) behind them. These agencies went to other statutory bodies (local councils, the Environment Agency [in England], Scottish Environment Protection Agency [in Scotland], Historic Scotland, English Heritage, water companies, port authorities) and asked them if they would be willing to be included in the partnership, often alongside environmental pressure groups (e.g. Royal Society for the Protection of Birds and the Wildlife Trusts). Often the partnerships received 'pump-priming' monies to appoint a project manager or secretariat to manage the day-to-day activities of the partnership. This pump-priming money may have come from a variety of sources, but often the main donor was either English Nature or Scottish Natural Heritage. As with all pump-priming money, this funding was given on the basis that it would allow the body to develop, stabilize and find its own funding in the future (McGlashan, 2003). The concept behind the majority of the partnerships is that decisions are made following a consensual approach, whereby

Box 11.2 Examples of the various types of coastal partnerships (after CoastNET, 2003: 4)

Whilst Estuary and Firth Partnerships are usually the focus of attention in the context of coastal partnerships, there is in fact a broad range of other partnerships. Many of these have a sectoral focus, but nonetheless have an important role in delivering sustainable development (through the pursuit of integrated solutions).

Estuary and Firth Partnerships and Coastal Fora – These are broad-based, voluntary groups focused on Integrated Coastal Zone Management (ICZM) covering from small areas to major estuaries and firths. They are usually set up by statutory bodies in the first instance, although maintaining a neutral role is an important feature. A number now have charitable status.

'Coastal Groups' – These usually comprise technical officers who are involved in shoreline management. These are usually linked to shoreline management planning of a recognized coastal sediment cell and have a sectoral approach, i.e. coastal defence, to sustainable development on the coast.

European Marine Sites – These have been set up under the EU Habitats and Birds Directives and are managed by voluntary partnerships of relevant authorities and user groups. They have a nature conservation focus although integration is the key to the management objectives. Some are established under the umbrella of an estuary or firth partnership.

Areas of Outstanding Natural Beauty/Heritage Coasts – Established to manage Countryside Commission (now Countryside Agency) designations, they typically comprise a management structure led by local authorities, but including other relevant interests (statutory and non-statutory).

Marine National Parks – At present there is provision for the establishment of Marine National Parks in Scotland under the National Parks (Scotland) Act although none have yet been designated. There is currently no legislation in England and Wales for the establishment of Marine National Parks. However, the level of consensus which would be needed to establish such parks makes a partnership approach essential.

Voluntary Marine Nature Reserves – Again a partnership approach reflects the need to bring organizations together to provide for effective management.

Other coastal projects – Many *ad hoc* projects are taken forward through partnerships of service providers, e.g. South-West Coastal Path.

Box 11.3 Examples of local issues driving the formation of coastal partnerships

Examples of a local need driving the formation of coastal partnerships are the Cromarty Firth Liaison Group (CFLG), the Loch Ryan Advisory Forum and a number of estuary partnerships in the south-west of England.

The CFLG was set up as a voluntary partnership prior to the *Focus on Firths* initiative as the Cromarty Firth harbour authority, local businesses and conservation bodies wished to take a less confrontational approach to the sustainable development of the Cromarty Firth.

Loch Ryan Advisory Forum was initially formed due to worries regarding the waves generated by 'fast ferries'.

Estuary management plans in South-West England have often been driven by a reduction in the commercial viability of ports and harbours, with increasing emphasis on recreation and tourism creating a need for more water and shore management (e.g. public access and zoning).

Table 11.1 Sources of information on UK coastal partnerships

Coastal partnerships	Sources
UK	Fletcher (2003); Edwards *et al.* (1997)
Scotland	McGlashan and Firn (2003); ITAD and BMT Cordah (2002); Burbridge (2001); Firn and McGlashan (2001); Gubbay (2001); Atkins (1999); Sankey (1999)
England	Fry and Jones (2000)
Forth Estuary	McGlashan (2002a); Jennison and Kay (1999)
Tay Estuary	Burningham *et al.* (2000)
Severn Estuary	Hoare (2002); Knowles and Myatt-Bell (2001); Ballinger and Brown (2000)
Dee Estuary	Jemmett (1998)
Solent	Inder (2001)
North-West	Baker (2002)
Isle of Wight	McInnes *et al.* (1998)
Thames	Kennedy (1995); Colclough *et al.* (2002)
Humber	Fernandes *et al.* (1995)

various viewpoints are aired and decisions can be made based on the various opinions round the table, not just the opinion of the body to make the decision. To reach this aim, the majority of coastal partnerships have produced (or are in the process of producing) a management plan or strategy.

The management strategies that currently exist have a variety of forms;

many are available on the Internet, some are glossy documents and some are very technical. One approach to the development of a management strategy is through the formation of topic groups. Various interests each have a topic group (e.g. coastal defence, nature conservation, fishing). The Forth Estuary Forum used such an approach, with ten topic groups. Each group undertook work and/or commissioned research (often sponsored by a partner body, or in many cases the European Commission through the ICZM demonstration programme). Once a consensus had been reached on the content of the topic group report it was released to the Forth Estuary Forum, and made available as a public document. Once all of the topic group reports were complete, they were used to identify the key issues for inclusion in the drafts of the Forth Estuary *Integrated Management Strategy* (Jennison and Kay, 1999). This was a long process and the final text was not agreed until 1999 (Forth Estuary Forum, 1999), the process having started in 1993 (McGlashan, 2002a). The South Devon coast provides two contrasting examples of approaches to drawing up estuary management plans. Whilst local government initiated both the Teign and Exe Estuary Management Plans, various factors led to different timescales between the initiation of work and adoption of the plans. Implementation rates are probably now broadly similar, but the way in which the plans evolved has affected the willingness of the user community to sign up to the ongoing implementation of the partnership's objectives (see Box 11.4).

Whilst the degree of complexity of issues may have some influence on the timescale for developing an estuary management plan, the contrasting approaches to consultation (above and in Box 11.4) appear to have had some influence on the ease with which a plan is adopted. It also appears to influence the longer-term perception amongst the local community of the need for and value of a management plan. In particular, it has been found that a more open participatory approach to the introduction of a management plan is likely to lead to improved trust between different interest parties when discussing problems, opportunities and resolving areas of conflict in the longer term.

Many coastal partnerships have now produced their own management plans and/or strategies. Despite the haggling over the specific wording and disagreement over what are key projects or aims, the production of a management plan is the easy part. What is more difficult is the implementation of the plan. The reason this is difficult is because these coastal partnerships do not have any statutory powers. They cannot force anyone to do anything. They are even powerless relating to the actions of their core partners (Box 11.5). Once the partners agree to the management strategy, they should then review all of their own internal policies to ensure consistency (policy alignment). However, this is easier said than done, as each partner will have official processes that have to be followed to review and change policy, which are often tight in the current economic climate. Therefore, unless something is of immediate priority or related to a regulatory change

Box 11.4 Examples of the development of a management plan

With over ten years of estuary management experience in the UK to draw from now, some lessons are clear in how best to work with local communities. One of the first estuaries in England to begin the process of preparing a management plan was the Exe Estuary in South Devon. Coinciding with English Nature's Estuaries Initiative in the early 1990s, consultants were commissioned by local authorities in Devon with the view to preparing a management plan for the Exe Estuary. The consultants, based at a remote location, undertook consultation with statutory and non-statutory representatives and local community representatives (e.g. boat clubs, conservation groups, parish councils). For various political reasons and some weak information, the draft management plan was not well received by the local community. Several years later the local authorities decided to employ a locally-based estuary officer to take a different, more locally-focused approach to progressing consultation for a management plan. However, it took three years of local officer time on the Exe Estuary to undertake consultation through a more participatory approach before the Exe Estuary Management Plan was approved in 1998. An estuary officer continues to be employed by the local authorities surrounding the Exe Estuary.

As a contrasting example, in 1998 Teignbridge District Council saw the need to prepare a management plan for the neighbouring Teign Estuary in South Devon. Instead of contracting the work to consultants they employed an estuary officer to initiate the management plan preparation. Techniques such as regular public exhibitions at locations around the estuary using a 3D model, newsletters, focus group meetings and a consultation video with repeated local media involvement were used. Within 18 months a management plan had been adopted and a partnership established. The local authority continue to employ an estuary officer to implement the Teign Estuary Management Plan.

Both estuaries now produce annual action plans to aid implementation of the management plan. The approach of employing full-time, locally-based estuary officers is now common practice in the UK. Corresponding partnerships have evolved to provide a continuing management framework for preparation and implementation of the management plans.

Box 11.5 The legal validity of a coastal partnership management plan

A theoretical coastal partnership management plan may have clearly stated that there is a presumption against new development on coastal land due to worries over relative sea level rise, flood risk and nature conservation. All the partners, including Council 'A', have agreed this. But, Council 'A' has a lack of land available for development; the local plan has not been changed since the management strategy was agreed. A developer proposes that they construct luxury houses, a school, a shopping centre and a community hall. The management strategy holds no weight in law. Under the local plan, the land is available for development; therefore, there is every likelihood that the development will go ahead. Indeed, if Council 'A' refused it because of the management strategy, there is a high chance that the developer would take Council 'A' to court, as their decision was based on a document with no legal force, as opposed to the local plan, which is a statutory document.

it is unlikely to be at the top of the 'to do' list. Furthermore, as budgets are cut, support for 'partnership' bodies may be one of the first aspects to have funding withdrawn. To counter this, the Forth Estuary Forum proposed that the (over 100) actions in the *Management Strategy* would each have a lead partner assigned to them. Over 65 per cent of the actions had a lead body yet; four years on (at the time of writing) few had been completed. This would appear to be entirely due to partners having to prioritize time; their main priority is their own workload, not that of the partnership. This is despite many being committed to the partnerships they support, but their own organizations must take priority; after all, that is where their salary comes from, and where their main responsibilities lie. To try and boost the implementation process, the Forth Estuary Forum has recently reviewed all of the actions in the *Integrated Management Strategy*. The forum staff asked each of the members of the management group to rank the actions in three categories (Environment, Economy and Society), from this the top 20 actions were identified. The majority of these have now been placed into broad categories, each with a topic group, thereby focusing the attention of the partners on the key achievable issues.

The representatives of the partner bodies, who are on the various management groups, steering groups, boards of directors and topic groups, do not get paid for their time by the partnership. They either attend during their normal working hours, or make up the time they give to the partnership. They are often much more committed than the organization they represent, and there are a number of reasons for this:

1   They are at the coal face. They see what is happening at the meetings, they can see the potential and they can visualize the benefits.
2   They develop a network of people that they can contact in other partner organizations; a friendly route into an organization when they would like advice and/or guidance.
3   The representatives are often (but not always) junior- or middle-level employees; they may not be the individuals who set policy, agree budgets or can say at the meeting 'Yes I can give you £1,000', rather they have to go to their boss and suggest that it may be a good idea to sponsor or donate, etc. More senior staff often perceive that they are too busy to attend meetings.
4   They often have difficulty 'selling' these benefits to their superiors. Partly because of point 3 (above), and partly because their superiors have not seen the benefits themselves.
5   Many of the partnerships are only just emerging from the 'planning' stage and moving towards 'implementation'. Until there are major implementation benefits to quantify, the qualitative benefits will always be speculative.
6   There have been many examples of 'partnerships' during the last two decades, many of which have been considered either 'talking shops' or failures. An example being the Cairngorm Partnership, which was set up to manage competing interests (e.g. forestry, sporting estates, mountaineers, offroad driving, skiers) in the Cairngorm mountains of Scotland.

The administrative structure in coastal partnerships usually follows a basic format, with a management or steering group, which often consists of the key funding partners and/or the main statutory agencies. The number of meetings a year depends on the partnership, most meet two to six times a year. This is the body that makes up the 'networking' component of the partnership. Decisions made by the management group will govern the work programme the project staff follow (if there are any) and/or agree policy issues. Beyond this, there may be a further group that oversees the business side of the partnership (i.e. financial and personnel issues), often called the steering group or the board of directors (though all of this may be rolled into the management group). This group needs to meet regularly enough to ensure that they can keep track of company or charity issues, probably at least quarterly. Often there are project staff, project officers and/or a project manager. The project staff usually act as a secretariat to the management or steering groups and/or board of directors. The project staff may also be responsible for the identification of funds to ensure their own post in the future (see below). Some partnerships use their annual general meetings to allow their members to vote for the individuals to stand as members of the various groups. However, as the majority of funding for coastal partnerships tends to come from a core of organizations, it is usual for these organizations to be represented on the various groups. Beyond the secretariat there may be a chairperson; this individual chairs meetings and may be the 'figurehead' of the partnership. This is usually a voluntary position, but one of responsibility. However, some partnerships have identified a 'patron' (e.g. the Thames Estuary Partnership). A patron should be a high-profile individual, much respected in the community, who is willing to be associated with and act as a champion for the partnership. Box 11.6 illustrates the approach taken by the Exe Estuary Partnership.

From a legal perspective coastal partnerships can be formal or informal groups. If they are formal organizations, they usually have a constitution and/or articles of association. This can be important in relation to funding bids as funding sources may require a constitution or some other form of legal document formalizing a partnership to ensure the partnership is a legal entity. A number of coastal partnerships are registered charities; there are various legal advantages to being registered as a charity (e.g. the ability to seek certain types of funding), particularly given the makeup of coastal partnerships. Even if registered as a charity, a coastal partnership may also register itself as a company limited by guarantee. This is considered to result in greater credibility and a more open and formal decision-making procedure; however, it also generates a larger administrative workload and requires that there are individuals that are responsible for the running of the company up to a predetermined level

---

Box 11.6 The Exe Estuary Partnership approach

The Exe Estuary Partnership in South Devon provides a typical example of the management framework established by a voluntary partnership. Implementation of the Exe Estuary Management Plan is undertaken by organizations and interest groups represented through the Exe Estuary Management Partnership.

The Exe Estuary Partnership is led by a Joint Advisory Committee (JAC) made up of members from the partnership's parent bodies, with advice and issues being raised by local community representatives through focus groups. Meetings of the public Exe Estuary Forum also help to inform the partnership of wider views on current issues. The priorities and work of the partnership are therefore led by a consensus view rather than the interests of any one group or body. An estuary officer is employed by the partnership to facilitate implementation of the management plan. The estuary officer is independent of any one organization or interest group, recognizing the importance of a neutral role to progress the overall objectives of the partnership.

of financial liability. If the partnership is registered as a charity, the directors, or nominated responsible individuals cannot be paid for their services (though they may be able to claim travel and subsistence costs associated with their role). These nominated individuals have a role akin to a non-executive director in a public limited company. Therefore, it is their duty to highlight issues that they believe may have an impact upon company operations, to ensure the organization is not in breach of the rules in relation to the running of a limited company. This highlights a quandary: should these individuals be those involved in managing the coast in the various partner bodies, or individuals who have experience in the management of the financial, legal and personnel issues that are associated with running a company? The voluntary nature of these positions, coupled with the responsibility means that it can be difficult to identify individuals with the appropriate company management skills to fill such posts. One of the strengths (and weaknesses) of being a charity and/or limited company is that a coastal partnership may employ its own staff directly. Very few partnerships have opted to do this as it requires that there are individuals in the partnership that need to be aware of employment law; there are also issues associated with tax, national insurance, pensions, sick pay, maternity leave, redundancy and health and safety. These drastically increase the liability of the directors, or nominated responsible individuals, as they must also ensure that these issues are being dealt with appropriately.

Informal partnerships (partnerships that do not have a constitution, or legal entity) may have difficulties in attracting funding directly. They are unable to employ staff in their own name. However, there are ways around these obstacles. By far the majority of staff in the partnerships are 'hosted' by other bodies (generally one of the main partners). An example of this are the estuaries in South-West England which are mostly hosted by local authorities. Devon County Council have hosted the Exe Estuary Officer since the mid-1990s, Teignbridge District Council hosts the Teign Estuary Officer and South Hams District Council provide the management co-ordination services for several estuaries in South Devon including the Salcombe-Kingsbridge and Dart. Cornwall County Council and English Nature have hosted staff for estuaries such as the Fal. Harbour authorities in the South-West have become increasingly involved in estuary management to the extent that, for example, Fowey Harbour Commission host the Fowey Estuary Partnership. There are usually additional costs to the host organization, which have been estimated by Devon County Council to be in the region of £3–£4,000 per year to host the Exe Estuary Partnership. Informal partnerships can also attract funding using a similar model, whereby one of the partner organizations 'hosts' the bank account and uses its legal status as the route to attract the funding. The importance of true partnership working becomes significant in this context. In a bid for European Interreg IIIb funding to sustain Exe Estuary Partnership work, the organization hosting the Exe Estuary Officer opted out of providing the legal lead role required to participate in a European-funded project. The Environment Agency, also a key player in the Exe Estuary Partnership, offered to provide the legal lead role enabling the partnership to draw down an additional £50,000 over three years.

The majority of partnerships are physically located in the building of one of their key partners, often one of their largest funders and/or the body hosting the employment. The authors are not aware of any of the partnerships having their own office. The closest examples include the Forth Estuary Forum (Box 11.7: McGlashan, 2000 and 2002) and the Dart Estuary Partnership that benefits from office space in Dartmouth in a building owned by Devon County Council. By far the majority of the other coastal partnerships retain strong links to their major funding partners.

Funding is a key issue in most coastal partnerships in Britain; without funding the partnerships cannot employ staff. Without staff it becomes difficult for the partnerships to develop and implement their policies and strategies. As previously stated many coastal partnerships were started with pump-priming monies (Burbridge, 2001; Gubbay, 2001; Knowles and Myatt-Bell, 2001; McGlashan, 2003). The pump-priming approach is that the main donor will gradually reduce the volume of funding available, and in time the project becomes self-sufficient, not requiring the pump-priming cash. However, many coastal partnerships are chasing the same sources for funding. There are many examples from across the world of challenges associated with the pump-priming model of funding coastal management (McGlashan, 2003). The project manager or officer is usually responsible for locating funding to ensure the survival of the staffing element of the partnership. It is in the interest of the project staff to identify funding for the future of the coastal partnerships. Often their work contracts are directly related to the money project staff can raise, as their contracts are unlikely to be renewed unless they can identify enough money for their salary and associated costs. This can result in a 'hamster wheel' approach to running the partnership where so much time is spent raising funding that the partnership does not develop and move forward (Firn and McGlashan, 2001). Fry and Jones (2000) undertook a survey of how the estuarine partnership staff used their time; they found that on average the project officers spent 50 per cent of their time identifying funding for the partnership to survive. This short-term funding loop results in staff being funded on short-term contracts. As a result, staff often look for new jobs before their contracts expire. This is understandable; a number of partnerships have lost capable staff as they have been unable to fund their posts or have identified permanent jobs, or longer contracts elsewhere. This results in low morale and a loss of corporate knowledge (McGlashan, 2000). Similar funding problems have been noted in non-profit organizations in Canada (Scott, 2003). A further funding issue relates to 'in-kind' donations. These are often quite substan-

Box 11.7 The Forth Estuary Forum

The Forth Estuary Forum was one of the partnerships that participated in the European Commission ICZM Demonstration Programme. During this time, the City of Edinburgh Council
accommodated the project staff, and held the bank account. Scottish Natural Heritage hosted the employment of the project staff. At
the end of the demonstration project, the partnership found that it
was seriously lacking in funds as throughout the length of the
demonstration project; the value of the euro had fallen relative to
the pound. As a result, many of the partners had to 'prop up' the
partnership financially. Many cost savings were identified and a
number of project staff left their posts. This was a particularly hard
time for the partnership, and there were worries at the time as to
whether or not it would survive. However, as a result of this crisis,
the management group decided that the partnership required to be
operated more independently. The partnership moved from having
a body to host its bank account (and therefore not worry about bank
charges or temporary overdrafts), its employment and associated
costs (e.g. post charges, photocopying, telephone), to being a completely independent body. The first obvious change was in location;
they moved from the centre of Edinburgh to an office in the Port of
Rosyth. Accommodation was provided as 'in kind' support by Forth
Ports Plc., but the partnership had its own telephone line, an old
photocopier (donated by a university) and had to buy its own
stamps. Scottish Natural Heritage donated many of the computers as
part of their rolling computer replacement programme. A bank
account was opened with a high street bank, and the staff became
employed by the partnership (though the payroll aspects were con-
tracted out to a private company). The result of this is that the directors are very aware of financial aspects, and continually strive to
ensure the partnership finances are healthy. This allows the management group to concentrate on the networking and development of
policy and projects to 'promote the wise and sustainable use of the
Forth' (the aim of the Forth Estuary Forum).

tial, and difficult to recognize or account for. The provision of accommodation, hosting of employment, banking etc. contains with it substantial
costs. However, there are other hidden costs; for example the time that
the various partners give to the partnership through attendance at meetings, organizing events, reading minutes and championing the partnership. These are arguably the most important form of support, and should
not go unrecognized.

The partnership approach to coastal management may be considered to be a form of 'bottom-up' coastal management, establishing partnerships where the need or wish arises. This is opposed to 'top-down', which would be due to the government directing bodies to act together or establishing a coastal management department. Crozier (1998) has highlighted that this mix of 'top-down' from government initiatives and 'bottom-up' (often involving stakeholder participation) are 'two parallel and potentially conflicting paradigms'. This is an interesting distinction as local priorities are often different from national priorities. It is often difficult to think strategically at the local level; as a result, the boundaries of these initiatives must be carefully drawn. As coastal partnerships are 'bottom-up', they are considered a way of engaging with the local stakeholders and local communities. However, given that the resources of these partnerships are often tight, can they afford to be consulting with the local communities? The partnership staff often have a full workload, adding public consultation could require more staff, and therefore more resources. Who will fund such activities? Furthermore, do the public want to be consulted?

Many coastal partnerships will consult their members in relation to their policies and management plans. The involvement of local communities and a broad a range of individuals and organizations is considered a key aspect of integrated coastal zone management (Cicin-Sian and Knecht, 1998; Kay and Alder, 1999; McGlashan, 2000). However, there are other policies that encourage or specify community involvement in relation to sustainable development (e.g. through Agenda 21: UNCED, 1992), of which coastal management must be a key component. However, including local communities in a meaningful way is a substantial task. Edwards *et al.* (1997) reviewed participation in a number of coastal partnerships in the UK; they identified relatively low levels of participation. This was particularly the case in urban areas, where the population is more removed from the natural resource base. They also emphasize that attempts to engage with local communities must be tailored to the communities in question, there is no universal 'best practice'. Coastal partnerships in the UK have a highly variable approach to including communities, decision-making and membership criteria, which could leave them open to challenge regarding their representativeness (Fletcher, 2003). There are problems associated with engaging with communities other than the costs, which can be substantial. Decisions take time, often the same people engage with different consultations and communities can eventually suffer from consultation fatigue. It must also be the case that the size of the estuary catchment or coastal area covered by any one initiative determines the feasibility of a participative approach being taken to management planning. Consultation and participation are time consuming.

Challenges in the short, medium and long term

Leach and Pelkey (2001a and b) have undertaken literature reviews of watershed partnerships (predominantly in North America and Australia). Interestingly, they found that the most regular issue which emerged as being of key importance to watershed partnerships were funding and having an effective co-ordinator, facilitator or leader. In total they located 210 separate lessons learnt from watershed partnerships that can affect the success or failure of the initiative (Leach and Pelkey, 2001b). One of the main issues that Leach and Pelkey (2001a) highlight in their conclusions is that local conditions are important and that it is difficult to identify 'hard formulas' for partnership success. Despite this, a key aspect in the success of a partnership is a dedicated leader or facilitator, sustainable funding and the co-operation and commitment of the participants to the process.

In Great Britain many bodies are involved in coastal management (generally the statutory bodies, councils, harbour authorities and NGOs). However, there are still many more who are yet to be convinced that coastal management is an important issue, particularly private companies (McGlashan, 2003), but even some councils (Allmendinger *et al.*, 2002). Until partnerships develop a more inclusive range of partners their inclusion and democracy will be questioned (Fletcher, 2003). The challenge is engaging those who currently appear uninterested. Many have championed the benefits of coastal management, but private companies are yet to be convinced. Individuals and private companies often cannot understand why they should pay for coastal management. There are a number of reasons for this, but the main issues are that many perceive managing the coast as an activity that should be funded by central government. It benefits the nation, not necessarily the individual, strategic decisions are required, and these are often best made at a national level. As a result of this, many have bemoaned the lack of institutionalization in the management of coastal resources in the UK (Hansom, 1995; Ducrotoy and Pullen, 1999) and in other countries (Fournier, 2001). Furthermore, ICZM is often considered to be 'conservation'. There is no doubt that conservation is a part of integrated coastal management, but partnerships must, and do, examine and tackle a broad range of issues. Increasingly so, the emphasis is now on sustainability of coastal resources with wildlife conservation being one of many interests considered by coastal partnerships.

One of the key aspects behind a successful partnership would appear to be stating clear aims and objectives and providing evidence of how they are met (Jennison, 2001). If a partnership knows what it is doing and what it wants to do, the ability to raise funds should be improved. However, also important is the ability to identify what previous successes have been and what the benefits of involvement are. McGlashan and Firn (2003) and FCR and GSES (2000) have illustrated that there are substantial financial benefits associated with ICZM (for the environment, organizations involved, and particularly tourism), but the partnerships have not been good at identifying these and using them to justify their existence both to existing partners and to prospective future partners.

The partnerships also require support at a higher level than just their management groups. In theory this could come from the various national partnerships (the Welsh Coastal Forum, English Coastal Forum and Scottish Coastal Forum). To date the Scottish Coastal Forum (Atkins, 1999) has been the most active. This could be because they have had a project officer in a full-time post for a number of years. The Scottish Coastal Forum organizes meeting for the various Scottish project officers and encourages networking and information sharing between each of the partnerships as well as commissioning work through its own partners. There could be benefits to coastal/estuary partnerships from the increasing focus on regional government in England. Devon, as the largest county in England (with the most estuaries), has a Devon Estuary Officers group convened by the County Council on a regular basis to encourage the exchange of information and experience. Such networking proves invaluable to individual estuary officers tackling similar issues in different locations (e.g. personal watercraft use, crab tiles).

At the British level, CoastNET (http://www.coastnet.org.uk) has recently become more active in supporting local partnerships, particularly through the organization of workshops. One of these tackled the identification of tangible benefits of the individual partnerships (CoastNET, 2003). Participants recognized that there was no nationally agreed role or purpose for coastal partnerships, save the initial remit to develop integrated management strategies and plans flowing from the Estuaries Initiative and Firths Project in the early 1990s. Whilst it was desirable that partnerships reflect local needs, a certain consistency of approach would ensure that integration and value remained central to partnership activity. This would aid the assessment of partnership performance.

The participants at the workshop compiled actions which have led CoastNET to draw up a prioritized action plan. The plan assigned responsibility for actions between the partnerships themselves (both individually and working together) to CoastNET (as a neutral facilitator) and to the government. The conclusions and recommendations of the workshop are reproduced in Box 11.8.

By far the biggest hurdles for coastal partnerships in the short to medium term are the identification of sustainable funding, convincing current and future partners that they are achieving integrated coastal management, ensuring the partners implement the various plans and strategies, increasing media profile and improving political will. The current short-term funding periods, coupled with high staff turnover, is not sustainable. How can an organization encourage the sustainable management of the coast if it is not sustainably funded itself? Currently, too

---

Box 11.8 Conclusions and recommendations from the CoastNET partnership workshop (CoastNET, 2003: 10)

1   There is a considerable body of evidence within coastal partnerships which demonstrates their ability to deliver sustainable development on the coast through ICZM and 'value-added' activity. Further work is planned to bring this information together in a comprehensive form.

2   The lack of a national framework for ICZM hampers the efforts of coastal partnerships to deliver, and during the workshop many potential actions were identified for the government in order to fill this vacuum. The national stocktaking presently underway as part of the EU ICZM Recommendation and preparation of a national coastal strategy should consider this issue in detail.

3   Coastal partnerships recognize the need for a clearly defined role and purpose, and practical performance indicators. The development of such is an urgent priority.

4   Coastal partnerships could improve their performance further by improved exchange of information between such groups. As a first step a standing conference for coastal partnerships will be organized and a good practice directory will be published.

5   CoastNET has been identified as the organization best placed to take a lead on behalf of coastal partnerships in certain key areas. CoastNET will respond to the action plan with a statement of what and how it can deliver.

---

few partnerships set themselves goals and targets and use these to monitor progress. This must change, as it is a key aspect of maintaining and improving support. When assessing partnerships the assessors must look beyond outputs and instead consider influence and outcomes (which are not the same as outputs). It is the partners that can enact the plans and strategies; they are the ones with power and the ability to change policy. This may be coupled to having a higher media profile (local newspapers should have regular features on how the local partnerships in the area are doing, what has changed, and how the local population can get involved). Improving political will must be high on the agenda – but it is not straightforward. Politicians must really see the need and worth of the partnership approach, for this to happen, we need to tackle the funding, assessing, maintaining support, implementation and the media awareness.

Annex 11.1: Coastal partnerships (kindly supplied by CoastNET)

- Anglesey Coastal Path Project
- Anglian Coast Authorities Group
- Blackwater Estuary Project
- Cardigan Bay Coastal Group
- Carmarthen Bay and Swansea Bay Coastal Engineering Group
- Charmouth Heritage Coast Centre
- Cleveland Way Project
- Coed Cymru Ynys Mon
- Cone Estuary Partnership
- Cornwall and Isles of Scilly Coastal Group
- Cromarty Firth Liaison Group
- Dart Estuary Management Group
- Dorset Coast Forum
- Dorset Countryside
- Dover Port Partnership
- Druridge Bay Country Park
- Duddon Estuary Partnership
- Durham Heritage Coast
- Durlston Marine Project
- Essex Estuaries Initiative
- Exe Estuary Management Partnership
- Exmoor Heritage Coast
- Fair Isle Marine Environment and Tourism Initiative
- Falmouth Bay and Estuaries Initiative
- Firth of Clyde Forum
- Flamborough Head Heritage Coast
- Forth Estuary Forum
- Fowey Project
- Glamorgan Heritage Coast Project
- Hampshire Coast
- Hamstead and Tennyson Heritage Coasts
- Humber Estuary Management Strategy
- Isle of Wight Estuaries Project
- Kingsbridge/Salcombe Estuary
- Liverpool Bay Coastal Group
- Lundy Island
- Lyme Bay and South Devon Coastline Group
- Medway Swale Estuary Partnership
- Mersey Strategy
- Millennium Coast National Park Project Office
- Moray Firth Partnership
- Morecambe Bay Partnership

- Norfolk Coast Partnership
- North Cornwall Heritage Coast and Countryside Service
- North Devon Somerset Avon Coastal Group
- North East Coastal Authorities Group
- North East Fife Estuary Project
- North Western Coastal Group
- North Yorkshire and Cleveland Heritage Coast
- Northumberland Coastal Group
- Northumbrian Coastal Group
- Orkney Coastal Studies Forum
- Pembrokeshire Coastal Forum
- Pembrokeshire Coast National Park Authority (Awdurdod Parc Cenedlaethol Arfordir Penfro)
- Poole Harbour Steering Group
- Romney Marsh Countryside Project
- Rye Bay Countryside Project
- Rye Harbour Nature Reserve and Two Bays Project
- Scottish Coastal Forum
- Sefton Coast Partnership
- Sefton Coastal Strategy Unit
- Severn Estuary Partnership
- Shetland European Marine Sites Project
- Solent European Marine Site (SEMS)
- Solent Forum
- Solway Firth Partnership
- Solway Rural Initiative
- South Devon Heritage Coast and South Devon AONB
- South Downs Coastal Group
- South Hams Coastal Group
- Spurn Heritage Coast
- St Agnes Heritage Coast
- St Bees Heritage Coast
- Strangford Lough Management Committee
- Strangford Shellfishermen's Association
- Suffolk Coast and Heaths Project
- Sustainable Development Unit
- Taw Torridge Estuary Partnership
- Tamar Estuaries Consultative Forum
- Tay Estuary Forum
- Tees Estuary Management Plan
- Teign Estuary Partnership
- Thames Estuary Partnership
- The Dee Estuary Strategy
- The Dorset and East Devon Coast World Heritage Site (Jurassic Coast Project)

- The Minch Project
- Wales Coastal and Maritime Partnership
- Wash Estuary Project
- Wear Estuary Project
- Yealm Estuary Forum
- Ynys Enlli to Llandudno Coastal Group

References

Allmendinger, P., Barker, A. and Stead, S. (2002) 'Delivering integrated coastal-zone management through land-use planning', *Planning Practice and Research* 17: 175–96.

Atkins, S.M. (1999) 'The progress, experience and potential of integrated coastal management projects for Firths', in Baxter, J.M., Duncan, K., Atkins, S.M. and Lees, G. (eds) *Scotland's Living Coastline*. London: The Stationery Office, pp. 81–92.

Baker, M. (2002) 'Developing institutional capacity at the regional level: the development of a coastal forum in the north-west of England', *Journal of Environmental Planning and Management* 45: 691–713.

Ballinger, R.C. (1999) 'The evolving organisational framework for integrated coastal management in England and Wales', *Marine Policy* 23: 501–23.

Ballinger, R.C. (2002) 'An evaluation of integrated coastal management in the United Kingdom', in Cicin-Sian, B., Pavlin, I. and Belfiore, S. (eds) *Sustainable Coastal Management: a Transatlantic and Euro-Mediterranean Perspective*. London: Kluwer, pp. 75–93.

Ballinger, R.C. and Brown, J. (2000) 'Coping with the undercurrents of national and subnational institutional reform: lessons from a UK non-statutory estuary management programme', *Periodicum Biologorum* 102: 625–32.

Burbridge, P.R. (2001) *Lessons Learnt from Coastal Management Partnerships*. Edinburgh: Scottish Coastal Forum Report No. 3.

Burningham, H., Duck, R.W. and Watt, A.M. (2000) 'Perspectives from a newly formed ICZM partnership: the Tay Estuary Forum (Scotland)', *Periodicum Biologorum* 102: 101–5.

Cicin-Sain, B. and Knecht, R.W. (1998) *Integrated Coastal and Ocean Management: Concepts and Practices*. Washington, D.C.: Island Press.

CoastNET (2003) *Partnership Approaches to ICZM: a Vision and Action Plan*. Colchester: CoastNET.

Colclough, S.R., Gray, G., Bark, A. and Knights, B. (2002) 'Fish and fisheries of the tidal Thames: management of the modern resource, research aims and future pressures', *Journal of Fish Biology* 61 (Supplement A): 64–73.

Cox, M. (ed.) (2002) *Planning Below Low Water? Proceedings of a Seminar*. Perth, 11 June, 2002, Scottish Coastal Forum.

Crozier, G.F. (1998) 'Fallacies associated with bottom-up management', Poster presented at the Soil and Water Conservation Society meeting, San Diego, Summer, 1998.

Department of the Environment (1996) *Coastal Zone Management: Towards Best Practice*. London: HMSO.

Ducrotoy, J.-P. and Pullen, S. (1999) 'Integrated coastal zone management: commitments and developments from an international, European and United Kingdom perspective', *Ocean and Coastal Management* 42: 1–18.

Edwards, S.D., Jones, P.J.S. and Nowell, D.E. (1997) 'Participation in coastal zone management initiatives: a review and analysis of examples from the UK', *Ocean and Coastal Management* 36: 143–65.

FCR and GSES (Firn Crichton Roberts Ltd and Graduate School of Environmental Studies, University of Strathclyde) (2000) *An Assessment of the Socio-economic Costs and Benefits of Integrated Coastal Zone Management*. Brussels: European Commission. http://europa.eu.int/comm/environment/iczm/socec_en.pdf.

Fernandes, T.F., Elliott, M. and Da Silva, M.C. (1995) 'The management of European estuaries: a comparison of the features, controls and management framework of the Tagus (Portugal) and Humber (England)', *Netherlands Journal of Aquatic Ecology* 29: 459–68.

Firn, J.R. and McGlashan, D.J. (2001) *A Coastal Management Trust for Scotland*. Edinburgh: Scottish Executive Central Research Unit.

Fletcher, S. (2003) 'Stakeholder representation and the democratic nature of coastal partnerships in the UK', *Marine Policy* 27: 229–40.

Forth Estuary Forum (1999) *Integrated Management Strategy*. Edinburgh: Forth Estuary Forum.

Fournier, R. (2001) 'Uruguay y su zona Costera', Presentation at the *Ecoplata 2001 Conference: Gestión Integrada de la Zona Costera Uruguaya del Río de la Plata*. Montevideo: 14–15 May, 2001.

Fry, V.E. and Jones, P.J.S. (2000) *The Development of Meaningful Indicators of Estuarine Management Partnership Success*. Report from UCL to English Nature under the Estuaries Review.

Gubbay, S. (2001) *The Role of Scottish Local Initiatives in Implementing the Principles of Integrated Coastal Zone Management*. Edinburgh: Scottish Executive Central Research Unit.

Hansom, J.D. (1995) 'Managing the Scottish coast', *Scottish Geographical Magazine* 111: 190–2.

Hoare, A.G. (2002) 'Natural harmony but divided loyalties: the evolution of estuary management as exemplified by the Severn Estuary', *Applied Geography* 22: 1–25.

Inder, A. (2001) 'Partnership in planning and management of the Solent', in Dixon-Gough, W. (ed.) *European Coastal Zone Management: Partnership Approaches*. Aldershot: Ashgate, pp. 155–64.

ITAD and BMT Cordah (2002) *Assessment of the Effectiveness of Local Coastal Management Partnerships as a Delivery Mechanism for Integrated Coastal Zone Management*. Edinburgh: Scottish Executive Central Research Unit.

Jemmett, A. (1998) 'Implementing estuary management plans: a case study from the Dee Estuary', *Geographical Journal* 164: 307–18.

Jennison, M. (2001) *Indicators to Monitor the Progress of Integrated Coastal Zone Management: a Review of Worldwide Practice*. Edinburgh: Scottish Executive Central Research Unit.

Jennison, M. and Kay, D. (1999) 'Estuarine management by partnership: its potential and implications', in Baxter, J.M., Duncan, K., Atkins, S.M. and Lees, G. (eds) *Scotland's Living Coastline*. London: The Stationery Office, pp. 93–103.

Kay, R. and Alder, J. (1999) *Coastal Planning and Management*. London: E & FN Spon.

Kennedy, K.H. (1995) 'Producing management plans for major estuaries – the need for a systematic approach', in Healy, M.G. and Doody, J.P. (eds) *Directions in European Coastal Zone Management*. Cardigan: Samara Publishing, pp. 451–60.

Knowles, S. and Myatt-Bell, L. (2001) 'The Severn Estuary Strategy: a consensus approach to estuary management', *Ocean and Coastal Management* 44: 135–59.

Leach, W.D. and Pelkey, N.W. (2001a) 'Making watershed partnerships work: a literature review of the empirical literature', *Journal of Water Resources Planning and Management* 127: 378–85.

Leach, W.D. and Pelkey, N.W. (2001b) '210 lessons learnt from the literature on watershed partnerships', *Watershed Partnerships Project*. University of California, Davis. http://www.ucdavis.edu.

McGlashan, D.J. (2000) 'Coastal management in the future', in Sheppard, C.R.C. (ed.) *Seas at the Millennium: an Environmental Evaluation*. Volume 3. Oxford: Pergamon, pp. 349–58.

McGlashan, D.J. (2002a) 'Coastal management and economic development in developed nations: the Forth Estuary Forum', *Coastal Management* 30: 221–36.

McGlashan, D.J. (2002b) 'Udal law and coastal land ownership', *Juridical Review* 251–60.

McGlashan, D.J. (2003) 'Funding in integrated coastal zone management partnerships', *Marine Pollution Bulletin* 46: 393–6.

McGlashan, D.J. and Firn, J.R. (2003) 'Perceived socio-economic and environmental costs and benefits of ICZM in Scotland', *Scottish Geographical Journal* 119: 103–19.

McInnes, R.G., Jewell, S. and Roberts, H. (1998) 'Coastal management on the Isle of Wight, UK', *Geographical Journal* 164: 84–101.

Norman, C. (2001) 'Planning for the Scottish coastline', *Scottish Planning and Environmental Law* 84: 31–5.

Penrose, J.P. (2000) 'Implementing a sustainable flood-defence strategy for London's tidal Thames', *Journal of the Chartered Institute of Water and Environmental Management* 14: 1–6.

Rees, G. (1998) Fractels: how long is the coast? in Cracknell, A.P. and Rowan, E.S. (eds) *Physical Processes in the Coastal Zone*. Bristol: Scottish Universities Summer School in Physics and the Institute of Physics, pp. 31–53.

Sankey, S. (1999) 'The Scottish Coastal Forum: an independent advisory body to government', in Baxter, J.M., Duncan, K., Atkins, S.M. and Lees, G. (eds) *Scotland's Living Coastline*. London: The Stationery Office, pp. 123–31.

Scott, K. (2003) *Funding Matters: the Impact of Canada's New Funding Regime on Non-profit and Voluntary Organisations*. Ottowa: Canadian Council on Social Development.

Scottish Coastal Forum (2002) *Coastal Economic Statistics*. Information Sheet 7. Edinburgh: Scottish Coastal Forum.

UNCED (1992) *Agenda 21 – United Nations Conference on Environment and Development: Outcomes from the Conference*. Rio de Janeiro, Brazil, 3–14 June.

12 Shoreline management

The way ahead

Jonathan S. Potts, David Carter and Jane Taussik

Introduction

Few, if any, national coastlines exhibit such a range and variety of biophysical forms and processes as the UK. This has provided, particularly over the past millennium, innumerable opportunities for the exploitation and development of resources, as well as locational advantages. Few of these, prior to the mid-twentieth century, were determined by deliberate planning or constrained by regulations enacted in the public interest. One consequence has been substantial investment in economic activity, property and infrastructure at and adjacent to coastlines whose capacity for dynamic change were either initially unrecognized or subsequently underestimated. In a few examples, storms and other natural high-magnitude events have resulted in substantial losses of life and livelihood, but at most locations the response has been to build more or less robust forms of defence and protection structures to modify forcing factors. There is abundant archival and documentary, but surprisingly little physical, evidence for the early construction of seawalls, dykes and embankments from the eighth century onwards. Some of these were undertaken as part of progressive schemes of land claim in inter- and supra-tidal wetlands, the results of which remain part of many modern coastal landscapes.

For many centuries, and indeed up until the closing decades of the twentieth century, there was a largely uncritical confidence in the ability of engineered defences to resist, for example, the force of breaking waves, 'train' river mouths and inhibit or modify longshore sediment transport. Many hundreds of kilometres of seawalls and other control structures were constructed between 1840 and 1900, by both private landowners and public bodies. Much of this defence stock was repeatedly repaired or replaced in subsequent decades despite the evidence of beach drawdown, downdrift sediment starvation and other negative effects on the natural coastal system (Clayton, 1989; Green and Penning-Rowsell, 1999). Thus, the response to the East Coast flooding induced by the storm surge in February 1953 was to build higher and more durable walls and dykes along the previous line of defence. It was not until the 1970s that the comparative merits of 'soft' engineering, such as artificial beaches, sediment replenishment and vegetation planting, began to make some tentative inroads into the domain of 'hard' engineering. While today this approach is still regarded by some professionals as experimental and has yet to receive general endorsement by public opinion (Myatt-Bell *et al.*, 2002; McGlashan, 2003), it is becoming an increasingly important element of coastal defence strategy. Furthermore, the appropriateness of universal defence of the land against the unremitting forces of the sea is being challenged and new approaches which allow the shoreline to move landward are under discussion.

One major reason for this historically conservative and usually *ad hoc* approach to coastal defence has been the national organizational and institutional structure (Ricketts, 1986; Pettit, 1999), which continues up to the present to make a distinction between defence against flooding and protection from erosion. Furthermore, there are over one hundred maritime local authorities and other agencies with statutory responsibilities for providing shoreline management. The system is thus devolved, fractured and politically delimited, and has mitigated against co-ordination and co-operation in the interests of managing coastal processes within natural units, such as littoral transport cells (Carr, 1988; Hooke and Bray, 1995). It is, however, encouraging that there has been significant recent progress in creating a strategic, longer-term view of the principles and priorities of shoreline management (Joliffe, 1983; Lee, 1993; Hooke and Bray, 1995; Bray *et al.*, 1995). Much of this initiative for change has come from the local operating authorities, with direct experience of the deficiencies of the current system (Carter *et al.*, 2000). Central government is now embracing this approach with increasing commitment and enthusiasm (MAFF, 1993a; 1993b; 1995; Defra, 2001a), recognizing the need to accommodate shoreline management to timescales of geomorphological and ecological change. This 'sea change' in attitude, approach and methodology is particularly timely in view of the perceived increase in coastal risk and hazard exposure due to predicted climate change and relative sea-level rise (Pethick, 1993; Bray *et al.*, 1997; Defra, 2001b).

Coastal defence in England and Wales

In the context of this chapter the 'coastal defence' process includes coastal protection (protection of land from erosion and possible subsequent inundation), sea defence (prevention of flooding of land) and tidal defence in estuaries. Process is taken to include all forms of structural (engineering-based) protection and non-structural (development planning) responses to coastal hazards (Pettit, 1999). The developed nature of over one-third of the coastline of England and Wales exacerbates the potential impact of natural hazard events. Currently, 5 per cent of England's population resides in areas at direct risk from flooding from the sea (House of Commons, 1998) and nearly 3,000 hectares of English mudflats and marshes were predicted to be lost from the failure of inter-tidal areas to adjust to sea level rise in the 20 years up to 2013 (Pye and French, 1993). Significant stretches of the soft sandstone and clay cliffs of eastern and south-eastern England suffer from intense erosion, which amounts to an estimated 12 hectares of land lost per annum (House of Commons, 1998; Rendel Geotechnics, 1998). Furthermore, problems associated with artificially imbalanced littoral cell sediment budgets are being experienced in a number of coastal areas, notably southern England and the Bristol Channel. Such concerns have produced a variety of responses to protect society and the conserved natural environment, without which it is estimated that the average annual value of physical damage from flooding and coastal erosion in England and Wales would be over £2.1 billion (House of Commons, 1998; Environment Agency, 1999).

The statutory framework for coastal defence

Between 1985 and 2001 the Ministry of Agriculture, Fisheries and Food (MAFF) was charged with overall central responsibility for coastal defence in England and Wales, with equivalent bodies in Scotland and Northern Ireland. This role was assumed by the Department of Environment, Food and Rural Affairs (Defra) in May 2001. As a result of the evolution of national legislation, the components of coastal defence, coast protection and sea defence are managed separately at the lower levels of the organi-zational hierarchy. Coast protection is generally undertaken by the 88 Maritime District Councils (MDCs), nominated as Coast Protection Authorities (CPAs). Each has jurisdiction over a relatively limited stretch of coastline, and is empowered by the Coast Protection Act (1949). In con-trast responsibility for sea defence is vested principally to one authority, the Environment Agency (EA), under the Water Resources Act (1991) and Land Drainage Act (1991) (Figure 12.1; Table 12.1).

In addition, a number of other organizations contribute to the adminis-trative framework. These include statutory consultees such as the Crown Estate, English Nature and the Countryside Council for Wales, private landowners such as the National Trust, most Port and Harbour Authori-ties (operating under independent legal sanction) and those other numerous formal and informal bodies with a responsibility to represent the interests of their members, e.g. the Country Landowners' Association (Pettit, 1999).

MAFF issued a national strategy document for flood and coastal defence in England and Wales in 1993, which was expanded in 1995 (MAFF, 1993a; 1993b; 1995). Its primary aim was 'To reduce the risks to people and the developed and natural environment from flooding and coastal erosion by encouraging the provision of technically, environmentally

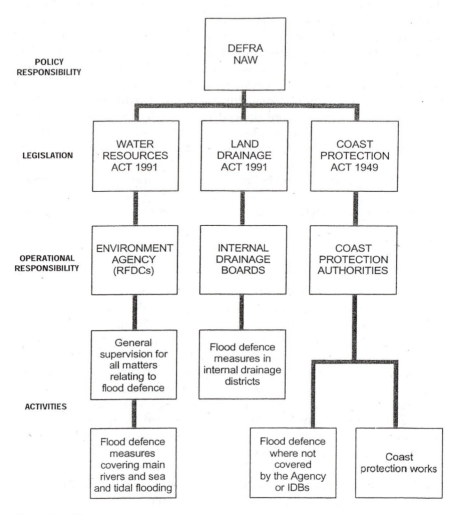

Figure 12.1 The structural administrative framework for coastal defence in England and Wales (modified from MAFF, 1993).

and economically sound and sustainable defence measures'. It sought to establish a comprehensive policy framework within which the key stakeholders could operate, plan and develop their own operational strategies, with particular reference to the need to incorporate a range of environmental objectives more fully, and improve integration with both the formal planning system and the wider spectrum of coastal-based activities and initiatives. This strategy is now recognized to require updating and Defra (in co-operation with HM Treasury, the Office of the Deputy Prime Minister and the Department of Transport) have embarked on a major consultation exercise 'Making space for water' (Defra, 2004).

Table 12.1 National legislation and policy relevant to coastal hazard management in England and Wales

Year	Events
	Planning
1947	Town and Country Planning Act 1947
1963	Government Circular to Local Authorities – *Coastal Preservation and Development*
1990	Town and Country Planning Act 1990
	(Planning Policy Guidance Note (PPG) 01 – General Policy and Principles
	PPG 07 – The Countryside. Environmental Quality, and Economic and Social Development
	PPG 09 – Nature Conservation
	PPG 12 – Development Plans and Regional Planning Guidance
	PPG 14 – Development on Unstable Land
	PPG 16 – Archaeology and Planning
	Planning Guidance Technical Advice Note (PG TAN) (Wales) – Development on Unstable Land
1991	Planning and Compensation Act 1991
1992	PPG 20 – Coastal Planning
1996	PG Wales – Planning Policy
	Coastal Zone Management: Towards Best Practice – Department of the Environment (DoE)
1998	Modernizing Planning: a Policy Statement
	Planning Guidance (Wales) Planning Policy
	PG TAN (Wales) 5 – Nature Conservation and Planning
	PG TAN (Wales) 6 – Development involving Agricultural Land
	PG TAN (Wales) 13 – Coastal Planning
	PG TAN (Wales) 14 – Development and Flood Risk
1999	PPG 11 – Regional Planning Guidance
	PPG 12 – Development Plans
2001	PPG 25 – Development and Flood Risk
	Coastal Protection and Sea/Tidal Defence
1930	Land Drainage Act 1930
1939	Coast Protection Act 1939
1949	Coast Protection Act 1949
1972	Circular 12/72 – *Planning of the Undeveloped Coast*
1973	Water Act 1973
1976	Land Drainage Act 1976
1982	Circular 17/82 – *Development in Flood Risk Areas* – DoE
	WO Circular 15/82 – *Development in Flood Risk Areas* – Welsh Office (WO)
1985	Food and Environmental Protection Act 1985
1989	Water Act 1989
1991	Land Drainage Act 1991
	Water Resources Act 1991
1992	Circular 30/92 – *Development and Flood Risk* – DoE/Ministry of Agriculture, Fisheries and Food, Flood and Coastal Defence Division (MAFF FD) 192
	Circular 68/92 – *Development and Flood Risk* – WO
1996	Policy Guidelines for the Coast – DoE
2001	Flood and Coastal Defence Policy Appraisal Guides – Defra

Benefits to date and challenges to address

Undoubtedly, this initiative has been instrumental in developing a robust, accountable and strategic approach to many aspects of coastal defence, and has established the foundations for a national policy framework based on a defined set of aims, objectives and targets (Purnell and Richardson, 2000). Its main achievement has been the creation of formal, non-statutory, Shoreline Management Plans (SMPs). In turn it has been of benefit to a number of the practical components of coastal defence, including strengthening the appraisal procedures for defence measures and flood warning systems (Defra, 2001b), clarifying the Grant Aid system (Purnell, 1996) and promoting the roles and operational activities of the Regional Coastal Groups (RCGs) (Potts, 1999).

There exist, however, a number of significant challenges, which impede the implementation of a national policy and the benefits that it seeks to deliver (House of Commons, 1998). Four key concerns have been identified. The first, often referred to as 'local dampening of national policy', is in respect of the increasing disparity between the approaches undertaken at the local and national levels. This has inhibited the effective translation of national policy objectives and subsequently hindered the progression towards a fully strategic and co-ordinated approach (House of Commons, 1998). Similarly, the legislative division between coastal protection and sea defence continues to aggravate not only administrative but also operational functions and capabilities (Lee, 1993; Bray *et al.*, 1997; Ballinger *et al.*, 2002; 2003).

Concern has also been raised over the ineffectiveness of current policy to consider adequately, and in an integrated manner, the full range of issues arising from the interface between defence and environmental attributes. More importance should be accorded to a number of key concerns, including amenity, landscape, the heightening of public awareness and participation in habitat creation and management (Huggett, 1996; Hooke, 1998). The latter issue is currently being addressed by the preparation of Coastal Habitat Management Plans (CHaMPs) which will have explicit links to SMPs (Lee, 2000; Worrall, 2002). In addition, and crucially, the current strategy has yet to establish a clear and substantive relationship with the statutory Development Plan process (Oakes, 1995; 1997; Potts, 1999; Ballinger *et al.*, 2003). Greater emphasis needs to be placed on integrating planning-based approaches and coastal defence initiatives, clarifying the niche that shoreline management should occupy in the formal planning process (Ballinger *et al.*, 2000; 2002; Brooke, 2000b; Cooper *et al.*, 2000; Taussik, 2000).

However, opportunities are presented by the proposed preparation of the second round of SMPs and the amendment of town and country planning legislation. The second round of SMPs is discussed further below but revised general guidance (Defra, 2001a) and interim procedural guidance (Defra, 2003) indicates that much closer integration of planning and shoreline management must be achieved and that SMP policy must be linked into the statutory planning system. The Planning and Compulsory Purchase Act 2004, which makes sustainable development the explicit objective of the town and country planning system and moves forward planning away from land use planning, as defined by the statutory definition of 'development', to the broader activity of spatial planning, should make it easier for shoreline management policy to be incorporated in town and country planning policy frameworks. The more flexible format of local development documents should facilitate the incorporation of shoreline management policy while strategic overview can be incorporated in the new regional spatial strategies (Taussik, 2004).

The non-statutory approach to coastal defence

Recently, a proliferation of non-statutory coastal and estuary management initiatives have sought to complement and bridge sectoral regulatory mechanisms (Table 12.2). Those most relevant to the planning and management of coastal defence are the RCGs and SMPs. These have been particularly important in the move towards a more sustainable and co-ordinated approach, although neither have statutory status.

Additionally, the wide-ranging, multi-sectoral Estuary Management Plans (EMPs) and Local Environment Agency Plans (LEAPs) play an important role in the management of coastal hazards (Jemmett, 1998). Coastal Defence Strategy Studies (CDSS) are local-authority sponsored approaches to detailed forward planning of the shoreline. They derive directly from SMPs and frequently form the basis of practical management, e.g. Beach Management Plans (BMPs), at the site-specific level. They provide both information and a strategic framework for beach managers, and extend from the relevant defence line down to the mean low water mark (Simm *et al.*, 1996) (Figure 12.2).

Presently, there are 18 regional RCGs in England and Wales covering 98 per cent of the coastline (Figure 12.3).

Although each of these has specific terms of reference, many common objectives and responsibilities may be identified. These include:

- the elimination or amelioration of the risk of defence schemes undertaken by one authority adversely affecting coterminous authorities;
- the development of compatible coastal defence management policies within and across sediment or sub-sediment transport cells;
- the provision of a forum for the exchange of information, ideas, experience and techniques;
- the establishment of effective liaison with and assistance for the

Table 12.2 Key events in the development of coastal hazard and shoreline management in England and Wales

Year	Event
1906	Royal Commission on Coast Erosion and Afforestation Vol. I
1911	Royal Commission on Coast Erosion and Afforestation Vols. II and III
1927	Royal Commission on Land Drainage
1944	*Coastal Preservation and Planning* – Department of Home Affairs ('Steers Report')
1949	Coast Protection Act
1953	Departmental Committee on Coastal Flooding (the Waverley Report)
1966–70	Countryside Commission – *The Coastal Heritage* and *The Planning of the Coastline Series*
1980	Department of the Environment – first *Coast Protection Survey*
1982	Welsh Office – *Coastal Defence Survey of Wales*
1985	Responsibility for Flood and Coastal Defence transferred to MAFF
	First Coastal Defence Group (RCG) established in Wales (Carmarthen Bay Coastal Engineering Group)
1986	First RCG established in England (Standing Conference on Problems Associated with the Coastline)
1989	National Rivers Authority (NRA) established
1990	Welsh Affairs Committee Report – *The Breach of the Sea Defences along the North Wales Coast*
1991	MAFF/WO Coastal Defence Forum established; Water Resources Act
1992	House of Commons Environment Select Committee Report – *Coastal Zone Protection and Planning*
	NRA – Survey of Sea Defences – Phases I–III
	National Audit Office – *Coastal Defences in England*
1993	MAFF – Survey of Coast Protection Defences (Biannual thereafter)
	DoE/WO – Consultation Papers: *Managing the Coast and Development Below the Low Water Mark*
	DoE – *Coastal Planning and Management – A Review*
	MAFF/WO – *Strategy for Flood and Coastal Defence in England and Wales*
	MAFF – *Flood and Coastal Defence Project Appraisal Guidance Note (PAGN)*
	MAFF – *Coastal Defence and the Environment: A Strategic Guide for Managers and Decision Makers*
	MAFF – *Coastal Defence and the Environment: A Guide to Good Practice*
	HR Wallingford Report SR 328 – *Mapping of Littoral Cells*
	MAFF: *Interim Guidance on Contents and Procedures for Developing Shoreline Management Plans*
1994	18 RCGs, covering 98 per cent of the coastline of England and Wales, established
	Coastal Group Chairmen Committee established
1995	MAFF – *Shoreline Management Plans: A Guide for Coastal Defence Authorities*
	DoE/Rendel Geotechnics Report – *Review of Earth Science Needs for Coastal Defence*
1996	Local Government Re-organization in Wales and parts of England
	Environment Agency (EA) established
	Shoreline Management National Advisory Service (SMNAS) established by the EA

Table 12.2 Continued

Year	Event
	Shoreline Management Plans Advisory Group (SMPAG) established by MAFF
	First Sub-Cell Groups formed via the Anglian Coastal Authorities Group (ACAG)
	First Estuary Shoreline Management Plans (ESMPs) developed (Humber Estuary)
	DoE – *Byelaws for the Coast* – Discussion Paper
	English Coastal Defence Forum established
	Countryside Council for Wales (CCW) publish *Seas, Shores and Coasts*
1997	Welsh Coastal Defence Forum established
	SMPAG – *Advisory Notes Numbers 1–5*
1998	Revision of Procedures for Licensing Offshore Aggregate Extraction – Crown Estate
	SMPAG – *Advisory Notes Numbers 6–12*
	House of Commons Agriculture Select Committee Review: *Flood and Coastal Defence*
1999	Completion of the 47 first generation SMPs for England and Wales
	MAFF publish *High Level Targets for Flood and Coastal Defence*
2000	Local Government Association Coastal Special Interest Group review of hazard legislation
	MAFF publish *Review of Shoreline Management Plans, Coastline of England and Wales*
2001	Defra publish *Shoreline Management Plans: a Guide for Coastal Defence Authorities*
	Defra publish *Flood and Coastal Defence Policy Appraisal* guides
2002	Defra publish *Future Evolution of the Coast*
2003	Environment Agency/English Nature – 6 provisional ChaMPs (Coastal Habitat Management Plans)
	Local Government Association's Special Interest Group on Coastal Issues publish *Managing Coastal Risk: making the shared responsibility work. Coastal Planning and Shoreline Management: a Review of Legislation and Guidance*

government in the development of national coastal defence policies (Oakes, 1995). This latter function is discharged through the national Coastal Defence Forum, convened by MAFF (now Defra) and informed by the Chairman of the RCGs Committee.

RCGs are informal consortia composed primarily of Maritime District Councils (MDCs), the appropriate regional division(s) of the EA and other agencies with statutory responsibilities, together with other interested parties co-opted for specific reasons or at particular times dependent on the range of issues and concerns (Figure 12.4). SMPs are progressed by cell and sub-cell groupings of MDCs and the EA, often including participation by English Nature and public, quasi-public and – occasionally – commercial organizations with a locally significant coastal

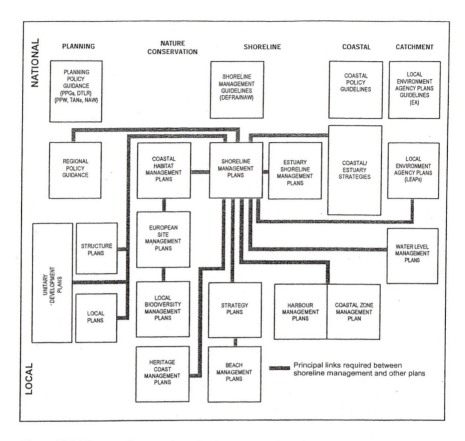

Figure 12.2 Plans and strategies of relevance to shoreline management (modified from Ballinger *et al.*, 1997).

land owning presence (e.g. Ministry of Defence; Associated British Ports; British Nuclear Fuels Ltd). Unlike RCGs, they have a specific remit and are funded by central government. However, the inspiration and pressure for the creation of SMPs came originally from the RCGs (Oakes, 2002).

SCOPAC – an example of a Regional Coastal Group

SCOPAC (Standing Conference on Problems Associated with the Coastline) is an informally-constituted consortium of 33 local and county authorities, and other regional agencies and organizations with various statutory responsibilities for the defence and protection of the coastline of south-central England (Figure 12.5). It was created in 1986 with a remit to advance the strategic management of the regional shoreline. This has

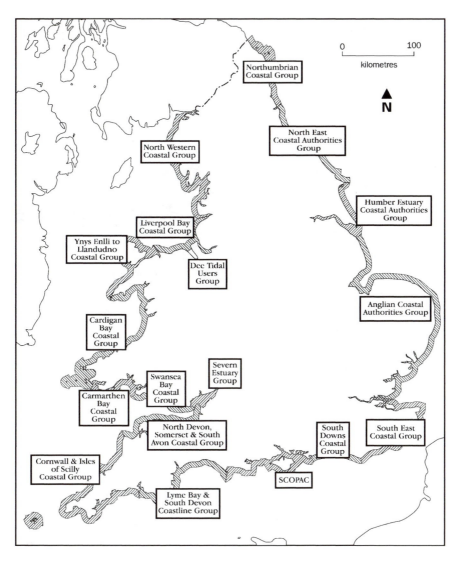

Figure 12.3 Map of England and Wales showing Regional Coastal Groups (source: Potts, 1999).

been very successfully achieved through: the exchange of information and experience on a wide variety of technical issues; promoting inter-authority consultation, co-operation and co-ordination on strategic shoreline planning; exerting influence on national policy, and commissioning research (Table 12.3). Full Conference involves delegated politicians and officers

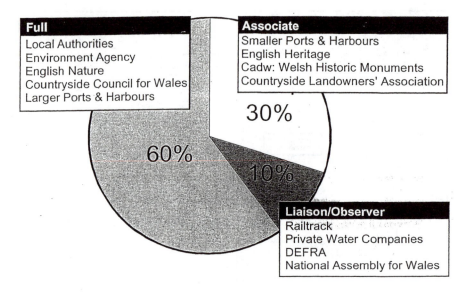

Full
Local Authorities
Environment Agency
English Nature
Countryside Council for Wales
Larger Ports & Harbours

Associate
Smaller Ports & Harbours
English Heritage
Cadw: Welsh Historic Monuments
Countryside Landowners' Association

30%

60%

10%

Liaison/Observer
Railtrack
Private Water Companies
DEFRA
National Assembly for Wales

Figure 12.4 Membership composition of Regional Coastal Groups (source: Potts, 1999).

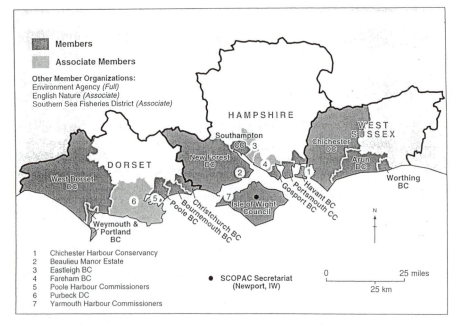

Members

Associate Members

Other Member Organizations:
Environment Agency *(Full)*
English Nature *(Associate)*
Southern Sea Fisheries District *(Associate)*

HAMPSHIRE

Southampton CC 3

WEST SUSSEX

Chichester DC

New Forest DC 4

Arun DC

DORSET

West Dorset DC

2

Havant BC

Worthing BC

6 5

Poole BC

Christchurch BC

Bournemouth BC

Isle of Wight Council

7

Gosport CC

Portsmouth CC

N

Weymouth & Portland BC

1   Chichester Harbour Conservancy
2   Beaulieu Manor Estate
3   Eastleigh BC
4   Fareham BC
5   Poole Harbour Commissioners
6   Purbeck DC
7   Yarmouth Harbour Commissioners

● SCOPAC Secretariat
   (Newport, IW)

0   25 miles
25 km

Figure 12.5 SCOPAC membership.

Table 12.3 SCOPAC – key roles

- Support the duties and responsibilities of member organizations relating to coastal defence and protection
- Promote and co-ordinate regional strategic shoreline management objectives
- Commission, disseminate and apply research
- Facilitate the communication of experience and best practice
- Influence the development of national and European Union policy

from each member organization, with the latter also meeting regularly to discuss technical and policy issues. This element of accountability ensures that SCOPAC has a strong presence amongst the RCGs in England and Wales.

Through the medium of a modest budget, SCOPAC has commissioned several independent research studies (Table 12.4) designed to improve the knowledge base informing future regional shoreline management. Amongst other issues, these studies have defined the scale, pattern and linkage of littoral cells and sub-cells (Bray *et al.*, 1995); begun the task of quantifying sediment budgets (Carter and Bray, 2003); made predictions of sea-level rise and a scoping of potential policy responses (Bray *et al.*, 1997); and reviewed the quantity and quality of regional tide gauge data. Most of these projects have been undertaken by specialist groups in regional universities, thus strengthening links between scientific thinking and management practice. They have also highlighted many areas of uncertainty that require further research, thereby introducing continuity and longer term objectives to SCOPAC's role.

SCOPAC has also used part of its budget to contribute to collaborative research undertaken by groups of professional consulting companies and public agencies (such as the British Geological Survey). Included here are major investigations into sea bed sediment mobility east and west of the Isle of Wight and a CIRIA-directed Beach Management Manual. Through

Table 12.4 SCOPAC – commissioned research studies

- Sedimentation and sediment transport database
  University of Portsmouth, 1998 (revised 1992, 1994, 1998, 2002)
- Coastal sediment transport study
  University of Portsmouth, 1991 (revised 2003)
- Sea-level rise and global warming
  University of Portsmouth, 1992
- Tidal information: relative sea-level rise on the South Coast of England
  University of Portsmouth, 1994
- Beach profile change and offshore sediment transport
  University of Southampton, 1995
- Sediment inputs in the SCOPAC Region
  Rendel Geotechnics, British Geological Survey and Posford Duvivier, 1996–9
- SCOPAC: a critique of the past, a strategy for the future
  University of Portsmouth, 1999

this, SCOPAC member authorities have had the opportunity to both influence and benefit from initiatives of national significance and considerable practical value. More recently, SCOPAC and other RCGs have been successful in securing central government support for a medium-term programme of coastal process and landform development monitoring.

Despite its reliance on the voluntary input of delegated officers, SCOPAC has been active in several other ways. It has organized a biannual conference dedicated to issues with implications for national and international strategic and sustainable shoreline management. It has also part-sponsored a wide range of regional initiatives, many of them concerned with the more intangible elements of shoreline defence and protection. Examples include a Solent Science Conference (Collins and Ansty, 2000), archaeological research into prehistoric coastal landscapes and nearshore ecological baseline mapping.

Although not directly responsible for the production of the seven SMPs within its regional area, SCOPAC has concerned itself with the policy issues involved in their implementation common to all plans. These have included the potential adoption of non-interventionist strategic coastal defence options: linkage to the processes of statutory planning at the coast, the vexed problem of compensation to landowners resulting from policy adoption, and the impact of defence works on coastal ecosystems and habitats. It is in this respect, perhaps more than any other, that SCOPAC has revealed a comprehensive awareness of the interaction between shoreline management and the interests and values of other coastal users (McInnes *et al.*, 1998). With its simultaneous initiative in promoting active contact with comparable informal groups in European Union member states, SCOPAC has now become a key organization in the advancement of national and international, as well as regional, shoreline management (Figure 12.6)

In 1999 SCOPAC commissioned a critical review of its achievements and its potential for future development (Carter *et al.*, 1999a; 1999b). Amongst its several recommendations (many of which are currently being implemented) it was proposed that retention of non-statutory status would best serve its interests. By that means, it maintains independence and objectivity, promotes the regional interests of its member organizations and engages constructively in national policy debate. SCOPAC has now adopted the revised Terms of Reference, suggested in the above report (Table 12.5), which might serve as a model for the other RCGs in England and Wales.

All regional RCGs – both individually and collectively – have had and continue to have an overview – of SMP production, both in relation to preparing individual plans and shaping national shoreline management policy (Hooke and Bray, 1995; Potts, 1999). Based on specified lengths of coast, SMPs provide a strategic framework for decisions on coastal defence management over the next 50 years, taking account of coastal evolution,

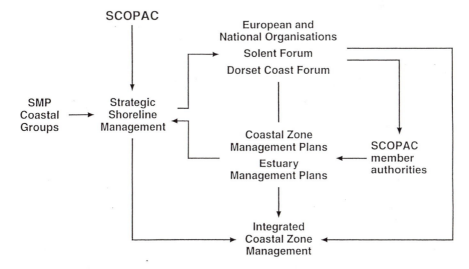

Figure 12.6 SCOPAC: relations with regional, national and European Union coastal zone and shoreline management organizations.

Table 12.5 SCOPAC – revised terms of reference (1999)

To promote sustainable coastal management in general, and shoreline management in particular, and facilitate the duties and responsibilities of local authorities and other organizations managing the coastal zone of south-central England by:

- Securing a consensus view of member organizations on regional strategic and sustainability objectives, and their means of delivery.
- Effecting consultation, co-operation and co-ordination between member organizations on issues of common concern.
- Promoting, co-ordinating and undertaking research to increase understanding of the regional shoreline environment, and in other ways expanding the knowledge base appropriate to regional policy and practice.
- Increasing awareness of the need to deliver national and international statutory obligations.
- Actively representing the interests of member organizations in the development of national and international policies relating to the implementation of shoreline management.
- Providing a forum for the communication of experience and best practice.
- Acting as a formal consultee on central government policy and guidance, and other nationally-directed initiatives.

present-day processes and other relevant environmental and human issues and needs (MAFF, 1995; Defra, 2001a). Since their introduction in 1995, 47 SMPs have been produced using a co-operative, multi-stakeholder approach (Figure 12.7). Although these plans promote liaison and co-ordination between authorities, agencies and other interested parties

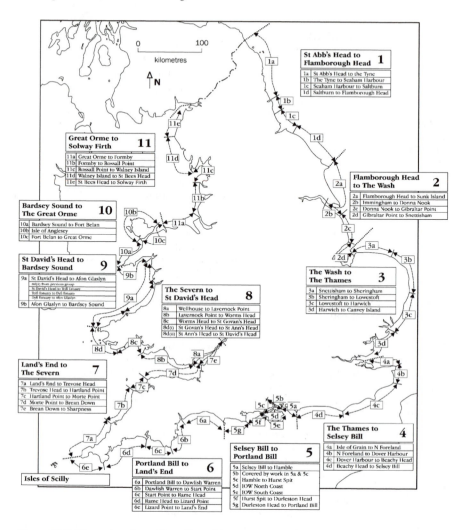

Figure 12.7 Map showing Shoreline Management Plans in England and Wales (source: Potts, 1999).

involved with coastal defence, they have been criticized for their limited interaction with the wider coastal community, including with the statutory planning system (Cooper *et al.*, 1999). Since then, guidance on SMPs has been updated (Defra, 2001a) and a substantial research exercise has been undertaken by a consortium of consultancies to establish the most appropriate approaches to be adopted in the preparation of a second round of SMPs. This included consideration of the scientific underpinning of plans; mechanisms to establish social and economic requirements as well as environmental needs and processes; and the means to develop transparency and inclusivity in SMP policy making. The resulting interim pro-

cedural guidance for production of SMPs has been available for consultation (http://www.defra.gov.uk/corporate/consult/smpguidance/index.
htm) and is being tested through three pilot SMPs in the South-East and
East Anglia before being finalized. Its publication will result in some
amendment to current Defra guidance on SMPs (Defra, 2001a; Fletcher,
1998; Cooper *et al.*, 2000; 2002).

National co-ordination of the non-statutory approach to coastal
defence is undertaken by the Defra Coastal Defence and the Welsh
Coastal Group Forums. These promote an active and constructive partnership between all levels of government and other parties with coastal
defence interests. They aim to provide a strategic understanding of the
common issues as well as developing a series of best practice guidelines
(Hathaway, 1992; Potts, 1999). In addition, two further national bodies,
the Shoreline Management Plans Advisory Group (SMPAG) and Shoreline Management National Advisory Service (SMNAS), have promoted a
more consistent, co-ordinated and informed approach to shoreline management through networking and the production of relevant guidance
(Leggett, 1996; Hutchison, 1997) (Table 12.2).

Examining elements of the shoreline management process

A research project which involved extensive interview and discussion with
key personnel examined the perceived benefits as well as shortcomings of
RCGs in England and Wales (Potts, 1999; 2000). Specifically, the study
examined the information needs and resource requirements of six of the
18 regional RCGs and the SMPs each accommodated. Six case study RCGs
were chosen: Anglian; North Western; Severn Estuary; Cornwall and Isles
of Scilly; South Downs; and the South East, as representative of both simil-
arities and diversity.

Benefits of Regional Coastal Groups

The findings of this research, as well as other analyses, indicate that there
is a general feeling of satisfaction from stakeholders with respect to the
role and achievements of RCGs. There have been, and should continue to
be, significant improvements in the planning and management of the
shoreline since the emergence of RCGs and associated SMPs (Potts, 1999;
2000; Carter *et al.*, 1999a; Smith, 2000; Cooper *et al.*, 2002). The most
significant benefit has arisen through the format and approach developed
by RCGs and SMPs. These have been successful in fostering a regional and
co-ordinated approach to planning and management for coastal defence.
Interviewees agreed that the co-operative, multi-skilled basis of RCGs provides opportunities for the full discussion of common issues of concern,
improved information dissemination and, importantly, joint strategic
management and planning. Similarly, the use of SMP sub-cell groups was

also identified as a highly positive development, as these groups have generated a more consistent, coherent and longer-term approach to the management of coastal defence.

The second key theme to emerge related to the substantial levels of information collected during the development of the first generation of SMPs. Interviewees considered that this factor has aided both strategic, regional level decision-making as well as addressing gaps in the knowledge base for specific coastlines. In particular, increased levels of information had markedly improved awareness of the need for more environmentally accountable engineering schemes and the need to proactively consider defence options other than 'hold the line', especially on previously contentious or controversial coastal frontages.

The third key benefit identified related to the role played by RCGs in improving the representation of local operating authorities at central government level(s). RCGs have provided a concerted and united approach by which to lobby, or liaise, with central government. This has arguably contributed to a heightened profile of coastal defence issues on the political, institutional and public agendas at national, regional and local levels.

Many stakeholders were of the opinion that the strategic approach developed by RCGs and SMPs has been a positive step in working towards the requirements of the European Union 1992 Habitats Directive 92/43/EEC. This is especially so in respect to addressing the crucial area of identifying and defining alternative strategic coastal defence options. Thus, although an individual strategic defence policy option may be incompatible with one or more environmental objectives, options adopted for adjacent co-management units in the overall SMP area may compensate for such adverse effects. As such a fully integrated strategy at the SMP level can be environmentally positive. This will be enhanced by the implementation of revised strategic defence options for second generation SMPs (Defra, 2001a) and ChaMPs (Lee, 2000; Worrall, 2002).

Limitations of Regional Coastal Groups

The development of a strategic, co-ordinated and multi-skilled shoreline planning and management process cannot be realistically achieved in the relatively short timescale of 14 years since the creation of the majority of regional RCGs and eight in the case of most SMP Coastal Groups. There have been, and will continue to be, a number of shortcomings which participants must seek to address.

The most prevalent shortcoming widely identified is that RCGs have no statutory recognition or powers. Interviewees argued that such a lack of power may limit the effectiveness of groups as well as restricting the time-span over which planning can be effective. Similarly, it is felt that their non-statutory basis may encourage an unstable or fluctuating management base with member organizations participating or leaving depending on prevailing circumstances. The experience of SCOPAC, however, serves to contradict this, with a steady increase in membership over its 16-year existence (Carter *et al.*, 1999a and b). It is also the consensus view of SCOPAC that its position preserves objectivity and status and encourages independent thinking.

There are two major criticisms that can be levelled at RCGs during their formative period: 1) the lack of a standard basis or format for each group in terms of membership and style of governance; and 2) a degree of bias towards engineering and other technical issues. In both cases, however, these problems have been or are being addressed. First, the development of the national level coastal defence fora has significantly improved consistency of approach. Second, the composition of the majority of groups has markedly expanded, more accurately reflecting the variety of matters relating to the interface between both coastal defence and coastal management and the diversity of organizations tasked with policy and practice relevant to the shoreline environment (Smith, 2000).

Review of first generation SMPs – benefits and shortcomings

The majority of interviewees were dissatisfied over various elements of both the procurement and consultation stages of SMP production. Although several of these factors have been previously reported (i.e. Child, 1996; 1997; O'Riordan and Ward, 1997; Fletcher, 1998; Potts, 1999) interviewees emphasized their significance. In terms of the procurement process interviewees focused on two main problem areas: the content and style of the brief, and the method of pricing. It was felt that these had both arisen through the differing perceptions of MDCs and consultants preparing the brief for these two main elements. The concern expressed in relation to the consultation process was that this phase of plan development was often overly focused on a limited range of participants, specifically statutory agencies and particular interested parties (O'Riordan and Ward, 1997). In addition, the task of consultation was underestimated, and inadequately funded, by MAFF.

A MAFF-commissioned research project has provided an objective review of a selected number of first generation SMPs (Cooper *et al.*, 2000; 2002). It identifies their key benefits and shortcomings, based on extensive discussion with personnel from organizations responsible for their creation, development and application.

Their principal strengths and benefits are perceived to be:

i   Synthesis of a previously very scattered and fragmented knowledge base.

ii   Provision of a robust foundation for progressing future strategic and proactive approaches to shoreline management, including recommendations for further research and monitoring.

iii Consideration of the environmental and amenity impacts of coastal defence and protection, predicated on the concept(s) of sustainability.

iv   Adoption of medium- to long-term timescales (usually in the order of 50 years) for the implementation of carefully and critically selected defence options.

v   Improvement of communication between local/regional and central government agencies.

Conversely, there are a number of weaknesses, in particular:

a   Lack of any national (and often regional) consistency of presentation format and analytical approaches.

b   Weak linkage between SMPs and the multiplicity of other statutory and non-statutory coastal zone plans, thereby potentially undermining the viability of strategic defence options for critical frontages (Taussik, 2000).

c   Conflict between the strategic vision of SMPs and the economic and social responsibilities of local authorities, often compounded by ambiguous or permissive guidance and legislation from central government. This factor tends to favour the maintenance of the status quo (often a 'hold the line' approach) in preference to more radical alternatives such as shoreline retreat and re-alignment.

d   Unrealistically high expectations of the immediate benefits of SMPs.

e   Vague guidance to operating authorities on the nature, purpose and organization of public consultation, heightened by lack of resourcing and under-estimation of the complexities of this task.

The last two points, in particular, are arguably more effectively dealt with at the level of CDSSs, which are undertaken for specific lengths of coastline with one or more clearly identified problems. These studies explore the issues and options in detail, using the appropriate SMP as the basic framework (Hamer *et al.*, 1999). Many are recently completed or currently in progress, and are an effective means of capitalizing on the strengths, and rectifying the weaknesses, of SMPs (Leafe *et al.*, 1998). The development of CHaMPs initially for selected areas of the English and Welsh coastlines (Lee, 2000; Rees, 2000) is a reassurance that the status and role of SMPs will be enhanced, whilst simultaneously addressing some of their deficiencies (Brooke, 2000a). The publication of revised guidance for second generation SMPs (Defra, 2001a) has addressed most of the major weaknesses listed above, but it remains general in nature. The detailed interim procedural guidance on producing SMPs should further address these problems but will only come into operation for the second round of SMPs once the pilot exercise, based on three areas, is complete.

Future tasks and responsibilities of Regional Coastal Groups

There are a number of key issues for RCGs to address as strategic shoreline management advances in its scope and technical complexity.

The status of Regional Coastal Groups

Although a lack of statutory power is acknowledged, in some respects, as a shortcoming of RCGs (House of Commons, 1998; Potts, 1999; Carter *et al.*, 1999a; 2000), it seems equally problematic as to how to grant formal powers to these groups. This is especially so given the consensus-based approach and multi-organizational format of RCGs, which may not be compatible with such powers. For example, a formally-constituted role might contribute to a bias towards existing statutory agencies and larger organizations, thereby isolating smaller or peripheral stakeholders; and a potential loss of autonomy, adaptability and dynamism. Furthermore, it seems difficult to envisage how statutory RCGs would be staffed and resourced, considering that membership is currently composed of a variety of independent organizations that contribute resources (principally officer time) on a voluntary basis.

Given these reasons and the evident degree of satisfaction with the status quo (Carter *et al.*, 1999a; 2000), it would seem most appropriate for RCGs to seek to consolidate and enhance their present style, and expand their approach to planning and management. This may be achieved by a more co-ordinated and consistent approach to shoreline management at the national level, working within a more clearly defined set of national guidelines and recommendations (Smith, 2000).

SMP implementation

RCGs should seek to ensure that individual SMPs within their areas of concern are implemented effectively. This requires SMPs to be designed and utilized as 'live', iterative documents adjusted to the evolutionary timescales of their natural coastal process regime, so far as these can be determined. Each SMP should be able to withstand exacting scrutiny and appraisal as well as continued updating and inclusion of new information. In essence, plans should be viewed as dynamic and flexible tools rather than documents that present a static picture. This may be more easily accomplished in the second round of SMPs with their requirement to consider a 100 year time frame over three epochs of up to 20 years, from 20 to 50 and from 50 to 100 years. RCGs should ensure that completed SMPs are adopted by the relevant operating authorities and that their recommendations are adhered to. In this respect, greater emphasis should be placed on attempting to remove any political, socio-economic or institutional bias that may occur when selecting preferred strategic policy options. This is especially so for frontages where closely-argued decisions between 'hold the line', 'managed retreat' or some form(s) of re-alignment are involved (Leafe *et al.*, 1998; Potts, 1999; Cooper *et al.*, 1999; Lee *et al.*, 2000).

Integration within and between adjacent SMPs

It will also be important to seek greater integration both within individual SMPs as well as between them. Notably, the individual management units contained within a specific SMP must be closely linked. Co-terminous management units should have the same, or similar, policy options in order to achieve compatible results. Compatibility between sub-cell management units is necessary, in order that full cells may be managed as coherent process units. Although the production of sediment cell-wide SMPs is usually viewed as impractical it should be possible to incorporate some form of cell-wide strategic overview (Hutchison and Leafe, 1996; Oakes, 1997). The conclusion of the Future Evolution of the Coastline Project (FUTURECOAST) (Burgess *et al.*, 2002; Defra, 2002) and the implementation of ideas expressed in the consultation exercise on a new strategy for flood and coastal erosion risk, Making Space for Water (Defra, 2004), should assist here. Within this a commonalty of objectives may be framed, in conjunction with longer-term aims and targets. These may embrace not only shoreline management, but also wider coastal management and other land-based issues at the regional level (Potts, 1999; Defra, 2004). Furthermore, RCGs and their individual members must continue to collaborate closely in order to work towards the co-ordination of individual CDSSs. The procedural guidance on SMP production should be particularly useful in providing a framework for this.

Co-ordination with other plans and programmes

The need for SMP policy to be integrated into plans of the statutory planning system has been mentioned. It must also integrate with other statutory plans, notably single schemes of management for European sites under the Birds and Habitats Directives. In due course, it must also integrate with river basin management plan policy.

Consideration also needs to be given to suites of other non-statutory coastal plans that collectively or individually may exist in particular areas (e.g. McInnes *et al.*, 1998; Oakes, 2002). Particularly important is to link the SMPs and the forthcoming catchment flood management plans. Improving integration between these plans should be seen as an attempt to reconcile the competing demands of different user interests caused by such obstacles as political bias, departmental barriers, operational inadequacies, lack of human resources and financial constraints within and between the various plans and stakeholders (Potts, 1999). Greater emphasis should be placed on developing common objectives, strengths and resources, multi-skilled teams, joint strategic planning initiatives and programmes of education, interpretation and training. Focusing on such areas may, therefore, help the next generation of SMPs interact more effectively with the plethora of current plans and those in preparation, as well as facilitating some degree of rationalization (Potts, 1999; Carter *et al.*, 1999b; Brooke, 2000b; Cooper *et al.*, 1999; 2000; Taussik, 2000; Lee *et al.*, 2000; Defra, 2001a; 2004).

Broadening the scope and definition of shoreline management

Recent research has established that existing policy, and much of its terminology, is either too narrow or inflexible to encompass the wide range of prevailing and future issues facing stakeholders. This is especially so in relation to the 'militaristic' phrases employed in first generation SMPs to describe responses to coastal hazards such as 'hold the line', 'advance the line' and 'retreat the line'. Such terms – although now modified by revised 2001 guidelines – have been viewed as somewhat contradictory to an anticipatory and sustainable approach. It is suggested that the management process must embrace a broader definition and scope, extending beyond purely structural defence considerations. This will require both an acknowledgement that coastal defence is only one, albeit an important, component of the planning and management process. As indicated by the interim procedural guidance (Defra, 2003) reference needs to be made to a wider range of issues that need to be reflected in shoreline management policy in order to move towards implementing the concept and practice of sustainability. A more holistic approach should include a broader suite of environmental objectives coupled with public concerns such as access, safety, ownership, development control, landscaping and community involvement.

Improved information management

Improvements to the management of information are of crucial importance if RCGs are to consolidate existing resources as well as address identified shortfalls. Particular emphasis needs to be placed on two key areas. First, efforts must be made to decrease the diversity of Information Communication Technologies (ICTs) employed both within individual RCGs and across the shoreline management process. Research has indicated that the wide variety of ICT systems employed has been detrimental to the availability, quality and compatibility of information resources. This is especially so within RCGs using more than one consultancy or consortia to prepare their SMPs. Second, although there have been numerous ICT systems employed, patterns of use have not been uniform across the full range of stakeholders (Potts, 1999; Defra, 2003).

Findings indicate that the most appropriate means of addressing these concerns is through the introduction of a series of formal guidelines on the roles and uses of ICTs for shoreline management. The systems adopted need to be evaluated for their effectiveness and compatibility to ensure that they provide an appropriate operating platform. Additionally, Defra intends to respond to the need for a complementary programme of education and training for consultants involved in SMP preparation. This should include familiarization with the ICT systems being used but will need to be supported at the RCG level with familiarization of the ICT systems employed by relevant stakeholders. RCGs may have a role in the latter.

Enhanced communication

Although the process of communication within and between RCGs is generally satisfactory, several factors need to be addressed to enhance this situation. Arguably, of most importance is the process of both consolidating and interpreting the work of the national level bodies. Greater emphasis should be placed on collaboration and co-ordination in order to pool specialist expertise and resources.

Continued effort needs to be focused on developing a consensus-based approach between all interested parties. Specifically, a clearer mechanism for integrating the views of co-opted members should be introduced. It is proposed that each member submits position papers and other information relating to their particular role so as to promote greater awareness of each organization's interaction with shoreline management. Similarly, the roles and responsibilities of RCGs and the objectives of the management process need to be more widely disseminated to other interest groups, such as non-statutory coastal initiatives, the formal development planning sector and the general public.

Education, interpretation and training programmes

As a means to complement and enhance the requirements outlined above, it is suggested that a standardized programme of education, training and interpretation is introduced. Research has indicated that such a programme would be of benefit to a number of areas, including: clarifying the components as well as the expectations of what may be achieved by the management process; improving the understanding of the roles and needs of the various organizations, plans and programmes involved;

increasing the familiarity and standardization of ICT use; strengthening the co-operative, multi-skilled approach; and developing a more effective means of 'selling' the concept and practice of sustainable ('soft') shoreline management to the public. The new two-year foundation degree in Rivers and Coastal Engineering, funded by the Environment Agency and operated through a consortium of universities, will provide an important contribution to this vision (http://www.environment-agency.gov.uk/foundationdegree).

To address these areas it is recommended that a national shoreline management information 'package' be developed. In essence, this would provide a 'core information pack' for all stakeholders to utilize as an aid to both policy implementation and practical management. To strengthen the regional approach to management this package should comprise subsections, which conform to a standard scope, format and media for ease of dissemination. In this way detail on local and regional conditions may be incorporated.

A standardized training programme to complement the information pack is also identified as a key future requirement. RCG members should be encouraged to attend workshops and seminars on various aspects of shoreline management, and where applicable wider coastal and environmental management (i.e. Heeps, 1996). A model approach has already been established by SCOPAC and adjacent RCGs, with specific reference to the co-ordination of approaches to sediment transport and process monitoring. Similarly, it is recommended that linkages be established with academic and professional institutions to offer courses on related subjects leading to formal qualifications or some form of continuing professional development.

Consolidate research, monitoring and review

Although the foundations of a centralized system for research and monitoring have been established through the SMPs and – more recently – through RCG co-operation with Defra, the need for greater effort in this area is an imperative for successful management. Particular attention needs to be given to several areas. First, it is evident that improvements to the quality and quantity of research are required to address the 'patchiness' of the existing knowledge base. Considerable concern has been raised over the lack of systematically-ordered information, especially in relation to physical processes (addressed by FUTURECOAST; Burgess *et al.*, 2002). Second, monitoring programmes should consider both strategic and local concerns to facilitate a more co-ordinated approach. This is especially important for the development of consistency between and across each management unit in single SMPs. Third, the monitoring and review process must be actively pursued after the completion of CDSSs.

Overall, a standardized system of comprehensive monitoring needs to be introduced, whereby each RCG develops a comprehensive regional dataset. These may then be integrated to produce a national resource base against which future changes of process regime and/or socio-economic policy may be assessed, and guidance amended accordingly.

Improved consultation and participation

An acknowledged limitation of RCGs, and the first generation of SMPs, has been their limited provision for wide consultation and participation (Child, 1996; O'Riordan and Ward, 1997; Cooper *et al.*, 2000; 2002). Consultation was often overly focused on a limited range of participants, specifically the statutory agencies and particular stakeholders, with little effort made to involve wider interest groups and the public at large (Child, 1997; Potts, 1999; Lee *et al.*, 2000). Experience from other national coastal management initiatives, such as those developed in Canada and New Zealand, have illustrated the advantages of deliberate and comprehensive stakeholder and community involvement (Rosier and Hastie, 1996; Hildebrand, 1997). Improvements in consultation and participation coupled with the consolidation and enhancement of communication between stakeholders are essential, so that further co-ordination and, eventually, integration with other coastal programmes can take place. Defra's procedural guidance of SMP production places considerable emphasis on this aspect (Defra, 2003).

Defra (2003) proposes that the RCGs responsible for SMP preparation prepare stakeholder engagement strategies before work on the plan starts. This will set out the duration of, and level at which, stakeholder involvement should be undertaken in order to ensure that inclusive and transparent approaches are developed to policy formulation and conflict resolution. Particularly important will be the links to the statutory planning system with its emphasis on sustainable development and spatial planning. Other research (Potts, 1999) has suggested that some form of semi-permanent RCG membership might be valuable as a means to incorporate a wider base of interested parties. Additionally, it is recommended that RCGs develop, or where applicable, strengthen links with other coastal and environmental (including flood risk) initiatives. While newly formed flood risk fora and groups may provide valuable links in estuarine and coastal locations, the Estuary Management partnerships and coastal fora are also identified as particularly effective mechanisms to facilitate greater participation and consensus-building. The broader approach and membership base of estuary management partnerships and regional coastal fora are seen as offering readily available means by which CGs could improve levels of dialogue with other stakeholders and the general public who were largely excluded from first generation SMPs.

The importance of mechanisms to educate public awareness of SMP preparation and review has been highlighted (O'Riordan and Ward, 1997;

Potts, 1999; Carter *et al.*, 1999a; Taussik, 2000). Defra (2003) proposes that RCGs should consider the widest possible means of information dissemination and exchange including use of the Internet, local media such as newspapers, radio and television, exhibitions and meetings and project specific newsletters. They could also involve themselves in other public events connected with the coastal zone to keep coastal defence issues fresh in the public mind. RCGs could contribute by actively encouraging the early involvement of the public in plan production and ensuring that such involvement is a two-way process based on active and regular interaction (Ballinger *et al.*, 2000). The procedural guidance being prepared for second generation SMPs (Defra, 2001a) should help to realize some of these needs and aspirations.

Conclusion: moving forward

Overall, the findings of recent research suggest that there is a general feeling of satisfaction from stakeholders with respect to the recent development of the shoreline management process in England and Wales, and in particular the work of RCGs. However, RCGs – and the SMPs they co-ordinate – should not be seen as panacea for resolving the diverse range of often competing issues that constitute shoreline management. Development, production and implementation of a strategic, co-ordinated and multi-skilled shoreline planning and management process cannot be realistically achieved in the short term. There exist, and will continue to exist, a number of challenges, which face those involved in both policy and practice. Proactive approaches achieved through the implementation of co-ordinated, regional-based initiatives, should be the foundation of the shoreline management process. Emphasis in the short term should focus on refinement of programme implementation and documentation, but over the longer term it must concentrate on improving the integration of SMPs with other key coastal zone management plans and programmes.

Several further challenges will also need to be addressed. First, policy-makers and practitioners need to develop a greater understanding of human behaviour, in particular how both individuals and communities respond to potential and/or actual hazard events, policy decisions and changes, information and education. This would reveal their understanding and acknowledgement of the range of possible adaptations and adjustments, particularly non-interventionist strategic defence options and 'soft' engineering techniques.

Second, RCGs should place greater emphasis on viewing shoreline management as an iterative, problem-solving process. The move, under Treasury Guidance in 2003, that second round SMPs should deal with a time scale of 100 years (divided into epochs of 0–20, 20–50 and 50–100 years) (Defra, 2003) should facilitate this approach. Encouraging certain procedures such as the employment of specialist consultants, regular and systematic policy appraisals, the utilization of education and interpretation tools and community involvement must be regarded as crucial to the quality and robustness of the final plan document. The representation, support and subsequent commitment of the full range of stakeholders advised by Defra (2003) will be valuable in ensuring that the prevailing strategy is routinely reviewed on a timely basis. The emphasis on shoreline management as a collaborative, continuing activity may afford added value to the end product for the full range of stakeholders involved. Importantly, such an approach may enhance the sustainability of both the overall shoreline management process as well as individual coastal defence strategies, especially when this long-term view is secured.

Third, implementing specific coastal defence strategies will require competent and consistent management to ensure that any chosen strategy remains focused. It is very possible that risks will increase in some areas in the longer term which will mean that the chosen strategy will have to change over the three epochs for which the plan is to relate. Care will need to be taken to manage this change which may generate considerable controversy.

Fourth, there is the need to ensure the 'understandability' and acceptability of specific adopted policy options to the general public. It is hoped that the proposed approach (Defra, 2003) for the second round of SMPs, based on (but not referred to as) the Quality of Life Capital approach will provide a means to balance more equitably public demands for 'inflexible' protection against their economic and environmental impacts. This will be of importance both locally and nationally (i.e. national and regional strategic interests versus local or individual concerns). The proposed greater emphasis on involving the public in the development, implementation and subsequent review of policy options and on the improved availability of the plan (e.g. on the Internet [Defra, 2003]) should contribute to better public awareness and perception of the dynamic shoreline environment.

Finally, there is a need to seize the challenges presented by changes external to the SMP planning process, for example to the statutory planning system; for integrated coastal zone management; and for river basin management planning. The amended town and country planning system, giving planning the statutory purpose of contributing to sustainable development and moving towards spatial, as opposed to land use, planning, provides a more flexible forward planning system in which shoreline management policy could be more easily incorporated and which can provide a vehicle for statutory public debate on shoreline management issues. Integration of planning and shoreline management policy will help ensure that new development does not exacerbate future problems of coastal risk management. The European Union's Recommendation on Integrated Coastal Zone Management has already enhanced the position of a more integrated approach to the management of coastal resources in the UK with the UK's stocktake undertaken by W.S. Atkins (2004) and current discussion on management regimes for coastal (and marine) resources. Shoreline management policy will make a major contribution to longer-term, more over-arching, strategies for the coast. The impact of the European Union's Water Framework Directive and the Water Environment (Water Framework Directive) (England and Wales) Regulations 2003 is to require the preparation of river basin management plans for England. These strategic plans will extend over the shoreline to one mile seaward and will, therefore, present an opportunity to link coastal and inland flood risk issues. If successfully linked, this would contribute to a more integrated, sustainable approach than is currently practised.

Despite these challenges there can be little doubt that there have been, and will continue to be, significant improvements in the management of the shoreline. In particular, the format of RCGs has been very successful in facilitating both a regionally and a nationally co-ordinated, formal approach to shoreline management. This has provided the foundations for a more inclusive and responsive approach to this key component of wider coastal zone management. The most recent ten to 15 years have witnessed the implementation of attitudes and methodologies that should eventually correct the numerous deficiencies of shoreline management of the past century, and more.

References

Atkins, W.S. (2004) ICZM in the UK: a stocktake. London: HMSO. http://www.defra.gov.uk/environment/marine/iczm/index.htm.

Ballinger, R.C., Potts, J.S., Bradly, N.J. and Pettit, S.J. (2000) 'A comparison between coastal hazard planning in New Zealand and the evolving approach in England and Wales', *Ocean and Coastal Management* 43: 905–25.

Ballinger, R.C., Taussik, J. and Potts, J.S. (2002) 'Developing shared responsibility for managing coastal risk: improving the shoreline management – planning interface in England and Wales', in Proceedings of *LITTORAL 2002, The Changing Coast*. EUROCOAST/EUCC. Porto, Portugal, pp. 303–11.

Ballinger, R.C., Taussik, J. and Potts, J.S. (2003) *Managing Coastal Risk: Making the Shared Responsibility Work. Coastal Planning and Shoreline Management: a Review of Legislation and Guidance*. A Report to the Local Government Association's Special Interest Group on Coastal Issues. London, p. 128.

Bray, M.J., Carter, D.J. and Hooke, J.M. (1995) 'Littoral cell definition and littoral sediment budgets: shoreline management applications, central-southern England', *Journal of Coastal Research* 11: 381–400.

Bray, M., Hooke, J. and Carter, D. (1997) 'Planning for sea-level rise on the South Coast of England: advising the decision-makers', *Transactions of the Institution of British Geographers, N.S.* 22: 13–30.

Brooke, J. (2000a) *The Extent to which First Generation Shoreline Management Plans Achieve their Natural Environmental Objectives*. Report to Royal Society for the Protection of Birds, p. 59.

Brooke, J. (2000b) 'Strategic coastal defence planning – the role of the planning system', *Journal of the Institute of Water and Environmental Management* 14: 140–52.

Burgess, K., Jay, H. and Hosking, A. (2002) 'FUTURECOAST: predicting the future coastal evolution of England and Wales', in Proceedings of *LITTORAL 2002, The Changing Coast*. EUROCOAST/EUCC. Porto, Portugal, pp. 295–301.

Carr, A.P. (1988) 'Geomorphology and public policy at the coast', in Hooke, J.M. (ed.) *Geomorphology and Environmental Planning*. London: Allen and Unwin, pp. 189–210.

Carter, D.J. and Bray, M.J. (2003) 'Coastal sediment transport study', *Report to SCOPAC, South Downs Coastal Group and Lyme Bay/South Devon Coastline Group*. Department of Geography, University of Portsmouth. 6 volumes.

Carter, D.J., Bray, M.J., Hooke, J.M., Taussik, J. and Clifton, J. (1999a) 'SCOPAC: a critique of the past – a strategy for the future', *Report to SCOPAC (Standing Conference on Problems Associated with the Coastline)*, Department of Geography, University of Portsmouth, 2 volumes (Vol. 1: Text, 188pp; Vol. 2: Maps, 11pp.).

Carter, D., Bray, M., Hooke, J., Taussik, J. and McInnes, R. (1999b) 'SCOPAC: a critique of the past – a strategy for the future', Proceedings of *34th MAFF Conference of River and Coastal Engineers*. Keele, pp. 9.1.1–9.1.12.

Carter, D.J., Bray, M.J., Taussik, J. and Hooke, J.M. (2000) 'Regional coastal groups in England and Wales: the way ahead', *Periodicum Biologorum* 102 Supplement 1: Proceedings of *LITTORAL 2000*. Croatia, pp. 215–20.

Child, M. (1996) 'Taking plans forward through consultation and participation: are plans sustainable?', in Fleming, C.A. (ed.) *Coastal Management: Putting Policy into Practice*. London: Institution of Civil Engineers, Thomas Telford, pp. 361–71.

Child, M. (1997) 'Wide consultation and non-engineering issues', Unpublished paper, conference on *Shoreline Management – Experience, Implications and Actions*. Co-sponsored by the Maritime Board of the Institute of Civil Engineers and the Ministry of Agriculture, Fisheries and Food, 6 February 1997. London: Thomas Telford.

Clayton, K.M. (1989) 'Sediment input from the Norfolk cliffs, eastern England – a century of coast protection and its effects', *Journal of Coastal Research* 5: 3, 433–42.

Collins, M.B. and Ansty, K. (eds) (2000) *Solent Science – a Review*. Amsterdam: Elsevier, p. 178.

Cooper, N., Bray, M., Carter, D., Barber, P., Taussik, J., McInnes, R., Lee, M., Lowe, J., Hooke, J. and Pethick, J. (1999) *Review of Existing Shoreline Management Plans Around the Coastline of England and Wales*. Volume I. Review Document. Report to Ministry of Agriculture, Fisheries and Food for project CSA5156 managed by J. Hutchinson.

Cooper, N., Bray, M., Carter, D. and Hutchison, J. (2000) 'A review of existing shoreline management plans around the coastline of England and Wales', Proceedings of *35th MAFF Conference of River and Coastal Engineers*. Keele, pp. 10.1.1–10.1.11.

Cooper, N.J., Bray, M.J., Carter, D.J. and Barber, P.A. (2002) 'Shoreline management plans: a national review and engineering perspective', Proceedings of *The Institution of Civil Engineers (Water and Maritime Engineering)*. 154: 3, 221–8.

Department of Environment, Food and Rural Affairs (2001a) *Shoreline Management Plans: a Guide for Coastal Defence Authorities*. PB 5519, p. 71.

Department of Environment, Food and Rural Affairs (2001b) *Flood and Coastal Defence Appraisal: Guidelines* (seven separate short publications).

Department of Environment, Food and Rural Affairs (2003) *Procedural Guidance for the Production of Shoreline Management Plans.* Interim Guidance May 2003 (Consultation version). http://www.defra.gov.uk/corporate/consult/smpguidance/index.htm.

Department of Environment, Food and Rural Affairs (2004) *Making Space for Water. Developing a New Government Strategy for Flood and Coastal Erosion Risk Management in England.* A consultation exercise. httpp://www.defra.gov.uk/environ/fcd/policy.strategy.htm.

Environment Agency (1999) *The State of the Environment of England and Wales: Coasts.* London: HMSO.

Fletcher, S. (1998) 'Shoreline management in England and Wales: implications for coastal development'. Proceedings of *LITTORAL 98*. Barcelona, pp. 191–7.

Green, C. and Penning-Rowsell, E. (1999) 'Inherent conflicts on the coast', *Journal of Coastal Conservation* 5: 153–62.

Hamer, B.A., Herrington, S.P. and Burgess, K.A. (1999) 'The benefits of a strategic approach to decision making', Proceedings of *34th MAFF Conference of River and Coastal Engineers.* Keele, pp. 5.4.1–5.4.14.

Hathaway, R. (1992) 'The role of the coastal defence forum', Proceedings of conference on *Planning for the Coastal Zone.* Institution of Civil Engineers, Birmingham, pp. 21–3.

Heeps, C. (1996) 'Sharing the secrets of the sea: new approaches to marine environmental education, interpretation and public participation', in Taussik, J. and Mitchell, J. (eds) *Partnership in the Coastal Zone.* Proceedings of *LITTORAL 96.* Portsmouth, pp. 581–8.

Hildebrand, L.P. (ed.) (1997) 'Special issue on community-based coastal management', *Ocean and Coastal Management* 36: 1–3.

Hooke, J.M. (ed.) (1998) *Earth Science Conservation and Coastal Defence.* London: Geological Society.

Hooke, J.M. and Bray, M.J. (1995) 'Coastal groups, littoral cells, policies and plans in the UK', *Area* 27 4: 358–68.

House of Commons (1998) *Agriculture Select Committee Review into Flood and Coastal Defence.* Vol. I, London: HMSO, p. 54.

Huggett, D. (1996) Strategic planning in coastal defence: a mechanism for sustainable habitat management', in Fleming C.A. (ed.) *Coastal Management: Putting Policy into Practice.* London: Institution of Civil Engineers, Thomas Telford, pp. 132–9.

Hutchison, J. (1997) 'Shoreline management plans: interim guidance, advisory notes 1–5. MAFF Flood and Coastal Defence Division, p. 16.

Hutchison, J. and Leafe, R.N. (1996) 'Shoreline management: a view of the way ahead', in Fleming, C.A. (ed.) *Coastal Management: Putting Policy into Practice.* London: Institution of Civil Engineers, Thomas Telford, pp. 352–61.

Jemmett, A. (1998) 'Implementing estuary management plans – a case study from the Dee Estuary', *Geographical Journal* 164: 3, 307–19.

Joliffe, I.P. (1983) 'Coastline erosion and flood abatement: what are the options?', *Geographical Journal* 149: 1, 62–7.

Leafe, R., Pethick, J. and Townend, I. (1998) 'Realizing the benefits of shoreline management', *Geographical Journal* 164: 3, 282–90.

Lee, E.M. (1993) 'The political ecology of coastal planning and management in England and Wales: policy responses to the implications of sea-level rise', *Geographical Journal* 159: 2, 169–78.

Lee, M. (2000) 'Coastal defence and the Habitats Directive: predictions of habitat change in England and Wales', *Geographical Journal* 167: 1, 39–56.

Lee, M., Cooper, N., Bray, M., Carter, D., Barber, P., Taussik, J., McInnes, R., Lowe, J., Hooke, J. and Pethick, J. (2000). *Review of Existing Shoreline Management Plans Around the Coastline of England and Wales.* Volume 2. A Guide for Coastal Defence Authorities. Report to Ministry of Agriculture, Fisheries and Food for project CSA5156 managed by J. Hutchinson.

Leggett, D.J. (1996) 'The work of the Shoreline Management National Advisory Centre (SMNAC) (UK)', in Taussik, J. and Mitchell, J. (eds) *Partnership in the Coastal Zone,* Proceedings of *LITTORAL 1996 (EUROCOAST)* conference, pp. 449–58.

Ministry of Agriculture, Fisheries and Food (1993a) *Strategy for Flood and Coastal Defence in England and Wales.* London: MAFF Flood and Coastal Defence Division. Publication PB 1471, p. 39.

Ministry of Agriculture, Fisheries and Food (1993b) *Interim Guidance on Contents and Procedures for Developing Shoreline Management Plans.* London: MAFF Flood and Coastal Defence Division, p. 11.

Ministry of Agriculture, Fisheries and Food (1995) *Shoreline Management Plans: a Guide for Coastal Defence Authorities.* London: Publication PB 2197, p. 24.

McGlashan, D.J. (2003) 'Managed relocation: an assessment of its feasibility as a coastal management option', *Geographical Journal* 169: 1, 6–20.

McInnes, R.G., Jewell, S. and Roberts, H. (1998) 'Coastal management on the Isle of Wight, UK', *Geographical Journal* 164: 3, 291–306.

Myatt-Bell, L.B., Scrimshaw, M.D., Lester, J.N. and Potts, J.S. (2002) 'Public perception of managed realignment: Brancaster West Marsh, North Norfolk, UK', *Marine Policy* 26: 45–57.

Oakes, T.A. (1995) 'The role of regional coastal groups in planning coastal defence', Proceedings of *LITTORAL 1994.* EUROCOAST. Lisbon, Portugal, pp. 63–76.

Oakes, T.A. (1997) 'Shoreline management plans – adoption and future', Unpublished conference paper, *Shoreline Management – Experience, Implications and Actions.* Co-sponsored by the Maritime Board of the Institute of Civil Engineers and the Ministry of Agriculture, Fisheries and Food, 6 February 1997.

Oakes, T.A. (2002) 'Flood and coastal defence and municipal engineers', *Proceedings of the Institution of Civil Engineers (Municipal Engineer)* 151: 4, 287–94.

O'Riordan, T. and Ward, R. (1997) 'Building trust in shoreline management: creating participatory consultation in shoreline management plans', *Land Use Policy* 14: 4, 257–76.

Pethick, J. (1993) 'Shoreline adjustments and coastal management: physical and biological processes under accelerated sea-level rise', *Geographical Journal* 159: 2, 162–8.

Pettit, S.J. (1999) 'The statutory approach to coastal defence in England and Wales', *Marine Policy* 23: 4/5, 465–79.

Potts, J.S. (1999) 'The non-statutory approach to coastal defence in England and Wales: coastal defence groups and shoreline management plans', *Marine Policy* 23: 4/5, 479–501.

Potts, J.S. (2000) 'Coastal defence groups in England and Wales: benefits, short-comings and future requirements', *Periodicum Biologorum* 102, Supplement 1: Proceedings *LITTORAL 2000.* Croatia, pp. 1–15.

Purnell, R.G. (1996) 'Shoreline management plans: national objectives and implementation', in Fleming, C.A. (ed.) *Coastal Management: Putting Policy into Practice.* London: Institution of Civil Engineers, Thomas Telford, pp. 5–17.

Purnell, R.G. and Richardson, B.D. (2000) 'Flood and coastal defence aims, objectives and targets', in Fleming, C.A. (ed.) *Coastal Management: Integrating Science, Engineering and Management.* London: Institution of Civil Engineers, Thomas Telford, pp. 228–33.

Pye, K. and French, P.W. (1993) *Erosion and Accretion Processes on British Salt Marshes.* Final Report to MAFF. Cambridge: Cambridge Environmental Consultants Ltd.

Rees, N. (2000) 'Coastal habitat management plans and shoreline management plans', Proceedings of *35th MAFF Conference of River and Coastal Engineers.* Keele, pp. 10.3.1–10.3.7.

Rendel Geotechnics (1998) *Investigation and Management of Soft Rock Cliffs.* Report to MAFF, p. 58.

Ricketts, P.J. (1986) 'National policy and management responses to the hazard of coastal erosion in Britain and the United States', *Applied Geography* 6: 197–221.

Rosier, J. and Hastie, W. (1996) 'New Zealand coastal planning: an issue-based approach', *Ocean and Coastal Management* 33: 1–3, 147–65.

Simm, J.D., Beech, N.W. and John, S. (1996) 'A manual for beach management', in Fleming, C.A. (ed.) *Coastal Management: Putting Policy into Practice.* London: Institution of Civil Engineers, Thomas Telford, pp. 229–47.

Smith, T. (2000) 'The future role of the Regional Coastal Groups', in Proceedings of *35th MAFF Conference of River and Coastal Engineers.* Keele, pp. 10.4.1–10.4.7.

Taussik, J. (2000) 'The role of town and country planning in implementing shoreline management strategies', Proceedings of *35th MAFF Conference of River and Coastal Engineers.* Keele, pp. 08.1.1–08.1.10.

Taussik, J. (2004) *Changes to the Planning System that Impact on the Management of Coastal Risk.* Research Briefing Paper No. 1 for the Local Government Association's Special Interest Group on Coastal Issues.

Worrall, S. (2002) 'Living with the sea – managing changing coastlines', Proceedings of *LITTORAL 2002, The Changing Coast.* EUROCOAST/EUCC. Porto, Portugal, pp. 23–8.

13 Designing a safeguard system for the marine environment

What do we really want?

Duncan Huggett   Φ ⌐ S

Introduction

If the amount of effort that had been invested in the production of books, guides, reviews and recommendations about marine protected areas (MPAs) had been invested in the conservation of the marine environment, maybe dying seas would not surround the island nation of the UK. Controversial? Maybe. However, despite the vast amount of work carried out on how to go about conserving the marine environment, there is still no clear vision of what it is we are trying to achieve. Take site safeguard in the marine environment. On the one hand, marine protected areas are seen as a tool to resolve all the conflicting interests and uses of specific marine areas in order to achieve some level of 'sustainability'. On the other, protected areas are seen as no-go areas representing both the best and last examples of what it is we value in the natural marine environment: areas that must be protected at all costs at the exclusion of all other interests.

Never before has the spotlight in the UK been turned on the conservation of the marine environment as it has been in the opening years of the new millennium. As the debate between the government, agencies, industry and non-governmental organizations (NGOs) continues as to how we should conserve the seas around the UK, the need to define the role of site safeguard in the marine environment becomes increasingly urgent.

The political impetus

The desire to make significant progress in the development of a site safeguard system for the marine environment is not limited to NGOs. At every level of governance, commitments are being made to establishing coherent networks of marine protected areas.

At the global level, the World Summit on Sustainable Development (WSSD) held in Johannesburg in 2002 agreed an implementation plan.[1] This commits to the establishment of marine protected areas consistent with international law and based on scientific information, including representative networks by 2012.[2] At the regional seas level, in June 2003,

Ministers at the OSPAR Commission meeting in Bremen agreed a recommendation to establish by 2010 an ecologically coherent network of well-managed marine protected areas throughout the OSPAR maritime area of the NE Atlantic.[3] Selection guidelines have been developed to assist with this. At the 'seas' level, in March 2002, Ministers at the fifth North Sea Conference agreed that by 2010, relevant areas of the North Sea would be designated as marine protected areas belonging to a network of well-managed sites that, amongst other things, best represent the range of ecological character in the OSPAR area.[4] Finally, at a national level, the UK government has committed to identify and designate relevant areas of the UK's seas as areas of marine protection belonging to a network of well-managed sites by 2010.[5]

But what are representative and ecologically coherent networks and how will we know in 2010 or 2012 whether we have achieved these political commitments?

The purpose of marine site safeguard – what are we trying to achieve?

Defining a purpose

The aims of a site safeguard system (as opposed to the objectives for sites themselves) can be summarized as (Pritchard, 1998):

- Mapping out on the ground, the right selection of places representing the best sites, the most threatened sites, those sites requiring restoration etc.;
- Communicating the results to those who need to know;
- Empowering relevant authorities with the ability to influence actions which would compromise the interest of the sites;
- Providing those with an interest in the sites with an opportunity in natural justice to challenge what the relevant authorities desire;
- Where a dispute persists, ensuring conservation prevails when necessary unless there is an urgent need in the public interest to override this.

This in effect describes what should be included in the network, what the main operational mechanisms should be, and how the network performs in practice. This is the approach the marine site safeguard system in the USA follows.[6] For example, the purpose of marine sanctuaries legislation in the USA can be summarized as:

- To identify areas of the marine environment of special national significance due to their resource or human-use values;
- To provide authority for comprehensive and co-ordinated conservation and management of these areas;

- To support, promote and co-ordinate scientific research;
- To enhance public awareness; and
- To facilitate, to the extent compatible with the primary objective of resource protection, uses of the resources of these areas.

However, as pointed out by Pritchard (1998), whilst domestic site safeguard legislation in the UK provides for the first four components of the system, it fails to define how the system should behave. Not only does it not express the way the system should behave, it fails to define why it should behave in a certain way. In other words, there is no stated objective for the site safeguard network in the UK.

At least two significant problems manifest themselves because of this shortfall in site safeguard law. First, consequently, there is no defined conservation end point. How do we know when enough sites have been designated and protected? Do we set some arbitrary area of the sea that should be designated? We will only know when to stop if reference is made to some stated objectives for the system. For example, the system might be considered complete when a basic minimum of the heritage is passed on to future generations (Pritchard, 1996). Second, without a sufficiently explicit reference framework of objectives and purposes for the safeguard system, arguments will remain as to how the system should be treated in the face of both natural and anthropogenic change (Pritchard, 1998).

When to stop – developing the objective of marine site safeguard

Existing marine site safeguard policy and legislation provides a useful starting point for developing an objective for a marine site safeguard network for the UK. For example, the Canadian Oceans Act defines the reasons for which marine protected areas may be designated. These include the conservation of: commercial and non-commercial fishery resources; endangered or threatened habitats and species; unique habitats; areas of high biodiversity and productivity.[7] Similarly, the National Marine Sanctuary Program in the USA establishes a Site Evaluation List using similar types of criteria.[8] However, whilst these illustrate how a purpose might be assigned to individual sites (i.e. the reasons for site designation), they do not in themselves provide a purpose for the network as a whole against which the adequacy of the site safeguard system can be measured.

There appears instead to be a tendency to provide this in policy rather than law. For example, Canada's marine protected area policy states that the objective of marine protective areas collectively is 'to conserve and protect the ecological integrity of marine ecosystems, species and habitats through a system of Marine Protected Areas' (Fisheries and Oceans Canada, 1999). Australia's oceans policy states marine protected areas should 'contribute to the long-term ecological viability of marine and estuarine ecosystems, to maintain ecological processes and systems, and to protect biological diversity at all levels' (Commonwealth of Australia, 1998).

The UK has yet to develop objectives for marine nature conservation and more specifically marine site safeguard. However, it has established an overall vision for the marine environment[9] and proposed a number of strategic goals for the marine environment as a whole:[10]

- Vision: Our vision for the marine environment is clean, healthy, safe, productive and biologically diverse oceans and seas. Within one generation, we want to have made a real difference.
- Proposed strategic goals:

  - To conserve and enhance the overall quality of our seas, its natural processes and its biodiversity;
  - To use marine resources in a sustainable and ecologically sensitive manner in order to achieve maximum environmental, social and economic benefit from the marine environment;
  - To sustain economic benefits and growth in the marine environment by enabling and encouraging environmentally sustainable employment;
  - To increase our understanding of the marine environment, its natural processes and our cultural marine heritage; and
  - To promote public awareness, understanding and appreciation of the marine environment and seek active public participation in the development of new policies.

Strategic objectives for marine nature conservation are still under development although NGOs have developed proposals for these (Wildlife and Countryside Link, 2002). This includes the overall aim to protect and conserve marine biodiversity, its natural processes and the overall environmental quality of our seas and restore these where they have been degraded.

The Ramsar Convention provides an example of where a vision for a network as a whole has been defined. The vision for the List of Wetlands of International Importance is 'To develop and maintain an international network of wetlands which are important for the conservation of global biological diversity and for sustaining human life through the ecological and hydrological functions they perform' (Ramsar, 2000). However, as with the marine policy statements, the vision does not provide a measure for establishing adequacy. Aiming to protect biological diversity is all well and good, but what contribution is site safeguard expected to make?

In the UK, defining when to stop in terms of site designation has become the root of much disagreement between agencies and NGOs. To begin with, under the Wildlife and Countryside Act 1981,[11] whilst there is a duty on statutory nature conservation agencies to designate Sites of Special Scientific Interest (SSSIs), they only have to do so when, in their opinion, a site is of special interest. Furthermore, whilst extensive guidelines on the identification of 'special interest' have been developed which ultimately allow an end point to designation to be defined in that all sites meeting the guidelines should be included in the network, change the values in the guidance, and the end point for site designation shifts. The weakness of this approach is even more apparent now that the agencies have powers to de-notify sites which in their opinion are no longer of special interest. Decisions concerning the validity of deletions from a network of sites can only be made within the context of a vision for the network as a whole (Phillips and Huggett, 2001).

Arguments about the adequacy of site networks in the UK spill over into the designation of European Wildlife Sites (Special Protection Areas [SPAs][12] and Special Areas of Conservation [SACs][13]). However, whilst guidelines have been developed both for the selection of SPAs (JNCC, 1999) and SACs (Brown *et al.*, 1997) legal imperatives in European law exist in the form of objectives, which help to define the discretion that may be exercised in implementing these guidelines. The objectives of the Directives help to establish both the role of the network of protected sites and how many are needed. For example, Member States must classify the most suitable areas both in number and area for Annex I bird species as well as for all regularly occurring migratory species in order to ensure their survival and reproduction in the area of their distribution.[14] Therefore, if a species is declining and areas important for that species remain undesignated, then it can be concluded that the network is deficient.

The Habitats Directive goes further. Like the Birds Directive, the objective of the Natura 2000 network of sites (which includes SACs and SPAs) is to enable the natural habitat types and the species' habitats concerned to be maintained, or where appropriate, restored at a favourable conservation status.[15] However, it goes further and, reflecting the Bonn Convention,[16] begins to define what favourable conservation status means and thus further reduces the level of discretion exercisable in terms of defining the end point for site safeguard.

Establishing a reference for marine site safeguard

As important as defining the purpose for marine site safeguard, is establishing how the selected sites should behave in relation to the defined end point when threatened with change (Pritchard, 1998). In other words, how do we decide whether an intervention, be it natural or anthropogenic, overrides the importance or value ascribed to the site and, if it is overriding, what do we do with the remaining sites?

A number of conventions and more recently EU law have addressed this point. In general terms, there are two steps involved. First, a test must be established which requires a comparison between the value and purpose of the designated site against the value or need for the intervention. Second, a consequence must be defined for overriding the interest of the site. This often requires the provision of compensatory measures (Di Leva and Tymowski, 2000).

The Bern Convention allows for exceptions to strict species protection so long as there are no other satisfactory solutions, and what is proposed will not be detrimental to the survival of the population and that the intervention is an overriding public interest.[17] The Ramsar Convention allows for deletions or restrictions to listed site boundaries in urgent national interest.[18] The Habitats Directive combines the concepts of urgency and national interest. Where there are no alternative solutions, then a damaging plan or project may only proceed for imperative reasons of overriding public interest.[19]

There are a number of important elements to this test which need be fully reflected in the design of marine site safeguard framework: what constitutes an 'imperative reason', what is 'overriding' and the fact that it is the 'public interest' which must be considered. In order to assess an intervention correctly, all these aspects must be addressed.

'Imperative' or 'urgent' relates to the nature and importance of the reasons. It is indicative of interest more pressing in nature than private interests. In order to assess whether there is an imperative for something to be carried out, one must consider what the consequences are of not carrying out the proposal. 'Overriding' relates to the nature of the public interest and its relationship to the ecological interest. Therefore, for something to be in the public interest, it must provide reasons described as imperative *and* be sufficiently weighty to override the ecological objective. Such interests must first be shown to stem from 'public interests' (i.e. wider than just private profit), then be shown to be 'imperative' and finally to be 'overriding'. Therefore, not every kind of public interest would be sufficient to override the interests of the site safeguard system (EC, 2000).

The UK government has suggested that something might be in the public interest without necessarily being in the national interest, and that something short of a national interest might be considered as imperative in that it has local or regional compelling needs (DETR, 1998). However, it is questionable whether it could be considered 'overriding' given the European importance of the ecological objectives.

The test refers to 'public interests'. Therefore, whilst a private body may promote a public interest, it is inappropriate for that body to demonstrate that their intervention constitutes an overriding interest. This is for a public authority. Furthermore, the interest of a private body should not constitute a public interest unless it could be demonstrated that it is of overriding interest to the public. It should aim to protect the fundamental values of citizens' lives, be consistent with the fundamental policies of state and society, and fulfil specific obligations of public service (EC, 2000).

A statutory purpose for marine site safeguard

Having considered in general terms what the objectives of site safeguard might be and how interventions can be assessed against these objectives, the two concepts need to be brought together as statutory purpose. There are two elements to this purpose. First a statement concerning the purpose of the framework, and second a statement concerning the purpose of the selected sites.

An example of a purpose for a marine nature conservation framework in the UK was suggested by Laffoley and Bines (2000) as 'to safeguard and promote effectively in the public interest the sustainable conservation of marine habitats and species'. This provides the purpose for legislation (i.e. measures should be taken in order to safeguard and promote) and the public interest test. However, it fails to engender action in order to achieve the objective. An alternative objective would be (Wildlife and Countryside Link, 1997):[20]

> Measures taken pursuant to this Act shall be formulated and carried out in such a way as to safeguard and promote to best effect the public interest in nature conservation and protection of wildlife.

> It shall be the duty of every public body in the exercise of any of its functions to further, in so far as it is consistent with those functions, the conservation purpose.

The purpose for sites selected, in pursuance of this purpose, would need to define what the end point would be, how to test interventions against the end point and who is responsible for ensuring it happens. This might look like (Wildlife and Countryside Link, 1997):

> It shall be the duty of the nature conservation bodies and the Secretary of State when discharging their individual functions, to ensure the establishment, conservation, maintenance and restoration of a nationwide network of marine areas sufficient in number, size and quality as will, in their opinion, meet the ecological requirements of the species and habitats and the requirements of any other nature conservation interests for which the sites have been notified, unless in the opinion of the Secretary of State it is necessary to act otherwise in any specific instance in order to further a superior urgent national public interest.

Establishing networks

Some considerable effort has been expended developing guidelines or criteria for the recognition and selection of marine sites of value. Often, these revolve around the identification of sites that include habitats or species which are rare, sensitive, declining, or of regional or global importance, or have the potential for restoration (e.g. Laffoley *et al.*, 2000; Connor *et al.*, 2002). Most recently, these have been developed as the Texel-Faial criteria under OSPAR for the North-East Atlantic.[21] Whilst such selection criteria are necessary, they generally fail to recognize that a site may be important not because of the interest found at that location per se, but for the value it has within a series of sites or network. In other words, a collective importance must be considered where the importance of sites stems from maintaining the integrity of a national series.

The concept of representativeness

To an extent, the need for a network approach is recognized by the Habitats Directive in that a fundamental objective is the establishment and maintenance of a 'coherent European ecological network of special areas of conservation'[22] although it is still far from clear how coherence will eventually be measured. One approach would be to assume that if a network is representative of all the functions and values or the marine environment, then a desired level a coherence would be achieved.

A representative system of marine protected areas has been defined as one that samples the full range of environmental gradients or habitat types at a given scale (Day and Roff, 2000). The advantage of the approach is that if the selection of areas were restricted to those that were distinctive or special, then the network as a whole would only consist of those communities, habitats and species where we have sufficient information to establish their value. Instead, by using broad physical attributes we can predict expected species assemblages based on geophysical characteristics.

The establishment of a National Representative System of Marine Protected Areas (NRSMPA) is being undertaken in Australia. The aim of the NRSMPA is to contain a comprehensive, adequate and representative sample of Australia's marine ecosystems (ANZECC, 1998). To more traditional selection criteria such as naturalness are added the criteria of (ANZECC, 1999):

• Comprehensiveness: areas that add to the coverage of the full range of ecosystems within and across each bioregion;
• Adequacy: a network that meets the required level of reservation to ensure the ecological viability and integrity of populations, species and communities; and
• Representativeness: areas that represent one or more ecosystems within a bioregion.

Within a bioregion, comprehensiveness is applied at the scale of ecosystems/habitats. MPAs should be selected in order to sample each of the ecosystems/habitats. Representativeness is achieved through each of the communities/individuals being sampled by at least one MPA. The adequacy of the MPAs will depend on several factors, including:

- The level of management within the MPA and outside the MPA;
- The size and shape of the MPA; and
- The natural/anthropogenic threats within or adjacent to the MPA.

The concept of network integrity

A fundamental question concerning the adequacy of a network of marine sites is that it provides ecological viability and integrity. Again, this is recognized by the Habitats Directive that attempts to define favourable conservation status as long-term viability of habitats and populations in terms of range, area, structure and function.[23] However, ecological integrity is not an absolute concept. It is so complex that its measure cannot be expressed through a single indicator, but rather a set of indicators at different spatial, temporal and hierarchical levels of ecosystem organization (De Leo and Levin, 1997). Indeed, considerable work is currently underway under the auspices of OSPAR to establish ecological quality objectives for marine interests such as seabirds (ICES, 2001) and other threatened and declining species (Gubbay, 2001) that should help to define marine ecosystem integrity.

Integrity can be defined as the quality or condition of being whole or complete (Huggett, 1997). But how do you apply this to site networks? The network of sites must consist of interconnected elements of physical habitats and the processes that create and maintain them so that they are capable of supporting and sustaining the full range of biota adapted for that region. A site network subject to external disturbance or intervention will retain its integrity if it preserves all of its components as well as the functional relationships among the components. Westra (1996) – who argues that an ecosystem can be said to possess integrity 'when it is wild and free as much as possible from human intervention, that is, when it is an unmanaged system, although clearly not a pristine one' – argues that it is the absence of influence by man that distinguishes the concept of 'integrity' from that of health. However, to assess this, the functional and structural aspects of the network must be characterized in detail to provide a conceptual framework for assessing the impact of human activities on the network and to identify practical consequences stemming from this framework.

Measures of network integrity may include:

- Physical attributes including spatial and temporal variation: implicit in the definition of integrity is the concept that specific physical measures can be used to assess the ability of the network to provide the physical template for the biological resources (a network that is representative);

- Biological attributes: implicit in the definition of integrity is the concept that specific biological measures can be used to assess the ability of the network to support and maintain the 'full range of biota adapted for that region' (the development of Ecological Quality Objectives or EcoQOs).

Whilst the criteria used to assess network integrity may be selected from any level of biological organization, more ecologically relevant criteria will be based on population, community and ecosystem responses to disturbance (De Leo and Levin, 1997):

- Population: estimates of population density, biomass, growth rates, age structure, sex ratios and genetic structure (use population models);
- Community: typical structural measures include reduced abundance, reduced species richness, community shifts from sensitive to tolerant species (a shift from k-selected to r-selected species) (use diversity indices);
- Ecosystem: typical functional measures include primary and secondary productivity nutrient cycling, energy flows.

Site networks that have high integrity are more resilient and self-correcting when subject to disturbance. Such ecosystems are characterized by three attributes: their inherent potential is realized; capacity for self-repair after a perturbation is preserved; and they require minimal external support from management. However, effects of disturbance on measures of network integrity are confounded by natural variation. The assessment of integrity requires the effects from anthropogenic disturbance to be distinguished from natural variation in structure and function. This is particularly difficult in moderately impacted systems and those with cumulative effects.

Expressing values and addressing ecological change

It is often argued that the need to account for natural variation in a marine site safeguard network fundamentally undermines the usefulness of establishing a site network. This is because 'natural change' in the marine environment is common, operates over large geographic and temporal scales and, even if it were possible to distinguish natural change from anthropogenic interventions, there is little we could do about it. This has led to the development of vague site management objectives such as 'subject to natural change, maintain the sandbanks which are slightly covered by seawater all the time in favourable condition' (English Nature, 2000). However, this is a fundamental misunderstanding about designated site networks. First, sites are designated because they are of recognized value, be it because they have threatened species or habitats, or they contribute to the integrity of the site network. What happens to a site, how it is managed and ultimately whether change within the site is acceptable or not, is a matter to be addressed once they have been designated. Second, ecological change within sites and across a network is not necessarily a problem and is certainly not incompatible with site safeguard.

How we desire a site network to react to change will hinge on how the value of component parts of the network is defined. The values involved are those that we choose to apply to the natural world (Pritchard, 1996). Change our view of the world and how we value it, and the nature and content of the marine site network changes. However, this does not mean the end product is of less value, just that it is different.

There has been a considerable amount of work carried out looking at the value of sites and whole ecosystems. For example, the mangrove wetlands of Bintuni Bay, Irian Jaya, Indonesia were estimated at Rp 9 million per year per household (Barbier *et al.*, 1997). The total global value of marine services has been put at US$577 per hectare per year (Costanza *et al.*, 1997). In these cases, it is easy to see how a change in the value of a site or network would be considered detrimental. However, it is not direct economic valuation that is of concern here, not the loss of monetary value but the loss of network integrity. Increasingly, the ecological values of marine protected areas are being quantified which allows changes in site networks to be evaluated. For example, from more than 100 marine reserves studies, population densities were on average 91 per cent higher, biomass 192 per cent higher, average organism size 31 per cent higher and species diversity 23 per cent higher within reserves (relative to the same sites prior to site designation or equivalent sites outside reserves) (Warner, 2001). Such work allows us to begin to assess what ecological values have already been lost and provide a baseline against which we can assess further ecological change.

Site safeguard legislation, at first glance, appears to be inflexible to ecological change, the objective being to maintain sites at some value that is identified at the point of designation. However, this is not the case. For example, there is no reason why European wildlife sites designated under the Birds and Habitats Directives cannot change. Indeed, the Habitats Directive requires sites where necessary to be restored.[24] Site objectives that detail our aspirations for a site, and management plans that indicate how the objectives are to be delivered, should be established. These should not preclude the possibility that the site will change. However, what is required is that the change must not be considered as detrimental.[25] Clearly, there are many facets to what 'detrimental' might constitute, but ultimately it is the integrity of the network and the favourable conservation status of the populations and habitats throughout the network that must be ensured.

At a site level, the Ramsar Convention has established a process by which change can be assessed. It requires Contracting Parties to be informed where the ecological character of a site is changing, or is likely to change because of technological developments, pollution or other human interference.[26] The 'Montreux Record' has been established to monitor sites undergoing ecological change.[27] The Ramsar Convention defines change in ecological character as:[28]

> Ecological character is the sum of the biological, physical, and chemical components of the wetland ecosystem, and their interactions, which maintain the wetland and its products, functions, and attributes.

> Change in ecological character is the impairment or imbalance in any biological, physical, or chemical components of the wetland ecosystem, or in their interactions, which maintain the wetland and its products, functions and attributes.

This provides a useful starting point for establishing a system for identifying and monitoring change in a marine site network. However, there is still a tendency to interpret any change as an imbalance in the system and thus an adverse effect that needs to be addressed. In terms of creating an imbalance in the site network and a loss of value, natural change may be just as detrimental as human induced change. It is not the cause of the change per se which should be of concern but what the change in value is, and whether it is desirable to do something about it.

Conclusions

Our understanding of the purpose of a site safeguard system in delivering nature conservation goals is sufficiently well developed for us to be quite explicit about what it is we wish to achieve through a network of designated marine sites. However, to date there has been little attempt to do this. Should we wish to clarify the role of marine site safeguard in order to assist politicians and decision-makers in the development of the legislative and policy framework necessary to protect the values we ascribe to the marine environment, then there are a number of points that need to be addressed.

In broad terms, the marine site safeguard system must define what it is we want included in a network of sites, what regulatory and management framework is necessary, how the desired network reacts to change, and why. In order to realize this, marine conservation must be explicit about the conservation end point: we need to know when we have arrived and when measures are adequate.

One way of achieving this in terms of marine nature conservation law would be to enshrine these concepts in a statutory purpose. This would provide a context within which a designated site network could be developed and against which change could be assessed. The purpose needs to be defined both at a site level in terms of site selection criteria and at a network level at which point the contribution site safeguard makes to the wider marine conservation goal can be elucidated. In short, the network should ensure the survival and reproduction of populations within their area of distribution, and maintain and enhance habitats to a predefined favourable state.

Having defined the purpose of the designated marine site network, the safeguard system must establish a mechanism for responding to change and rules for deciding when change overrides the stated purpose of the network. This requires two distinct features. First, a test of 'urgent overriding national public interest' must be enshrined in law. Second, what happens when a superior interest arises which is considered overriding must be defined (for example, the provision of compensation).

It is essential that the concept of networks provides the foundations to the marine site safeguard system. It must be more than just a collection of sites that harbour rare or declining species. Instead, the value of sites in contributing to and maintaining the integrity of a national (or international series) must be recognized. However, to enable this it will be essential to develop an understanding of network coherence or integrity in the marine environment. The problem is that the level of information required (unlike for terrestrial site safeguard systems) is unlikely ever to be available. Instead, a proxy approach is needed; one where it is assumed that a fully representative site network will provide the desired level of integrity. Due to the complexity of ecological integrity, indicators of coherence (perhaps ecological quality objectives) would be required.

The concept of site network integrity must account for the fact that integrity is often masked by ecological variation or change, both natural and anthropogenic. The site safeguard system must be designed to react to change, both in terms of values as well as ecological change (both natural and human induced) without ultimately losing network integrity. In order to do this, we have to be explicit about the values we wish to maintain in the marine environment, and what changes to these we would consider detrimental. And now, we have come full circle. We need to define what it is we want from marine nature conservation and the part marine site safeguard has to play.

Acknowledgements

Particular thanks goes to Dave Pritchard, Euan Dunn and Gwyn Williams at the RSPB for all their constructive comments and help in the development of this chapter.

At the time of writing, the author was with the RSPB. He may now be contacted at the Environment Agency, Kingfisher House, Goldhay Way, Orton Goldhay, Peterborough PE2 5ZR.

Notes

1 http://www.un.org/esa/sustdev/documents/WSSD_POI_PD/English/POIToc.htm.
2 Paragraph 32(c) of Chapter IV of the WSSD Plan of Implementation.
3 OSPAR Recommendation 2003/3 on a Network of Marine Protected Areas agreed at the OSPAR Ministerial meeting held in Bremen, 23–27 June 2003.
4 See paragraph 7 of Chapter II of the Bergen Declaration (http://www.dep.no/md/nsc/).
5 See paragraph 2.44 of *Safeguarding Our Seas: a strategy for the conservation and sustainable development of our marine environment.* Defra, May 2002a.
6 § 1431 of United States Code, Title 16 Conservation §§ 1151 to 3100, Chapter 32 – Marine Sanctuaries.
7 § 35(1) of Statutes of Canada 1996, Chapter 31, an Act respecting the oceans of Canada.
8 See appendix I to Part 922 of the Code of Federal Regulations, Title 15, Chapter IX – National Oceanic and Atmospheric Administration, Department of Commerce: National Marine Sanctuary Regulations.
9 See chapter 1 of *Safeguarding Our Seas.*
10 See paragraph 2.19 of *Seas of Change: the Government's consultation paper to help deliver our vision for the marine environment.* Defra, November 2002b.
11 The Wildlife and Countryside Act 1981 as amended by the Countryside and Rights of Way Act 2000.
12 Classified under Council Directive of 2 April 1979 on the conservation of wild birds (79/409/EEC).
13 Designated under Council Directive 92/43/EEC of 21 May 1992 on the conservation of natural habitats and of wild fauna and flora.
14 Article 4.1 and 4.2 of the Birds Directive.
15 Article 3.1 of the Habitats Directive.
16 The Convention on the Conservation of Migratory Species of Wild Animals, Bonn 1979.
17 Article 9 of the Convention on the Conservation of European Wildlife and Natural Habitats, Bern 1979.
18 Article 2(5) and 4(2) of the Convention on Wetlands of International Importance especially as Waterfowl Habitat, Ramsar 1971.
19 Article 6.4 of the Habitats Directive.
20 See Section 28G of the Wildlife and Countryside Act 1981 as amended by the Countryside and Rights of Way Act 2000.
21 Reference Number: Agreement 2003–13, date of adoption: 2003, Bremen.
22 Article 3.1 of the Habitats Directive.
23 See Article 1e and 1i of the Habitats Directive.
24 See Article 3.1 of the Habitats Directive.
25 See Article 6.2 of the Habitats Directive.
26 Article 3.2 of the Ramsar Convention.
27 Resolution 5.4 of the fifth Meeting of the Conference of the Contracting Parties, Kushiro, Japan, 9–16 June 1993.
28 Resolution VII.10 of the seventh Meeting of the Conference of Parties, San José, Costa Rica, 10–18 May 1999.

References

Australian and New Zealand Environment and Conservation Council (1998) *Guidelines for Establishing the National Representative System of Marine Protected Areas.* ANZECC Task Force on Marine Protected Areas, Environment. Canberra, Australia.

Australian and New Zealand Environment and Conservation Council (1999) *Strategic Plan of Action for the National Representative System of Marine Protected Areas: a Guide for Action by Australian Governments.* ANZECC Task Force on Marine Protected Areas, Environment. Canberra, Australia.

Barbier, E.B., Acreman, M. and Knowler, D. (1997) *Economic Valuation of Wetlands: a Guide for Policy Makers and Planners.* Gland, Switzerland: Ramsar Convention Bureau.

Brown, A.E., Burn, A.J., Hopkins, J.J. and Way, S.F. (1997) *The Habitats Directive: Selection of Special Areas of Conservation in the UK.* Peterborough: JNCC Report no. 270.

Commonwealth of Australia (1998) *Australia's Oceans Policy.* Canberra: Commonwealth of Australia.

Connor, D.W., Breen, J., Champion, A., Gilliland, P.M., Huggett, D., Johnston, C., Laffoley, D.d'A., Lieberknecht, L., Lumb, C., Ramsay, K. and Shardlow, M. (2002). *Rationale and Criteria for the Identification of Nationally Important Marine Nature Conservation Features and Areas in the UK. Version 02.11.* Peterborough: Joint Nature Conservation Committee (on behalf of the statutory nature conservation agencies and Wildlife and Countryside Link) for the Defra Working Group on the Review of Marine Nature Conservation.

Costanza, R., d'Arge, R., de Groot, R., Farber, S., Grasso, M., Hannon, B., Limburg, K., Naeem, S., O'Neill, R.V., Paruelo, J., Raskin, R.G., Sutton, P. and van den Belt, M. (1997) 'The value of the world's ecosystem services and natural capital', *Nature* 387: 253–60.

Day, J.C. and Roff, J.C. (2000) *Planning for Representative Marine Protected Areas: a Framework for Canada's Oceans.* Report prepared for WWF. Toronto: Canada.

De Leo, G.A. and Levin, S. (1997) 'The multifaceted aspects of ecosystem integrity', *Conservation Ecology Online* 1: 1, 3. http://www.consecol.org/Journal/vol1/iss1/art3/.

Department of Environment, Food and Rural Affairs (2002a) *Safeguarding Our Seas: a Strategy for the Conservation and Sustainable Development of Our Marine Environment.* Defra, May 2002.

Department of Environment, Food and Rural Affairs (2002b) *Seas of Change: the Government's Consultation Paper to Help Deliver Our Vision for the Marine Environment.* Defra, November 2002.

Department of Environment, Transport and the Regions (1998) *Guidance on the Application of Article 6.3 and 6.4 of the Habitats Directive.* DETR, May 1998.

Di Leva, C. and Tymowski, W. (2000) *The Ramsar Convention on Wetlands: the Role of 'Urgent National Interests' and 'Compensation' in Wetland Protection.* Bonn: IUCN Environmental Law Centre.

English Nature (2000) *Wash and North Norfolk Coast European Marine Site: English Nature's Advice Given Under Regulation 33(2) of the Conservation (Natural Habitats &c.) Regulations 1994.* Peterborough: English Nature.

European Commission (2000) *Managing Natura 2000 Sites: the Provisions of Article 6 of the 'Habitats' Directive 92/43/EEC.* Brussels: European Commission.

Fisheries and Oceans Canada (1999) *Marine Protected Areas Policy.* Marine Ecosystems Conservation Branch of Fisheries and Oceans Canada. Ottawa, March 1999.

Gubbay, S. (2001) *Development of Ecological Quality Objectives for the North Sea: Threatened and Declining Species.* Report to BirdLife International, March 2001.

Huggett, D.J. (1997) *Implementation of the Habitats Directive – Significant Effect and Adverse Effect on Site Integrity.* In Marine Environmental Management: review of events in 1996 and future trends, London: 22–23 January 1997.

ICES (2001) *Report of the Working Group on Seabird Ecology.* Copenhagen: ICES Headquarters, 16–19 March 2001.

Joint Nature Conservation Committee (1999) *The Birds Directive: Selection Guidelines for Special Protection Areas.* Peterborough: JNCC.

Laffoley, D.d'A. and Bines, T. (2000) *Protection and Management of Nationally Important Marine Habitats and Species.* Prepared by English Nature based on the views of a sample of the members of the DETR Working Group on the Review of Marine Nature Conservation. Peterborough: English Nature Research Report 390.

Laffoley, D.d'A., Connor, D.W., Tasker, M.L. and Bines, T. (2000) *Nationally Important Seascapes, Habitats and Species: a Recommended Approach to their Identification, Conservation and Protection.* Prepared for the DETR Working Group on the Review of Marine Nature Conservation by English Nature and the Joint Nature Conservation Committee. Peterborough: English Nature Research Report 392, p. 17.

Phillips, M. and Huggett, D.J. (2001) 'From passive to positive – the Countryside Act 2000 and British wildlife', *British Wildlife* April 2001: 237–43.

Pritchard, D. (1996) 'Site safeguard concepts and systems: a design guide for the next millennium', *RSPB Conservation Review* 10: 19–24.

Pritchard, D. (1998) 'Spelling it out in statute', *ECOS* 19: 1, 67–72.

Ramsar (2000) *Strategic Framework and Guidelines for the Future Development of the List of Wetlands of International Importance.* Ramsar handbooks for the wise use of wetlands no. 7. Gland, Switzerland: Ramsar Convention Bureau.

Warner, R.R. (2001) *Using Past Marine Reserve Performance as a Guide for Effective Design.* Paper presented at AAAS meeting: The scientific theory of marine reserves, San Francisco: 17 February 2001.

Westra, L. (1996) 'Ecosystem integrity and the "fish wars"', *Journal of Aquatic Ecosystem Health* 5: 275–82.

Wildlife and Countryside Link (1997) *Proposals for Improvements to Wildlife Protection in Great Britain.*

Wildlife and Countryside Link (2002) *Proposals for Strategic Goals for Marine Nature Conservation.* London: September 2002.

14 Putting sustainability into practice

Bob Earll

Introduction

Since 1994 a series of annual conferences has been run on environmental and broader issues covering the coastal and marine environment of the UK and Europe by the author. At the start of the millennium, it seemed appropriate to reflect upon this process in general and on one important area in particular – sustainability and how this could be translated into practice. The original core ideas for the conference – annual review, the growing use of management in environmental practice and the importance of sustainability – have stood the test of time. In addition, the multi-sectoral, inter-disciplinary nature of the papers selected has been notable, as have the drive and innovations of many of the speakers to find practical solutions to a very real and growing set of environmental and sustainability issues.

Throughout this time however, one concept – sustainability – has continually underpinned not only speakers' papers but also the policy agenda from a global to a local scale. A list of changes that have taken place over this seven-year period is illustrated in Table 14.1. This list is not put forward to be in any way comprehensive. Indeed, others might wish to assess these trends more systematically. What they do highlight however, is that the scale and range of serious issues we face is growing, and that on a worldwide scale, solutions need to be found. The conferences have been supported by a variety of well-respected figures and in his keynote presentation in 1998, Bud Ehler from NOAA reflected upon the challenge we face as follows:

> The doubling of the world's population will be of far greater significance in terms of the energy, resource consumption and stress on the environment especially in the coastal zone. Today's vague concept of 'sustainability' will take on very real proportions as we move into the next millennium.

This chapter puts forward pragmatic ideas to help convert the 'vague concept' of sustainability into the solutions and practice that will be needed to meet the challenges of the future.

Table 14.1 Changes between 1993–2000 that have affected the coastal and marine
environment

Deleterious changes – man made
- Population growth 1 billion/11 yr
- Climate changes (droughts, increased natural disasters of all sorts and billion-dollar storm events)
- Enlarging Antarctic and Arctic ozone holes
- Ecosystem collapse (Canadian cod fishery, Black Sea)
- Increased changes to ecosystem fluxes – nutrients, freshwater, sediment – into the coastal zone
- Declines in commercial and migratory fish stocks, the demonstration of dramatic seabed effects of fishing
- Resource depletion – oil and aggregates
- Pollution by toxic chemicals and endocrine disruption
- 'Events': tankers *Braer, Sea Empress* and *Erika; Brent Spar*

Positive changes
- Greater capacity (ICZM)
- Process, stakeholders involvement and enabling processes
- Marine Nature Conservation – growth
- Growth in awareness and legal forces management solutions, information
- Law of Sea – accession by UK
- Drift net bans etc.
- Wind Energy offshore, in Europe, particularly Denmark – not UK

Organizational and policy changes
- International – Rio Earth Summit (sustainability, precaution and ICZM)
- Global trade and WTO
- European (governance and directives – 80 per cent of all UK environmental legislation results directly from the EU)
- UK – devolution – Scotland, Wales, NI and English Regions – agencies
- Legal measures, styles of government and governance
- Re-organization of regulatory bodies – agencies, research

Life style changes
- The Internet and information revolution
- Growing car use
- Growing global tourism
- Growing consumerism
- Food scares: BSE and GM foods

Sustainability – moving beyond definitions

Sustainable development was being discussed well before the Brundtland Commission in the 1980s but this provided one key formalizing step. The other and more recent affirmation was the Rio Earth Summit in 1992. Since then, many countries including the UK and Europe have begun to incorporate sustainability concepts into policy.

Whilst sustainability has been with us for well over two decades, in the popular jargon of environmentalism, it would probably be fair to say that it still hasn't really taken off in guiding our activities – as Ehler (1998) put

---

Box 14.1 Deconstructing sustainability – beyond definitions

There are hundreds of definitions of sustainability; indeed, the author once saw a 40-page report that comprised *just* definitions. The *definition* of a definition might be 'a very clever use of a small number of words to express a complex concept'. The definitions of sustainability fall into this description. However, arguing over definitions of sustainability is a complete waste of time. Alternatively, if one asks, 'What are the key concepts that underpin sustainability implied by the definitions?' then most people can answer this. These ideas include precaution, integration, holism, inter-generational equity, the need to integrate social, economic and environmental issues and so on. Even though the result is a very long list of concepts, the type of delegates attending these meetings could all give a list of constructs that they see as important in the concept of sustainability. What is more interesting from a pragmatic point of view is that these constructs can be applied to real projects and translated into action.

---

it, too many people still see it as a 'vague concept' which they find difficult to apply in practice.

Without digressing into why this breakthrough has not happened, there does seem to be light at the end of the tunnel. This chapter puts across the view that there is a pragmatic framework for the routine application of sustainability that can be derived from our understanding of environmental management.

From cradle to grave

In the 1980s, it became routine to discuss the 'life cycle' of products or, in a similar vein, 'cradle to grave' aspects of production or industries. This was probably a direct result of looking at the longer-term horizons flowing from thinking about sustainability. This provides a powerful basis for considering the many phases that projects or developments move through (Figure 14.1). Put another way, it provides a clear structure on which to base many developments in relation to environmental management. This idea can be summarized simply to describe the main stages of environmental management that have been developed and refined over the last decade. This includes scoping, assessment, monitoring through development, management systems for routine operation and assessment and monitoring for decommissioning (Earll, 2000).

An excellent example of this was presented in an early paper in this meeting series by John Hartley (1995), then of AMOCO – the major oil

Environmental Management

Stages				
	Proposal	Construction	Routine operation	Decommissioning
	Time line			

Techniques				
	Env. impact assessment	Feedback monitoring	Env. management systems	Env. security and restoration

Figure 14.1 Sequential stages and application of techniques in Environmental Management.

company. That paper described environmental management in the cradle to grave context of oilfield development (Figure 14.2). Hartley showed that over the entire lifespan of the oilfield from prospecting, installation, production and decommissioning, different environmental management techniques were being applied routinely. This emphasizes the connected nature of environmental assessment, construction and routine operation of a development through to decommissioning.

This meeting series started under the title Marine *Environmental* Management. However, as has been highlighted earlier, the environmental movement in all its many forms has grown spectacularly during the last two decades and has moved 'environment' from a peripheral to a mainstream consideration in virtually every walk of life. However, as many environmentalists would point out, *sustainability* should be the key goal to which we aspire. In pragmatic terms, sustainability includes 'environment' as well as economic and social dimensions.

What happens if we simply replace 'environment' with the word 'sustainability' in our cradle to grave management framework? This can be, and is being done and a number of examples illustrate this below.

The application of sustainability concepts within this framework

The application of the sustainability concepts such as integration, precaution, holism etc., can have a logical place in the cradle to grave framework. It may well be that at different stages of projects or developments the concepts need to be applied with greater or lesser efforts. Put another way, the practical implications of scoping or assessment in relation to looking at issues of integration, resource use, holism and precaution would be quite different from applying these ideas to a well-established factory operation. Some of the main concepts and how they are expressed would include:

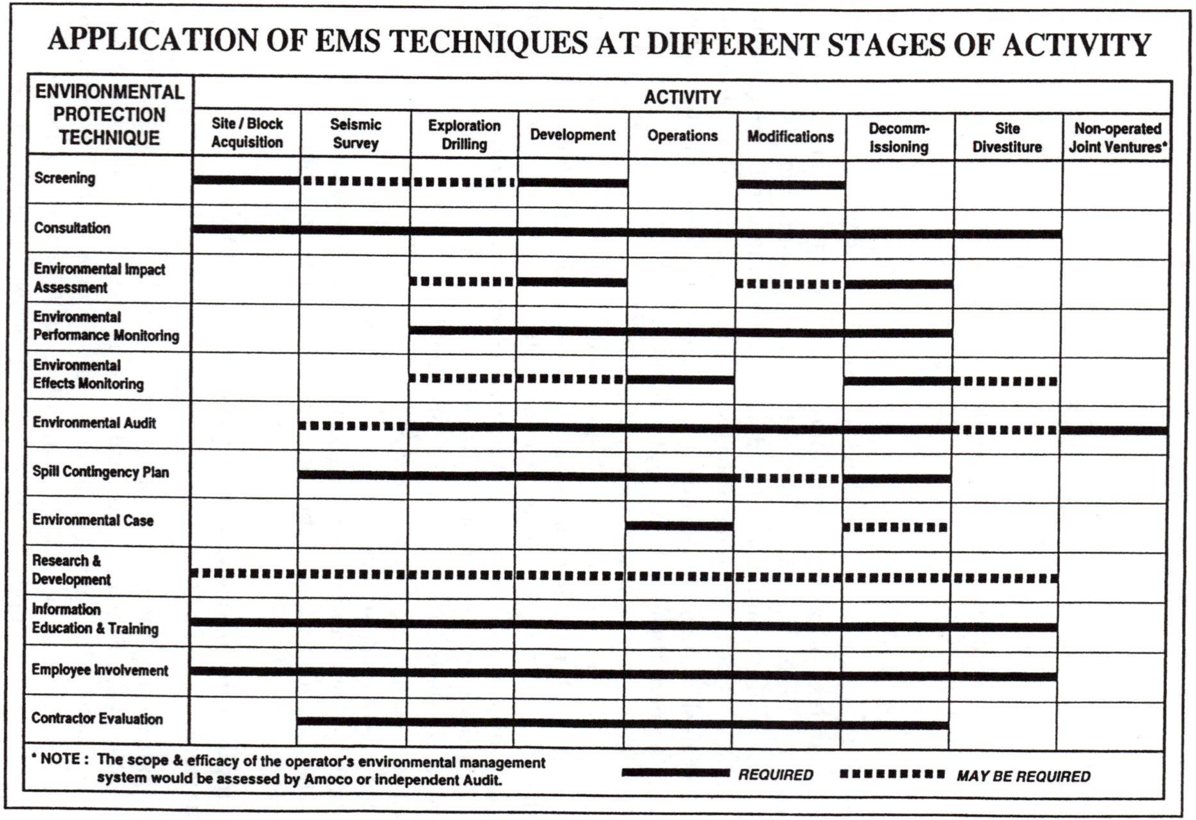

APPLICATION OF EMS TECHNIQUES AT DIFFERENT STAGES OF ACTIVITY

ENVIRONMENTAL PROTECTION TECHNIQUE	ACTIVITY								
	Site / Block Acquisition	Seismic Survey	Exploration Drilling	Development	Operations	Modifications	Decommissioning	Site Divestiture	Non-operated Joint Ventures*
Screening	REQUIRED	REQUIRED	MAY BE REQUIRED						
Consultation						REQUIRED		REQUIRED	
Environmental Impact Assessment			MAY BE REQUIRED	REQUIRED		MAY BE REQUIRED	REQUIRED		
Environmental Performance Monitoring			REQUIRED				REQUIRED		
Environmental Effects Monitoring			MAY BE REQUIRED	REQUIRED	REQUIRED			MAY BE REQUIRED	
Environmental Audit		MAY BE REQUIRED	REQUIRED			REQUIRED		MAY BE REQUIRED	REQUIRED
Spill Contingency Plan		REQUIRED	REQUIRED			MAY BE REQUIRED	REQUIRED		
Environmental Case					REQUIRED		MAY BE REQUIRED		
Research & Development	REQUIRED	REQUIRED	REQUIRED	REQUIRED	REQUIRED	REQUIRED	REQUIRED	REQUIRED	
Information Education & Training		REQUIRED						REQUIRED	
Employee Involvement		REQUIRED						REQUIRED	
Contractor Evaluation		REQUIRED					REQUIRED		

* NOTE : The scope & efficacy of the operator's environmental management system would be assessed by Amoco or Independent Audit.

━━━━━ REQUIRED ▪▪▪▪▪▪▪▪ MAY BE REQUIRED

Figure 14.2 The Amoco UK Environmental Management System (EMS).

Integration

This is a key concept and there will be many approaches. One version of this involves actively considering economic, social and environmental issues in developing practice. Integration in terms of 'integrated coastal zone management' can imply a variety of approaches to both structural mechanisms (horizontal and vertical) or processes to develop so that more effective integration takes place. The way sectors work together – joined-up government – and the need for more effective management of issues is another expression of this topic. 'Process' is increasingly being recognized as key in developing integrated approaches – not least in helping people develop shared values or vision of how to proceed.

Holism

The need to consider issues in the broadest perspective – the holistic view – is often raised at the outset of issues or in scoping new projects. ICZM can often only be considered effectively once a full assessment of issues affecting the area a long way outside management boundaries has taken place.

Not considering issues beyond one sectoral perspective often is highlighted as a failing of organizational performance.

Precaution

The need to act cautiously in situations of uncertainty and incomplete science has become a centrepiece of legislative development on many levels and within many sectors. Every discipline and sector has ways of expressing precautionary action and acting upon it. This is hardly surprising since 'precaution' is a fundamental trait of human behaviour. Risk assessment and management has become one way of formalizing approaches to precaution in routine matters.

Resources

Air, water, energy, renewable or non renewable resources are the subject matter of differing approaches to sustainability. They are often at the very core of sectoral operations and the functions of organizations. Sustainability will often need a clear assessment of flows and cycles of these components.

Biodiversity

In its broadest sense and the 'goods and services' it provides to the marine environment have been frequently highlighted, as have the steps being taken to meet its conservation. The role of the nature conservation sector is now well defined and will continue to be to work to protect and restore biodiversity both in general and for particular species.

Equity

The need to ensure equity, both within existing society and between generations, is a major component of sustainability. The concept of not constraining the options of future generations in terms of resources or pollution is often highlighted. In the coastal defence sector for example, the need to consider the long-term consequence of projects and activities – that covers inter-generational issues directly – is at the core of current thinking and long-term planning.

It is not suggested that this list of concepts and the accompanying descriptions are in any sense complete. They have been included to illustrate how the major sustainability concepts impinge on current coastal issues.

These concepts provided – listed on the vertical axis of Figure 14.3 – will need to be considered in working through the management stages.

Sustainability management – evidence of the developing approach

It is evident from the popular environmental press that work is currently being undertaken that supports this thinking; four examples:

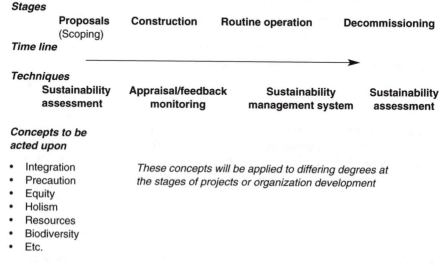

Figure 14.3 Sustainability management from cradle to grave.

- The DTI and Forum for the Future are investigating the possibility of 'a sustainability management system' for routine operational practice (ENDS, 1999a).
- The regional Development Agencies are now commissioning 'sustainability appraisals' (assessments) in relation to their proposals (ENDS, 1999b).
- The Marine Stewardship Council has been developing what is, in effect, a sustainability management system for fisheries involving social, economic and fishery-environment issues (MSC, 1999).
- The government has also been promoting sustainability reporting for businesses, and powers for local authorities (ENDS, 1999c and d).

Conclusion

No breakthroughs – just applying what we know

In looking to apply the concept of sustainability, it is very easy to get sidetracked, not least by the semantics of definitions. This chapter develops the view that we now have in place a framework for testing and applying most of the constructs of sustainability through a cradle to grave, management systems approach.

Translating sustainability into routine practice will not be done by magic. Nor are there likely to be any 'eureka' breakthroughs. Two decades have shown us there is unlikely to be any point that suddenly enables sustainability to be put into practice. The translation of sustainability concepts into practice lies within our current thinking.

Over the last two decades, we have become increasingly at ease with the concept of environmental impact assessments. Over the last decade, we have become increasingly happy with the idea of management systems and environmental management systems. We can see how these are linked by time and it is routine business practice to do this in many sectors. At the end of the next decade, it is suggested that that stakeholders will be happy to talk about sustainability management in this cradle to grave way and will be at ease with the component parts – sustainability assessment, management systems, etc.

This approach has the virtue that it explicitly links our current thinking and the language of management towards translating sustainability into practice.

Environment into the heart of organizations and projects

It is interesting to note that as major sector players have thought about and developed their environmental agenda, they have seen this to be at the very heart of why they are in business. In practice, this means that having 'environmental management' bolted on to their operations as some kind of novel appendage looks increasingly out of place. Incorporating 'environment' *within* existing management systems saves unnecessary duplication and more effectively illustrates the totality of what organizations do.

Counter to intuition, it will be easier to arrive at sustainability management approaches, because it is easier to solve problems by considering their totality rather than just worrying about the environmental component in isolation.

Of course, this does not mean that explicit evidence of environmental and social performance is not required. Reporting, for example, should amply illustrate the performance of environmental and social indicators as well as the usual economic analysis. Performance indicators are yet another product of management systems and objective driven approaches. Coffey (2000) describes how this thinking – putting environment at the heart of policy – is being embodied into European thinking through the Cardiff process and highlights how indicators are seen as being a key way of demonstrating this.

What and who will be involved?

This approach can be applied to projects of all sizes and complexities, from local to national and international. Put simply this would include policies, organizations, projects, new and existing developments – anywhere in fact where 'environmental' management might be deemed to be appropriate.

There will be those who have responsibility for the 'whole' who have the role of bringing together many facets that sustainability involves into these areas. Other people will have a stronger expertise in how sustainability applies to parts of the whole process, sectors or issues. The people who will be needed to work in this way will be happy with a range of disciplines and will be able to bridge the traditional sectors to find sustainable solutions to the major challenges that now confront us.

References

Coffey, C. (2000) 'Environmental integration and the common fisheries policy', in Earll, R.C. (ed.) *Coastal Futures 2000: Coastal Management for Sustainability – Review and Future Trends.* Volume 7, paper 11: 53–6.

Earll, R.C. (2000) 'Putting sustainability into practice', *Coastal Futures 2000: Coastal Management for Sustainability Review and Future Trends 2000.* Volume 7, paper 1: 3–6.

Ehler, C. (1998) 'Managing for sustainability in the coastal environment', in Earll, R.C. (ed.) *Marine Environmental Management Review of Events in 1997 and Future Trends.* Volume 5: 167.

ENDS Report (1999a) *DTI Starts Work on 'Sustainability Management'.* 293, 9.

ENDS Report (1999b) *DETR Consults on Sustainability Appraisal in Regional Planning.* 295, 43.

ENDS Report (1999c) *Big Firms Try Out Sustainability Reporting Guidelines.* 298, 10.

ENDS Report (1999d) *Government Backslides on 'Sustainability' Duty for Councils.* 299, 35.

Hartley, J.P. (1995) 'Integration of environment into offshore oil and gas industry management', in Earll, R.C. (ed.) *Marine Environmental Management Review of 1994 and Future Trends.* Volume 2, paper 10: 49–52.

Marine Stewardship Council (1999) *Our Empty Seas: a Global Problem a Global Solution.* London.

Index

eBooks – at www.eBookstore.tandf.co.uk

A library at your fingertips!

eBooks are electronic versions of printed books. You can store them on your PC/laptop or browse them online.

They have advantages for anyone needing rapid access to a wide variety of published, copyright information.

eBooks can help your research by enabling you to bookmark chapters, annotate text and use instant searches to find specific words or phrases. Several eBook files would fit on even a small laptop or PDA.

NEW: Save money by eSubscribing: cheap, online access to any eBook for as long as you need it.

Annual subscription packages

We now offer special low-cost bulk subscriptions to packages of eBooks in certain subject areas. These are available to libraries or to individuals.

For more information please contact webmaster.ebooks@tandf.co.uk

We're continually developing the eBook concept, so keep up to date by visiting the website.

www.eBookstore.tandf.co.uk